You Can Call Me Al

Photos: Front cover, Al McGuire Enterprises. Back cover, Marquette University Sports Information Department.

"I've always been a flower child. I've always been free."

You Can Call Me Al

The Colorful Journey of College Basketball's Original Flower Child, Al McGuire

Joseph Declan Moran

PRAIRIE OAK PRESS
Madison, Wisconsin

First edition, second printing, 1999
Copyright © 1999 by Joseph Declan Moran

Prairie Oak Press
821 Prospect Place
Madison, Wisconsin 53703

Typeset by Quick Quality Press, Madison, Wisconsin
Printed in the United States of America by BookCrafters, Chelsea, Michigan
Cover design by Flying Fish Graphics, Blue Mounds, Wisconsin

Library of Congress Cataloging-in-Publication Data

Moran, Joseph Declan.
    You can call me Al: the colorful journey of college basketball's original flower child, Al McGuire / Joseph Declan Moran. -- 1st ed.
        p.   cm.
    Includes bibliographical references (p.).
    ISBN 1-879483-52-1 (pbk.: alk. paper)
    1. McGuire, Al. 2. Basketball coaches -- United States -- Biography. I. Title.
GV884.M27M67 1999
796.323'092--dc21   99-18577
[B]   CIP

DEDICATION

This book is dedicated to the memories of M. Paton Ryan, James P. Murphy, and Jackie Smith. Sister Ryan, in her role as associate dean of admissions at Marquette University, convinced me that Marquette was the place for me during an interview with my parents in her campus office on a hot August afternoon in 1975. After my graduation in 1980, she continued to encourage me in my career and in this book project.

James P. Murphy was my first journalism professor at Marquette. It was through his persistent constructive criticism that I learned how to write well by incorporating the four C's (Clear, Correct, Colorful, and Concise) and to keep it simple. I owe my career to Jim Murphy.

Jackie Smith not only encouraged me in my efforts to write this book but helped re-create the Rockaway Beach and "Irish Town" of Coach McGuire's youth. Jackie worked as a bartender at a tavern near McGuire's and knew Al's parents. Through my interviews with Jackie, I was able to lay the foundation for this book. Thank you, Jackie, for re-creating that wonderful time and such fond memories. I am forever grateful.

Contents

FOREWORD

Many people, I think, when asked about Al McGuire would say something to the effect that he has been one of the great personalities in the game of basketball.

I would not in any way disagree with this.

Al's unique way of going about and doing things created an aura that I think was quite singular in all the history of basketball.

However, I would go beyond the personality that Al created for himself to say that he quite simply was one of the best coaches ever in college basketball.

He had an understanding of what was important as far as the game was concerned that few coaches have. He had the ability to get kids to play extremely well together at the offensive end of the court without making mistakes and, at the same time, working to get good shots.

It did not seem to make a lot of difference to Al's players who scored points or who took shots, which I think is the true mark of a coach who understands offensive play.

At the defensive end, his players played hard and were always difficult to score against. I don't think Al ever paid much attention to the Xs and Os of the game or different offenses or different defenses, but he had this exceptional ability to get across to his players that on offense it was important that you didn't throw the ball away and that you got good shots and played hard on the boards.

At the same time, at the defensive end, it was always clear to me that Al's emphasis was simply, "Let's not let these other guys score easily against us." In the simplicity of this approach, I think, really lies Al's true greatness as a basketball coach. He went right to the core of what makes a team good and how players have to play together to develop into a good team, and this is not done by using all kinds of different offensive and defensive approaches.

I have always enjoyed Al's many unusual comments and the things he does relative to both basketball and other aspects of his life. Throughout Al's career as both a coach and a broadcaster, the very uniqueness of his personality was a tremendous asset to college basketball.

When basketball was in the developmental stages of becoming as popular as it is today, both during the college season and throughout the NCAA tournament, no one brought more attention to college basketball than Al did. Both Al's style and lack of style have, I think, been central to the great contribution he made over many years as a coach and as a broadcaster to popularize the college game.

From the first time I met Al when I was a young coach at West Point until today, I have been a great admirer of his and have a tremendous respect for what he is and who he is.

It is a great honor to write the foreword to this book about Al McGuire, a coach I greatly respect, a man I admire, a personality I have thoroughly enjoyed, and a friend I treasure.

Bob Knight
Head Basketball Coach
Indiana University
Bloomington, Indiana

ACKNOWLEDGMENTS

Many people have been very helpful and forthcoming over the past several years in helping me write this book on Coach McGuire. I thank my parents, Joseph and Mary C. Moran, for giving me the opportunity to attend Marquette University. Through their efforts I was given the chance to learn my journalistic trade. From the beginning of this project through the end, they have provided inspiration and reminders of the importance of patience. Mom and Dad, this is my gift to you.

I owe the greatest debt of gratitude to my wife, my soulmate, and my partner in life, Kristen Janet, who encouraged me every step of the way, assisted me in research, and believed that this book would come to fruition through all of my research, late night interviews, unreturned phone calls, and the uncertainty of getting a publisher. Thank you, Kristen Janet, for your love and patience as you indulged me in my passion for Marquette basketball and telling this story. Thank you for believing it could come true. I love you bunches.

To my in-laws, Allan and Nancy Edwards. For the past few years they have allowed me to work on their computer, use their paper, and stay at their home into the wee hours of the morning writing, rewriting, editing, and printing out chapter after chapter of this book. In addition they provided lunches and dinners too numerous to mention, and their hospitality and love made me feel welcome as a part of their family. I will forever be grateful to Mr. Edwards for keeping late hours with me to make sure everything came together. To my brother- and sister-in-law, Kurt and Tammy Edwards, for their continued encouragement. I will always appreciate your buying the Bob Knight book. Thank you, all.

For my brothers and sisters and immediate family, who continued to encourage me throughout this process. Your love and understanding of my efforts were heartening and made me feel proud. This is for you.

Former Marquette University archivist John Ledoux and his fine staff made every effort to accommodate me from the very beginning. John and Phillip Runkel provided scrapbooks, videotape, and photographs to peruse during my research, and stayed long hours so I could do my work. This book would not have been possible without your help, patience, and support.

To Dr. Kathleen Fitzgerald for believing in my talent and helping me prepare my book proposal in 1991. You have been an inspiration to me during this journey.

To George Reedy, my advisor at Marquette when I was a senior. Thank you for putting me in touch with Mike Hamilburg, who became my agent with your good words and help. To Mike and his secretary, Joanie, who showed enormous patience in dealing with my impatience. Thank you for believing in the book and sticking with me through thick and thin.

To Mary Durkin and Andrew Greeley, who took the time to review my proposal and offered support and encouragement.

To my publishers, Jerry Minnich and Kristin Visser of Prairie Oak Press, for having the courage to take a chance on an unknown writer and turning him into an author. Your patience with me has been a godsend. Thank you.

To Edith Duncan for taking the time to help edit my manuscript.

Among the Belmont Abbey alums, I owe a debt of gratitude to Jim Lytle for taking the time to be interviewed on the phone and for allowing me to use his home as my base when I went to New York to conduct my initial research in 1993. And to the Belmont Boys, Danny, Hank, "the Poet," Bobby, Johnny, Dock, and "the Spook," thank you for your stories. To Ebb Gantt of Belmont, North Carolina, whose background stories of Coach McGuire's early days at Belmont Abbey were instrumental in writing that chapter. Also to Coach Dean Smith, his secretary, Linda Woods, and Duke coach Mike Krzyzewski, Lou Carnesecca, and Bob Knight for working with me in putting together your dust jacket statements and foreword for the book. Thank you.

To all the other coaches: Ray Meyer, Joe Meyer, John Wooden, Bobby Cremins, Red Auerbach, Gene Sullivan, and John Kundla. Thank you for sharing your time and insights.

In New York, many thanks go out to Norman and Betty Ochs for inviting me into their home and sharing their stories of Coach

McGuire's youth. To Gene and Kathleen Mann who shared the McGuire family's Rockaway days with me during my trip to New York in 1995. Thank you, Dick McGuire, for sharing your basketball memories of growing up on McGuire's Playground.

In Milwaukee, many thanks go to Hank Raymonds and his wife, Jinny, for their hospitality during our interview sessions. Also, Goran Raspudic, Tom Collins, Bob Bach, Joan Bohmann, George Thompson, Dave Delsman, Gary Brell, Dean "the Dream" Meminger, Howie Fagan, Bob Wolf, Tom Flynn, Earl Tatum, Bo Ellis, Butch Lee, Gary Rosenberger, Dick Nixon, Lloyd Walton, Ric Cobb, Jim Chones, Blanton Simmons, Pat Smith, Rick Majerus, and all the Marquette players, coaches, trainers, and managers past and present who took the time to be interviewed and share their stories of Coach Al. Also at Marquette: Ed Pepan and Jim Scotton, dean of journalism during my undergraduate days, for encouraging me and being there when I needed someone to talk to about "the Book." And Marquette AD Bill Cords and SID Kathleen Hohl.

And to Coach Al McGuire and his secretary, Jeannie, for giving me the go-ahead to speak to your players, past and present, as well as your family members in putting together this tribute to your life and times. I feel privileged as a Marquette alumnus to have been allowed to write this story of your life. Coach McGuire, you gave me the opportunity of a lifetime. The good wishes, patience, and support that you showed me from our first meeting in Pewaukee in 1994 will never be forgotten. Thank you.

And to all of the Marquette alumni and students, as well as all the fans of Marquette basketball near and far who value the tradition, dignity, and respect for which Marquette has stood.

This one is for you.

Joseph Declan Moran
Winter 1999

Chapter One

A Rainy Night in Georgia

The grown man was crying on the bench, as a packed arena and millions of television viewers looked on. They were at first surprised, but soon became caught up in the moment, as the man's team put the finishing touches on his first—and only—NCAA basketball championship.

With less than a minute remaining in the 1977 national championship, Marquette University coach Al McGuire could not control the emotional rush. While he rubbed his eyes, McGuire's longtime assistant Hank Raymonds put an arm around his shoulder and vigorously congratulated the man in his finest hour as a college coach.

McGuire had announced his retirement early in the 1976–77 season and the impact of winning it all in his last game was sinking in quickly. The realization struck an untapped reservoir of emotions that fell on him like the steady rains outside Atlanta's Omni the night of March 28, 1977.

McGuire's cocky, New York street-tough façade was melting. Humbled by the magnitude of his team's achievement, the retiring coach, his face buried in a towel, revealed a vulnerable side few had ever seen.

As the final seconds ticked away, Marquette's players and fans flooded the court to celebrate the Warriors' 67-59 upset of the University of North Carolina Tar Heels and its coach, McGuire's friend Dean Smith.

During the 1976–77 season disco was king and so were underdogs. Jimmy Carter was elected president. The Portland Trail Blazers won the NBA title. And, later that evening in Hollywood, *Rocky* won the Academy Award for best picture.

In the midst of the full-court celebration, Al McGuire left the floor. A loner by nature, he wanted to enjoy the moment. Or to paraphrase a couple of McGuire-isms, he wanted to "go barefoot in the wet grass" and "congratulate the temporary."

When a reporter asked why the victorious coach was leaving the scene of his greatest triumph, he replied: "I'm not ashamed of crying. I just want to cry alone."

The emotional display by the 48-year-old coach overshadowed the fairy-tale finish of the Warriors' championship season. Only two other coaches have won the NCAA title in their final college game: John Wooden at UCLA (1975) and Larry Brown at Kansas (1988). Actually, the fact that McGuire was walking away from the sport at the top of his profession—and at a relatively young age—made him the focus of the '77 NCAA tournament.

Earlier, he had declared that his final Marquette squad was not nearly as good as some of his earlier teams—"I must have had six or seven clubs better than this one."

The 1976–77 Warriors had lost their final three home games en route to a 20-7 record. The seven losses were the most ever by a team selected for the tournament up to that time. Even the most faithful Warrior fans seriously doubted that McGuire would get one last shot at the brass ring before driving off into the sunset on his motorcycle.

While some preseason prognosticators had picked Marquette to win it all that season, the Warriors almost did not make it to the Big Dance. "We got in by the side door," insisted McGuire, who started planning his vacation after the team lost its final home game to Wichita State.

"After we lost our final three games at home I thought the carnival gates would close. Nothing was expected of us," he said. But Marquette won four of its last five road games, and was the final team selected for the 32-team tournament.

McGuire's last hurrah became one of the most memorable moments in the history of the Final Four, as indelible as John Wooden's tenth title when UCLA defeated Kentucky in his '75 swan song, and the late Jim Valvano's mad victory dash after North Carolina State defeated the University of Houston and Akeem "the Dream" Olajuwon in 1983.

"It was like the guy on the street making it to the top of the Empire State Building," said Jim Chones, one of McGuire's blue-chip All-Americas from the early 1970s. "Here's Marquette, a small independent in Milwaukee, beating big North Carolina. We were always competing against and beating schools that had million-dollar athletic budgets."

Al McGuire arrived at Marquette in 1964, the season after Wooden won his first NCAA title. In those pre–Proposition 48 days, freshmen were not eligible to play varsity ball, there was no shot clock or three-point shot, and only 24 teams were invited to the NCAA tournament. The only question each season between 1964 and 1975 was who would play UCLA in the finals?

While McGuire's Warriors always trailed the Wizard of Westwood's Bruins in the weekly basketball polls, his outspoken personality and unconventional coaching style made McGuire stand out from his more famous coaching brethren, such as Wooden and Kentucky's Adolph Rupp.

Wooden, the teacher, schooled his players in the "pyramid of success." McGuire, the curbside philosopher, relied on street smarts, common sense, and the School of Hard Knocks to make his men successful on the court and in the game of life. Though he did not have the basketball dynasty that Wooden enjoyed at UCLA, every one of his Marquette teams from 1969 to 1977 finished in the top 15 of the final Associated Press poll. Only the Bruins could make the same claim.

"Until I got to know Al, all I knew was a certain reputation," recalled Wooden. "A reputation about him—flamboyancy, outspokenness, and a few things of that sort. And that he was fiery on the bench and left the bench a lot, and was prone to pick up technical fouls. And all of these things that I didn't quite understand and wouldn't care too much for.

"Until I got to know him. Once getting to know the real Al McGuire, he's entirely different in the sense that he's sort of a Jekyll and Hyde in some respects. But not in other respects because he's honest all the way. He's an extremely honest person. One of the most honest I've ever known. You know exactly where he stands."

Al McGuire was one of the first white coaches to actively recruit inner-city ballplayers. "Marquette had a reputation at that time as a haven for the black athlete offering them education and television exposure," said Rick Majerus, one of McGuire's "co-coaches."

"What impressed me about Al was that he knew how to take the subway to get to Harlem," commented Pat Smith, one of the first players McGuire recruited to Marquette. "What impressed my mother about Al was that he talked about education, while all the other coaches who came to see me talked about basketball."

Al McGuire was one of the first to use the television timeout and technical foul to his strategic advantage. He was the first $50,000-a-year coach in college basketball, one of two goals he had upon arriving in Milwaukee. (The other was to become a millionaire.) McGuire was the first to reject a bid to the NCAA tournament (1970) and win the NIT, after the tournament committee decided to send the Warriors out of their region. His team was also the first to have its uniforms banned. He was the first to call for a coaches union, declaring that they should get tenure like any professor on their campuses.

With apologies to Earvin "Magic" Johnson, Al McGuire was really the father of "showtime." He understood the entertainment aspect of sports long before television had discovered college basketball and, from his playing days with the New York Knickerbockers, how hype could sell out stadiums. A salesman more than a coach, McGuire promoted himself and his teams by any means possible. He was equal parts Bill Veeck and P.T. Barnum.

It was a point of pride for McGuire that his Warriors consistently sold out the Milwaukee Arena, or the Mecca, as it came to be known. It was also home to the NBA's Milwaukee Bucks. McGuire filled the Mecca to capacity on a regular basis as Marquette drew more than a million fans over his 13 seasons. His teams created excitement and a winning basketball tradition.

"I like SRO. You need charisma. There should be electricity," he said of the games. "When I walk into the arena, the first thing I do is look at the four [most distant] corner seats. If those are sold, I've done my job. If I had a 25,000-seat arena, I guarantee I would fill it every night. I guarantee it."

Whether it was good timing or the luck of the Irish, McGuire seemed to be in the right place at the right time during his 23-year coaching career. One of the true characters of American sport, he arrived on the scene at a time when personalities were grabbing the headlines. Individuals, not teams, were becoming the main focus of the nation's media. In the mid-1960s, Muhammad Ali, Joe Namath, and Howard Cosell were "telling it like it is" and backing up their boasts. And McGuire, the native New Yorker, fit right in with his colorful speaking style, which would probably be considered politically incorrect today.

"Al was the quintessential New Yorker," noted Chones. "He talked to get an effect. Al once said, 'The brothers can jump higher because they have bigger butts.' If someone else had said that they'd be kicked out of Marquette. No one took him seriously as far as verbal slurs, because actions speak louder than words. He was loyal to all his kids. He stood by everyone."

McGuire coached in an era he described as "burn, baby, burn" and "hand grenades in your hands," when race relations in America were very volatile. It was a time when not only the color of the basketball was changing but the color of the players as well. His way of bringing black and white ballplayers together in a successful mix, which he called the "checkerboard," emphasized the overall team concept.

"People say, 'How do you handle blacks?' I don't handle black players. I don't even know they're black. If I knew how to handle blacks I'd sell it to GM and Sperry-Rand and IBM and go live on an island in New Zealand," he said.

"Al understood what we were going through because of the discrimination the Irish went through," said Chones, referring to what McGuire's immigrant parents encountered when they came to New York before the 1920s.

McGuire made it clear to his players that he was the boss, but he was secure enough to let them speak their minds and talk back to him if they disagreed. He followed a simple mantra: "Be straight with your ballplayers and they'll be straight with you."

A lightning rod for controversy, McGuire deliberately drew attention to himself so his players could concentrate on playing the game. His way of causing a distraction was to draw a technical.

"Sometimes Al did things to get people mad," recalled Raymonds, McGuire's successor at Marquette. "He used to do it on purpose to get you mad at him. This is what he did on the road to take your mind off the pressures of the game."

During a game against Loyola University at the Chicago Stadium in 1971, McGuire talked to the team in the huddle, ignoring beer bottles as they flew past his head.

"Al calls a timeout," recalled Chones. "We're behind by 12 points. LaRue Martin, who was a number one NBA draft pick in 1972, was having a great game. The fans started throwing bottles from the stands. I said, 'Coach, they're throwing bottles at your ass!' He slapped me twice and said, 'Listen up!' Nothing fazed him. He was fearless."

He described the relationship with his players as a "push"—or a standoff—but it was forged with mutual respect. He treated them like men and expected them to behave as such. He was determined not to be a babysitter.

"I can help them, but I won't be a social worker or a man of the cloth. I'm more like a mother figure to my players than a father figure." And "You don't come into my office unless it's close to a felony. Don't come to me for misdemeanors, haircut money, or garbage."

He did not discourage his stars from taking the "hardship" route to the NBA or ABA when it was to their advantage to do so. Chones was the second college player to leave school and enter the pros under the hardship rule (Spencer Haywood of the University of Detroit was the first in 1969).

"I looked in my refrigerator and it was full. I looked in Jimmy's refrigerator and it was empty," McGuire said, rationalizing Chones's decision to turn pro in the middle of his second collegiate season.

The one aspect of coaching that McGuire disliked was recruiting. He felt that he was lowering himself by chasing 17-year-old high school players. "I don't think any decent human being enjoys recruiting," he has said. "I never saw a ballplayer play in high school that I recruited, and I only recruited blue plate specials."

When asked if he looked for anything special in the players he recruited, McGuire said: "If they can look me in the eye, and the way that they treat their parents. That's how I know how they will treat me."

He usually relied on his co-coaches, childhood friends, former players, and "bird dogs" to let him know who was good. After he established himself in Milwaukee, McGuire went after one blue-chipper a year to develop his "senior star" system.

One of those was guard Alfred "Butch" Lee, who became All-American and Most Outstanding Player of the '77 Final Four. A native of the Bronx, Lee wanted to know how McGuire knew he was so good if he had never seen him play.

"Butch, you come from DeWitt Clinton," said McGuire. "There's 5,000 brothers in that school. You've been startin' for two years. You're the best. I don't have to go hug you. I said, you come with me and we'll make some nice music."

But McGuire never coached with the idea that he needed any one player to be successful. In fact, he insists that his life never depended on anyone but himself. He told recruits, "If you can have harmony and hug each other, that's beautiful. But if you don't join in the parade, I'm gonna get there anyway, with or without you."

McGuire always joked that he could not recruit a player who had grass in front of his home. He was more comfortable in the inner city. A self-described "kitchen" recruiter, McGuire preferred to talk to the players on their turf. Always looking for an edge with the parents, the unconventional McGuire was not above bringing his wife and kids or even his mother along on a visit. His recruitment of Danny Nee epitomized the McGuire touch.

"It was a Saturday afternoon in May or June 1964," recalled Nee, now head coach at the University of Nebraska. "I had been recruited by Seton Hall and Providence. I had an 875 SAT score. I couldn't go.

"Al shows up at my house in Bay Ridge, Brooklyn, on 67th Street. I didn't know he was coming. He brings his mother. My mom and dad were from Ireland. I walk into the little kitchen. Here's Al and his mom drinking tea and eating Irish soda bread. I'm stunned. My father didn't know where Milwaukee, Wisconsin, was. My father wanted me to get a good job after high school and get in with the Teamsters. After the visit, my father said, 'You should go with your own kind.' It was done in my kitchen. That's how I met him."

McGuire did not consider himself an Xs and Os or a "salt and pepper" coach, referring to those coaches who move the shakers around a table to demonstrate a new play or defensive wrinkle. He left that to his "co-coaches," Raymonds and Majerus. But what McGuire lacked in Xs and Os he more than made up for with wits and instinct. He was at his best at game time, when he thrived on the pressure, and established a reputation as one of the best game coaches in college basketball.

"You never talk basketball to me. I dictate basketball. I don't talk it," he used to say. "When you ask me what do they [players] think of it, I don't know what they think of it. Because it's not up to them to think of it. If you're gonna run a show, you've got to run it."

During the three stops on his coaching compass—Dartmouth, Belmont Abbey, and Marquette—McGuire claimed never to have worked from a blackboard or blown a whistle. When he arrived for practice, McGuire would invariably look at his players and say, "OK, let's scrimmage." The practices were usually open to anyone, including opposing coaches and the media. Most days the wrestling team could be seen running laps on the wooden track above the court where the Warriors went through their paces at the old gym on Clybourn Street in Milwaukee.

"Coaches would leave our practices in a cold sweat," recalled Raymonds. "They couldn't believe that a team that was so organized on the court could be so disorganized in practices."

At least once a week during practice, McGuire would give his "philosophy of life" talk, which sometimes went on for 45 minutes. He told the players stories from his days growing up in New York to drive home the point that they should use basketball and not let basketball use them. The talks were intended to bring some perspective to their lives and remind them that "sports is a coffee break."

"The other guys would laugh, 'There's Al bullshittin' us again,'" said Chones. "I listened to him. I wasn't from the streets [like Al]. You can't bullshit a bullshitter, he used to say."

"I think it's a different approach to coaching," commented Indiana University coach Bob Knight. "I think Al was a personality coach rather than an offensive or defensive coach. I don't know whether there's been anybody in coaching since I've been in college coaching that [did] a better job of handling personalities and getting more out of players."

"Dealing with problems, differences. That is what coaching is. Running patterns is not coaching," McGuire insisted during his career, where he used tolerance to deal with the many issues raised with his teams.

The self-described "original flower child," McGuire followed no road map in life or on his many motorcycle treks to the "pools and meadows" where he collected antiques and toy soldiers. The motorcycle trips helped him escape the trappings of coaching, which he considered a means to his real goal in life: making money. "Coaching is not the ultimate. I never liked coaching. There's got to be more to life than hangin' up jock straps."

McGuire grabbed life by the handlebars and rode without an itinerary on a magical mystery tour filled with characters from all walks of life, with names like "Spook," "The Dream," "Cupcake Man," and "The Evil Dr. Blackheart."

A major intangible in McGuire's success was his personality. His charisma attracted ballplayers, fans, and media to him and, by extension, to Marquette. By the sheer force of his personality, McGuire transformed a losing basketball program into a national power.

Just when Marquette was becoming competitive with the Kentuckys and UCLAs of the college basketball world, television discovered the sport in the late 1960s. The game that started it all was the classic 1968 matchup between Lew Alcindor's UCLA Bruins and Elvin Hayes's Houston Cougars.

The charming Irishman was a perfect fit at a time when television, specifically Eddie Einhorn's TVS syndicate, was searching for something to sell to the networks and the nation's sports fans.

Einhorn, now vice chairman of the board of the Chicago White Sox, put together the package of regional games at a time when there were still powerhouse teams among the independent ranks. Some of these included the University of South Carolina, Notre Dame, and Marquette. Long before "March Madness," ESPN, and billion-dollar TV paydays, Marquette was one of the first teams to play televised games on Sunday afternoons.

"He was smart enough to use that personality and smart enough to use it against the other guy. He used eccentricity as a game plan. He's maintained being a personality. He has a way with words that no one else has. Being a little different, there was an advantage to it," said Einhorn.

Whether by design or not, the quick-witted coach was always good for a quote or a story, which endeared him to the national media. He coined memorable phrases by combining simple words with colorful imagery into his own stream of consciousness. An original, McGuire did not fall back on the familiar cliches or hackneyed phrases other coaches spouted when being interviewed. He added color to the hoops lexicon with such terms as "prime time," "numbers," "run," "blue chip," "goin' uptown," "cupcake," "white knuckler," "French pastry," "thoroughbred," and "aircraft carrier," not to mention his "Hail Mary" passes, among other Catholic metaphors.

His colorful and straightforward speaking style brought the game down to a basic, bottom-line level, which has helped McGuire stand out in his broadcast career from the homogeneous, blow-dried broadcasters who parrot overworked phrases and cliches. But it is not a shtick. It is how he talks, a manner of speaking. Even the *New York Times* dubbed him the James Joyce of the airwaves before the 1995 NCAA basketball tournament. During the 1997 tourney, the *Chicago Tribune* described him as "properly skeptical . . . he remains a broadcasting gem."

"I never really learned how to spell, and this is genuine," McGuire said. "And so I guess I've always played with words, related words. I've never had a good vocabulary, even at board meetings in the private sector of my life.

"A lot of times I feel inadequate. And a lot of times I'll ask what that particular word means, or those initials or that phrase. And a lot of times, especially around accountants, they're great for using initials. And I'll never stop askin' what it means. And a lot of times you get smirks and this and that. But it's a way of sayin' 'Hey, this is me. This is what it's all about.'"

The result is that McGuire has always spoken in pictures, using such phrases as "elevator man," "cloud piercer," "ballerina in the sky." He has always been, in a sense, colloquially articulate, never using words "that a shoeshine boy couldn't understand."

"He makes the abstract concrete," explained Chuck "the Poet" Sullivan, one of his former players at Belmont Abbey College. "Those things that we can't see, he makes clear with pictures."

Even today he peppers his broadcasts and speeches with street-corner aphorisms that make listeners do a double-take—"If the waitress has dirty ankles, the chili is good." "Never undress until you die." "You're born alone, you die alone." "The stool's too close to the boardwalk." "You can always tell the Catholic schools by the length of the cheerleaders' skirts." He is college basketball's answer to Yogi Berra. "You can't figure out what he means. You either laugh at him or laugh with him. It's Al," remarked childhood friend Norman Ochs.

These and other streetwise witticisms roll off the tongue of the voluble Irishman in a lyrical, spontaneous, and rapid-fire delivery, spiced with a salty Queens accent. So much so that longtime NBC broadcaster Dick Enberg dubbed him the Leo Gorcey of College Basketball, referring to the late star of the *Bowery Boys* movies. Tournament and Marquette invariably are turned into "toonament" and "Mahquette" by McGuire's Noo Yawkese, where the letter "r" seems to get tangled in his tongue along with the other vowels and consonants.

"My father talks like he's lived on the street all of his life, but a lot of that comes from working in a bar," said Allie McGuire, a guard for the Marquette Warriors from 1970 to 1973. Added Ochs: "Al stayed so down to earth in his speech patterns and mannerisms. He was very much a neighborhood product."

Spontaneity is another McGuire attribute. He insists that he is never afraid to make a fool of himself. Who can forget the head-bobbing impromptu hip-hop that he danced with the Syracuse basketball team after they advanced to the 1996 Final Four, or when he kissed Minnesota coach Clem Haskins after the Golden Gophers earned their first trip to the Final Four in 1997?

McGuire was really a more charming version of Indiana's Knight. When they were both coaching, both had short fuses, especially when it came to talented ballplayers who never lived up to their potential. It incensed McGuire and Knight when players who had much more talent than they had during their playing days did not take advantage of it.

While McGuire wanted to win just as much as the next coach, he never took himself or basketball too seriously. It was just a game, and when it was over—win or lose—he did not second-guess himself or look for anyone to blame. "Winning is only important in war and major surgery," declared McGuire, who still won 78 percent of his games and was twice named national Coach of the Year.

However, he was one up on Knight when it came to the media. McGuire both entertained and took advantage of the media to promote himself and his players. With the press he established an accommodating, symbiotic relationship, tempered by his Irish sense of humor. McGuire courted the press at a time when most coaches had little use for sportswriters.

While many of the aphorisms and barroom expressions McGuire sprinkled in his stories were often laughed at or dismissed as simplistic, they were for him a philosophy of life.

"Everything that I get is picked up in relation to something I'm doing. And then the expressions I use are out of those areas and connected into basketball. But when they come out, they come out. I don't say, I'm gonna say this or that. They're just back there. Then, all of a sudden, like the other day I said, 'cracked sidewalks.' And I meant the bad part of town," he explained. "The rundown part of town."

Another attribute is his up-front honesty. He has always spoken his mind and never backed down from anyone, including the "memos and pipes" (university administrators and professors), "zebras," and the NCAA.

"A lot of times, being relatively honest, you become brutal. Being truthful is not always the nicest thing in the world," he said. "It's not nice sometimes. You're better off treading water, allowing room to move, and so on."

"I think Al subscribed to the notion that the only absolute defense is the truth and you don't have to memorize it. Al spoke what he truly felt," observed Bob Bach, former "Voice of the Warriors" on Milwaukee's WISN radio.

It was during games that McGuire played the court jester and ringmaster to the circus that was Marquette basketball. Always looking for an edge, he relished the role of the underdog as he played the "us against the world" angle to perfection, mercilessly working the referees, the crowd, opposing coaches, and players. When an opposing player was getting ready to shoot a free throw, McGuire's voice could be heard echoing through the Mecca: "*Get da shootah!*" McGuire's big top was every arena in which the Warriors played around the country from 1964 to 1977.

A master showman and psychologist, McGuire played up his image of "Dirty Al" in opposing arenas. His strutting, shouting, step-right-up coaching style helped put people in the seats. "You cannot have a bland feeling about me. Either I'm a showboating son of a bitch, or I'm the darling that everyone picks on."

He was as much a performer as his players—a mixed bag of inner-city black All-Americas and white complementary players from Wisconsin burgs. All of his teams played a rugged, in-your-face defense, born of the New York style of playground ball he grew up on. He brought the city game to the Dairy State, making sure that his teams never let anyone take anything from them without a fight, including home-court winning streaks. In fact, the Warriors 81-game home winning streak from 1967 to 1973 is the sixth longest in NCAA history. "A team should be the extension of the coach's personality. So my teams are obnoxious and arrogant. Being a fellow originally from the streets, when I am punched, I punch back."

"We were perceived as a bunch of bandits," recalled Gary Rosenberger, a guard on the '77 championship team. The Warriors were usually dressed in discofied uniforms with the shirttails hanging out, a no-no in today's corporate college basketball world. "At Marquette, I put people in the seats. We're more like productions. *Annie Get Your Gun, South Pacific*," said McGuire, who was not above resorting to gimmicks to get attention, including retiring a uniform number in honor of the Apollo 11 astronauts.

For the 1976–77 season, the Warriors' uniforms were designed by Jule Campbell, senior editor of *Sports Illustrated*'s annual swimsuit issue, in cooperation with Medalist Industries, a Milwaukee-based sports equipment company for which McGuire served as an executive after leaving Marquette. Those were the days when basketball shorts were really shorts, light-years away from the pajama bottoms that today's players wear.

Many observers of Marquette basketball thought that much of McGuire's behavior—the tantrums, the technicals, and the rest—was simply an act. "It's no act," corrected Raymonds. "He just gets caught up in the excitement of the game." But his courtside demeanor never degenerated into bullying or buffoonery.

While McGuire ran what appeared to many fans and the media to be a loose ship in which players openly disagreed with him, he somehow knew what was going on, even when he was not around. He exercised what could be described as a hands-off "institutional control."

"I was the Houdini, who did his disappearing act," said McGuire. "I know that 85 percent of me is buffalo chips, and the other 15 percent is rare talent. I'd stay in that 15 percent, in the mental toughness, the media, keeping an eye on the elephant, not the mice, and extending the life of the extinct kiwi bird, which is nocturnal."

During one practice in 1973, Dave Delsman, a walk-on guard and one of McGuire's complementary players, and All-American Marcus Washington, started fighting. McGuire issued a challenge that anyone who wanted to fight had to fight him. Delsman called the coach's bluff and sucker-punched him. As McGuire lay on the floor dazed, the stunned Delsman stood above him in disbelief, thinking that he would be thrown off the team. But McGuire liked Delsman's guts and kept him on the team. Delsman reminded McGuire of himself.

McGuire remained steadfastly loyal to his players. The seniors in his "star system" usually wound up with professional basketball contracts, or "two loaves of bread under their arms" (good jobs). "We tried to make them aware of life and business. We don't run a [basketball] factory."

Long before Proposition 48, McGuire insisted that his players go to class and earn their degrees. In his opinion, "they should be starting Proposition 48 back in the fifth grade, never mind the high schools." While it took some of them longer than four years, McGuire continued to harp on how important their education would be after basketball. The only promise he made to the parents of his players was that their sons would graduate. And he was determined to fulfill that promise while they played for him, and even after their pro careers ended.

"My players got degrees before it was *fashionable* to get a degree," he said. "I don't know what influence I had [on their lives], but from the batting averages of their lives, it's a pretty nice batting average."

The charismatic side of McGuire's personality cast a positive aura that transcended race, talent, winning and losing, and even college basketball itself. The way he touched people's lives seemed mystical because of the flip side of his personality—the sentimental introvert who kept his distance and enjoyed his time away from the spotlight. This is not to say the man does not have an ego. "I don't really know what it is not to be a celebrity," he said the day he announced his retirement. "I like to have smoke rings blown at me."

As he became better known nationally as a broadcaster, the perception emerged that the former coach was becoming more withdrawn—from Marquette, his former players, and others in his life. While on television McGuire comes off as a glad-handing sort, in everyday life he keeps people at arm's length. This has expanded the McGuire legend and made him seem almost larger than life.

But this "distance" is really a healthy detachment from his past that has allowed McGuire to move on with his life without regrets or excuses. "When my father closes the door on a part of his life, he just does not look back," explained his youngest son, Robbie.

"While he loves the limelight, by nature [Al] is a loner. He likes to go on his motorcycle. He likes to take walks. He likes to think," said Raymonds, who was never invited to the McGuire home for dinner. "So there's a big contrast on the court and off the court. And what the people see in him I do not believe is the real Al McGuire. The real Al McGuire is a compassionate man. He likes to do little things for people, whether it be a janitor or anyone."

Even with all of his success, McGuire has stayed close to his blue-collar roots. He has lived in the same house since 1964, has the same telephone number, drives a nondescript car, and has given back a great deal to the community through his involvement in charitable causes. He remains so close to his roots that when he has breakfast with his friend Herb Kohl, U.S. Senator from Wisconsin and owner of the Milwaukee Bucks, they meet at a McDonald's for Egg McMuffins. "He could relate as easily to the bum on the street as he could the millionaire. He was a man for all seasons," added Raymonds.

Jim Chones, former voice of the NBA's Cleveland Cavaliers, recalled a practice when a street person wandered in to watch the Warriors go through their paces.

"This guy would be shadow-boxing in the corner during our practice. And as the practice wore on he made his way behind one of the baskets. All of a sudden, Al yells out, 'Hey, fella.' We thought, oh, oh, Al's gonna kick the shit out of this guy.

"But he goes over and starts asking him where he boxed and who he fought, and they went on for 45 minutes while we practiced. Then the guy just sat and watched us practice. I guess Al had seen the worst of life growing up in New York. So this was nothing new to him."

During his Marquette heyday the dapper McGuire, decked out in three-piece suits, jet-black hair combed straight back, was usually better dressed than most of his contemporaries. This was at a time when coaching and haute couture were not synonymous. Most coaches of the day wore sweaters or two-button sports coats, test-pattern plaid being the design of choice.

McGuire had a flair for the dramatic. He was usually the last to enter an arena before a game. During games he paced intently at courtside, as if looking for someone to plead his case. When he did not get a call or lost a game, McGuire simply shrugged, turned his palms up, and looked skyward with an expression that said, "Why me, God?"

Moving back and forth, walking the tightrope that was his imaginary coaching box, McGuire barked out instructions and taunts, while animatedly gesturing with his arms and hands. He would kick a chair or a water bottle. When anyone crossed him—players, officials, fans—McGuire's green eyes became fixed in a piercing, hawklike stare that seemed to say, "Let's go outside and settle this," as he had a number of times at his father's bar at Rockaway Beach, New York.

A quick-trigger Irish temper led to outbursts well known to basketball fans across the country. During one NCAA tournament game in the early 1970s, he became so incensed at a call that he stomped around in a circle like a child having a tantrum, literally pulling out clumps of hair. His invective-laced tirades drew costly technical fouls, especially at tournament time.

While some of his technicals may have been calculated to get his team psyched up, more often than not they put the Warriors in the "minus pool." His two "Ts" during the 1974 NCAA finals cost Marquette the national championship against David "Skywalker" Thompson and the North Carolina State Wolfpack.

"I would say that I lost the game there. I would say that I gave them two five-point plays and that was it. I had a bad day."

During the 1976 Mideast Regionals in Baton Rouge, Louisiana, McGuire drew a technical during a loss to eventual national champion Indiana. After that game he vowed never to coach Marquette if it was invited to another NCAA tournament. He would let his co-coaches take the team. "My only worry is that they'd win without me," McGuire declared.

But there he was a year later on Peach Tree Street coaching in the national championship. There would be no technical fouls on this rainy night in Georgia. Before the final, McGuire guaranteed he would not get hit with a technical. He had announced his retirement and he was determined not to blow his "auld lang syne," as NBC's Dick Enberg described it that night.

There were only tears on this night. Tears of joy. Tears of a clown, not unlike the portraits of the sad Emmett Kelly that lined the walls of his office. "If I knew crying on the bench would mean a million dollars, I would have started crying ten years earlier," he joked.

McGuire parlayed the national championship into a lucrative broadcast and speaking career. He became an even bigger star after leaving coaching—first as a color analyst with NBC, and now as a self-styled hoops guru for Conference USA's college basketball telecasts and for CBS during the NCAA basketball tournament. "He brought a new meaning to analyzing games," said his friend and former DePaul basketball coach Ray Meyer.

"When Al was coaching, anytime he gave a recommendation for someone it was considered the kiss of death," laughed Raymonds. "But all of a sudden after he begins broadcasting, he's a genius."

But unlike many of the antics that characterized his successful 13-year run at Marquette, McGuire's emotional swan song did not appear to be an act. It looked like a genuine display of emotion from a man who suddenly realized that it was all over. "Curtains." "Tap City." "That's all she wrote." All of those McGuire-isms now applied to his own career.

Al McGuire, the eccentric who rode his motorcycle around the Georgia backwoods the day of the NCAA championship game and almost did not make it back in time for the tip-off, and who fought with everyone from the drunks in his father's bar to the NCAA establishment, finally had his career validated with a national championship. Nobody could take that away.

He went out a winner, just like UCLA's Wooden in whose shadow he paced and pranced to draw attention to his teams. During his final ten years coaching at Marquette, no coach—Wooden included—averaged as many wins (25) as McGuire. He took his Warriors to the NCAA or NIT tournament every year, his players graduated, and he ran a powerhouse basketball program with no hint of scandal.

"Seashells and balloons," his trademark imagery for victory and happiness, were finally his. Al McGuire could leave the Big Top even though he did not think he would win at the Big Dance. His hoop dreams had become a reality.

"I've always been a bridesmaid. More like a lunch pail, tin-hat type of person. I never thought I'd really win. I'm a positive thinker, but I always thought I'd come in second," he said.

"I started to think back to all the PALs and CYOs as a kid. And all the wet socks and jocks and T-shirts and all the sprained thumbs and I said, why me? I still do to this day. Why me? Then I started to enjoy the moment. The next thing I knew I was crying where Sherman burned down the city."

When he returned to the court at the Omni to join in the celebration with his players, family, and fans, McGuire was smiling broadly and wearing the face of a winner as he clutched the sheared white strings of basketball net. A happy clown.

The memories of joy, pain, and frustration that washed over McGuire in this, his greatest moment, seemed to make everything he experienced in his merry-go-round career worthwhile. The NCAA championship was not a destination for McGuire, but another stop along his colorful journey. The national championship and his longtime success as a broadcaster led to his induction into the Basketball Hall of Fame in 1992.

All of Al McGuire's worlds seemed to converge in that one magical moment, providing a grateful, sentimental perspective on his magnificent run.

"All love affairs end. Eventually the girl is gonna put curlers in her hair."

Chapter Two

Early Days

The bright colors of that triumphant night in Georgia were a much different hue from the cloudy sepia tone of the Great Depression during which Al McGuire grew up on the streets of New York.

Alfred Emanuel ("Just like God") McGuire was born September 7, 1928, in the Bronx, the third of John and Winifred McGuire's four children. It is not entirely certain what his middle name is because the family didn't keep records. Depending on the circumstances, he could be Alfred E. or Alfred J. (Joseph or James) McGuire.

His father, John Richard McGuire, had emigrated from the family farm in Loch Key, a village in County Roscommon, Ireland. "That's where the sheep stealers come from," McGuire joked. His father came from a family of property owners in the ould country. The former Winifred Sullivan, born to an Irish father, arrived in New York from Hereford, England. Both came by boat to America before the Roaring Twenties. Like so many others who passed through Ellis Island, they came here to make a better life for themselves and their families.

"I was always proud to be Irish," noted McGuire. "I think that we brought a comfortableness and a sense of humor to the U.S."

The Irish who came to Americay, as many newcomers pronounced it, were fortune seekers. They wanted the freedom to vote and more important, the freedom to practice their religion. The Catholic Church was the one institution that held Irish families together in the new world. As a result, it was the Irish who started the parochial school system in the United States.

Winifred, who had always dreamed of coming to America, came in 1917 or 1918, when she was 16. Like many young Irish women of the time, she worked as a domestic for wealthy families in Manhattan and earned enough money to bring her other sisters to America.

In 1921, John and Winifred met at an Irish dance in New York City, according to family members. They were married when she was 21; he was ten years her senior. Not long afterward they settled in a railroad flat on 167th Street in an area of the Bronx known as Irish Harlem. There they ran a small bar and grill, where Mrs. McGuire made lunches for the local railroad workers.

Al McGuire's older brothers, John and Dick, were born in 1924 and 1926, respectively. Their sister, Kathleen, was the youngest, born in 1932.

Al McGuire was reportedly named for New York Governor Alfred E. Smith, another son of immigrants and, in 1928, the first Irish Catholic nominated for President of the United States. Smith, a.k.a. "the Happy Warrior," was best known for his phrase, "Let's look at the record." Al Smith campaigned against GOP nominee Herbert Hoover and Prohibition, which endeared him to tavern owners like John McGuire. But Smith could not overcome the anti-Catholic bias of the time and the prosperity of the party in power. Hoover won the election, polling 58 percent of the vote.

America in 1928 was a vibrant, exciting place where change seemed to be the only constant. The stock market was soaring to unprecedented heights, fueled by nonstop speculation. The underlying current of that wildly prosperous era was a notion of permanent prosperity for all Americans, even immigrants.

Americans were quickly becoming seduced by the latest fads, novelties, games, and also by spectator sports, which were broadcast on the nation's newest entertainment medium, radio, and shown in movie theaters. People were tuning out the social and political problems of the day and tuning in the exploits of the Kings of Sport: Jack Dempsey, Babe Ruth, Red Grange, and Bobby Jones, as well as Amos 'n' Andy.

The post–World War I boom produced cars, electric refrigerators, phones, vacuum cleaners, washing machines, and other household conveniences on a seemingly endless assembly line, a virtual capitalist cornucopia of consumerism.

The flip side of the boom could be seen in the ramifications of Prohibition, enacted with the passage of the 18th Amendment in 1920.

Rumrunners, bootleggers, homemade booze, and the elevation of gangsters such as Al Capone to front-page status were areas of concern to ordinary Americans. As writer Milton Meltzner described the times, it seemed that thriftiness and other old-fashioned virtues were giving way to "a dollar down, a dollar forever." The bottom line was to achieve success by whatever means possible.

Not all Americans were sharing in the promise of prosperity, however, especially immigrants. Even though the standard of living in the U.S. exceeded that of their homelands, the future was not particularly bright for those from the ould country who took any work they could find. Unfortunately, what many of them found were signs that read, NO IRISH NEED APPLY.

What helped the early Irish immigrants survive was not only a willingness to work hard but an ability to communicate. Americans jokingly referred to it as blarney, but it was really a gift. The newly arrived Irish quickly picked up the American tongue and warmed it with a brogue. This gift of gab eventually helped the Irish thrive in politics and union organizing.

In the Bronx, the Chamber of Commerce was touting the borough as "the Nation's Sixth City," as it was already bigger than St. Louis, Boston, or Baltimore. The New York Yankees were packing crowds into "the House That Ruth Built" (Yankee Stadium), which opened in 1923. Irish immigrants helped build not only the Brooklyn Bridge but the Bronx Democratic machine, a formidable bookend to longtime political monolith Tammany Hall.

In 1925 the first truly "national" basketball league was formed, the American Basketball League. Two years later, Abe Saperstein formed the Harlem Globetrotters in Chicago. And as far as basketball was concerned in the Big Apple, the all-black New York Rens made quite a name for themselves. The team compiled an 88-game winning streak in 1933, which was snapped by the Original Celtics, another team that rarely lost a game.

Bronx Democrats helped elect Jimmy "Night Mayor" Walker to lead New York City and Franklin Delano Roosevelt to govern the state, succeeding Al Smith.

It was into this roller-coaster world that Al McGuire was born.

"We were a close family," recalled John McGuire, "but not lovey-dovey. Mother was a big woman, 260 to 280 pounds—tremendously strong and a hard worker. I remember her bottling beer by hand and makin' bathtub gin in the basement in the old days in the Bronx. We'd never answer her back."

Any profile of Al McGuire is not complete without noting the influence of his mother, Winifred. She not only ran the family, she ran the business.

McGuire and his sister, Kathleen Mann, recalled that their mother had a feel for people and a knack for making and holding on to money. In fact, she would not go to sleep at night until the day's cash was tucked safely under her pillow.

Her world was ruled by common sense, honesty, and frugality. She instilled these values in her children and also passed on her athletic prowess. Before coming to America, she had established herself as an athlete in her native Hereford, England.

"She was quite a swimmer," said Mann, who recalled that the mother, like Al, tended to exaggerate when telling a story. "She told us that she swam the English Channel. But it was actually the River Wye in England.

"She had a philosophy of life and business, and he [Al] inherited all of that. She never took a vacation. She was a very hard worker. But she was a woman for zero detail. She never kept family records or photos."

"Al never remembered anyone's name. He'd call you anything. Mrs. McGuire didn't remember anyone's name either," said Gene Mann, a boyhood friend who grew up with McGuire and later married Kathleen. In the grand scheme of things, names, birthdays, and phone numbers just did not seem to matter to Winifred McGuire.

"She had a two-plus-two-is-four philosophy," McGuire explained in a 1986 *Milwaukee Journal* story by Roger Jaynes. "Mother's background was people. She was always touching people. There was a singleness in her approach. She always used to say, 'The best manners in the world are to be natural.' You can't get a sense of humor or common sense from a computer."

"But there was a shyness to my mom," Kathleen Mann added. "She was OK on her home turf, very much in control. But if she was in situations where she was around people with more education or where she might use the wrong word, she was shy.

"But if it was business or on her home turf, she was always in control. She was more of a business person than my dad." Mann guessed that her parents probably came to America with no more than an eighth-grade education.

America was reaching the end of the Roaring Twenties in 1929. According to Meltzner, national income was up to $87 billion—a 44 percent jump from 1922. One half of American families owned a car, and 71,000 stockbrokers were doing business in the U.S. But more than three fourths of the country's 27.5 million families earned less than $3,000 a year and had no savings.

When the stock market crashed on Tuesday, October 29, 1929—panic spread throughout the country. The next day, President Hoover assured the country that "the traditional business of the country, that is the production, distribution of commodities is on a sound and prosperous basis."

Bread lines and job lines began to snake around the big cities of the U.S. "Hooverville" centers were springing up from coast to coast, filled with men, young and old, down on their luck. Astrologers, soothsayers, and readers of tea leaves began to flourish as people looked to anyone who might tell them that things would get better.

While things were tight in the McGuire household, the family was not on government relief. There was enough to eat, and Winifred McGuire was boss.

One of young John McGuire's favorite stories about his brother growing up was the day their mother caught Al with his hand in the money jar that she kept hidden in her bedroom, retold in a Roger Jaynes' feature in the *Milwaukee Journal* in 1976.

"Dick and I heard someone coming, so we crawled under Mother's bed, and here comes Al. No more does Al get the jar opened than in comes Mother.

"She grabs him by the ear and lets him have it, and then she opens the window and hangs him out, shakin' him, holdin' him by one leg. At that time we were living five floors up. And so mother shouts at him, 'Don't you ever do that again, or I'll let go.'

"Dick looked at me and I looked at Dick, and we both gulped. And we never went near that money jar again."

By 1930 New Yorkers found something to take their minds off the Great Depression: a group of basketball players from St. John's University nicknamed the Wonder Five. Some 12,000 spectators filled the old Armory to see Jack "Rip" Gerson, Max Posnack, Allie Schuckman, Mac Kinsbrunner, and Matty Begovich beat a CCNY squad 26-21.

Edward "Ned" Irish, a sports reporter for the *World Telegram*, saw great financial potential in the Wonders and booked them as part of the first tripleheader played at Madison Square Garden in 1931.

The tripleheader, which was backed by Mayor Jimmy Walker, drew some 16,000 fans to the Garden. Columbia defeated Fordham, Manhattan beat NYU, and the Wonder Five upset CCNY, coached at the time by former Original Celtic great Nat Holman.

By 1932, America was still digging itself out of the Great Depression. Americans were embittered and disenchanted with the conditions of their lives and the country's future. New York City alone had 15,000 homeless men, and unemployment in Harlem was at 50 percent. Virtually the only hero on the American scene was the Brown Bomber, heavyweight boxing champion Joe Louis.

That summer, the GOP renominated Hoover and the Democrats picked New York Governor Franklin Delano Roosevelt. The wheelchair-bound Roosevelt received 22 million votes to Hoover's 15 million, and the New Deal soon began.

In 1933, Prohibition was repealed. Two years later at the Summer Olympics in Berlin, Dr. James Naismith was on hand for the first international basketball game between Mexico and the Philippines, which was played outdoors. It was a far cry from the game Dr. Naismith had designed specifically for indoor play. At that time, most former collegians wound up playing in the annual AAU tournament in Denver or in the World Professional Tourney in Chicago.

Dick McGuire recalled that his brothers did not start to play basketball until the family moved to the Rockaway area of Queens, an ocean resort on a strip of Long Island between the Atlantic Ocean and Jamaica Bay. In 1937 their father sold his tavern in the Bronx. John was 12, Dick 10, Al 8, and Kathleen 5 when the McGuires went uptown for the first time.

The family moved into a ten-room hotel and bar in a Seaside section of Rockaway called Irish Town. Eighteen blocks long and three blocks wide, it attracted families on vacation during the summer, or "the season," as it was known.

Rockaway at that time was "mostly Irish Catholic," recalled Gene Mann, who added that most of the residents worked for the courts and for the police and fire departments. Civil service jobs were big on the beach. "In politics you voted for Democrats. You took care of the guy who got your son a job in the summer. Patronage went to the local people. John and Winifred were probably Democrats."

While happy days were not exactly here again in the late 1930s, people were slowly being put back to work. It was in this atmosphere that the Rockaway Beach section flourished. Hotels, motels, bungalows, and the boardwalk attracted people from all over New York during the season.

The bungalows were organized into courts of eight on each side facing each other, and all of them were adjacent to the bars. The two-bedroom bungalows had walls that did not reach the ceiling.

"The distance between the bungalows would be six to eight feet, and a lot of them had a little white picket fence," remembered Gene Mann. "They had outdoor showers with cold water. The sinks had one tap because there was only cold water."

"Everything was a court back then," said Kathleen Mann. "Everything was lanterns, balloons, music, and little ones crying. It was a happy time."

The innocent and carefree life growing up on Rockaway Beach was where Al McGuire discovered his seashells and balloons.

"Seashells and balloons is bare feet and wet grass. It means a light breeze. You know, a light breeze that would maybe move a girl's skirt a little," explains McGuire. "It's sweater weather. A malted, you know, a shake. The gentleness of it. The wholesomeness of it. It's tender. That type of thing.

"I don't know where in the devil I came up with it. People when they hear it, if they are of that certain type of quality, they understand what a seashell is and what a balloon is."

Back then, Queens had one fifth the population of Manhattan, three times as many people as Milwaukee, and a half million more than Detroit. In summer, Queens offered the beach and all the dances.

It was a carnival atmosphere with something for everyone. Millions came down to Rockaway every weekend during the season from all the boroughs except Staten Island, which was a major reason all of the taverns survived year-in and year-out. People filled the 13-mile stretch of beach from Breezy Point to Far Rockaway. Priests, judges, policemen, and firemen, even NBA referee Sid Borgia, lived in the bungalows during the summer. Party lights were strung up from bungalow to bungalow from Memorial Day through Labor Day.

People made their way to Rockaway by bus, car, the Long Island Railroad, or hitchhiking. Guys usually wore a T-shirt and dungarees, with their swimsuit rolled up in a towel stuffed into a back pocket.

But the beach was not just a summer place. It was where people grew up, hung out, worked, met their wives, and eventually brought up their families.

"The Irish Catholics who were civil servants were all products of the Great Depression," recalled Gene Mann. "The Democrats treated them well with the WPA [Works Progress Administration]. Mixed in were bankers and lawyers and CPAs, and young families on their way up who ultimately did well," he said, referring to the diversity of people who came to the beach during the summers. "Ninety-nine percent of the inhabitants were Irish," recalled Lou Carnesecca, long-time Saint John's University coach. Aspiring civil servants went to the Delahanty Institute to take the qualifying exams after finishing high school.

The journey began at Playland, a combination playground and carnival at 98th Street, where the aromas of corn on the cob, caramel corn, hot dogs, and French fries comingled with the salty breeze. Only the happy noise of children interrupted the steady sound of the waves slapping the shore. Playland was a miniaturized version of Brooklyn's famous Coney Island.

Many high school boys hung out under the boardwalk, either playing cards or making time with their best girl. That was their indoctrination to the beach.

The college crowd also hung out at Rockaway. After college, most of the 21-plus set headed to the Jersey Shore or the Hamptons.

In the Irish Town section of Rockaway, all of the taverns were wooden sheds except McGuire's. The bars served food, and an appetizing aroma wafted from the bars between 102d and 103d Streets.

Radio was king back then as Americans were entertained by Bob Hope, Jack Benny, George Burns and Gracie Allen, and such programs as *Fibber McGee and Molly* and *Gangbusters* (produced by Norman Schwarzkopf Sr.).

Beachcombers also found entertainment in the dance halls and bars located on 103d Street from the Boardwalk down to the Bay. People moved from place to place and hopped to the Big Band sounds and Irish dance bands every weekend. A lot of the bars in Irish Town had floors that could hold 100 dancers. "When Irish Eyes Are Smiling" was heard from Memorial Day to Labor Day. In these establishments you could get as much to drink as you wanted and no one asked your age. It was also on this street that the happy sounds of the revelers were interrupted by the wail of the paddy wagons, taking away those who had imbibed a wee bit too much of the crather.

During the 1940s and '50s, differences between residents of the boroughs were based on baseball, ethnicity, or both. Queens was a melting pot of people from Brooklyn, Manhattan, and the Bronx. "If it wasn't ethnicity, it was the team you rooted for," said Jackie Smith, a bartender at nearby Fitzgerald's. "The Yankees, Brooklyn Dodgers, or the New York Giants. Guys would be on street corners arguing who was the best centerfielder in New York: Mickey, Willie, or Duke."

At 106th Street were the handball courts, and at the 108th Street playground was the asphalt court where the McGuire boys learned their basketball trade. It became known as McGuire's Playground.

The Catholic church was St. Camillus, located in the Seaside section of Rockaway at 100th Street. Mass was held every Sunday in the upper chamber, lower church, and gymnasium. Girls coming from the beach in shorts were not allowed in church; they had to wear skirts. "Everybody went to church, no matter how drunk they got on Saturday night," said Mann.

"I thought everyone was Catholic when I was growing up," added McGuire. Smith recalled that there were always a few guys outside the church taking bets on what time each mass would end. "Part of growing up in New York was gambling, on anything," Smith said.

McGuire's was located at 108th Street and Rockaway Boulevard in Irish Town. Wall-to-wall taverns lined the boulevard from 102d to 108th Streets, none taller than two stories. Rockaway's commercial district ran from 108th to 116th Street. Bars were scattered here and there. Mann's on 114th Street was operated by Bill Mann, Gene's father.

"There was the Leitrim House, O'Reilly's, Fitzgerald's, and our place," said McGuire. The seven-block strip was also home to such ould-country-sounding places as the Blarney Castle, Gildea's, Flynn's, O'Gara's, Healy's, Innisfail, the Sligo House, and the Dublin House. For the college crowd there was Mike Reilly's, while the more sophisticated set preferred Cooney's.

Immigrants who worked as domestics cleaning the homes of the well-to-do in Manhattan would come down to the taverns named for their respective counties in Ireland, simply to hear a familiar brogue and see an Irish face.

All of the taverns got a fresh coat of paint just before Memorial Day weekend and the opening of the season. McGuire's, however, was open year-round. John and Winifred lived in the basement and rented out the ten rooms above the tavern. After Labor Day Rockaway resembled a ghost town. With the Empire State Building looming 18 miles across Jamaica Bay, Rockaway looked like Alaska in winter.

"What you have to realize," noted Al's oldest brother, John, "is that you lived all year on what you made during the summer. So summers we slept in the cellar. But we kids loved it down there. Sleeping next to the beer boxes, stealing soda from the crates, playing hide-and-seek. When you're young you don't realize how bad things are."

"I remember falling asleep and hearing the Irish songs where we lived behind the tavern. I remember the drunks interrupting our dinner to ask where the restroom was," said Al. "Everybody worked. Money was tight."

Since both Winifred and John worked in the bar, the children were partly raised by Winifred's parents, whom she brought to the U.S. in the late 1930s.

"In those days, grandparents lived in the extended family," explained Kathleen Mann. "My father's Aunt Kate and Grandpa and Grandma Sullivan lived in the house. Mom and Dad had no sentimentality. Everything was business."

In 1939 college basketball was still in its infancy when Oregon defeated Ohio State to win the first NCAA basketball championship at Northwestern University's Patten Gymnasium, in Evanston, Illinois. The National Invitation Tournament took its bow a year earlier as Temple defeated Colorado in the first NIT championship. The first professional basketball association, the National Basketball League, was just two years old, the jump ball after each basket had been eliminated—as had the use of ropes and chicken wire to separate fans from basketball courts—World War II was still several months away, and the World's Fair came to New York City.

After the family moved to Rockaway, John McGuire purchased the former Mr. Bowe's Restaurant and began to put his imprimatur on the establishment. Between 1937 and 1940 the old brick boardinghouse was remade into a tavern. "He was very stylish," noted Gene Mann. "He bought the back bar and mirrors from the Schaefer Pavilion at the '39 World's Fair. Schaefer was the biggest beer at the time."

Other top brews of the day were Piels, Guinness, and Rheingold. Rheingold featured Dalmatians and New York City fire trucks in its advertisements and was famous for the beauty contests it sponsored in the 1940s and '50s. Photos of the Miss Rheingold finalists covered the walls of Irish Town bars, and each establishment had a ballot box. McGuire's parents used to make Al drink the Guinness Stout to fatten him up because he was so skinny, remembered Ochs.

"McGuire's was a big family bar in 1939. It had singing waiters. There was this big bar behind the rectangular windows. But then you went into a major back room. Every bar had a back room, many of which had basketball courts in later years. We played a lot of our games in old back room bars and grills," said Mann.

The vertical green neon sign on the front of the tavern read McGuire's. The back room of the bar had leather seats, booths, and tables. An Irishman played the piano, and singing waiters with handlebar mustaches and garter belts on their sleeves served draft beer on metal trays. There were no bottles. It was all keg beer.

"It was a boom time in Rockaway Beach during World War II. Everyone was looking for relaxation. Everyone had a few dollars because they were working," said Mann, who traveled from bar to bar selling pretzels and potato chips out of the back of a station wagon during the season. At the time, you could buy a portable radio for $25. A glass of beer was 15 cents, Seagram's 7 and ginger ale was 35 cents, a shot of scotch was 50 cents. A movie was 35 cents. People were earning $15 a week. Milk was still being delivered in horse-drawn carriages, and whole generations of people had never been on an airplane.

"In 1945, when the war ended, you started to see a change in the clientele because you had the veterans coming back from the war," remembered Smith. "Not drastically at first, but then as the [McGuire] boys went to college, it started to become a college hangout versus the family, singing-waiter-saloon type of atmosphere. But it was not an ethnic beer hall. It was a long bar at McGuire's. It had a big window where you could stand and look outside. It was a standing-up bar."

"We'd take out the stools in the bar every weekend so the customers would become tired of standing and move somewhere else," McGuire said. "One time, a lady said she stood all day at work and wanted to sit down when she had a drink. My father told her to quit her job."

McGuire's did not have air conditioning, but it was the first Rockaway bar to have television. John McGuire purchased his first set before World War II: a six-inch television whose image was reflected onto a large screen for all to see. In 1946, there were 6,000 sets in America. That number jumped to 190,000 the next year, and to a reported 1 million by 1949. Tuesday nights people lined up three- and four-deep outside the large window overlooking Rockaway Boulevard just to watch Milton Berle's *Texaco Star Theater*. Also popular among patrons at McGuire's were heavyweight prize fights and college football games telecast on Saturday afternoons.

Al's Grandma Sullivan actually thought that the people brought into her home via television could see her, so whenever she watched, Mrs. Sullivan dressed up in her black dress and pearls. "I don't like your friend, Cousy," she once told Dick. "I waved to him and he didn't wave back. I think he's getting to be a big shot."

Other entertainment during the season included fireworks on Wednesday nights and an Indian minstrel show and church bazaar, both sponsored by St. Camillus.

"At that point, the McGuire brothers were just starting to become known as a couple of real good athletes. Al was 17 at the time. The playground started to boom," recalled Mann. Basketball and club football were popular, but golf and tennis were not real big with the Rockaway crowd.

The asphalt playground and basketball court overlooking the beach were installed in 1939, about a block from McGuire's. There were no silky white nets hanging from the rims. The steel backboards were pockmarked with holes, and the Atlantic Ocean breeze played havoc with most shots. A thin yellow line painted on the asphalt hemmed in the court. On a hot Sunday afternoon you hoped that someone brought a ball for the famous three-on-three contests renowned in New York City as the Rockaway Game. And to get the water in the drinking fountain to shoot higher, you had to push a match stick into the tap.

"[Basketball] fed the dreams of the Irish athletes on famous playgrounds such as the one at 108th Street in Rockaway, Queens," noted the late Pete Axthelm in his book *The City Game*. "New York," he said, was "the most active, dedicated basketball city of all . . . and basketball is the city game."

Before the dunk, the shot clock, or the three-point shot, the Rockaway Game emphasized the extra pass, tough defense, setting picks, and looking for the open man. Anything more fancy than the give-and-go or pick-and-roll on offense was considered showy.

It was the East Coast-style hoops of the weave-and-pass as opposed to the West Coast run-and-gun style made famous by Stanford and its star Hank Luisetti. It was Luisetti who popularized the one-handed shot. Later, Kenny Sailors of Wyoming took Luisetti's idea one step further when he introduced the jump shot during the 1942–43 basketball season.

That playground is where the McGuire brothers learned basic basketball and mined their personal hoop dreams. "It was more of a team game back then," said Dick.

"We all played on the asphalt playground in 1946, 1947," said Mann. "They [McGuire brothers] were playing there in high school at 16, 17, 18 years of age. Al was at St. John's Prep and Dick went to LaSalle Academy near the Bowery."

"I basically did not touch a basketball until I was a junior in high school," conceded Dick, the most self-effacing of the brothers. "I played only one year in high school—my senior year."

The McGuire boys often played as a team, and people on the beach could tell when they lost a game by their behavior as they left the court. "John would take the ball and throw it at Dick while cursing him. Dick would mumble something about John, and Al would say, 'Hey, Johnny, whadya complainin' about?' And they would prance out in single file after the game the same way every time [they lost]," remembered Ochs.

They played basketball every day during the summer with their friends Norman Ochs, Jimmy Weston, "Eddie Boy" Bacalles (known for having the "best shot into the wind"), and Mann, who later went on to play with Bob Cousy at Holy Cross College.

Ochs, known as the Jewish McGuire son because he spent so much time with John, Dick, and Al, would pry the ball from Jackie Craven, who had the only basketball on the beach, by promising to get Craven into a game after he returned from church. Most times there were so many players ahead of him, Craven had to wait hours to get into a game, if he was ever picked at all.

"None of us ever bought a ball," declared Ochs. If the basketball was deflated or the bladder was ruptured, the boys simply stuffed newspapers into the lining. Or they just rolled stocking caps into a ball. After all, in the Rockaway Game to score was human, but to pass was divine. In fact, the term "Rockawayitis" was coined to describe the affliction of making one pass too many. The games were generally physical, and players called their own fouls.

The half-court games were played to seven baskets and the victorious team had to win by two points. Winners took the ball out and held court until they lost. Players waiting for a chance to play leaned against the chain link fence that surrounded the court, wearing just their bathing suits and Converse Chuck Taylor high-top sneakers. This was where the phrase "We got next" first gained popularity. If a team lost a game, the players would slip off their sneakers, go up on the boardwalk or go for a swim until it was their turn to play. "We used to go down there during the summer. Rockaway was one of the hot spots. If you lost, you couldn't come back for a week," noted Lou Carnesecca. "People would come and go. It [three-on-three] was an event. Later on the Knicks would come down."

But summer was not the only time of year they played hoops. "We all played quite a bit, three-on-three mainly," recalled Bacalles, a long-time New York City bartender, whose high-rise now overlooks the Rockaway of his youth. "I remember shoveling the snow off the playground so that we could bounce the ball in the winter."

The Sunday games usually were played after 12:15 mass (the last and shortest mass at a summer resort). Crowds poured down from the Bronx and Manhattan for the three-on-three action, featuring some of the finest college players in New York City. By the late 1940s college basketball was the most popular game in town and the NBA was yet to be born. Professional basketball was governed by the old Basketball Association of America, founded in 1946. In the BAA's inaugural game, the New York Knicks defeated the Toronto Huskies at the Maple Leaf Gardens in Toronto, 68-66. That year a seat in the front row at Madison Square Garden cost $5.

"The college game remained THE draw during the early days of pro basketball," wrote Axthelm in *The City Game*. "The Knicks usually played in the 69th Regiment Armory. College teams played in the old Madison Square Garden."

"Everyone on that half court would be a starter at CCNY, NYU, Columbia—all college athletes," said Mann, who recalled the greats who graced the court. They included Bob "Zeke" Zawoluk and Ray Wertis (St. John's), Hank Poppe (Manhattan), Ray Felix (Long Island University), Bobby Wanzer (Seton Hall), Frank Layden (Niagara), George Kaftan and Tom Heinsohn (Holy Cross), Sid Tanenbaum and Dolph Schayes (New York University), Carl Braun (Colgate), Bobby Davies (Seton Hall—first player to dribble behind his back), Ray Lumpp (New York University), Richie Guerin (Iona), Chuck Connors (TV's *The Rifleman*), Gil Clancy (boxing manager and analyst), and, of course, Cousy (Holy Cross), the future Celtic Hall of Famer who hailed from St. Albans, Queens.

What the Field of Dreams in Dyersville, Iowa was to baseball, that asphalt court in Queens was to the game of basketball, featuring what was certainly the game's original "Dream Team."

"Al and Dick and Tommy Heinsohn had the court all afternoon one summer day," recalled Charlie Parl, a Rockaway regular. "In 1957, Heinsohn had just finished at Holy Cross. He came down for the weekend. They controlled the court."

"We didn't know it at the time, but we were laying the foundation for the modern NBA," quipped McGuire in a Nostalgia piece about Rockaway Beach that appeared in *Sports Illustrated* in 1973. "It was the top guns coming in from everywhere."

"We never even thought about being pros when we played at McGuire's playground," said Layden. "Nobody thought about it. Kids are playing for all the wrong reasons now."

But *the* top gun was Dick McGuire. The basketball court became known as McGuire's Playground for his ability to dribble and pass a basketball without peer. He was credited with being the first player to dribble a ball between his legs. The playground was where he earned his reputation and developed the skills that turned him into the prototype point guard. Back then, however, they were known as playmakers.

"My instincts gravitated toward playmaking," remarked Cousy. "And in those days, I thought Dick did it better than anyone. Back then there were shooting guards and playmaking guards, but there was no such thing as a point guard.

"In terms of the skills he and I had, we weren't point guards. It fell on us to create plays for the other four players. You took great pride in being able to make a play. [In that way] you were showing off your skills.

"Both Dick and I had all these God-given talents and we exploited them for one goal. That goal—winning—is what team sports is all about."

"When it came to basketball in the Rockaway area, nobody even touched Dick," said Mann, who described the soft-spoken McGuire as a "finesse player" with the two-handed set shot. "He was so smooth, it was said, that he could play wearing a tuxedo."

"John could have been a first-rate collegiate football player," Mann continued. "A tough guy. Al was a good rebounder who was fleet of foot, always hustled, and played good defense. However, most of his baskets were garbage points. He was a good runner and had a tremendous upper body build. He had endless energy."

While Al was generally referred to as "Dick McGuire's brother," he established his own reputation as a disciplined athlete and tenacious defensive ballplayer, although he was self-conscious about not only his athletic and academic abilities (or lack thereof) but his physical appearance.

"Everything came hard for Al, but everything for Dick came easy," said John, who became notorious for his gambling exploits and for his careers as a policeman and a saloon keeper. "Al was competitive, but clumsy. Back then, Al was a skinny kid, brash, short on talent, but long on muscle. A guy who would beat you with his mouth, if not his jump shot."

"Al was the ugly duckling kid brother made good," said Ochs, who pointed out that McGuire's awkward appearance made him very self-conscious.

"He was a tall and skinny kid who wore orthopedic shoes because of bone problems in his feet, and knickers [grade school uniform]. And he would walk the long way home on Bay Road from St. Francis de Sales grade school in Belle Harbor so people would not see him."

While McGuire was not considered a good student at St. Francis de Sales or St. John's Prep, he respected those who fell in love with Shakespeare and calculus. And though Dick was no great fan of school, he was sharp enough to do the *New York Times* crossword puzzle. "Al got through St. John's Prep," commented Frank Layden, who attended Niagara with Hubie Brown and Larry Costello, "so he had to be pretty smart. But the selling point with the parents was to get your degree. The Irish guys who got their degrees were able to go further in their lives," added Layden, whose grandfather was from County Cork, Ireland, and whose father was a longshoreman.

"The nuns at St. Francis de Sales couldn't do anything with me when it came to reading," said McGuire. "My sister, Kathleen, did my papers for me in grade school and high school."

St. John's Prep was a part of the Brooklyn/Queens Diocese, which included St. Francis Prep, Brooklyn Prep, St. Augustine, Holy Trinity, Bishop Loughlin, Monsignor McClancy, Xaverian High School, Chaminade, Holy Cross, Cathedral Prep, and Archbishop Molloy. Dick played for LaSalle Academy, a school in the Manhattan Diocese, which included St. Simon Stock, St. Nicholas of Tolantine, Mount St. Michael's, Cardinal Hayes, Manhattan Prep, Fordham Prep, Mount St. Helena, All Hallows High School, Power Memorial, Regis High School, Brother Rice High School, St. Ann's, and Xavier High School.

The two McGuire brothers played together so often in the local Police Athletic Leagues and Catholic Youth Organizations of their grade school that their first names were almost always pronounced as one: DickandAl.

"They [Rockaway Beach] had Easter tournaments at St. Francis de Sales," said Cousy. "We'd just get a team and go to the tournament. [During the summers] we'd go to the beach. We used to go ogle the girls, then play three-on-three [at the playground]. And afterward, if you were of age, you'd go to McGuire's to hoist a few."

"All the great players came to McGuire's, and it was a chance to meet the ladies and gather after mass," said Layden. "You could see one guy dressed in a suit and tie and the guy sitting next to him was in his baseball uniform."

Al played with the CYO teams during and after high school and into college, especially the Easter tournaments. "Al was very competitive," Mann said. "Every time he played he'd be all over you. It wouldn't be unheard of for Al to get into a fight. No one would be surprised if he took a swing at someone. But Dick would walk away from a fight."

It was Al McGuire's never-give-up tenacity that made his reputation in both basketball and football.

"We had a very good football team then," said Bacalles. "We were champions of our division at 16 [years old]. On that team we had an undeveloped, gangly 13-year-old, who through sheer competitive desire played with us. Al was a such a fierce competitor that we had no choice but to put him on our team as a tackle."

Gil Clancy, now a boxing analyst for CBS, recalled McGuire's determination and guts. "When he was a kid, I think he was 14, another guy kept knocking him down. Al kept getting up. Finally, Al dragged himself up off the ground and the other kid said, 'I give up. You win.'

"On Sunday nights, we played at Smythe's Bar and Grill," continued Clancy, who ran a Police Athletic Center in Queens at the time. "The coach of one of the teams was a detective. His son played center on the team. This guy would sucker-punch the other centers at the tip-off.

"We got to play these guys in the last game of the year. Al jumped center with him. We get the tap, and Al goes in to score. Two possessions went by, and then Al hit the guy right in the mouth. Then he hit Al. The game was more like football. It just goes to show you what a scrappy guy he was," said Clancy.

The games at Smythe's, Renaissance Hall in Harlem, and other establishments were known for very long halftimes, because the players, fans, and coaches went to the bar. They were having such a good time they sometimes forgot there was a second half.

"Al always had a very competitive desire to win," said Bacalles. "Al did not like to lose. He was a disappointed loser, but he wasn't a sore loser. He was a good sportsman."

"We waited all weekend for Sunday night to play basketball games," said Mann of the indoor CYO and PAL games that pitted parish against parish.

"I used to go to three games on a Sunday," recalled Winifred McGuire in an interview a few years before her death in 1986. She always had her famous seat against the back wall of the gyms in such far-flung locales as Rockaway, Howard Beach, and New Jersey. "The boys would be in these leagues. People used to think I was coming out to collect money."

But television eventually killed Sunday night basketball in New York. "Ed Sullivan on Sunday nights was the start of the downfall of basketball," said Mann. "It was a social event, with the game, a dance at halftime, and a dance after the game. The number of adults watching the game was large. But as television became more widespread, attendance at the games slowed down, and then it was over."

Dick and Al were not the only basketball stars in the family. Kathleen was a standout for Stella Morris Girls School, which played by "girls" rules: six to a side and just one dribble. She also played in the CYO for St. Francis de Sales and the Equitable Life Insurance Company team, which played by "boys" rules. The basketball bloodlines extended to Gene and Kathleen's daughter, Laurie Mann, who played for Immaculata's NCAA tournament teams during the late 1970s. And McGuire's grandson, A.J., marked the third generation of McGuires in college basketball when he joined Cornell for the 1998–99 campaign.

Both Dick and Kathleen enjoyed going to movies, but Al preferred to make his own entertainment. He never attended a major league baseball game. But just for kicks, he would hitchhike with his friends to Albany, just to go to Albany. There was no other reason, according to Ochs. The following Monday morning, Ochs would receive a postcard with greetings from Albany and Al.

McGuire was a practical joker who would always try to get away with something, and he never seemed too concerned with the consequences of his actions. And he would always try to get in the last word.

"We worked construction one summer," recalled Mann. "And the workers complained that Al wasn't dumping the bricks close enough to them. So, Al dumped the next load over the guys' legs, and we took off."

He once took the keys to Dick's new Chevy, which he had received as a signing bonus from the Knicks.

"Al says to me, 'Let's go to Lake George,'" Mann recalled. "'We'll take Dick's car. How much money do you have?' Al asked me. I said, 'I don't know. I think I have $25 at home.'

"So I go home and get the $25, and Al's in the kitchen with his mother, who referred to him always as 'Alfie.' When she asked where we were going, Al said, 'We're going to Brooklyn to pick up the suits.' He went upstairs and took the keys to Dick's car off his dresser while Dick was sleeping.

"We headed to Lake George and everywhere we stopped for a drink, Al would say, 'There's another cuff. There's another sleeve.' Al was a funny guy. He was the life of the party."

When he was a senior in high school, he drove up to the Cross Bay Bridge toll booth, shook the collector's hand and hit the gas. The police followed him all the way back to 108th Street, where his father had to give the officer two bottles of scotch to keep Al from getting arrested.

"It was not a normal household," recalled Kathleen. "My grandfather and grandmother lived with us and our Aunt Kate, who was on my father's side. We had 12 or 13 people here for dinner. What was our dinner every night was most people's Thanksgiving.

"One night my father was standing up carving turkey, and he was standing a long time carving for 12 people. When he went to sit down he thought that Al had moved the chair under him, but Al had pulled out the chair.

"Well, when my father went, he went hard. I remember my father getting up and Al running from him. He got up, took the turkey to the kitchen and threw it out the window and said, 'Big Al! Big Al!' Why Al did it, I never knew."

Like his father, McGuire was very well dressed when the occasion required it. But if he did not have to dress up, "he was a disaster," laughed Gene Mann, who recalled that among McGuire's many firsts, he was the first on Rockaway to wear Bermuda shorts.

Growing up, McGuire was not the most patient person. One evening, recalled Kathleen, she was sitting on the hood of his car in her bathing suit as Al was getting ready to pick up his girlfriend, Pat Sharkey.

"Al said, 'OK, Kath, get off. I'm leavin'.'

"'Take it easy, Al. You're always in a rush,' I told him.

"'I'm leavin', Kath. Get off!'

"When I didn't get off the car, Al hopped in, turned on the car, and drove off with me on the hood holding on to the car's hood ornament."

"He took her all the way to 120th Street," said Gene Mann, picking up the story. "He was doing 40 to 50 miles per hour with the police chasing him all the way to Pat's house.

"When they arrived at Pat's house, Pat and her mother went inside and locked the door. Now, Pat's family was very reserved and very quiet. Pat wore white gloves to church on Sunday. Al was on the wild side," said Mann.

McGuire always seemed to be testing how far he could push figures of authority. Mann remembered a time when Al brought a boat to Rockaway Beach, along with sandwiches and beer. Al was reportedly headed to the next bar across the Atlantic—an Irish village called Knock, in County Mayo.

"Al and his friend, Johnny Monks, take the boat from an area on the beach lightly patrolled by lifeguards, sometime after 6 p.m. They get into it and begin moving down the beach. The lifeguards on duty see them and begin to go after Al and Johnny as they row farther away from shore.

Then the Coast Guard helicopters come out and the police helicopters with the bullhorns warning them to get out of the water.

"At 110th Street the Coast Guard helicopter dropped a rope ladder down to the dinghy for Al and Johnny, arrested them, and brought them into night court, wearing their bathing suits. When the judge asked where the two miscreants thought they were going, Monks smartly answered: 'We were going to Ireland,'" laughed Mann at the memory. Winifred McGuire reportedly had to pay the Coast Guard $500 to bail out her Alfie.

"Al was much more outgoing, much more gregarious than Dick. Al was a wise guy," said Mann. "Dick was quiet. But nobody ever gave it a thought, or tried to figure out or analyze why they were so different. They just were."

John McGuire described Al as "skinny and wild. A roaring maniac," in a 1976 feature in the *Milwaukee Journal* by Roger Jaynes. Added Mann, "You'd have to kill Al before he quit fighting."

McGuire's street-fighting image was born on the beach. He would not allow anyone to take anything from him or hurt anyone close to him without a fight. One day a bully kicked sand in the faces of Pat and Kathleen, and McGuire became incensed.

"Al dropped the basketball and ran down to the beach, and he held this guy's head under water. If we didn't stop Al, he would have killed the guy. If something didn't go as Al thought it should, he would fight to the death," said Mann.

The three boys could also be seen together on the lifeguard stands during the summer months. John, Dick, and Al patrolled the beach front at 107th, 106th, and 105th Streets. Al spent his pre-bartending days on the beach, where he met Pat Sharkey. Her family rented a bungalow across from McGuires' each summer.

"I sat on the beach as close to the lifeguard stand as possible," said Pat. "I don't know how he ever sat still on that lifeguard chair so long." Her father owned a livery service for the local funeral homes.

"Pat was ultra, ultra class," commented Mann. Concurred Ochs: "Patricia Sharkey was a perfect lady. She was as sweet and ladylike when she was 14 as she is today."

When Al and Pat began dating in their teens, McGuire took a train and transferred to two buses to get to Queen's Village, where Pat's family lived.

Recalled Pat, "I'll never forget our first date. We got back at 11 o'clock. My grandmother said to Al, 'Oh, glory be. I thought you kidnapped her.' I was so embarrassed. I thought that was the last I'd ever see him," she recalled in a 1976 *Milwaukee Journal* feature by Roger Jaynes.

After she was graduated from high school, Pat worked as a receptionist while Al played college basketball for St. John's University. They were married in 1950, his junior year.

As a schoolboy at St. John's Prep, McGuire was All-City in basketball and football. Despite a lean build, McGuire played tackle his first three years, and was switched to running back his senior year.

One of St. John's big football rivals was Brooklyn Prep. The games were so intense that fistfights usually broke out. Thanksgiving Day was the biggest game of the year when the teams played in the Turkey Bowl, which was referred to as the little Harvard-Yale game because the crowds were so large at Brooklyn's Boys High Field. In the 1945 game, Joe Paterno caught the winning touchdown pass in Brooklyn's 7-6 win over St. John's. "If I got by that one guy [to score the extra point after touchdown]," rued McGuire, who played halfback, "I would have been the hero of that game. It would have been tied."

The first basketball coach to make a strong impression on McGuire was Herb Hess at St. John's Prep. Hess was a stern man who did not want his players dribbling the ball between their legs or attempting other extraneous moves. "If you want to get fancy with the ball, take it across the street to the college," Hess would say. After having played three sports in four years, the only words McGuire heard from Hess were a terse "thank you."

The 1940s were the heyday for basketball in the old Madison Square Garden, at 50th Street and 8th Avenue, and the gestation period for college basketball. Playing for the championship in the Garden was considered the ultimate for New York schoolboys. At that time the Garden was considered the mecca, the big top. McGuire played in the last Catholic high school basketball championship held at the Garden, when his St. John's team lost to LaSalle.

Those were the days of the high school quintuple headers and college doubleheaders, which were put together by sports impresario Ned Irish, who later became president of the New York Knickerbockers. After watching five high school games, fans could get a spaghetti and meatball dinner with bread and a Pepsi at Romeo's restaurant, on 49th and

Broadway, for 30 cents, and for another quarter watch two college games that night in the rafters of the Garden. The whole day cost less than $1—including carfare.

The first NIT was played in "the Gahden" back in 1938. In 1943, the younger (by one year) NCAA championship game moved to Madison Square Garden, where it stayed until 1950. Only eight teams were invited to each tournament. During World War II, the NIT and NCAA champions squared off three times in the annual American Red Cross War Fund series, also started by Ned Irish, to determine the overall national champion. The NIT champ lost each time.

It was not unusual to have 18,000 basketball fans pack the Garden to see such local favorites as St. John's (first back-to-back NIT champs, 1943, 1944), City College of New York, St. Francis, New York University, Fordham, Manhattan, Seton Hall, Long Island University (which won the NIT in 1939 and 1941), and occasionally St. Peter's of New Jersey. The New York Knicks, which did not play their first game until 1946, were still playing in the old Armory when the National Basketball Association began its first official season in 1949–50.

"That whole era from 1947 to 1957 is really the roots of the McGuire family," said Mann. "Everyone wanted to be in McGuire's. Dick was the famous one back then." While it was Dick McGuire and basketball that turned McGuire's from just another bar on the beach into *the* place to be, it was Winifred and John McGuire who made the bar a financial success.

"When you lived in a summer resort [area], the stars of the family were the stores. I mean, if the store did well, everybody did well. It was like the parents were the stars of the family, not the kids," said Ochs, whose family owned a deli on 109th Street, just down the street from McGuire's.

"It was a very strict bar," remembered Mann. "Mr. and Mrs. McGuire were on the floor all night long. When kids from other areas were asked by their parents where they were going during the summer and they said, 'McGuire's,' their parents would say, 'Well, OK.'

"Mrs. McGuire ran the family and the business. John McGuire basically patrolled the bar, collected the empty glasses, and kept the place orderly. He was not bashful about throwing punches if the situation required it," said Mann.

"He [John McGuire] was very tough," said Norman Ochs. "One night I came late to see some guys in the bar. And just as I get there, they're carrying out some guy from the back room. And John McGuire says, 'Stand him up a second.' And the guy was totally under control. They stand him up and Mr. McGuire gives him one last shot to remember him by. And I made the mistake of saying to whomever I was with, 'Gee, that wasn't necessary. They seemed to have the guy under control.' It got back to him somehow.

"He called me aside the next day, and he said, 'How long you know me?' All my life. He says, 'How long you know the guy that I hit?' I never saw him before. 'Well, don't you think I should have gotten the benefit of the doubt?' So I said he was right. 'Do you know what that guy was doing to our back room before you got here? He was driving us nuts for two hours.' He had a very common sense, street smart way about him. Very smart," said Ochs.

It was easy to recognize John McGuire at the bar. He was the strong, silent one in the old-fashioned undershirt with his arms folded across his chest. When he was there everyone behaved. Before he opened for the season he would quietly announce, "Well, we have a clean ladies' room and the cleanest [beer] pipes in New York. I guess we're ready for business."

Most of the Irish Town taverns had plastic hoses running from the beer kegs to the tap. When the bars closed on Labor Day, many of the hoses were left uncleaned. John McGuire used leaded coils and made sure everything in the bar was kept spic-and-span. Kathleen Mann remembered her father being a stickler for detail.

"He would always be walking around the bar with a cloth wiping off something. 'If you leave one mark, you'll find a hundred,' he used to say."

"Al's got more of his dad in him," said Mann. "The sternness, very well dressed, very well groomed." Remarked Ochs: "Mr. McGuire would wear his suit and tie on Sunday, even to watch us play football. Your father earned the money. You respected him, but you didn't use bad language in front of him. Al's father was very proper. The father had the attitude that everyone who came into the bar was capable of being a potential problem."

Another attribute Al McGuire picked up from his father was fair play.

"One Sunday, Johnny was coaching our [football] team and Mr. McGuire comes out in his suit and tie to watch us play," recalled Ochs. "I thought that I got across the goal line, and then the officials moved back the ball six inches. I went over [the goal line] a second time, and they moved the ball back a few inches.

"We're in the huddle for the third time, and I look up and there's Mr. McGuire talking to the officials right there on the goal line. 'Why don't you let the boys just play. Whoever wins, wins. It's not that important. But don't cheat.' He made his speech, and he turned and walked off the field," recalled Ochs, who played his college football for Lou Little at Columbia.

McGuire's father felt that Al came the closest to living up to what he expected of his sons, according to Ochs, and he gave Al his pinky ring. The father believed that since his children were born in the United States and had more opportunities than he did, they should achieve higher status. "If I were born in this country, I'd be president," he once told Ochs.

"Mr. McGuire said a customer once told him how lucky he was that his kids learned how to dribble a basketball," said Ochs. "'You know what I should have told the S.O.B.? I came to Rockaway Beach with a quarter of a million dollars before they even touched a basketball.'"

He was a shrewd businessman. There were no neon beer signs in the windows at McGuire's. When a Rheingold salesman wanted to put a beer sign in the window, McGuire asked how much they would pay him for the privilege. The salesman said that Rheingold couldn't pay anything due to concerns about kickbacks.

"Bring your boss down. I'd like to talk to him." When the distributor came down the next day, McGuire said to him: "I like your salesman. I'll still let you put a sign in my window. But it must read John McGuire's."

"He always wanted 51 percent of the deal," Ochs said. "He didn't want emotion or friendships to enter into it. This was business. He was a tough negotiator. Both he and Al did not want to be made to look like fools when they were making a deal." But when it came time to do business, John McGuire took out the best booze. "My father drank a bottle of scotch a day for business," McGuire recalled. "And when he became successful he continued to drink that bottle of scotch a day."

Ochs also recounted the time that a customer in the bar was down on his luck and asked Al if he could borrow $30. "When Al told this to his father, he replied, 'I'll give him $15.' 'But Dad, the guy really needs it.' 'No. I'll give him $15; he loses $15, I lose $15.'

"The mother could always play to an audience," Ochs continued. "She was very good with the public. Al and John both had that ability, but Al was not on stage all of the time. John was one of the world's greatest bartenders. Dick was the quiet one. Al used to say, 'The next bad thing [Dick] says about anyone will be the first.'"

"There's one thief in every family," McGuire said. "In our family, it was my brother John. My brother Dick was the saint, and I was the con man." But of the three McGuire boys, Fat Johnny, as he was affectionately called, was the real bartender of the family. After learning his trade at the family bar, he successfully operated Pep McGuire's in New York with Norton Peppes for seven years, and other establishments during his tenure as New York's resident bon vivant. "John could take care of one side of the bar by himself, while it took two bartenders on the other side," recalled Ochs.

"John was tending bar when he was 15 or 16 years old," said Dick. "We all started there. John did most of the work [at the bar]. Al had to work. I was the worst bartender. John and Al were very good with people," said Dick, whose elocution was so poor that he was tagged with the moniker Mumbles. John was more loquacious than Dick and Al, and liked to be in charge, whether it was at the bar or in athletics. He especially liked to take credit for his brothers' athletic achievements.

"My brother John lied to the priests at St. John's. He told them I was a good player and then I received a scholarship at St. John's," remembered Dick, who won the Haggerty Award his freshman year at St. John's, presented annually to the outstanding collegiate player in the city. He won it again in 1949, and was considered among the best basketball players in the school's history.

But it was said of John that his real job as a New York City policeman interfered with his time at the track, and the ponies usually won out. One day he was on such a roll at Yonkers Raceway that he hired a private plane to fly him to Saratoga to continue his winning streak. Mrs. McGuire reportedly helped him get out of some serious straits that were the direct result of his gambling habit.

While Johnny never saw a spread that he could not beat, the gambling bug did not bite Al. He enjoyed a good game of poker or gin rummy, but said he would never bet on the horses or the roulette wheel because "you can never beat the house." Instead, he played the percentages in all aspects of his life and remained frugal.

"Al was naturally frugal," joked Jerry Savio, a longtime friend of McGuire's from their days in Rockaway, when Savio worked as a delivery driver for Wonder Bread. "The next dollar Al loses will be the first. He gets it from his mom. His mom used to bum cigarettes from me every time I made a delivery. By the end of the week, she had bummed a whole pack from me. And then you had to light the cigarette for her. She'd buy me a beer once every two trips."

Winifred McGuire, or Mrs. McGuire as she was respectfully known, held court at the bar from 8 P.M. to 4 A.M. "She usually hung out at the side door, near the kitchen," recalled Jackie Smith of Rego Park, a bartender at Fitzgerald's. "Whenever you needed money, if she knew you she would lend it to you."

"She did like to play the numbers," noted Savio, who was raised in Jamaica, New York. "She'd play a dime, a nickel, a quarter. It was usually the last three numbers of the parimutuel that day, wherever the horses happened to be running, Belmont or the other tracks."

She sat in her little corner by the side of the bar with her arms folded. During the hot summers, the McGuires kept the beer taps open and lined glasses on top of the bar. John, Dick, and Al then handed beers to customers as they came in from the beach. Beer and Tom Collins were the popular summer libations at McGuire's.

Bartenders always doubled as bouncers at McGuire's. All of the McGuire boys took turns behind the tapper. Frank Deford wrote that when it came Al's turn, he took a cue from his father, whose advice whenever trouble started was to "always come over the bar feet first." Al said, "The best piece of advice my father gave me was always to get paid and never co-sign."

"In Rockaway, Al was a showman," recalled Savio. "Al would be there behind the bar when I arrived with the cases of bread and buns for the long summer weekends. He was cocky then."

McGuire stood 6'2" behind the bar, where he worked during the off-seasons of his college and pro basketball careers. He believed that life experience was the ideal complement to education. And it was in the tavern where he witnessed human nature in the raw.

"In order for a person's education to be complete," McGuire said, "he should work six months driving a cab and six months as a bartender after graduating college. You can't con a con. You can't fool a bartender. If you've been one, you've heard every story in the world."

As a bartender, he was considered a regular guy, according to those who worked in nearby taverns. "Al always welcomed people," remembered one area barkeep. "But he would say hello to you while he was looking out the window at something else."

"I can remember in there a couple of times, Al practicing play-by-play on TV when the sound was off during a game. The impression was that maybe someday he might want to try that [broadcasting]," said the bartender.

Much of Al McGuire's quick wit and the colorful nicknames he uses are a result of his experiences behind the bar. His nicknames aptly described the personality traits and habits of those who frequented McGuire's. Those who were known for not buying drinks became frequent targets of his rapier wit. McGuire called one regular "corks," because he would not pop for corks, never mind a bottle. Another he tagged "elbows" because the customer kept his arms on top of his money on the bar. "Hey, elbows," McGuire yelled. "It's your turn to buy."

"He could go from tending bar until three in the morning to breakfast, and go out and play golf," marveled Ochs. "He'd come back from golf, go to the playground, play a little basketball. I don't know if he ever took a nap. And then he'd be back behind the bar again."

"My mother went on three hours' sleep," added Kathleen Mann. "She worked 20 hours a day. But Al wasn't much of a sleeper. Neither was my brother John. Dick was the sleeper, and my father."

"In a family business you always have to sleep with one eye open," warned McGuire. "And nobody handles the cash register but family. And then you have to watch them, too."

"Every night people poured into McGuire's," remembered Gene Mann. "You served them beer but you didn't know who they were. Maybe the first name, but that was it." Lines of people snaked outside the door, and beers were handed to customers out the window and door. "When he [Mr. McGuire] had to raise the price of beer from 10 to 15 cents, he thought he was going to lose his whole trade," said Ochs. "He thought that everyone was going to stay away."

Mrs. McGuire controlled the bar. If anyone acted up they were tossed out. She paid her bartenders $15 a night. At the end of the season, if she felt that it was a good summer for the bar, there would be a lump-sum bonus check for the bartenders.

Besides the burgeoning college crowds, quite a few Catholic priests rented rooms at McGuire's, "because it was considered a legitimate place to stay," according to Gene Mann.

"A lot of the rooming houses up through Irish Town were party houses. Here, Mrs. McGuire guarded the door to the rooms so it was a very controlled type of place. So we had a lot of priests, a lot of FBI agents, a lot of judges. That caliber of person," said Mann, who added that newspaper columnist Jimmy Breslin would occasionally drop in for a drink and conversation at the bar.

"It [McGuire's] was family," said Layden, who was introduced to his wife, Barbara, at the tavern by McGuire. "It was hospitality. You don't have that anymore. This was our club. This was our church. You could always go there to find friendship."

Cliffie Jones, a friend of McGuire's, helped out behind the bar while Al handled the physical aspects of the job. "But there were no real donnybrooks," said Mann, who had a couple of teeth knocked out during his time behind the bar.

While McGuire's biggest assets behind the bar were his physicality and an ability to make money, he was a sloppy barkeep, according to Mann. When he came in for the evening shift, Johnny had clean glasses and fresh water in the stainless steel tank. "When Al would put the glasses in the water, he would take up half the sink with him, and there'd be water everywhere behind the bar. And Johnny would be furious. By 8:30 or 9 o'clock there would be no water left."

The summer months saw Mann, Jones, and the McGuire boys locked in at the bar from 7 P.M. until at least 1 the next morning. Mrs. McGuire fed them lettuce, tomato, and meat sandwiches, and eggnog sprinkled with nutmeg, to keep their energy up.

Mrs. McGuire usually put the sandwiches on the back bar until the boys had a break. Never one to miss a chance at a prank, Al took the meat out of Dick or Johnny's sandwich, replacing it with a napkin. When the piece of napkin was stuck in their teeth, Al had a great laugh at their expense. If he actually wanted their sandwiches, he would tell them they had a phone call, and then take the sandwich.

McGuire's was open until 4 A.M., but Al's first "last call" of the night was usually at 2 A.M.. "OK, last call. Get it now!" he would yell out over the din of the crowd and the jukebox. "Some of the customers would shout out, 'Give me 10, Al. Give me 15, Al.' And he would line the glasses up on the bar," said Mann. At 3:15, McGuire would issue his next "last call." "'Give me 10, Al. Another 15, Al.'

"At 4 A.M., Al would pull the plug on the jukebox and say, 'OK, every-body out!' and he'd empty out the bar," Mann continued. "At last call the customers would carry the glasses out to the beach. In that last hour, some-times we took in more money than we took in during the three hours before." But the bar would lose a gross of glasses every weekend.

When the bar opened at 8 A.M. it was filled with the sounds of Eddie Fisher, Glenn Miller, and Frank Sinatra, as the unplayed songs from the night before bellowed from the jukebox.

"[But] in the 1950s, when Dick was playing with the Knicks, the world started to change," noted Mann. "There were barroom fights. Knives. It was a rougher and tougher atmosphere."

McGuire had his share of fights. If his father did not take a trouble-maker outside, he usually sent Al. But by the time Al's first son, Allie, was born in 1951, McGuire had had enough of the fisticuffs. As he told Frank Deford, "I was handling this guy, but I couldn't put him away, and I knew I couldn't get away with this." A policeman happened on the scene and broke up the fight.

Upon returning to the bar, McGuire threw down his apron and told his father, "Dad, that's it, Dad. I'm never gonna go outside again. For $15 and tips, I'm not going to work and fight too!"

John Richard McGuire died of a stroke in December of 1957. He was in his early 60s, according to family members. It was after his father's death that McGuire drew closer to his mother.

"What I tried to do when I was listening to her was to pick up words, thoughts, ideas. I don't think I ever came away that I didn't have a Will Rogers or Einstein thought that was done in a very simple, common sense way."

Frugality was part and parcel of Winifred McGuire's business and life sense, a carryover from the days of the Great Depression. In order to save a buck, she would buy items that were a day old.

"My sister, Kathleen, said when we were growing up we never had a yellow banana because mother always bought things a day old. We were never poor. The biggest problem my mother had with us was getting us to go get the two pair of pants with the suit, not the suit. I remember when my wife, Pat, had a new dress. My mother would say, 'That's a nice dress.' Then five minutes later, she'd say, 'How much did it cost?'" according to a 1976 Roger Jaynes feature in the *Milwaukee Journal*.

"We never received a wrapped present from my mother," recalled Kathleen. "Mother was not into saving things. But she would put four turkeys in the oven and give them to those people in the neighborhood who didn't have one."

McGuire always understood what his role was on any team for which he played. "He scored a lot of points in high school," Dick remembered of Al's schoolboy days at St. John's Prep. "I think he was highly rated. Al was a very good high school player. He could run like hell. They [his teammates] thought he was all right. But Al was more of a defensive player. Al wasn't afraid to talk. Al has a way of getting along with people."

Before making his decision to attend St. John's University, the brash high school junior considered going to the University of Notre Dame. The interest was mutual, and basketball coach Ed "Moose" Krause agreed to meet McGuire at the Commodore Hotel in New York one evening at 5:30. Later that night, Ochs dropped by the McGuire household and inquired about the interview.

"'He didn't show,' McGuire said. 'I went there at 5:30. I gave him until 6, and he didn't show.' Not long afterward, Krause called to explain that he did not arrive at the hotel until 6:10. Could they meet the next night? 'No,' McGuire said indignantly. 'I gave you a half hour. If you don't think enough of me to be on time, I don't think you're that interested in me.' And that was that," Ochs said.

In addition to basketball offers, McGuire was offered football scholarships to Holy Cross and Notre Dame. When Fighting Irish coach Frank Leahy came a'calling, he liked McGuire's football talent but was not impressed with his academics.

"Well, why don't ya throw my basketball marks in with my grades?" McGuire suggested. But McGuire was not going to make the grade at Notre Dame, so he joined his brother Dick at St. John's.

Photo courtesy of Frank Gallagher

Photo courtesy of Marquette University Sports Information Department

Top: McGuire's tavern at Rockaway Beach. *Bottom:* Al McGuire (#59) chases Joe Paterno during the "Turkey Bowl" classic at Boys' High Field in Brooklyn, in 1945. Paterno's Brooklyn Prep edged McGuire's St. John's Prep, 7-6.

Photo courtesy of Marquette University Sports Information Department

Above: Al (left) and Dick McGuire (right) with their St.John's coach Frank McGuire. *Right:* Al McGuire meets one of his fans, P.J. O'Dea, after a speech in Chicago.

Photo courtesy of P.J. O'Dea

Above: Kentucky's venerable coach Adolph Rupp looks on during Kentucky's 85-69 defeat of Marquette at the 1972 regionals in Dayton. This was Rupp's final NCAA basketball tournament. *Right:* McGuire used his promotional skills to sell the Marquette basketball program to Milwaukeeans during his first two years.

LADIES DAY
WITH
AL MC GUIRE

BANK of MILWAUKEE & TRUST

HOTEL PFISTER

Opposite page top: McGuire leaps atop the scorer's table after a last-second shot defeated the Wisconsin Badgers in February of 1974. Hank Raymonds is to McGuire's right. Badger coach John Powless walks off dejectedly.
Opposite page bottom: Al and Pat McGuire honored at Alumni Hall in Chicago before McGuire's last game at DePaul, with Gene Sullivan, then DePaul athletic director.

This page right: Dean Meminger and Gary Brell in their "bumblebee" uniforms.
Below: Al breaks down while assistants Hank Raymonds and Rick Majerus celebrate Marquette's victory over North Carolina in the 1977 NCAA title game.

Opposite page top: Al McGuire and some Marquette basketball players get set for the annual Al's Run benefit for Milwaukee Children's Hospital. *Opposite page bottom:* President Jimmy Carter welcomes Coach Al McGuire to the President's Council on Physical Fitness in 1979.

This page: The famous NBC college basketball trio of Al McGuire, Dick Enberg and Billy Packer take a break for a commercial during Al's early days as a network analyst.

College basketball's original flower child and easy rider continues on his colorful life's journey, wherever that might take him.

Chapter Three

Dance Hall Player

McGuire chose St. John's in Jamaica, New York. As a freshman, he described himself as a "dance hall player," one short on talent but long on effort. He was not a good shooter and usually was assigned to do the rough work on the opposing team's top scorer. He also ran track at St. John's, where he was clocked at 4:34 the first time he ran the mile.

Dick preceded Al at St. John's and had already established himself as a star with his finesse and ball-handling skills. He won the Haggerty Award as a freshman, but left the team before the 1944 NIT. Dick went into the Navy and began a training hitch at Dartmouth College, where he also played basketball with the Big Green. During World War II, every branch of the military fielded a basketball team. (The war was over by the time Al could enlist.)

During that year's NCAA, first-round loser Utah was called back to New York when members of the Arkansas team were seriously injured in a bus accident. Utah and Dartmouth advanced to the finals, with Utah winning the NCAA in overtime, 42-40, behind Arnie Ferrin's 22 points. Utah then met St. John's—NIT champ for the second straight year—in the Red Cross charity game to determine the undisputed champion of college basketball. As Dartmouth's guard, Dick McGuire came very close to playing against his own St. John's team.

Al harbored no jealousy toward his more talented brother. "I got jealousy out of my system when I was 14 years old because I knew I would never be as good as my brother Dick." As their father succinctly put it when asked to compare the brothers: "The difference between Dick and Al is that Dick can play."

Al felt that St. John's had cheated Dick out of his degree after using him for his basketball talent. Dick finished his four years of college with only 60 credit hours. Al, who majored in economics, was not going to let the same thing happen to him. When his basketball eligibility was up, he earned his last two credits in summer school.

While Harry Truman was "giving 'em hell" as president, Al McGuire was giving opponents hell on the basketball court with his tough, hard-nosed style of play between 1947 and 1951. "Al was a tough, tough player. Very strong defensively," remembered former DePaul University coach Ray Meyer, whose Blue Demons team won the 1945 NIT behind the 53 points of George Mikan, the first high-scoring center in college basketball. Mikan's domination forced the basketball powers to widen the lane from 6 feet to 12 feet. He was also voted the greatest player of the first half of the twentieth century. Luisetti finished second. Also that year, Oklahoma A&M, behind National Player of the Year Bob Kurland, became the first team to win back-to-back NCAA championships in 1945 and '46.

During his first season at St. John's (freshmen were not eligible to play varsity ball), McGuire scored 232 points for coach Al "Dusty" Destefano's undefeated freshman squad.

McGuire's reputation for telling it like it is preceded him to St. John's. He became particularly angry after one game when the fans turned ugly, yelling epithets at some of the opposing team's Jewish players. The next day in his speech class, McGuire addressed his peers on "Sportsmanship, Politics and Bigotry." "Was that a basketball game I played in last night or a Bund rally?" Throughout the rest of the speech, he went on to castigate the crowd for its unbecoming behavior.

The summer prior to his senior year at St. John's, McGuire worked as a busboy at a Jewish resort in the Catskills in South Fallsburg/Monticello, New York. "We used to call that area the 'Jewish Alps,'" McGuire laughed. "He made $1,000 in ten weeks," remembered Ochs, a total that broke the record for busboys. "He was so much in demand that they begged Al to work in the cocktail lounge.

"Al knew how to mix. He had this flair for public relations and people. As wild as he was at that time, he could be adaptable. He was extroverted, energetic, good-looking. He was fun."

The most influential coach in Al McGuire's career was Frank McGuire (no relation). He replaced Joe Lapchick as varsity coach during

Al's freshman year at St. John's, when Lapchick took over the New York Knicks, and had played and coached at Xavier High School in Manhattan.

Frank McGuire hailed from Greenwich Village, and later helped Al get the head coaching jobs at Belmont Abbey and Marquette. "Al's coaching and clothes style were from Frank McGuire," noted Fred "the Spook" Stegman, one of the many "street scouts" Al used during his coaching career.

At the University of North Carolina in the late 1950s, Frank McGuire helped make college basketball big time on Tobacco Road. The turning point was the 1957 NCAA finals when his undefeated Tar Heels defeated Wilt Chamberlain's Kansas Jayhawks in triple overtime, 54-53. That came five years after McGuire's St. John's team lost to "Phog" Allen's Kansas Jayhawks in the finals, 80-63. In addition to All-America Clyde Lovellette, the Jayhawks had a player on that team named Dean Smith. Allen had played for Dr. James Naismith. So Smith played for the man who played for the man who invented the game of basketball.

Frank McGuire recalled a scrimmage that epitomized Al's toughness while at St. John's.

"We were playing Long Island [University] at the Garden. It was a great rivalry, and the game was played hard. There was a fast break early in the game. It was four-on-four. Al's speed was unbelievable, but he wasn't there on the break. I looked at the other end of the court in time to see Al duck under a right from the huge Long Island center.

"Soon, everybody was around these two guys. I took my time getting to the fight, figuring the refs would end it. By the time I got there, players were pulling Al's legs, and he had the big guy around the head. 'Al,' I said, 'let him up.' 'Not until he says I give,' Al said. 'He can't, Al, he's turning blue,' I said. 'Oh,' was Al's reply as he let go."

Years later, Al gave Frank an autographed copy of one of his favorite clown prints with the inscription: "Frank, thanks for putting the calliope in my life."

After Frank McGuire's death in 1994, Al recalled that the coach was a fighter who motivated his players and always had them prepared. "Those of us on Frank's teams knew the enemy was NYU or CCNY. Frank got us to play. We were part of a unit, almost like blood brothers . . . like kamikaze pilots."

"I remember Al as a student," said Lou Carnesecca, who played at St. John's from 1946 to 1950. "Him and Danny Finn would fight every single day in practice at the old DeGray gym. It was maybe about an elbow or something. In practice, Al was very tough. He always took the high scorer of the other team. He was a good rebounder, a good, tough defensive player."

While admitting that he was not much of a playmaker as a guard/forward during his college days, McGuire produced statistics at St. John's that the university described as "unusually impressive." He missed just three games and averaged 8.1 points a game in his three varsity seasons. During that time, the Redmen averaged 22 wins a year, finishing 66-19 with four postseason appearances.

In his sophomore season (1948–49), Al joined Dick on the varsity, which included such players as Danny Buckley, Ed Redding, and Gerry Calabrese. In his first game, St. John's defeated Ft. Monmouth, 93-27. St. John's finished 16-9 that season and received a berth in the National Invitation Tournament, which was still considered the preeminent post-season college tourney in the country. The Redmen lost in the first round to Bowling Green University, 77-64. That season college teams used glass backboards for the first time.

"Zeke" Zawoluk joined St. John's for the 1949–50 season when the Johnnies defeated Adolph Rupp's University of Kentucky Wildcats in Madison Square Garden, 69-58. Kentucky was still reeling from a point-shaving scandal in the previous year's NIT. The Wildcats' star center, Alex Groza, admitted that he and other members of Rupp's "Fabulous Five" took money to shave points in Kentucky's 67-56 NIT loss to Loyola in 1949.

In that season's NIT, St. John's defeated Western Kentucky 69-60, but lost in the next round to Bradley, 83-77. In the consolation game, the Redmen beat Duquesne 69-68 in overtime to take third place.

During the 1949–50 season CCNY, which was known at the time as the poor man's Harvard, became the first and only college team to win both the NCAA and NIT titles. After that, the NCAA prohibited conference champions from playing in the National Invitation Tournament. However, they allowed runners-up to participate in the NIT.

But another basketball scandal tarnished CCNY's twin titles as Nat Holman's boys—Irwin Dambrot, Norm Mager, Ed Roman, Ed Warner, Floyd Layne, Al Roth, and Herb Cohen—pleaded guilty to shaving points.

Kentucky and CCNY were not the only schools implicated in the fixing scandals. Players from LIU, NYU, Manhattan, Bradley, and Toledo were also implicated between 1947 and 1950. As the scandals became more widespread, the stock of college basketball dropped while that of professional basketball began to rise.

Al was named team captain his senior year (1950–51) when the Johnnies won 26 games, which was the most wins for a team in one season up to that time. St. John's played in both the NIT and NCAA tournaments that year. In McGuire's final college game, St. John's defeated Seton Hall in two overtimes, 70-68, to finish third in the NIT for the second straight year.

In the NCAA tournament, St. John's defeated Connecticut and lost to Kentucky before beating North Carolina State in the consolation game of the third round, 71-59. McGuire was named to the East squad in the annual East-West Fresh Air All-Star Game, which was played at Madison Square Garden after the season.

McGuire was not drafted by any NBA team, but Big Al still thought he could play pro basketball. He went up to the New York Knicks camp at Bear Mountain, New York, and talked coach Joe Lapchick into giving him a tryout. "I think I can make the team," he confidently told Lapchick.

The reticent Lapchick had been a 6'6" center for the Original Celtics, a roving team of professionals who were considered one of the greatest teams in the early days of professional basketball. They were a barnstorming team that rarely lost and were referred to as the white Globetrotters. Joining Lapchick on the Original Celtics was Nat Holman. It was the Original Celtics who pioneered such innovations as the pivot play, defensive switching, the give-and-go, and the weave.

"His [Al's] biggest problem was that he didn't score, which made it difficult for him to make the team, never mind that he went undrafted," noted Dick, who was already established with the Knicks, and would eventually become a seven-time all-star during an 11-year career with the Knicks and the Detroit Pistons.

"The summation of Al McGuire is that he was the worst shooter in the world," recalled Vince Boryla, a 6'5" forward who played for the Knicks from 1949 to 1954. Boryla was also recognized as the Knicks tough guy, and was a highly sought after player, according to McGuire.

"They called me the Moose," Boryla said, "but he [Al] was a tough sonofabitch. He had great street sense. He played better than average defense. He was tenacious. But when choosing up sides to shoot 21, he was the last guy chosen."

"I think what happened is that when Al went to camp, he realized that he couldn't make it on his ability," said Ochs. "So, he had a couple of agendas. One of them was to pick a fight with somebody that Joe Lapchick felt was tough. Lapchick thought that Vince Boryla was the gorilla. And so Al probably figured, 'If I start a fight with Lapchick's tough guy, maybe he'll think I'm a tough guy. And maybe I'll make the team that way.'"

Not long after McGuire began working out with the Knicks, he picked a fight with Boryla. As it turned out, Lapchick liked McGuire's aggressiveness and decided to keep him on the team. He called McGuire his mix master, because he was the one Lapchick turned to when he wanted something started.

Ray Lumpp, a teammate of McGuire's and a guard on the 1948 U.S. Olympic basketball team, remembered it differently.

"The first trip we made, Al carried the basketballs. Al was the reserve, the eleventh man. The first two or three games Al didn't play. We had a young player from St. Peter's who left us in Fort Wayne, Indiana. After that, Al was the tenth man. He didn't make the team until after that kid left the Knicks."

The Korean War was in full swing and Dick McGuire was already a star in the three-year-old NBA when Al joined the Knicks for the 1951–52 season. The new league was formed in 1946 when the 11 teams of the Basketball Association of America absorbed the six teams left over from the old National Basketball League.

"Al exemplified everything about a New York street guy. There wasn't anyone who didn't have a fight with him," Boryla said. "He was mouthy. Dick and Al were like night and day. It was hard to believe they had the same parents. There couldn't be two more opposite people.

"But Joe [coach Lapchick] liked Al. He admired the fact that he was a scrappy guy. He didn't have one-fourth of the talent that Dick had. He was a helluva guy to have on the team. That same type of mentality and toughness has stood him in good stead during his coaching career. He was the king of the elephant balls," Boryla said. "He actually played basketball so much he was never out of shape. Al was hard as nails."

"My role on the Knickerbockers," said McGuire, "was to go in and disrupt the opposition, to throw off their rhythm, change the game. They called me a scrambler, and that's where I got the idea for 'scrambled eggs' at Marquette, a whole unit that would go in to change the rhythm of a game."

During another practice, McGuire was guarding Ernie Vandeweghe too closely for the star's liking, and he began calling fouls. "Oh, Ernie, don't be a crybaby," McGuire teased. "You're five times the player I am. You're just not in shape yet."

"Al wasn't afraid to say anything to anyone," said Vandeweghe, who attended medical school at Columbia University while coming off the bench for the Knicks. "When the rookies came to Bear Mountain, McGuire would say, 'Here's the ball. If you want it, ya gotta fight me for it.' I could manage playing in the NBA, going to medical school, and marrying a Miss America [Coleen Hutchins, 1952], but I couldn't keep up with Al McGuire."

After making the team, McGuire made his presence known to the other Knicks. During game timeouts there were usually two people talking in the huddle, Lapchick and McGuire, and Al was not even playing in the game.

Toward the end of games the Knicks were losing, McGuire would start chirping at the other team. "During a timeout, he'd go to the other team's huddle and say: 'Hey guys, we got you now. Here we come. We're in position now. Pack it in. The game's over. We got ya where he want ya.' They'd look at him like he was crazy. He challenged everybody," said Vandeweghe, who was usually teamed with McGuire to press the opposing guards. "Al's spirits were always up. He had an opinion or a saying, or he was ragging someone. We were gonna win, no matter what. His laughing was infectious."

At that time, NBA players were making anywhere between $5,000 and $10,000 a year. Boryla noted that his first "guaranteed" contract with the team was $49,000, spread out at $16,500 a year. Dick McGuire's first contract with the Knicks was $6,500 and a car.

"We had $8 a day for meals: $1.50 for breakfast, $2.50 for lunch, and $4 for dinner," said Boryla. "Our pregame meal came out of our per diem meal money. The Knicks gave us an envelope with our meal money before a road trip." Al McGuire was paid the league minimum (approximately $5,000; $6,000 including playoff monies).

Like most teams of that era, the Knicks' mode of transportation was trains, planes, and automobiles, but not necessarily in that order. There was no such thing as a training table and the showers were very small. "It was train, bus, and plane a distant third. We carried our own bags," said Boryla, who presently works in an investment business in Colorado building shopping centers.

What kept the team sane on the long road trips was card playing, according to Boryla, who noted McGuire's prowess.

"He was a helluva card player," Boryla said of McGuire. "We were probably the most notorious card team in the league. It kept us together. Those six, seven, eight of us would play cards, poker. Al and I and Dick and Connie Simmons and Sweetwater Clifton were the ringleaders in card playing.

"The card games to us were a great pacifier. With good guys and good teams things don't carry over. I always liked Al. You didn't stop going to dinner or playing cards with him just because you had a fight [with him]."

"It was Al who organized the late-night poker games that began past midnight and usually lasted until just before the tipoff of the game the next night," said Vandeweghe, who was usually sent out to get food for the players. "Al could stay up all night and get ready to play the next day, but I couldn't. They were still playing hands of poker as they were getting ready in the locker room."

"You know, traveling by train we'd play cards all night, but we would not allow Sweets into our games. He was so bad, he'd draw two to an inside straight. It was too much like stealing, so we had to try not to let him know if or where there was a game," recalled McGuire, who roomed with Clifton on the road but usually hung out with Simmons.

"It was Sweets who taught me that 'aunt' didn't mean you're related. If he told me an aunt (a great looking woman) was coming to visit, I knew that meant I'd have to make a trifecta and sleep in a room with two other guys," laughed McGuire.

It was not until three years after Jackie Robinson had integrated baseball that the NBA had its first black player, Earl Lloyd. Chuck Cooper of the Celtics was the first black drafted, and Clifton, a former Harlem Globetrotter, was the first black to sign an NBA contract. But it was Lloyd who was the first to actually play in a game, in October 1950, for the old Washington Capitols.

While Sweets was accepted as one of the guys by McGuire and his teammates, he still could not eat in the same restaurants or stay in the same hotels as the rest of the team. McGuire befriended the powerful forward, who was considered the Wilt Chamberlain of his day. "Sweets was our number one muscle man," recalled Boryla. "Al was in the middle of a lot of brawls," said Ochs. "Anytime Al got in trouble, Sweets would come over to bail him out."

"A lot of people give me credit for having a special rapport with blacks, especially when I was coaching," explained McGuire. "But I was no crusader. It was just that racism never came up with me in my life in basketball, as a player, a coach, or whatever. At the end of the day, I'd go where I lived and they'd go where they lived. But during the day I can honestly say I was never aware of the color of anyone's skin."

One teammate with whom McGuire did not have an especially close relationship was Harry "the Horse" Gallatin, a 6'6" power forward/center, from a small town in the Midwest. Gallatin did not drink or play cards. "Al probably rubbed Harry the wrong way more than anyone on the club. But Al never took himself seriously," said Boryla.

"Harry Gallatin was the big man on that Knicks team," said McGuire. "A workhorse, a Clydesdale. He was Midwest, very straight, and we called him Farmer. A nice person but with a lot of competitiveness, a kind of silent assassin. Harry was slow on the court and slow with money, too. He and Vinny Boryla would always sit on the outside in cabs, with a rookie sandwiched in between, because the last one out had to pay."

Carl Braun and Max Zaslofsky were also members of that pioneer Knicks squad. Zaslofsky, a forward, led the league in scoring during the 1947–48 season with the Chicago Stags. When the team folded in 1950, Zaslofsky was coveted by the Celtics' Red Auerbach when Stags players were dispersed to other teams. But the player that Auerbach wound up getting was not half bad: a guard named Bob Cousy, or "Cooz" as he was affectionately referred to later by denizens of the old Boston Garden.

"Tricky Dick" McGuire was the polar opposite of Al. He enjoyed a reputation as a gentleman of the game. He later went on to coach the Knickerbockers and the Detroit Pistons before becoming a scout for the Knicks. He has been associated with Knicks basketball for over 50 years, and was inducted into the Basketball Hall of Fame in 1993.

Al, on the other hand, was not a good shooter. So he concentrated on being an "enforcer" or, as he put it, a tailender: playing defense by hanging onto the shirttails of the other players. "I stayed in the league three years by diving over press tables and starting fights.

"I know some people called me a designated fouler, but I was more like a tackler. I remember once, when I had a fight in three games in a row (one of them with Bill Sharman in Boston), Lapchick said to me before the next game in Rochester, 'Al, please, no fight tonight.' Was I obnoxious, arrogant, surly? I don't know what I was in those days. I guess I was Al McGuire."

Knicks games were always a big family outing for the McGuire family. Winifred usually took the wheel and quiet John would sit in the front seat. The father enjoyed watching his sons play.

"He never missed a game. He liked the idea of going to a game," Dick said of his father. "They liked going to the Garden. He brought a bottle of rye or scotch to the ushers. He wandered around the Garden and didn't come back to his seat until the last two minutes because that's what he felt was the best part of the game."

"Whenever Dick left the game to a standing ovation, John McGuire would retreat to the concession stand and cry by himself, he was so proud," recalled Ochs, who added that neither Al nor his father "wore softness on their sleeves" very well.

Whenever the Knicks were on television and brother John, a.k.a. "Fat Johnny," was bartending, he would scream instructions at the set. When customers would yell at him to keep it down, his reply was: "Hey, that's Dick's body running around up there with my brains." But Johnny was also the one who negotiated Dick's contracts with Knicks' president Ned Irish.

During the 1951–52 season, the Knicks finished 37-29, good enough for third place in the Eastern Division of the NBA. After eliminating the Celtics and Syracuse Nationals in the playoffs, the Knicks advanced to the NBA finals for the second straight year. The team had lost the previous season to the Rochester Royals. This time it was against George Mikan and the Minneapolis Lakers, coached by John Kundla, who coached the Lakers to four titles in five years during the early 1950s.

"We split the first two games in Minny [Minnesota]," Boryla recalled. "We really should have won two. We were jubilant [though]. We really had a good series. We never played well in Minny. So, after splitting the first two games in Minnesota, Al proclaimed, 'They won't see us back here again.'" And, as it turns out, he was right. But not with the outcome McGuire had in mind.

In keeping with his reputation, the rookie McGuire was involved in a controversial play in the first game of the NBA finals, April 12, at the St. Paul Auditorium.

Late in the first half, according to McGuire, he drove the lane and was fouled by Laker Pep Saul as he put up a shot, which swished through the net. Most of the 10,000 in attendance, including the players from both teams, saw the ball go in. The only ones who did not see the ball go through the hoop were the two officials working the game, Sid Borgia and Stan Stutz, who once played for the Knicks. As a result, the basket was not counted.

"Sid called a two-shot foul. He was underneath the basket watching for contact, not watching the ball," said Ray Lumpp. "Kundla gets off the bench and asks Borgia how it could be a two-shot foul when the ball went in the basket."

Borgia still signaled for a two-shot foul even after the players tried to convince him that the basket was good. However, after he talked to Stutz, Borgia did not allow the basket, insisting that he did not see the ball go through the net.

Knicks coach Lapchick became apoplectic. NBA president Maurice Podoloff and Walter Kennedy, the league's supervisor of officials, were dragged into the discussion. When the referee's decision stood, Lapchick played the game under protest.

McGuire made just one of the free throws. The score was tied at 71 apiece at the end of regulation. But the Lakers' Jim Pollard scored seven of his 34 points in the overtime period, giving the home team the win, 83-79.

"He had a fantastic series," Boryla said of Pollard. "Sweetwater Clifton was assigned George Mikan for that series. He was too tough for Sweets physically. And the Lakers beat us three straight in New York."

"We had a guy named Slater Martin and he did a good job of guarding Al during the finals," recalled Mikan, who was named the greatest player of the first half of the twentieth century. "Through the newspapers we had heard about his antics. If you put a little spice in the league, that didn't hurt.

"Al was a very fiery player," added Mikan. "He ran at top speed. We used to call him the outer space man when he wore that mask on his face. We didn't pay any attention to him during the finals. We actually ignored him. He gets out there and he's real fired up, and he'd do anything to win.

We looked at him as a solid sixth man. He was very entertaining and instilled the power to win in his team. Al was a good competitor, that's the best thing that I can say about him."

Lapchick's protest was ultimately disallowed by Podoloff, and the Lakers took the series 4 games to 3. "The blown call was one of the most critical officiating gaffes in NBA history," according to Bruce Nash and Allan Zullo in their book *The Basketball Hall of Shame*. "It directly affected the outcome of the entire championship series."

One of the few highlights of McGuire's pro career was being the first player to sell out Boston Garden. He boasted before a Knicks-Celtics game that he would "stop" Bob Cousy. His famous "I own Cousy" boast, which was carried in the *New York Post* and the Boston papers, was nearly as famous as the *Chicago Tribune*'s Dewey Defeats Truman headline in 1948.

"After a Knicks-Celtics game in the Boston Garden, Al saw *Boston Globe* sportswriter Cliffie Keane come into the visitors' locker room," recalled Leonard Lewin, now executive director of the Knicks' Alumni Association.

"Al knows that Keane thinks the sun rises and sets on Cousy. So for Keane's benefit, Al hops up on the training table and points at Dick and says, 'You can't cover Cousy. I own Cousy.' Keane wrote the story and it was picked up by all the newspapers," said Lewin, who covered the Knicks at that time for the *Daily Mirror*. "Al said that statement kept him in the league two years. It was typical Al McGuire theatrics," said Lewin, who tagged McGuire with the nickname Alley Cat during Al's days at St. John's.

At the time, the Celtics were drawing about 4,000 fans a game in Boston Garden. This night it was packed to see the cocky young Irishman try to stop the 6'2" all-star guard who was beloved in Beantown and a 13-time all-star during his career. McGuire did stop Cousy while he was in the game, by fouling Cousy or the man who set picks for him, Bob Brannum, whose job it was to keep McGuire away from Cousy.

"Al fouled out against me," said Cousy. "Al knew where his strengths lay. Defensively, he would offer a change of pace if a guy got the hot hand and physically intimidate the player. The aggressor has the advantage.

"For the time it took him to commit five fouls, he played a role," Cousy said. "He couldn't stop me from penetrating or making the pass. I remember that he fouled out a few times, and playing against him was physical in that he didn't let you do what you wanted. Against me, he was more of a clutch-and-grab player because I was quicker.

"Al was a very physical defensive player. It was through the combination of his hard work, dedication, and promotional abilities that we sold out every Knicks-Celtics game at the Garden for two years," remembered Cousy, now a television analyst for the Celtics. "Our games drew good crowds in New York, too. We played each other often during the three seasons Al was in the league—maybe five to seven times a season."

Before one Knicks-Celtics clash, "Al brought a knife, a fork, and a plate to the middle of the court and said, 'I'm gonna have Cousy for dinner!'" recalled Vandeweghe, who added that a photo of McGuire at center court appeared the next day on the *New York Post*'s sports page.

Before McGuire's boast, Cousy did not know much about Al, except that he was Dick's younger brother. "Dick was the talent in the family. Every coach he ever played for pleaded with him to shoot more. He was the whole package. But after Al told the world he was going to do a number on me, we became aware of him."

Not long after his boast, McGuire attempted to back it up at the old 69th Regiment Armory, where the Knicks played some of their home games.

"It was early in the game," recalled McGuire, "and someone was setting a pick for Cousy. It was usually [forward Jim] Loscutoff, but it might have been Jack Nichols. Nichols was the second player to wear low-top shoes. I was the first. Anyway, whoever was picking for Cousy, I ran over him, tackled him really, and that started a brawl.

"Now, my rule is always stay close to a bigger guy in a fight. He can't hurt you if you stay close. In a bar fight or street fight, you never go down, but on a basketball court you go to the floor and grab and you don't get hurt.

"That's what happened. We went to the floor, grabbed and rolled around a little, and it was over. But here comes my brother Johnny out onto the floor, a cop carrying a gun. I stopped Cousy all right on that possession because some other guy went on the line. But the fight was stopped when Johnny McGuire came onto the court with his gun."

Neither Cousy, his teammates, nor Celtics coach "Red" Auerbach considered McGuire's boast "trash talk." In fact, they never really took what McGuire said that seriously. To them it was just another New Yorker talking.

"When I was coach in those days, that [McGuire's boast] was the biggest joke of all. That's all it was," recalled Auerbach. "He was trying to justify their existence. We didn't pay any attention to it. We laughed about it. Russell, Sharman, they used to laugh about it, too. His conversation and picking a fight was his forte of trying to hang on in the NBA. He was full of energy. He energized the team.

"Al was no factor. We cared about who won," Auerbach continued. "We didn't care about this exploitation. Being from New York, we took special delight in beating them [the Knicks]. The rivalry was there because of the proximity of the cities. The writers felt that anything outside of New York City was camping out," he said.

"Al was always, in his playing and endeavors in life, an opportunist," said Cousy. "And he exploited whatever abilities he had to take advantage of the opportunities in his life. [But] on a professional level, the fans and the media respond to that. The players don't take it too seriously. In a team sport, it's like they built up the Russell-Chamberlain matchup to sell tickets. I didn't take it [too seriously].

"For Al or anyone else to say 'I'm gonna stop him'—hey, I was extremely confident about my abilities. But once I got out on the floor, I knew what I could do. There was no one in the sport I was concerned about. But you could not ignore Al.

"Trash talking was not in, in those days. Other than getting into it [fighting], we would have been insane to try to intimidate someone personally. I don't remember Al trash talking. I'm sure he didn't. His talking was usually reserved for the media. Once the game began, you just went out and did your thing. It was hype. Arnold's [Auerbach] concern was winning the damn game. We were all wise-ass New Yorkers. Not only survivors, but we'd use whatever skills to our advantage."

"He [Al] rubbed some guys the wrong way with his mouth, but in general everyone liked him," added Boryla.

McGuire's fisticuffs were not always confined to the basketball court. One night, he and his partner in crime, 6'8" forward Connie Simmons, were, according to McGuire, in a tavern under the Third Avenue "El" during the wee hours one morning.

"Connie or I said something someone didn't like and I was blindsided with a punch. I knew right away it was bad, the jaw was broken in two places, but I said to Connie, 'We gotta get out of this joint before reporters show up.'"

According to Vandeweghe, the story of McGuire's legendary dustup is not as glamorous as he made it out to be. "I examined his jaw," stated Vandeweghe. "We were at a bar in Baltimore. We came out of the bar, and there's a trolley coming down the road. Al says that he'll flag down the trolley but he slips and falls, and that was how he broke his jaw.

"The next day his jaw was swollen. He says to Connie, 'Bump into me in the warmup drills to make it look like it happened then so I won't get in trouble for doing it the night before.' So he goes to the trainer, Danny Fredericks, and says: 'Connie broke my jaw when he bumped into me.

"'Connie got me to some hospital with a lot of foreign docs, and I had one from, I think, the Yucatan Peninsula. It was five in the morning, he was probably thinking about some native relics or artifacts, and I'm thinkin', How good can he be?

"'So my jaw was wired shut, and the story we gave out to the press was that I was hurt in a traffic accident on my way home at 11 the night before. Anyway, when I showed up at the Garden with that big brace to protect my head, that's when I really earned the name of 'space cadet.'"

During surgery doctors wired his jaw shut but removed a tooth so that a straw could be slipped into his mouth to feed him. McGuire's mother mixed liver and various vegetables into a liquid paste for nourishment because he could not chew.

"Al still played with that broken jaw," said Ray Lumpp, longtime athletic director of the New York Athletic Club. "With that white mask, he looked like the masked marvel running around out on the court."

"Al's buddy was Connie Simmons," recalled Vandeweghe. "He teased Connie the most. He said to Connie, 'I'll bet you that you can't walk through the revolving door without touching the glass. I'll bet you five dollars,' Al said as the team was leaving the hotel for a game.

"Connie goes in the revolving door. He's standing in there and he isn't moving. Al stops the door and puts up the Out of Order sign on the door so that no one would use the door. And if Connie touches the glass, he loses the five dollars. We're on our way to the game and they argued all the way to the game about who won the five dollars. Al was thinking all the time," Vandeweghe said, laughing at the memory.

McGuire's only other claim to fame during his playing career was that he was the first player in the league to have a shoe contract and not receive any money for it. Converse had asked him to wear the low-top sneakers for publicity purposes. But he later claimed that he was forced to wear low-tops after he broke his ankle attempting a high jump during his track days at St. John's.

The 1952–53 campaign saw the Knicks finish 47-23, good enough for third in the East. After defeating the Baltimore Bullets and the Celtics to win the division, the Knicks again advanced to the finals, losing to the Lakers 4 games to 1. It was the Knicks' third straight trip to the finals. The Knicks would not reach the finals again until 1970, when they finally beat the Los Angeles Lakers 4 games to 3.

McGuire's last full season in the NBA (1953–54), the Knicks finished first in the East with a 44-20 record, but were quickly eliminated in the playoffs. During the 1954–55 season, the NBA introduced the 24-second shot clock and McGuire was traded to the Bullets, along with Simmons, in exchange for Ray Felix.

"A dozen or so games into the season, I knew the Baltimore franchise was going belly up, and not just because we played our games in some kind of roller rink," recalled McGuire.

"About a week before it became official, I was in our bus in Baltimore riding through those white stoops and crab sandwiches, and I was sitting next to our coach, Clair Bee [former Long Island University coach and author of the Chip Hilton sports books], who was always a nifty dresser. He took his handkerchief out of his breast pocket, wiped his brow, carefully rearranged it in his pocket, and threw his fedora out the window. That's how I knew the end was in sight."

The Bullets folded 14 games into the season, and Al was out of a job. While it was a short-lived pro career, McGuire said that he enjoyed the life. He also had the opportunity to play in two NBA finals, made the most of his limited skills, and, most important, made a name for himself.

"Al was different in a smart way," noted Ray Lumpp. "He made the most of his abilities and took advantage of the opportunities that came his way. You have to take your hat off to him. He was a success anywhere he went."

By this time, Al and Pat had a second child, Noreen, who was born in 1953, and Al went back to tending bar at his father's tavern in Rockaway while he contemplated which career path to take on his road-less-traveled journey.

Chapter Four

Whistle Blower

McGuire could have opted for the FBI, or for the police department, like his brother John, who ticketed the mayor's car twice and was eventually fired after reportedly falling asleep on the job.

He was scheduled to take the FBI test one day, but decided to play golf instead. On his way home, thinking he'd made the biggest mistake of his life, he reportedly threw the golf bag and clubs over the Cross Bay Bridge. Twenty-four hours later he was asking a friend if he could borrow his clubs.

"I could have been a policeman or a bartender or a construction worker. You know what success is? It's when you can do the things you really want to do outside your job." But he also felt that success was born not of confidence, but of fear of failure. The fear of having to go back to where he came from is what drove McGuire, who was not content to sit still and wait for opportunity to come knocking on his door. "Al was always in a hurry to get to the next part of his life," observed his friend Norman Ochs.

When asked whether the family thought that Al might become a coach someday, Dick said no. "Everyone thought he was going to be a bartender." He added that their parents never talked about aspirations they had for the boys, if they had any at all. "They probably would have liked us to run the bar," he said matter-of-factly.

Al did have coaching prospects at West Point and Yale. When he interviewed for the West Point job, McGuire said he brashly told Hall of Fame football coach and athletic director Red Blaik how much money it would take to hire him.

"He listened to me and then said, 'Mr. McGuire, hand in your expenses on your way out the door.' That's it. End of interview," he recalled.

It was Boston Celtics owner Walter Brown who gave McGuire his first break. Both he and Joe Lapchick recommended the out-of-work ballplayer for the freshman coaching job at Dartmouth College, before the start of the 1954–55 season.

Dartmouth had earlier selected Joe Mullaney, an all-star at Holy Cross and with the Celtics, to replace the retiring Chick Evans as its freshman coach. But before the season started, Mullaney accepted a head coaching job at another school, opening the door for McGuire.

"Walter Brown said to me, 'Al, you were the first guy to pack the Boston Garden. I owe you one.' That's because I said I could stop Cousy," said McGuire. "I lied. Only God could stop Cousy."

Back in 1955 the nation still liked Ike, and a double-breasted, pointy-shoed, brash city slicker named Al McGuire invaded the preppy environs of Hanover, New Hampshire.

McGuire joined the staff of Alvin "Doggie" Julian, who was in the stretch run of a Hall of Fame career. Julian won an NCAA title when Cousy was a freshman at Holy Cross in 1947, and earned his nickname for the manner in which he worked over referees. Julian came to Dartmouth originally as a football coach, and was offered an extra $500 to coach the basketball team. Cousy recalled that Julian "literally did not recruit any players, but he certainly got the most out of the talent that he had."

Julian drilled his players in the fundamentals—passing, moving without the ball, making the extra pass. He was, in McGuire's words, a "whistle blower"—a coach who uses a lot of drills and wants his players to dress in lookalike sports coats.

"He [Julian] was a great pregame, inspiring guy. He loved coaching, loved winning," said Rudy LaRusso, a star power forward in the early 1950s at Dartmouth. "He was a great fatherly type."

"I remember Doggie being a character," said Cousy. "He was extremely superstitious. He had a real thing about diet. And just before the game would start, he would rub the foreheads of the individual players."

Julian was also known for his one-liners and catch phrases, many of which McGuire incorporated into his own hoops lexicon.

"If practice was going badly, Doggie would yell, 'How much rice can a Chinaman eat?'" recalled LaRusso. "And Doggie's phrase when a guy threw the ball behind his back was, 'Forget the French pastry, play bread-and-butter basketball.'" *Bread and Butter Basketball* was the title of a book that Julian wrote about the game. Cousy recalled that whenever a player made an unnecessary pass instead of taking the easy shot, "Doggie would say, 'You can never get closer than close.'"

"I think he was a good coach for Al to be around," recalled LaRusso, who was later a defensive standout during a ten-year professional career with the Minneapolis and Los Angeles Lakers. "This was Julian's last [coaching] stop. He had a world of experience behind him. Doggie taught a solid game of basketball. He was good at making personnel work."

"Al was at the tail end of the character coaches," remembered Dave Gavitt, who played on McGuire's freshman team and is now president of the NCAA Foundation. "He was just coming out of the NBA.

"Red Rolfe [Dartmouth athletic director] hired him for four months. Al arrived in Hanover. It was really remote. It is a three-hour drive from Boston. Here's Al out of Queens. He thinks he's been put in Alaska.

"Al comes to practice wearing black pointy shoes and a red V-neck sweater. We're about four games into the season, playing Holy Cross in Hanover."

In the second half of that game, McGuire inserted Gavitt. "Down the stretch, I hit seven jumpers. He subs for another player. He's streaking in front of the bench. He gives me a pat on the back and says, 'Good job, George.' The next day, I'm still sitting on the bench," recalled Gavitt, whom McGuire nicknamed Butterball for his corpulence. "I was a little stocky in those days," laughed Gavitt, who added that nicknames were the only way McGuire remembered people. "He never remembered anyone's name."

McGuire warned his freshmen that referees always want to control the game, according to Gavitt. "He told us: 'No jump shots the first five minutes of the game. Take the ball to the basket.' He wanted to see how the referees were going to call the game."

"He [McGuire] insisted on hustle," said LaRusso. "He was a great believer in conditioning. We did a lot of running and sprinting. He was very casual about lots of stuff. At Dartmouth, he was cool, calm, and collected. His philosophies were simple and direct."

In addition to coaching the freshmen, McGuire assisted Julian with the varsity. Since the part-time position paid only $2,000 a year, McGuire lived alone in Hanover and returned to his family in Queens after each season.

McGuire stayed in Dartmouth's Davis Varsity Field House near the 2,000-seat Alumni Gym, where the Big Green played its home games. He had the only room on the third floor. It was said to be so small that even the mice were hunchbacked. McGuire slept with the window open in the middle of winter. "In the morning, I'd wake up and there'd be snow on my blanket. The only time it was exciting [there] was Winter Carnival weekend," he recalled.

In order to supplement his "Catholic" salary, McGuire earned $100 a game as a player/coach for a basketball team in Pittsfield, Massachusetts, called the Lenox Merchants. It grew from a town league team to a semi-pro club, but was more like a poor man's CBA team, according to McGuire's teammate Frank Mahoney.

"Lenox was operated by William 'Butch' Gregory, whose family owned a local meat market. He ran the club," said Mahoney, whose other claim to fame was that he and his wife were the subject of a 1955 *Saturday Evening Post* cover by Norman Rockwell entitled, "The Marriage License." Slater Martin also played on the Merchants with McGuire.

"He [Gregory] became friendly with Red Auerbach of the Boston Celtics. For $500 the Celtics came up and played us in a small gym. At the time, Bob Cousy was Babe Ruth of the Basketball Association of America," said Mahoney. "The pro teams would play teams like Lenox in between games against such professional outfits as the Syracuse Nationals, Minneapolis Lakers, and the New York Knicks. Teams like the Celtics would play because the owners needed the money."

McGuire, who played guard, was a "confirmed basketball nut," said Mahoney, who added that the Merchants played twice a week during the regular basketball season. "He [McGuire] was married with kids. He lamented the travel and schedule, and he was blue at times that he couldn't be home with Pat, Allie, and Noreen."

"They always paid us in the dark and we'd have to count the house ourselves," joked McGuire. "If we didn't get paid, we'd threaten to leave at halftime."

The Merchants also played the St. Louis Hawks, who were coached by Red Holzman. The Red Head, as he was affectionately known, later went on to coach the New York Knicks to NBA titles in 1970 and 1973.

One night, Hawk rookie Cliff Hagan lit up McGuire and the Merchants for 42 points.

Meanwhile, back at his day job in Hanover, McGuire's freshmen teams went 8-2 and 11-2 during his two seasons coaching the Big Green. "We had an unusually good freshman team with Rudy LaRusso. We played when freshman basketball was very competitive," said Gavitt, who later became head coach at Providence, the first commissioner of the Big East, and a vice chairman of the Boston Celtics.

"We played a mixed-bag schedule," remembered LaRusso, now a professional basketball consultant in Europe. "We played Colby College from Maine, Assumption College, Harvard, and Pennsylvania."

McGuire tried to get Julian to implement his newfangled triangle-and-two defense, but Doggie would have none of it, claiming it would not work. Julian's own switching defenses incorporated aggressive man-to-man and zone philosophies. McGuire later used his triangle-and-two defense with great success at Marquette.

"In a place like Dartmouth, you don't have anyone else to talk basketball to," said LaRusso. "They would argue about rules or what was legal. Al and Doggie were always chewing about something at practice.

"Al was trying to invent new things in the game. He would put a three-man zone in the key, one man at midcourt and another player under the basket at the other end," said LaRusso, who played for McGuire during the freshman coach's second season (1955–56) at the Big Green.

"When Al coached at Dartmouth for two years, he learned a lot about running practice and Xs and Os," said Ochs. "What Al learned from Joe Lapchick and Frank McGuire was dealing with people and the press.

"Doggie also taught him a lot about economics," Ochs continued. "Al scratched Doggie's car one time and Doggie wouldn't talk to him for a month. Doggie also told Al not to spend his own money." But "Doggie loved Al," added Gavitt.

"He had the feeling that they [the Dartmouth administration] were watching him closely. He had this brash reputation. He thought that they didn't want this street-smart kid influencing their values," said LaRusso.

"They are ashamed to admit that I coached there because they didn't like the way I talked," McGuire joked in a 1989 interview on NBC's *Later with Bob Costas*.

During the 1955–56 season the Dartmouth varsity squad advanced to the second round of the NCAA tournament. It was the farthest the Big

Green had advanced in the Big Dance since the 1942 and 1944 seasons when they reached the Final Four. That '55–56 season, Phil Woolpert's University of San Francisco Dons, led by Bill Russell, won their second straight NCAA title.

The games at Alumni Gym were usually sellouts, including the freshman contests. It was at Dartmouth that McGuire started to entertain on the sidelines to get the fans into the game. Just as Red Auerbach would light up his famous victory cigar, McGuire would take off his jacket like a matador, which brought the students to their feet.

"He developed his routine of taking off his jacket when he knew the game was in the bag. [Usually] in the middle of the second half. It had a psychological punch to it. It gave you positive vibes," recalled LaRusso, whom McGuire considered to be the first great player that he coached.

Also at Dartmouth he began to use the media to draw attention to his teams. Two or three days before a game against St. Michael's of Vermont, coached by Doc Jacobson, McGuire was asked by a sportswriter to name his All-NBA team, and he left Bob Cousy's name off the list.

"The story hits the wires," Dave Gavitt said. "We get to a sold-out arena. People are hanging over the balcony with signs telling Al to go home and other things."

With no athletic scholarships, minimal meal money, and traveling by bus, McGuire used bottom-line tactics to keep his players on their toes. On less than successful road trips, Gavitt recalled, McGuire would send the starters to one part of the restaurant and the reserves to another. The reserves were fed steak while the losing starters were given cold chicken sandwiches.

"I was influenced by four coaches," said Gavitt. "Al, Doggie, Dean Rowe, and Joe Mullaney. You didn't forget Al. He was more of a defensive coach. The bottom line with Al McGuire is win. In this day and age, it might be different."

Asked what he learned from McGuire, LaRusso mentioned fierceness and the importance of defense and team play.

"Al wanted players playing as a unit. Make the pass, the give-and-go. Playing without the ball is a lost art. A lost skill. Instinctive basketball. The instinctive part is just physical."

McGuire's experiences at Dartmouth convinced him that amateurism in its purest form existed in remote places like Hanover, New Hampshire, and other Ivy League outposts.

"The Ivy League is really the utopia of sports. They keep sports in proper perspective."

Chapter Five

Vaudeville: Character Building at Belmont

McGuire left Dartmouth after two successful seasons in Hanover. When he returned to Rockaway Beach in 1956, Ike was heading for reelection, the oral vaccine against polio was developed, gas was 16 cents a gallon, and Grace Kelly married Prince Rainier. McGuire went back to bartending and making money any way that he knew how. According o family friends, he sold insurance, trophies, anything to make a buck. "I have always had a 'golden thumb' in my life. I have always been able to make money," noted McGuire.

The next door to Al McGuire's coaching career was opened by his mentor, Frank McGuire.

"My dad called Frank," recalled Howard "Humpy" Wheeler Jr., whose father, Humpy Sr., was the athletic director at Belmont Abbey, near Charlotte, North Carolina. "The Abbey had dropped football in 1950. They were looking for a coach and they were putting the emphasis on basketball. 'Al is who you need to get,' Frank told my father. 'He's the guy who'll bring a whole lot of wins here.' My dad said Al was a wild enough Irishman that he might make something happen at Belmont Abbey," noted Wheeler Jr., now president of the Charlotte Motor Speedway.

"I met with the priests of Belmont Abbey in Charlotte," remembered Frank McGuire in a 1977 radio interview. "I said there's one fella I think can coach at Belmont Abbey. Right now he's out of basketball. I know he was a freshman coach at Dartmouth and didn't particularly like it. I know he went back to work for his father. I think he's tendin' bar. That's Al McGuire."

Frank McGuire originally wanted Al to become his assistant at the University of North Carolina. But Al wanted to be a head coach and instead took the job at Belmont Abbey, the second point on his coaching compass. Not long after Al took the job, Brooklyn's beloved bums—the Dodgers—and the New York Giants played their last games at Ebbets Field and the Polo Grounds, leaving New York to the Damn Yankees.

"Can you imagine what a great basketball tradition North Carolina could have had if I took the assistant coach's job at North Carolina?" Al joked years later. But there is some question as to whether Frank would have taken him under his wing, according to Dean Smith.

"Frank thought that Al really was something. [But] Frank thought that maybe Al was too much like himself," said Smith, who was an assistant basketball coach at the U.S. Air Force Academy in 1958 when Frank McGuire asked him to become his assistant at UNC.

"I knew Al pretty well," recalled Red Auerbach. "But I knew he had great motivation. I knew he could be a leader someday, but I had no way of knowing he had the patience to be a head coach."

Only two Belmont Abbey priests and local newspaper reporter Max Muhleman showed up in Charlotte for the press conference to introduce the Crusaders' new coach. After 20 minutes, Muhleman recalled McGuire saying, "Well, father, it looks like nobody else is gonna show up. Why don't I just take this young guy out and buy him a couple of beers?" Muhleman was later responsible for bringing professional basketball and football to Charlotte with the Hornets and the Carolina Panthers, respectively.

"He lived with me two or three months," recalled Muhleman. "We lived in an apartment a short walk from my newspaper office. I was his friend and I would cover his games. Lefty Driesell was coaching Davidson at the same time Al was at Belmont Abbey." Also coaching on Tobacco Road were legends Vic Bubas (Duke) and Everett Case (North Carolina State). Horace "Bones" McKinney arrived at Wake Forest the season after the McGuire era began at Belmont.

"When Max and Al got together, they forgot the time of day," said Wheeler. "They were notorious about forgetting time, space, and possessions. They were like Mutt and Jeff. It was like 'The Odd Couple' when they lived together," Wheeler said.

At that time, Belmont Abbey was a small school (enrollment 1,000) run by the Order of St. Benedict monks in Belmont, North Carolina (population 5,000), a textile town eight miles west of Charlotte.

Baptist Belt Belmont was a far cry from Hanover, New Hampshire, which looked downright sophisticated by comparison. The city boy had to go country in order to become a head coach. For a man who had known the glare of the media in New York City, it was quite a drop-off from NCAA Division One to the National Association of Intercollegiate Athletics (NAIA).

The tiny hamlet of Belmont did not even catch the reflected glow of big-time hoops on Tobacco Road, where Duke, North Carolina State, and the University of North Carolina were kings. Not only that, Al was paying his coaching dues in the long shadow of Frank McGuire.

On the ladder of college sports, NAIA schools such as Belmont Abbey were a rung below even the smaller NCAA schools. The Abbey made the jump to the NCAA Small College Division during McGuire's second season when soccer was added to its sports offerings.

Belmont Abbey's success in athletics was limited to a single football championship in 1939 when the school was still a junior college. The all-male school did not become a senior college until 1952. But Humpy Wheeler, who had played football at the University of Illinois with Red Grange, dropped the Abbey football program before McGuire arrived. Wheeler acquired his nickname after Illini head coach Bob Zuppke caught him smoking Camel cigarettes. While he was running laps for his punishment, Illinois students began calling him Humpy.

The first basketball coach at Belmont Abbey was Al McClellan and the next was Humpy Wheeler Sr., who coached for a number of years before Neil Gordon was hired. Gordon lasted just one year before McGuire was named the fourth coach in Abbey history for the 1957–58 campaign.

McGuire's salary was under $7,500 a year, according to the Reverend Raphael Bridge, Belmont Abbey's athletic moderator, or academic liaison. In order to collect what was owed him at the end of the season, McGuire had to chase a monk who kept the money hidden under his robes.

But if the 28-year-old McGuire thought he was out of place in Ivy League Hanover, he was really a fish out of water as an Irish Catholic in Baptist Belmont. Everette "Ebb" Gantt, radio voice for the basketball team on WCGC and a Belmont native, described the town as a "closed little community." It was also dry.

"They were a clannish-like people. It was a remote village back then. It was an ideal little college town. People were not as receptive to Belmont sports," remembered Gantt, who pointed out that most of the student body was comprised of Catholics from northern and eastern cities, especially New York and New Jersey. "There were so many students who knew of Al from New York before he came to the Abbey," added Wheeler. "Al couldn't have been in a better place than Belmont. Here was a Yankee New York coach with a team runnin' its mouth, and it could get nasty.

"You have to understand that at that time," said Wheeler, "North Carolina was a Jim Crow state. Very southern, anti-Catholic, the Civil War wasn't over yet. They could not tolerate someone from New York City. Coaches of that era tended to be extremely reserved and never lost their temper."

But throughout his career, McGuire found a way to make a home wherever he was living. "He became popular from the first day," said Gantt. "He didn't shun the quiet people downtown."

As the new coach quickly learned, however, bigotry was still strong 30 years after Al Smith ran for president. When McGuire went into town for a haircut, the barber asked him: "Are you the new Catholic coach?" McGuire shot back: "I came in for a haircut, I didn't come to talk religion."

After McGuire touched down in Belmont, he moved Pat, Allie, Noreen, and Robbie, who was born in 1956, down to Charlotte. It was the first major relocation for the family because Pat and Al were leaving their families behind in New York.

Not long after, McGuire parlayed his cachet as the area's newest coach into basketball camps. He ran the camp on Providence Road with the help of Tom Brennan, basketball coach at Charlotte Catholic High School. Pat operated a children's day camp during the summers in Charlotte, which was slowly becoming a sports center, according to Gantt.

"Al had a day camp that we were all involved in," recalled Pat McGuire. "The children would pass out fliers promoting the camp. I would cook. Al would drive the bus. He built tree houses where the campers would stay. He thought he should be around the camp as much as possible."

"It was a great area to start a basketball camp," Gantt said. "At that time Duke, UNC, and North Carolina State were all going great. And so were the smaller schools."

"At Al's day camp, I remember Pat was busy making peanut butter and jelly sandwiches," remarked Dean Smith. "I did a clinic for him at his basketball camp. That's when we got to know each other."

Davidson's Lefty Driesell also worked McGuire's camps during the Belmont Abbey days. After four and a half hours of basketball, the two stopped for lunch. While eating, Driesell was moving salt and pepper shakers around the picnic table, which prompted McGuire to ask if Driesell ever took a break from basketball.

The closest thing to major league sports in that area at the time was minor league baseball. The old Charlotte Hornets of the "Sally League" was the Double-A affiliate for the Minnesota Twins and featured such future stars as Harmon Killebrew, Tony Oliva, and Bobby Allison.

While McGuire would later become renowned for his successful recruitment of All-Americas at Marquette, he was not able to attract that caliber of ballplayer to Belmont Abbey. But he knew so little about high school talent, even in his native New York, that he was forced to rely on street scouts and friends for tips and leads. "Al had a labyrinth of spies watching the high school basketball scene in New York and New Jersey," noted Wheeler. "He made a couple of recruiting trips to New York. I've never seen anyone make his way around New York and New Jersey like Al."

Wheeler recalled that the Division One college coaches in North Carolina—Bubas, McKinney, Driesell, Case—knew McGuire could get players out of New York, which resulted in some jealousy on their part toward him and Belmont Abbey.

While the cupboard was not exactly bare when McGuire arrived at Belmont, he did not have a whole lot to work with in terms of basketball talent. He inherited a pretty good ballplayer in Francis "Bevo" Clair, a football and basketball legend from Charleston, South Carolina. Other holdovers included Bobby Hodges and Mike Ross. "Basketball is a huge sport in a few parts of North Carolina," explained Wheeler, who attended the University of South Carolina from 1959 to 1963. "High school basketball was not big, so they didn't produce that many great players in the state."

McGuire wanted to bring New York players down to Carolina who reflected his street-tough background: aggressive, hard-nosed, underdog types who were mentally tough.

Since Frank McGuire already had his "underground railroad" of talent coming to Chapel Hill from New York City, Al needed his own New York connection. That turned out to be Fred "the Spook" Stegman, whose claim to fame was that he had the telephone number of every college coach in America.

McGuire included Stegman in his list of the most interesting basketball people he had ever met. "He knows where the bodies are buried," McGuire said of Stegman, who was tagged with his moniker by Al's brother Dick. "Every time I turned around, there was Freddie. Just like a ghost. Like a spook."

"I only met him [Stegman] once," said Gantt, now retired in Belmont. "You could have said that guy lived on the street. Al dressed him up. He didn't miss a game that he could get to. He was a hired Hessian who recruited high school ballplayers for just about any college coach," said Gantt of Stegman, who started his career recruiting for the late Seton Hall coaching legend "Honey" Russell.

"Al told me, 'You get the players and I'll charm the mothers,'" Stegman recalled of McGuire's double-barreled recruiting strategy.

"The Spook" helped recruit McGuire's first class of players to Belmont: John von Bargen, Danny Doyle, Jimmy Mullen, and Jimmy Sparrow (Gene Mann's cousin). They were Belmont's version of the Fab Four.

"The type of kids he brought down mixed well with the students," said Gantt. "Al was that perfect person to fit in with the common talk of the boys. He was tough enough and personable. I called them a scraggly bunch of boys from New York. It takes a damn good coach to put them in line."

McGuire referred to his players as freckles—white, usually first-generation Irish, German, and Italian with names like Sullivan, Roche, Dockery, Doyle, Steincke, and Affuso. Few were taller than 6'5". And they came from such Big Apple hoops hotbeds as Archbishop Molloy, St. Francis Prep, Brooklyn Prep, DeWitt Clinton, and Power Memorial.

They also shared an unconditional love for basketball that was spawned on concrete courts such as McGuire's Playground in Queens. One of those players was Chuck Sullivan (1961–65), who played for Jack

Curran at Archbishop Molloy High School. Lou Carnesecca preceded
Curran there before moving on to coach at St. John's. But Sullivan and
the others learned the game on McGuire's Playground, and their nostalgia for the Rockaway game was reflected in a poem Sullivan penned years
later entitled, "Longing for the Memories."

> This fall not even one
> shooting stars soul is ghosting
> off the pick and roll
> nothing gives nothing goes
> on the chipped coal asphalt
> of McGuire's Park
> where time out o mind
> we once courted our Lady
> of Rockaway Hoops
> teeming with suitors
> of three on three
> in this salty cage by the sea
>
> And alone I replay that day
> a quarter century ago
> When we three in low black "cons"
> found our mortal feet winged
> as we rose in the blue leap
> of air breezing above the sweep
> of the roundball rookery flying
> high with the half-court feather
> touch of August excellence gliding
> free of losses of three epic hours
>
> Caught in the tall dance of flesh
> and shadows larger than life
> our moves were the sweaty tunes
> of our bodies keeping the once
> in a lifetime time of the soaring
> score of most arcing music
> whose sphere would drop banked

Lyric clean again and again to be
recalled through the past plunge
of a summer rim without a net
on a backboard with a dead spot
alive in the pressing sun's
most burning trophy won

By luck's all-stars shining
in the broad daylight skilled
in the hustling game of true fakes
A chance team of champions graced
with the free-lance fate
of friends becoming legends

In our minds our hearts breaking
time into song as we sang in our beers
like the sea in rim rounds
rounding the hoop of lost harmony.

"We traveled all over the city looking for games. When we were in high school, we played every Saturday and Sunday in the summer at McGuire's Playground. There were 30 to 40 people waiting to play. We won for three straight hours. If you dove for the ball, Al loved you. Then we went down to McGuire's. If you were 18, you could drink," recalled Sullivan. "But they never bought us a beer at McGuire's," laughed Bob Kopf, one of Sullivan's teammates at Molloy and the Abbey.

Sullivan added that McGuire had a feel for who could play the game that was uncanny. "Al gave scholarships to four of us just by seeing us play once. Bobby, me, Bill Dockery, and John Murray."

"Al could spot talent that was about to break loose," noted Wheeler. "My father knew that if you could get kids out of New York and New Jersey, he knew that you had to get a guy who could talk the language of the players. That was Al."

McGuire's players at the Abbey were not the best and the brightest, but most majored in accounting, pre-law, and chemistry, and all earned their degrees. McGuire promised them room and board, books, tuition, laundry money, and a chance to play in a climate warmer than New York. He gave them an opportunity they would not have had otherwise.

"We were an intelligent group of players," said Jim Lytle (1958–62), a tough 6'3" guard from Rego Park. "If it weren't for Al, none of us would have gone to college."

One of the first players Stegman brought to McGuire was Danny Doyle, a 6'7" forward from Astoria in Queens. Doyle had been expelled from high school before the Spook and McGuire set him on the straight and narrow.

"In early August of 1957," said Doyle, "this gentleman [Stegman] and him [McGuire] went to my mother and father's house. And they said, 'Listen, this kid can go to school four years at Catholic school.' My mother and father were Irish-Catholics from the other side, not the swiftest human beings in the world. They said it was great," he said of their reaction to the arrangement, which allowed Doyle and his brother Duke to attend Belmont on what amounted to a partial scholarship.

"I was in a schoolyard shootin' dice, and I look up and there's the Spook. I say, 'What's goin' on, Spook?' And I see this guy next to him dressed in a blue suit, and I figured I was goin' to jail. Then Spook tells me I'm goin' to Belmont Abbey. I asked him if that was a toothpaste. I went down there and had four of the most glorious years of my life. It was absolutely sensational."

But McGuire was not always enthralled with Stegman. Toward the end of McGuire's career at Belmont, Stegman was supposed to recruit a 7-foot center for the Abbey. When Stegman arrived at Belmont, he drove up in a new car. And instead of a 7-foot giant, out stepped a 5'1" guard, according to Chuck Sullivan.

"Freddie brings in this guy, the son of a car dealer in New Jersey. He's trying to pass him off on Al. And Al says, 'Nice car, Spook. Is that what you're getting for bringing him down here? Where's the 7-footer?' That guy never played at the Abbey," laughed Sullivan.

"McGuire said himself the guys he got at the Abbey were all the misfits, the rejects," said Hank Steincke (1958–62). "All the guys he went for were the fifth or sixth guys on the high school team. The first four went on to the big schools. The fifth and sixth guys were borderline or maturing late, as he used to say. Those are the guys that he and Freddie would grab. As far as recruiting, I'm the only guy he actually found on a playground."

McGuire discovered Steincke in a summer league game in Queens. "We were playing against a bunch of tough Irish kids," remembered Doyle, who was playing for a McGuire squad called Alan's Animals.

"A fight started. Steincke banged a guy and knocked a guy down. I remember Al ran on the court and said to Hank, 'You got a scholarship, kid, with me,'" said Doyle.

"Let me burst your bubble on his recruiting abilities," Steincke said. "His wife, Pat, said she remembers recruiting with Al, coming into neighborhoods like where I grew up in Glendale, New York. And he did. He came down with the car, with the kids, the blue suit.

"And all the guys in my block were there with the bomb-thrower T-shirts on, they were drinkin' the quart bottles of Schaefer's. And he shows up in a blue suit. So, he comes up the steps into the house. There's my father and mother, both German immigrants.

"So now Al goes into the pitch. 'I would like to send Hank to a nice Catholic school. He'd be taught by priests, he'll go to mass every day.' He goes through this, that and the whole thing. All of a sudden, he's lookin' around and he sees a lot of faces goin', 'What's he talkin' about? Mass? Taught by priests?'

"Al was all red in the face. He turned around and he said, 'Are they Catholic?' Four people shook their heads 'nope.' Then he quickly says, 'Well, he doesn't *have* to go to mass every day. And he can pick his own classes.' He lost it. It's the only time I ever saw the guy really, totally embarrassed. His whole sales pitch went right down the tubes. He turned it right around," laughed Steincke.

It was a New York police department friend of McGuire's who discovered Jim Lytle (pronounced Ly-TELL in McGuire's Noo Yawk speak), a quick ball-handling guard who arrived from Power Memorial, the school later to be made famous by alum Lew Alcindor.

"We called Al the Fox because he stole so many games. He was vaudeville at Belmont Abbey. He didn't go legit until he went to Marquette," said Lytle, who was an Abbey captain.

"He'd say, 'You cannot outfox a fox,'" added Steincke. "And he always thought that he was one up on everyone. It was always Fox. We never called him *Coach*."

Max Muhleman once asked McGuire how he could recruit players from New York to little Belmont. "He told me, 'I'd buy postcards of the

Charlotte Coliseum and tell 'em this is where we're playing. And once I get 'em here, I got 'em.'"

That was how he was able to con one of his later recruits, 6'5" center Bill Dockery of Brooklyn, into coming to the Abbey.

"He would say anything. He was big on talking to the immigrant parents about how the monks were gonna take care of you, and they're gonna look out for you.

"You know that classic postcard of a girl water skiing on the lake?" Dockery asked. "I was down there about a month lookin' for the lake. And finally, I went over to him and told him, I said, 'Fox, where's the lake?' He said, 'Hey, forget the lake. Get outta here and get to the gym for practice.' 'Where's the lake, Fox?' I asked him. 'Where's the lake?'"

"Al had a loaded brochure," laughed David Wheeler, another of Humpy's sons who attended the Abbey toward the end of the McGuire era. "He went down to Davidson, North Carolina, and took pictures of the Davidson campus and put them in an Abbey brochure he would send to the players."

McGuire also promised the mothers of his New York recruits that he would bring them home once a month. "He told my mother that since his wife and kids were here in New York that he would be coming here once a month. The first time I came home that year was at Christmas," laughed John von Bargen.

Kenny Sears, a former Knicks teammate of Dick and Al, helped recruit the 6'11" von Bargen out of Mt. Vernon, New York. McGuire kept talking about what a great Catholic school Belmont Abbey was. von Bargen, who knew Dick, begged him to get Al off his back. "Dick, would you please tell Al that I'm Protestant?"

Von Bargen began his college career at Santa Clara University, but returned home because he was homesick. When McGuire learned that the big center was back home, he paid a visit. After making his pitch, McGuire gave von Bargen ten days to make up his mind. "My mother told me that I shouldn't leave Mr. McGuire hanging. So, I decided to go to Belmont Abbey." The irony of it all is that von Bargen eventually converted to Catholicism.

At Belmont, McGuire was not only the head coach, but the trainer, doctor, and driver. It was not just a coaching job, but an apprenticeship. It was character building and the building of characters.

"It's where I learned to pick up towels, where I drove the team bus, taped ankles. It was all the things that made me a coach," Al said at his induction into the Belmont Abbey Hall of Fame in 1992.

"Al used to drive the station wagon. Humpy Wheeler drove a station wagon," said von Bargen. "And Father Raphael drove a station wagon or a bus. Al would take the starting five because the other guys didn't know what they were doing. They might get lost on the way to the game."

"We were driving down to Mississippi Southern once for a game," recalled Bob Kopf. "We'd rented a couple of cars. And Al wanted to see if he could get all of the electrical stuff working in the car at the same time. The windshield wipers, horn, turn signals, radio, air conditioning, heat. He did it just to amuse himself." Joked Chuck Sullivan, "Al did it so that we wouldn't notice how bad of a driver he really was."

"Al was a pioneer," noted Wheeler. "Basketball was a game where players had to be loose. Al had that ability to keep his players loose. Al was so focused on basketball that everything else was secondary. He wouldn't know where he parked his car. He'd lose cars. He expected the bus to run, but he forgot that you had to put gas in it. He would forget where he lived."

"One particular time, we played Friday night and then went to Jacksonville to play Saturday night. Monday we left for Quantico, Virginia, for a tournament," the Reverend Bridge recalled of the Crusaders' extended road trips.

"Usually, they were seven- to nine-passenger station wagons," said Bridge, who noted that the Belmont administration liked to have a member of the clergy go along on the road trips.

After the team arrived at its destination, the players went right to the motel. "And instead of going to the court and warming up and everything, we would get dressed at the motel," recalled Doyle. "We'd run right onto the court, take layups, and start the game."

Trips to road games that were three hours or less were called sprints by the players. "That meant you sprint three hours, you eat a shit 'n chicken meal, you play and get your head beaten in, maybe, and then you gotta eat another chicken meal after it," explained George Affuso (1962–66). "And then you drive back until three in the morning."

Von Bargen remembered when the Crusaders first hit the road in 1957.

"We were going to a place in Georgia. But before we went over a little bridge, we had to get out of the bus and take all our luggage, because the bus might have gone down in the river. That bus driver drives about three miles [ahead of us]. We still had our traveling coats and ties on, and we walked in 95-degree weather in the Georgia backwoods."

"This is our first game ever," said Doyle. "Me, John, Jimmy Mullen, and Stewart started. The score, I can remember it like it was yesterday, was 69-67 and there were 12 or 15 seconds to go. They had the ball. I stole the ball and called a timeout.

"We went in the huddle and he [McGuire] says, 'What did you call timeout for? What are we gonna do?' I said, 'Give me the ball and get out of the way.' I wasn't that good. But I drove the basket, made the basket, and was fouled. I went to the foul line to win the game. I missed the foul shot. Stewart caught the rebound, got fouled, and made one, and we won 72-71."

When the team did stay overnight on road trips, they stayed in "a lot of dirt-bag hotels," according to Steincke. When they stayed at Campbell College, for example, the Crusaders were forced to sleep on the floor of the college gymnasium on cots. The Campbell football team banged on the doors of the gym all night long and the Crusaders could not get any sleep, which was the general idea.

Humpy Wheeler Sr. booked most of the games during the first two years of the McGuire era. Belmont's biggest rivals were Lenoir-Rhyne and Georgia Southern. The Crusaders also played the Oglethorpes, Presbyterians, and Pfeiffer colleges of the small basketball world.

After McGuire took over the scheduling, he would occasionally get Jacksonville, Kentucky Wesleyan, Evansville, Austin Peay, Southern Illinois, and St. Bonaventure to tangle with the Abbey boys during his lucky seven years at Belmont.

McGuire's office, located in the basement of Haid Gym, along with the team locker room, had no heat. So during the winter months, McGuire wore a coat while conducting business, which included recruiting and making sure that his money back home was earning good interest.

"Almost every morning he would be on the phone to his stockbroker in New York," said Gantt. "Al was always a money maker. He was in touch with his broker at least two to three times a week. Al was a great poker player. He would have a whole roll of checks from the night before."

And, New York hustler that he was, McGuire was shrewd enough to play cards only with those he knew he could beat, like southern gentlemen, according to his players. And he would play golf only for money.

McGuire's first three Crusader teams went 24-3 (1957–58), 21-2 (1958–59), and 19-5 (1959–60). People were coming out of the woodwork to see the Abbey, and the crowds at Haid Gym were growing more raucous. It was not long before word filtered down Tobacco Road about the burgeoning success of the little Catholic college that could. "Seems like you got quite a show down there," Duke's Bubas remarked to Gantt.

Haid Gym's small size drew comparisons to various sized boxes. "The townies referred to it as a cracker box; the newspapers called it a bandbox; and McGuire, falling back on his Catholic metaphors, called it a small confessional box. It was so small that the bleachers almost touched the sidelines. The seating capacity was 500, but there were standing-room crowds of as many as 1,000, according to Gantt. The old brick gym's basketball court was 88 feet long by 45 feet wide, with the court's end lines hard by the walls.

Because many of the bigger schools refused to play at Haid, the Crusaders played a number of their "home" games at the Charlotte Coliseum and the Ray High School Gymnasium in nearby Gastonia. "It was unusual to have over three home games a year [at Haid]; four tops," Gantt said. "His [McGuire] only hope of getting any teams here were junior college teams." McGuire likened his Crusaders to an "orphan" team in a 1960 story in *Sport* magazine: "We don't ask for games. We beg for them."

Big-time colleges refused to play games in Haid because the "crowd noise was just deafening," remembered the Reverend Bridge, affectionately known to the players as the Bridge. His main responsibilities included bed checks, keeping track of the players' eligibility, and helping drive the players to road games.

"They [students] rang a large bell in the bleachers when they wanted a rally," said Gantt. "At home, the boys were wild about that team. There were usually 15 to 20 monks at each game that raised hell. When all these people got together, screaming and hollering, we were likely to beat the hell out of you [opposing teams]. They didn't play a home game that wasn't packed."

"It was really electric when they were playing a good team," noted Humpy Wheeler Jr. "Haid Gym at the Abbey was like the Blue Horizon of small college gyms," he said, referring to Philadelphia's famous boxing arena.

As the Crusaders wound up a hugely successful (24-3) 1957–58 campaign under first-year coach McGuire, the Kentucky Wildcats' "Fiddlin' Five" defeated Elgin Baylor and Seattle University in the NCAA championship game. It was the last NCAA championship that Adolph Rupp would win as Wildcats coach, and the last title game Kentucky would appear in until 1966. Also that season the "bonus" free throw after seven fouls was implemented, offensive goaltending was outlawed, and the University of Cincinnati's "Big O," Oscar Robertson, became the first sophomore to lead the nation in scoring when he averaged just over 35 points a game.

During McGuire's second season (1958–59) at the Abbey, one of the Crusaders' most memorable games at Haid featured what would now be considered a Jordanesque performance by Bobby Stewart.

"Stewart had lost his eligibility midyear of my freshman season," explained Lytle. "In the last game he played in Haid he scored 64 points. The rest of us scored seven total. At halftime, McGuire told us, 'Nobody else shoot except Stewart.' Stewart collapsed from exhaustion in the locker room after the game."

In the 1959 NCAA Finals, Pete Newell's University of California Bears nipped Jerry "Zeke from Cabin Creek" West and the University of West Virginia Mountaineers, 70-71.

Meanwhile at little Belmont Abbey, the one player who was the star of the show was Danny Doyle, the team's designated clown prince of basketball. McGuire called him Sunshine.

"He gave me the nickname Sunshine because he said I was always smilin' and laughin'," said Doyle. "And then before each game, they [student body] used to sing 'You Are My Sunshine,' and I used to come out and act like a moron, and he [McGuire] told me half the things to do."

Some of Doyle's antics included wearing clown hats and other items during a game, simply as a distraction. "Al had Danny dressed up like Emmett Kelly during the games," remembered Gantt. "Danny would wear a hat or come out with one red sock and one black sock. Or one sock high and one sock low. We had Batman capes," said von Bargen (1957–61). "I think Doyle's majoring in vaudeville," McGuire told *Sport* magazine.

"I could do something at that time that they thought was phenomenal," said Doyle. "There were no black guys allowed to play for the University of North Carolina, Wake Forest, or anywhere. I went there and I could dunk, and they thought that was great."

Doyle would come out early for warmups. He dunked with two hands, and then he would ride a bicycle down the center of the court, jump off, and dunk.

"There was only one problem," he said. "The bike stayed right there when I fell down. He [McGuire] wrapped the ankles tight and said, 'You're all right. Keep playin'.' The ankle was fractured in about five or six places. We didn't really know. It wasn't his fault. He just taped it."

If Doyle was the designated clown, McGuire was the ringmaster of the Abbey show. "His courtside demeanor was showmanship," remembered Gantt of station WCGC, which McGuire dubbed Radio Free Belmont. "I was impressed that he could fire the team up the way he did."

"He could play a crowd better than anyone I've ever seen," remarked Wheeler, whose future wife was a Crusaders cheerleader. "He put theatrics into everything he did. He'd wear a dark suit and a tie. Twenty-five percent of the time he looked like a tall, thin Frank McGuire. Both Al and Frank were cut from the same cloth."

"It was his personality," Bridge said. "It just attracted people. He had a way of being so outgoing, never at a loss for words. He was streetwise."

McGuire's Noo Yawkese and storytelling also helped fill up the only class that he taught on campus: Health and Hygiene.

"He didn't really teach health," recalled Paul Poschmann, who took the class as a freshman in 1961. He noted that as with the players, McGuire's students also called him Fox. "The guys went to his class because they wanted to hear Al talk. The first 15 minutes of his Saturday morning freshman class may have been about health, but the rest of the time he warned us about drinking and driving, prostitutes, and what bars not to go into in Charlotte. It just got into a conversation about life."

When McGuire the teacher graded his students' tests, he invariably used the famous "McGuire curve."

"[After we handed back our tests] he walked over to the window on the second floor," Poschmann continued. "And then he chucked the tests out the window. He then said, 'OK, the first five guys back here with their tests get A's; the rest get B's.' And everyone would dash out of the classroom to pick up their tests outside. No one would believe me when I told that story," said Poschmann, now a schoolteacher in Syosset, New York.

During another test, two students in front of Poschmann were looking at each other's papers and talking while McGuire was going through his grade book. McGuire looked up and warned them that the next time he saw them talking they would get B's.

After the test Poschmann approached McGuire about his final grade. "Fox, I need an A to stay in school," he said. "He kinda looked at me funny, and then went back to his grade book."

Poschmann wound up with a B for the class, while another classmate, who simply wrote the words to the Catholic prayer "Hail Mary" on his test paper, received an A, he said.

On the basketball court, part of McGuire's act was a carryover from his days at Dartmouth. "Al would shed that coat and it was like you'd wave a cape in front of a bull," said Gantt. "There were only a couple of times he lost when he shed his coat."

"At the right moment, he'd swing that coat by the sleeve over his head," recalled Poschmann, who would occasionally be recruited as a Crusader practice player. "If we were up by two or three points, they'd reel off 10 or 12 points in a row" after McGuire took off his coat.

McGuire would hand the coat to Mario Manorino, who was considered the team manager. "He was a guy from the Bronx," said Doyle. "He knew nothin' about trainin' or managin', but he was our friend, so he came with us on all our trips."

Even after generating excitement and wins for the basketball team in Belmont, McGuire had a tough time getting press coverage for the Crusaders. But competing against the major schools in the area was tough. McGuire would stay on Max Muhleman of the *Charlotte News* to get more publicity for his team. Before the Duke-Carolina contest, which is *the* biggest basketball game of the year in the state, McGuire teased Muhleman: "Max, can't you get me a little coverage on the first page?"

"Al was good copy," said Gantt. "The press was crazy about him. But promotion was something that they [the basketball team] never had. The old Southern Protestant attitude wouldn't cooperate with Catholics. But it changed. Al McGuire had a lot to do with the change. All the papers in North Carolina and South Carolina were picking up his quotes. Wherever he went, there was a packed house."

The team really had no official trainer. "The only piece of equipment we had when you got hurt, [was] you put on the Ace bandage. And that was it. That was the only piece of equipment. Take two aspirin and go to bed," said von Bargen. "We had six pieces of tape to tape our ankles."

"Our team physician was a guy named Dr. Duke," said Steincke. "He was a chiropractor. It's a true story. Now, if it really hurt he would put you on this table."

And regardless of how injured an Abbey player was, he never missed practice. "You break your leg, you never missed practice," said Steincke.

In practices, McGuire was more like a drill sergeant than a coach or a teacher, according to his players. He spent more time at practice getting the team in shape than actually teaching basketball.

"He never blew a whistle. He'd come to practice with a golf club and a $500 suit," said von Bargen. "He wouldn't show up half the time," added Dockery. "At practice, we would come in and play four-on-four and three-on-three. And he would go and play golf," said Doyle.

Some of the players recalled with fondness McGuire's "knockout drills," where he had them jump over and crawl under ten benches that he arranged in the shape of a wheel. "He would make us jump up and over them until we were exhausted," said Kopf. "It was punitive." "There was no rhyme or reason to the drills," added Affuso. "Practice was always a physical confrontation." The workouts included early morning runs in the fog around the soccer field.

"Al was a tactician," said Lytle. "He was a head coach. He taught us how to rebound, how to play defense. He was one of the first coaches who understood spacing. He taught people how to box out." The coach even played in scrimmages when an extra player was needed.

On a more humorous note, there was McGuire's famous "cursing chart," which was designed to curb vulgar language by the players. This was very important at a Catholic college. "If we cursed, he put an X on your name," said Steincke. "For 15 minutes of practice it was the cursing chart," because the players would continue to curse simply to annoy McGuire.

Before each season he took the players to Parris Island to play various Marine basketball teams to make sure the Crusaders were in top physical condition. They also played tournaments at Quantico, Virginia, during the season. The players would not touch a basketball the first two weeks of practice. "The guy really was ahead of his time as far as getting us in physical condition," said Doyle.

During scrimmages McGuire forced the losing team to do ten wind sprints, with the next scrimmage starting right after the losers finished their sprints.

"Twenty baskets would win the game," explained Kopf. "You had to win the first scrimmage. They were bloody matches. Nobody in the country practiced harder than that. We never dogged it. He used to suit up and practice with us from time to time. That's the way he played. He had to take it. He got his lumps."

McGuire would also pick a player to shoot free throws at the end of practice, and if he missed one the team would have to do extra sprints. It was another head game to see who would crack in a pressure situation.

"He'd say, 'C'mon, line up for wind sprints.' We'd say, 'We're tired,'" remembered Steincke. "He'd say, 'C'mon, line up for wind sprints.'" Occasionally, Steincke would make a wager with McGuire so the team could get out of doing the sprints.

"I'll make you a bet," Steincke dared McGuire. "If you hit a foul shot, we'll double the wind sprints. Instead of 50, we'll do 100. And he'd go to the foul line to take the shot, and we'd all start walkin' out of the gym, down the stairs and we'd say, 'See ya later, Fox. See ya tomorrow.'"

"You could leave him there for days and he wouldn't hit a foul shot," said Dockery. "It was automatic. We'd be downstairs in the locker room and you'd hear, 'Fuck!' reverberate through the gym when he kept missing free throws."

"Al was such a bad free throw shooter, he makes Shaq [Shaquille O'Neal] look like Bill Sharman," joked Sullivan.

According to his players, McGuire was no Knute Rockne when it came to halftime speeches. Actually, he would talk about anything but basketball.

"Now, if we were losing, he'd say, 'You guys can't even get up and down the court. I know you've been drinkin','" said Lytle. "He'd bust your balls," added Steincke, whose benching during a game epitomized how McGuire kept his players off balance.

"I'm playin' a game my senior year. It was the first half. He pulls me out of the game. When I get my wind back, I say, 'OK, coach. I'm ready to go back in.' And he doesn't pay attention. I wait a few more minutes.

I say, 'Coach, I'm ready to go back in.' Then he looks at me and says, 'You're not that good. Go take a shower.'

"I had to walk the length of the court to watch the whole second half. Then I'd look down the bench, wondering 'What'd I do wrong?' I took two shots, made them both, got four rebounds, and got an assist and beat up a guy. And now he told me I'm not playin' the rest of the game," said a still incredulous Steincke.

"I was the captain of the team at the time," said Sullivan. "When I asked Al why Steincke couldn't go back in, he said, 'Hey, you can take a shower too. Both of ya, get outta here and take a shower.'"

"Al psyched them up," Doyle said of the second team. "Because when the second team came in, the other [opposing] team used to get more petrified. Guys [Belmont second team players] would come in, rough a guy up, then hit two jumpers and be having a good game. And Al would go, 'Yeah, you're out.' And he didn't play you the rest of the game.

"His psychological effect was the good guys play, the second team came in to rough guys up, bang guys up. But when the second team played real good, he would never give them any respect," he said of McGuire's philosophy of sticking with his starting five, which he picked up from Frank McGuire.

"He did not show any favoritism," Gantt countered. "He had a funny way of relating with his players. He had their respect. He had their fear. He wasn't afraid to tell them off. He had as good a relationship as you need to win."

"The players would do anything for Al," added Wheeler. "It was a much more structured time in coaching back then, but Al gave his players room. But he did discipline them. And when it came time for them to play, they were ready."

"Al ran a seven-man team," Lytle explained. "Al really knew how to substitute by need. If he needed a rebounder, if he needed defense, if he needed someone to give a foul. He was a counter puncher. If I can stay close in the first half, I'll get you in the second half. A four-point lead to McGuire was like a ten-point lead to any other coach."

Another tactic to keep his players on their toes was to introduce other players who McGuire said were going to take their place the following season.

"He would bring a new player up to your room and say, 'I want you to meet Lou Grasso from Long Island. He's gonna take your position next year,'" said von Bargen. "You would say but two words to him, and it [wasn't] Merry Christmas or Happy Easter. He'd turn around and you'd walk out of the room. That was a ploy he'd always use. He'd do it just to get you goin'."

Belmont Abbey's NAIA label did not fool a lot of the bigger NCAA Division One schools. The Abbey was no "cupcake." McGuire's teams played a disciplined, tough, defensive brand of basketball, and the major powers along Tobacco Road refused to play the Crusaders for fear of losing.

Al and North Carolina's Frank McGuire, however, would get their teams together for closed-door, preseason scrimmages. While this was illegal for the Abbey, it was legal for the Tar Heels. Both coaches felt that it would be a good tuneup for the players. During one of the scrimmages, the Belmont boys were taking it to the Tar Heels. Frank McGuire ordered the team manager to lock the doors of the old Woolen Gym on the UNC campus so that no one would see the whipping his Tar Heels were getting at the hands of an NAIA team.

"They were rough scrimmages," Dean Smith said. "They helped us get ready for the [ACC] season. Their best team was in 1959. My first year as North Carolina head coach was in August of 1961. In November of that year we scrimmaged Belmont Abbey."

"Our freshman year (1961–62) was the last year that we scrimmaged the University of North Carolina," remembered Sullivan. "I was playing against Donnie Walsh and Larry Brown, UNC's starting backcourt."

"I remember Al telling Sullivan during one scrimmage, 'If you throw the ball away one more time, I'll kick you in the tail,'" laughed Smith. "Sullivan throws it away and Al chased him around the gym yelling. We were laughing all the way out of the gym," said Smith, who ended a 36-year career in 1997 as college basketball's all-time winningest coach.

"Each guy on North Carolina had his own ball," said Steincke. "The leather was peeling off our basketball. They'd come out in their practice uniforms. We had those bar shirts that said 'Joe's Bar & Grill.' When they went to the showers [after the scrimmage], we stole their uniforms."

But McGuire always counseled his players against getting caught up in petty theft. "Al told us, 'If you steal a towel, don't tell me about it. But if you rob a bank, I'm in with you,'" laughed Steincke.

After some of the players stole towels during one hotel stay, the players were told that their two-dollar meal money would be withheld until the towels were paid for.

The Belmont boys did have curfews, and the Bridge always conducted bed checks. "We had study hall until 9 p.m.," said von Bargen. "Father Raphael was always walking up and down the halls."

Since Belmont, North Carolina was located in a dry county, the city boys had to find their entertainment in other places besides the local Stuckey's and Paul's Ice Cream Fountain.

"We had to go into Mecklenburg County [across the Catawba River Bridge, which connected Gaston and Mecklenburg counties] to get a couple of beers and a cheeseburger. A pickled egg was a dime, a cheeseburger was a quarter, and Black Label beer was 40 cents," remembered von Bargen.

"When we went to the movies it was 25 cents. Danny had a blue Dodge, and I had a '57 white Impala convertible," continued von Bargen, who went to the dances on Friday nights at the local women's college, Sacred Heart, affectionately referred to as the Convent.

Another drinking hole for the boys was the Quonset Hut near the Catawba River. "You ate as much fish and drank as much beer as you wanted for $3.95, and then sat on the dock of the river. It was like mud," von Bargen said. "When you came out of it, you had to take a shower."

The boys listened to Elvis, Paul Anka, the Earls, the Platters, and Tony Bennett. Keep in mind this was at a time when compact discs, computers, and Walkman headsets were well beyond even George Orwell's imagination. People back then were still listening to 78 rpm albums. It was an era that predated eight-tracks, cassettes, and cable television, never mind MTV and ESPN.

During his seven years at Belmont Abbey, McGuire earned his apprenticeship and honed a style that was centered on a tenacious defense, which for McGuire was like money in the bank. It was a constant with his teams. Offense took a back seat. It was here that he could experiment with plays and defenses like the triangle-and-two that Doggie Julian dismissed during his Dartmouth days.

"A lot of what McGuire did with us, Phil Jackson did later with the Chicago Bulls," said Lytle. "The day before a game, he would put in defensive plans, but we would rarely work on an offense. He did an awful lot of defensive maneuvering, which was unheard of back then.

"Going from man-to-man to zone. He did something that was known as the scramble, which became the 'scrambled eggs.' We were the first trap defense. In fact, he was so interested in defense that when he chose his bench at home for the second half, he wanted to make sure that he was on our defensive end [of the floor]."

But the defense was made much more effective when combined with intimidation tactics.

"He was a chaos coach," said George Affuso, now a high school teacher. "He didn't scout the other teams. He didn't have any idea how to beat those teams. He never watched film. He had a philosophy that he carried on for winning. What he used to do was intimidate. He wanted to get into the head of the leading scorer. He didn't want the other guy to take a shot or handle the ball.

"And I used to cover the guy [opposing player] and intimidate the guy. Muscle him, hit him, but follow him all over the place. If the guy was in the huddle, I'd follow him to the huddle. I got thrown out of the first game that I played for him [McGuire]. I walked over to the sidelines and Father Raphael says, 'That wasn't very Christian.' Then Al says, 'You should have hit him another time.'"

"And if the guy was a good offensive player and we had the ball, he [Affuso] would cover the guy," said Doyle. "So the other guy would say [to Affuso], 'What are ya doin'? Your team has the ball.' 'But my job is to cover you,' George would tell him." "It changes someone's game when you get pounded," said Dockery of McGuire's physical defense.

"You gotta understand, these teams were small Southern schools. Most of them weren't great. They were like Southern white boys. Nice guys. They were strong, but they weren't tough. You have to give Al credit, he was psychologically ready. He was not a good coach as far as offense [was concerned]. He was a good defensive coach, a good psychological coach," said Doyle.

"His whole thing was to take the refs, the other coach, and the star player out of the game just by psychological means, and it worked," said Lytle. "If we had an Xs and Os coach, we would not have been success- ful. Because we were so individualistic we thought we knew the whole world, and McGuire allowed us to run our own show. He never crowded us. He allowed us to be ourselves. That's the way he wanted us. He liked the intellectual give and take. What we allowed him to do was to grow in his relationships with people."

McGuire's psychology extended to the printed game program, according to Lytle. "He listed bogus items in the program for each of us. For example, Bill Dockery came from San Juan, Puerto Rico, and Bill Ficke was a world renowned bird caller who could imitate 64 different bird calls. All this he did on the road. Anything to work an edge." One of the players, Bobby Hodges, even brought his pet goat with him to road games. During the week, he kept the goat on a farm adjacent to the Abbey.

Al McGuire had to be creative at Belmont in order to get teams to play his Crusaders. For example, to convince Evansville University to host his team, McGuire promised to buy ice cream for the crowd if the Abbey lost the game. "Al McGuire wouldn't buy your mother an ice cream bar," joked Doyle. "Yeah, even if it was a hot day," added Affuso.

"The local dairy company caught on to the thing and came out with the McGuire Booster Bar. They said they'd provide the ice cream. We lost the game and everybody got an ice cream bar. At first I thought the whole idea might be a mistake, but you rarely succeed in anything without a few mistakes."

Just as he sold out the Boston Garden during his pro career, McGuire sold out 11,000-seat Roberts Municipal Stadium in Evansville. McGuire had a following, and he produced crowd numbers that Belmont Abbey never would have imagined. In fact, some 200 rabid Abbey fans followed the team to Evansville in station wagons and any other car they could find to make the trip. "Evansville ran out of ice cream before Al ran out of money," joked Max Muhleman.

McGuire took advantage of every psychological ploy just to get an edge on the opposing coaches, teams, and their fans. When the Crusaders played on the road, especially in the South, McGuire had the ballboy bring out a phonograph with the ball rack to midcourt before the team came out for its warmups.

As the fans settled into their seats, the ballboy took out a 45 rpm recording of "When the Saints Go Marching In" and played the record as the Crusaders began to go through their paces.

"*Bong, Bong, Bong*," resounded through the gym as each of the Abbey players dunked the ball in succession during layup drills. "The ball would never touch the floor during the entire drill," said Lytle. "After the warmups, the home team was already so psyched out that the game would be over before it started."

"We'd warm up," said Doyle. "I'd be dunkin', he'd [von Bargen] be dunkin'. The other kids [team] would be down at the other end sayin' 'What is goin' on?' And we'd play defense. Zone. Nobody on the other team would make a shot, except a layup. And we'd be winnin' 27-4. And the game would end and the other team was dead."

As tough as McGuire was on his players, he was very loyal to them. During one game Lytle was assigned to guard Jacksonville's star, Roger Strickland, who was one of the leading scorers in the nation at that time. In the weeks preceding the game, McGuire continually reminded Lytle that if he stopped Strickland, Belmont could win the game. "He [Lytle] was so pumped up about getting this guy," said Kopf.

"He was pumping in about 32.6 points a game that season," said Lytle. "If a confrontation flared up, Strickland was scoring 35 a game and I was scoring 10. In Al's strategy that's a win-win situation for the Abbey if both of us get thrown out of the game.

"My job was to get the guy I was guarding frustrated so he would get thrown out of a game," continued Lytle, who played Strickland so tightly that he could not get a shot off. "They [Jacksonville] were bouncin' us around the court. We played very aggressively. We were changing defenses on every foul shot."

Lytle's in-your-jersey defense so frustrated Strickland's uncle, who was sitting in the stands, that he came down to the court and broke Lytle's nose. Hank Steincke followed the uncle back into the stands and began pummeling him. "The stands emptied onto the floor," said Kopf. "There were only two cops in the gym. The refs folded. They were intimidated by the home fans."

After the fracas ended, McGuire wanted assurances from the referees that it was safe for his players to continue playing the game, according to Kopf. The officials offered to clear the fans from the gym so the game could go on. But McGuire would have none of it.

"If you're gonna give us this screwin' in front of 5,000 people, I can't imagine what you would do to us if there were no one in the stands," McGuire angrily told the referees as he forfeited the game.

"They had to bring the team bus right up to the door with police on both sides," said Ebb Gantt. "We walked right through to the bus. We get in the bus and they gave us a police escort to the hotel. The police were staying right outside to watch. The boys didn't get beat up. The defense by Jim Lytle was perfect on their star player."

Before the Belmont boys arrived in Georgia for a game against Albany State, the local newspaper headlines screamed: "The Catholics Are in Town!"

"We were Irish-Catholic, German-Catholic, Italian-Catholic. We were white Catholics," stated Doyle. "They really didn't like us down there." Added Gantt, "When the boys played in the South, they were called 'Yankee Catholics.' When they played in the North, they were the 'Southern Rebels.'

"During one game at Georgia Southern in the late 1950s, when the home team band blared 'Dixie' all the crowd rose to attention. A big ugly guy looked down at the Abbey boys on the bench who were still seated and said, 'Don't you know the national anthem when you hear it?' The Abbey boys then stood up," Gantt laughed.

Gantt, who was announcing the game on radio, became involved in one of the Belmont brouhahas at Newberry College in South Carolina. "That day we were packed in. The other team's fans were shouting at Al. Some were drinking. I couldn't get away from them.

"[Toward] the end of the game, the score was in favor of the home team. Al sent his team into the dressing room—everyone except the starters. Belmont won the game on a last-second shot. The crowd went off," Gantt said.

"I had to start swinging," said Gantt, who earlier in his youth was a boxing coach. "I had a cheap watch. I swung at a guy and the watch sailed across the floor and wound up in pieces. In a puffing sort of way, I said [on the air], 'Well, that's it from here. Al's boys came out and won it, and now we'll send you back to the station.'"

"I was in one of the station wagons with Al after the game," recalled Wheeler. "He was riding in the front and the players were in the back. There was a cold box next to me in the car." McGuire waited until the car was safely out of Newberry, South Carolina, which was dry, according to Wheeler. "Al said, 'OK, open the box.' He had iced down a case of beer. The guys didn't abuse that privilege. They were ready to play again."

McGuire promised Gantt after the game that he would replace the watch. As it turned out, McGuire gave Gantt his 1970 NIT championship timepiece at the dedication of Wheeler Auditorium that same year.

Gantt was also impressed with McGuire's control under less than ideal circumstances. "I heard them call Al a name on the home floor against Kentucky Wesleyan. I was excited myself. They [Abbey] lost the game. I told Al, 'When we get through, I'm not too old to lay a good punch.' But Al said, 'No, Ebb. We won't do that. I've got other things more important. Maybe we can ask the priests to pray for us. Ebb, you know, in New York, we could give someone $100 to knock 'em off,' he said laughing.

"Al had come to the conclusion that he had to be prepared to handle it. The one good thing that occurred was that he went through all these rough times. He got bad calls, mostly from opposing teams. Yet he brought his teams through with flying colors. That was where Al knew the game. He had to play against the odds year after year. It was basic training all the way," explained Gantt.

McGuire also learned how to get a loss out of his system during his tenure at Belmont, according to Gantt.

"He had a burning desire to win. He hated to lose. He'd walk after a loss. After a game in South Carolina, he started walking. No one knew where he was going. When I heard that Al was gone, I decided to take a little trip. One of the routes led to farm territory. And there's Al.

"I said, 'Hey, Al, they're waiting in the bus.' Al said, 'Let's stop in this joint.' It was crummy; a pool table in the corner. We sat down. Al had to go to the bathroom. They had an outhouse. Al gave me some money while he went to the outhouse. I stood in the [bar] doorway waiting. Finally, here he comes back. 'We'd better go,' he tells me. He had a way of getting the loss out of his system. He then started talking about the next game."

McGuire could get a loss out of his system, but if he felt that his players did not put out the maximum effort in that game, they would find out exactly how he felt about it on the bus ride back to the Abbey.

"He stops the bus on the interstate at one or two in the morning," recalled Bob Kopf, "and he told us to walk the seven miles back to the school." Recalled Poschmann, "I remember the players walking in just before breakfast that morning."

McGuire also was pretty good at making the best of poor accommodations. During a 1961 game at Southern Illinois, coach Harry "the Horse" Gallatin, a former Knicks teammate of McGuire's, gave Al the treatment.

"Al says, 'Harry, you have a better team than I do, a bigger team than I do, but I'll beat you tonight because I think better than you do.' Gallatin would just walk away," recalled Bridge.

"He's [Gallatin] tryin' to get control of the refs before the game even starts," said Lytle. "The ref turns to McGuire and says, 'Coach, you have 30 seconds to get your team on the floor.'

"So we walk out. We do the jump ball and no warmups. The first whistle, the first timeout, Al's lookin' around, and he can't hear because Gallatin has taken the band and put it behind our team bench. The next timeout, Al moves the bench behind the band, five rows up into the stands, and takes the fans and puts them down on the bench.

"Here's Bernie Brennan, who's substituting for me, going, 'Excuse me, excuse me,' as he makes his way down from the stands onto the floor. It must have taken him 30 seconds to get down from the bench, which is now up in the stands. And the guy [referee] comes over to McGuire and asks, 'What are ya doin'?' Al says, 'Get the tubar out of my ear, and I'll move my bench down,'" Lytle laughed. And, yes, the Abbey won.

"Opposing coaches had a disdain for him because he was so flamboyant and he tried to control the games with the refs," said Sullivan. "We never walked into a place like we weren't going to win. We had a little bit of an arrogant attitude that we got from Al. The people at Charlotte loved him."

During a lopsided loss to Lenoir-Rhyne College in Hickory, North Carolina, McGuire took a shovel over to coach Billy Wells and said, "Why don't you just bury us?"

Long before former Northwestern University coach Ricky Byrdsong started roaming the stands and talking to fans, McGuire was using it as a tactic on the road to get the crowd behind his Crusaders.

"Al would go into the stands and start talking to people," recalled Steincke. "[He would say] 'Look at 'em out there, the referees are a bunch of lumberjacks.' He always called the refs lumberjacks. 'Look, a bunch of lumberjacks pickin' on my kids. My kids wash their own jocks and socks,' which we did.

"And he would start tellin' these people, 'Look at 'em. My kids have to room with 500 kids in a little Catholic school. We're up here, and these lumberjacks are pickin' on us.'

"The next thing you know, we come out at halftime and have three or four sections rooting for the Abbey. Opposing fans rooting for the Abbey."

McGuire's way of working officials was also different. As an unknown in his early days in the South, he had a tough time being taken seriously. During one game, the Crusaders were called for so many fouls that McGuire just took off his jacket, handed it to the referee, and said, "Here, take this, you've taken everything else from me tonight."

"Al would take a 'T' in the first half," recalled Lytle. "He had us start the game with a layup to see how the refs were going to call the game. He didn't want any jump shots."

At times, it became frustrating for McGuire, as Muhleman remembered during a game against Pfeiffer College. "Al invited me to sit on the bench. Belmont Abbey had been getting robbed by the refs. Two officials were working the game. As one of them ran by the bench, Al jumped up and said, 'I'm gonna kill you when the game is over.' That ref avoided Al the rest of the game."

"I think Al felt he could get through to the referees by working them over psychologically," said von Bargen. So when the Crusaders were having a tough night, McGuire made sure that the referees were within earshot during timeouts.

"'You know you guys are brutal. These officials are doin' a great job and you guys stink.' Sure enough, the next two fouls called after the huddle were against the other team," said von Bargen. "It worked almost every time. He was the most dangerous man in college basketball with four minutes on the clock."

Concurred Doyle: "He was a psychological genius."

"Al's greatest single attribute was his ability to focus out there," noted Wheeler. "Especially in the latter part of games, the last three minutes. Everybody overlooked his brilliance."

And to give his teams a breather, McGuire would have his players tie up one of their shoes with a worn lace so that it would break easily during a game, forcing an official timeout.

In McGuire's fourth season (1960–61) Chubby Checker shook the country with "The Twist," a guard named Billy Packer began playing at Wake Forest, and the Crusaders added a new basketball event to their schedule: the Winged Foot Tournament.

The brainchild of Ray Lumpp, a former Knicks teammate of McGuire's and athletic director of the New York Athletic Club which sponsored the event, the tournament allowed Al's players to come home to New York for the holidays. "But there was no Christmas vacation," corrected Kopf. "We had to practice every day."

"Al asked me if I could come up with a holiday tournament. So we were able to get St. Peter's, St. Anselm, Belmont Abbey, and our team to play," said Lumpp. "In the early days, we would end up in the finals against Belmont Abbey." But regardless who won, both teams wound up at Pep McGuire's on Queens Boulevard, for a Yuletide bacchanalia.

When his boys arrived in New York for the tournament in December of 1960, McGuire convinced John Goldner, then manager of Madison Square Garden, to let the Crusaders work out on the Garden floor for a couple of hours.

After one holiday practice at Madison Square Garden, the players dressed quickly and were hurrying out the locker room to get home to their families and girlfriends when McGuire stopped them in their tracks.

"'Hey, you guys, don't leave. You know that I'm the only coach in America who didn't get a Christmas gift from his players. I took you guys out of New York,'" von Bargen recalled of the coach's guilt trip. "We laughed at him as we left the locker room."

"I was always good at taking the parade off the side streets and puttin' it on Fifth Avenue," McGuire said later. By giving the players a chance to practice on the floor of the world-famous Madison Square Garden, he was showing them that they should not settle for second best in life.

"He used to tell us, 'Do things first class. Go to a nice restaurant,'" said Steincke. "He wouldn't allow us to do any different," added Lytle. "There was an image he wanted to create: 'Be better than you are.'"

Toward the end of the 1960–61 campaign, the 17-5 Crusaders were riding a 12-game winning streak into their finale at Oglethorpe.

"This is a perfect example of how the Fox coached," Steincke said. "It comes down to the wire and we're down by a point. We made a big comeback at the end of the game. We're kind of laid back. It was, basically, we're down a point, let's steal the ball.

"So we go in the huddle. We say, 'What are we gonna do, Fox?' 'Slow down, slow down. What do you mean, what are we gonna do?' 'What are we gonna do, Fox?' we asked him. 'Calm down. Let me think, let me think.'

"Then he starts like this: 'Clap your hands. C'mon, everybody, clap your hands.' 'What?' we said to him. 'No, just clap your hands.'

"Then he starts clapping his hands and he starts sayin' 'We're gonna win. We're gonna win.' So we all started in. And the Twist was in at that time, so we have guys doin' the Twist and clappin' our hands. Then the fans start to get into it. The other coach is on the floor diagrammin' a play. And he looks up at us like we're nuts. At the end of the timeout, we ask: 'What are we gonna do, Fox?' 'Ah, just go out there and play.'

"So we set up a shot for Jimmy Lytle, and the ball goes off the rim and we lose the game. After the game, we said, 'Fox, you are the worst coach in the history of basketball.' 'But did you see the fans?' McGuire asked. 'Did you see the smiles on their faces? They loved it,' he said, as if all that mattered was that the fans were treated to a good show."

"He was always confusing the hell out of the opposing coaches," Lytle said of McGuire's antics. "We set up a shot that was 50/50 at best. I blew the shot. We were on a 12-game winning streak, and he didn't like to lose. However, he didn't like to go into the tournament on a winning streak. He never liked to go into the postseason on a winning streak," said Lytle.

One of the few highlights of that season was an overtime loss to highly ranked St. Bonaventure, in January 1961, which McGuire described as "the best competition I ever coached." The Brown Indians of St. Bonaventure featured the Stith brothers and were coached by Eddie Donovan.

In 1961 the CIA's attempt to overthrow Castro in the Bay of Pigs backfired, Alan Shepard was the first American in space, another point-fixing scandal beset college basketball, this time at Seton Hall, and the University of Cincinnati won the first of its two straight NCAA titles over Fred Taylor's Ohio State Buckeyes, which featured Jerry Lucas, Larry Siegfried, John Havlicek, and a guard named Bob Knight.

Also that year, four black college students in Greensboro, North Carolina, refused to move from a Woolworth's lunch counter, prompting sit-ins.

With all of the changes taking place under the New Frontier administration of President John F. Kennedy, the integration of college basketball teams was moving very slowly in the early 1960s. The white picket fence of segregation extended to sports teams, especially basketball, where black and white teams remained separate. It was especially difficult in the South, where Babe McCarthy's Mississippi State Bulldogs were leading the way.

While Belmont Abbey had no black players, it was the only college that played black schools like J. C. Smith, according to Steincke, which did not sit well with some of Abbey's opponents south of the Mason-Dixon line.

"They'd [fans] be screamin' at us. Danny would spit at them. We're Catholic. We're from New York. Even the *Charlotte Observer* looked down on us. When Max Muhleman came, it changed."

"We had a job to do," said George Affuso matter-of-factly. "This was the game and that was it. He [McGuire] never explained all the problems that we would encounter," referring to the religious and racial abuse the Crusaders faced on the road.

Before the Abbey played J. C. Smith, McGuire visited the school's gym. As he gazed at the beautifully appointed arena, he slumped against the wall and slowly slid down to the floor, awed by the magnificent gym.

In 1962, a popular guard named Billy Packer helped lead the Wake Forest Demon Deacons to the Final Four. That same year, McGuire used distractions to take his players' minds off important games and tournaments. For example, before he took his 16-8 team to Kansas City for that season's NAIA tourney, he decided not to put his players through their regular practice regimen.

"Every other coach is going through drills [with their teams] and Al would disappear," said Steincke. "Most coaches would have been looking at tape and preparing, but he was nowhere to be found."

"The day before we leave he was directing his basketball camp," continued von Bargen. "He has us there working two days straight clearing rocks, and all we're doing is raking pebbles and horse manure. We were exhausted."

"I think he did it to keep our minds off the tournament rather than running us through practice," surmised Lytle. "We were a lot looser going into the tournament."

When the Crusaders attended the pre-tournament banquet, their table was pressed against the back wall of the restaurant. "Chuck Sullivan said, 'Fox, when they call our name, I'm gonna stand on the chair,'" recalled Kopf. "When Chuck stood up, it looked like he was 7'6". You could hear oohs and aahs all through the hall. It was psyching these people [other teams] out." The Abbey lost to eventual tournament winner Pan American, which was led by Lucius Jackson.

During his seven years at the Abbey, McGuire took the Crusaders to five small college postseason tournaments, including the NAIA and NCAA College Division tourneys. But after the first four years, the thrill was gone.

"Something happened to him," noted Steincke. "He went from having a record his first four years that was fantastic to almost nothing." Steincke and the other players noticed a change in his attitude his last two years, even though he had talented ballplayers from New Jersey in Joe McDermott, Bernie Brennan, and Joe Butts.

"But he was really pointing to go somewhere else," said Sullivan, who was paired in the backcourt with Brennan for the 1962–63 season. "In some ways, he was marking time. He wasn't recruiting. The kids he got after we came were not all that good."

While he may have been marking time, Sullivan recalled that McGuire could still work over the referees pretty well.

"We played Davidson when Lefty [Driesell] was there. Joe Butts cold-cocked a guy with his elbow. Lefty went nuts. Joe was bald with an acne-scarred face. Al comes out to center court with his arm around Joe and Lefty's yelling at the ref. Al says to the ref, 'Is this the face of a guy who would hurt another boy?' We went back to playing because both refs didn't see it," Sullivan said, laughing at the memory.

McGuire's last two Crusader teams finished 7-21 and 6-18, respectively, in the 1962–63 and '63–64 seasons. In McGuire's defense, *Charlotte News* reporter Max Muhleman explained that the schools Belmont Abbey defeated in McGuire's first five years refused to schedule any more games.

"Belmont Abbey was a member of no conference and therefore at the mercy of all opponents for games," he told the *Marquette Tribune*. "When McGuire burst upon the scene with a 20-game winner, they began dropping him, refusing to play for one political reason after another, except in their own lairs, where of course the house was packed."

In the NCAA finals those two seasons, respectively, George Ireland's Loyola Ramblers ended Cincinnati's NCAA reign and UCLA began its dominance of college basketball by defeating Duke. At that time, the country was still trying to deal with the trauma of President Kennedy's assassination, and the escalation of the Vietnam War was in its early stages.

In McGuire's last appearance at the Winged Foot Tournament, during the 1963–64 season, the frustrations of his final two years boiled over when the Crusaders lost in the finals. And one Abbey player wound up on the receiving end of the infamous McGuire temper.

"[Before the tournament] Bobby Kopf [6'3" junior forward] told Al that he would be late for practice in New York because he was helping his family move," recalled Sullivan. "But he was [really] going to see his girlfriend in Virginia Beach. So Bob misses our first practice." In the interim, McGuire had learned the truth of Kopf's whereabouts from another player.

"My junior year, I was failing out of school," explained Kopf, who was a pre-med major. "I was resigned to the fact that I would be leaving anyway. So, I got the word from Chuck that the Fox knew I was blowin' practice off."

Before the game against St. Michael's of Vermont, "I showed up for the game loaded. The locker room was set up with two or three rows of lockers. When I snuck into the locker room I got in the next row of lockers behind the rest of the team so he wouldn't know I was there. When we left, I got on the end of the line of players leaving the locker room."

"Al doesn't even look at him in practice," Sullivan continued. "Bob tries to dunk but gets his hand caught on the rim. And Bobby is the type of guy who was such a good jumper that he could get his elbows over the rim. But before the game, Al goes up to him and says, 'Bobby, you're startin' tonight.'"

Kopf recalled that he was surprised and thought he was back in McGuire's good graces. He then proceeded to have "one of the best games he's ever played. He has eight points," according to Sullivan.

"I sobered up at the half," said Kopf, "and I wasn't feeling good. A couple of times I would get rebounds and the guys on the other team took the ball right out of my hands. We lost the game."

"He [McGuire] calls us into this little room off the locker room after the game. He comes crashing through the door and starts screamin' at me," said Kopf. "He was in a rage. A crazy Irishman. He grabs the front of my jersey and rips it right off of me. I took my shorts and kicked them off onto the floor. So I'm standin' there in my jock and sneakers."

"Al turns around and Bob steps out of his jock," Sullivan said. "'Hey, Fox, do you want this, too?' Kopf said as he kicked his jockstrap toward him. Al walked toward him as he grabbed his crotch and fumed, 'Hey, Bobby, do you want my balls, too, since you got none of your own?'

"He [Kopf] runs out the door into the locker room in just his gym shoes and McGuire throws another chair at the door," said Sullivan.

"We then went on the road," said Kopf, picking up the story. "In Erie he threw one of the sportswriter's typewriters onto the floor during a game. He was losin' it big time. He was very abusive to everyone. He could have had a real good team." Not long after, Kopf left the team and the Abbey.

McGuire's overall record at Belmont Abbey was 109-64. But as successful as he was, McGuire seriously considered giving up coaching and doing something else with his life, such was his frustration. "He felt he did all that he could do at Belmont," said Sullivan. "He was really pointing to go somewhere else." Echoed Dean Smith: "Al was afraid that he was dying there at Belmont Abbey."

Despite the disappointing finish, McGuire looked back on his time at Belmont as an important learning experience. "I learned so much from the monks there. It was like a window opened up. They really opened a stained glass window inside of me. They didn't save me, but they got me on my way."

As far as some of his players were concerned, the feeling was mutual.

"When you played for Al, you were taught how to combat any problem that involved life. You were totally prepared to go out and face life. If he didn't teach you, he told you," said von Bargen.

To this day, the Abbey players who played for McGuire remain close. In fact, a number of them march in New York City's St. Patrick's Day parade under the Belmont Abbey Alumni banner. It is a bond they treasure to this day, and they were all brought together by Al McGuire. "A week does not go by when we call each other that somebody does not bring up some story about the Fox," said Lytle.

Ebb Gantt believed that McGuire was brought to Belmont, North Carolina, by a higher power. "There was never a dull moment with Al McGuire. It was as if he was placed here by a higher being to face the adversities and realities of coaching," said Gantt, who believed that McGuire would get a head coaching position at a major Catholic college. "We were just happy the man passed our way. He put us in the limelight."

"The only thing truer than truth is legend," noted Sullivan. "He invented the myth of himself. He really compromised very, very little, and he managed to be accepted for himself while giving up very little at all. The Abbey never recovered their profile after Al left."

If times were tough at little Belmont Abbey, they were even more disheartening at another Catholic school: Marquette University, located in the heart of the Midwest, Milwaukee, Wisconsin. Unlike Belmont, Marquette was a Division One NCAA program that enjoyed a successful basketball tradition as a major independent.

The Warriors had put together six winning seasons under coach Eddie Hickey, a serious, no-nonsense coach who was known as Little Caesar for his diminutive size (5'4"), tyrannical ways, and the fact that he served as a lieutenant colonel during World War II. The stereotypical whistle blower, Hickey was a perfectionist and strict disciplinarian. His first Marquette team finished 23-6 in 1958–59. His 1962–63 team finished 20-9. Hickey, a lawyer by training, also served as athletic director, which gave him the power to schedule games.

"Hickey spent 20 out of 24 hours at his office," recalled Dr. Sam Sauceda, a language professor at the university who was also a member of the athletic board. "You could go by his office at 16th and Wisconsin at 11 o'clock at night and the lights were still visible. But nobody ever saw Hickey on campus."

"My sophomore season (1960–61), Marquette played in the Dixie Classic, a holiday tournament held in Raleigh-Durham," recalled guard Dick Nixon. "We couldn't stay in the hotels in Raleigh-Durham. We had to stay in the infirmary at North Carolina State. Don Kojis played on that Marquette team, as did Bob Hornak and Ron Glaser.

"Hornak and Glaser were walking with me in the airport," said Nixon, "and the bathrooms were marked COLORED and WHITE. We all went in the COLORED ONLY bathroom," he said.

"The first night of the classic, we played Wake Forest, which was led by center Len Chappell and guard Billy Packer. They loved Billy Packer down there. He was the darling of the team. He was a very good technician, as far as passing and setting screens," said Nixon. "[But] we ran 'em off the floor 91-83. However, we lost to Duke in the next round and to Villanova in the consolation game.

"After the Wake Forest game I'm in the hallway, and all these white kids were asking me for an autograph," Nixon recalled. "A white guard says to the kids after I gave them autographs: 'Aren't you going to thank the good man for the autograph?' Then the kids say, 'Thank you.' And ten steps down the hall is the 'colored only' bathroom," said Nixon, noting the irony. "I had not experienced such overt racism in Milwaukee during my four years at Marquette.

"My final year [1962–63] was good," recalled Nixon, who noted that the students always supported the team and there was no booing at the Milwaukee Arena. "We went to the NIT that year and finished third. Dave Erickson, who was a high school All-America, had to play with a cast in the NIT. The Providence Friars, led by John Thompson, defeated us in the NIT."

Hickey was known for the three-lane fast break offense and matchup zone defense. He never believed in the bonus situation, even when his team had fouls to give, according to Hank Raymonds. It was Raymonds and "Easy" Ed Macauley who helped lead Hickey's first St. Louis University squad to a 24-3 record and the NIT title in 1948. Raymonds was the first player in St. Louis basketball history to win four straight letters. He was also a good baseball player, so much so that he became a property of the Milwaukee Braves. Raymonds joined Hickey's staff at Marquette in 1961.

"He was a brilliant coach as far as getting teams prepared. Very thorough. Tough. He ran the show. He treated everyone alike," remembered Raymonds.

"Hickey didn't treat Hank well at all," noted Bob Wolf, a 6'2" freshman guard from Menomonee Falls, Wisconsin. "Hickey was nuts. He was outlandish. He used to go on tirades. He wasn't a happy man."

"With Hickey," Nixon added, "there was never a game when we were not prepared or didn't know what the other team was going to do. He was very organized."

"The game had kind of passed him by [though]," remarked Tom Collins, radio play-by-play man for the Warriors' broadcasts on WEMP-AM. Added Bob Harlan, then sports information director at Marquette, now president of the Green Bay Packers, "Eddie had treated his players so poorly that when he brought kids on campus he was recruiting, the host players on the Warrior team told the recruits that things were not that great in Milwaukee.

"His recruiting started to suffer. There was a real problem on the team with respect to the way he treated the players. When he yelled at a player during practice, some of the other players laughed at him behind his back. He would grab players by the shirt. That wasn't seen in those days," said Harlan.

When he took over Marquette from Jack Nagle in 1958, Hickey had the good fortune of inheriting Don Kojis, a 6'6" forward who became a

Converse All-America and the eighth leading scorer in Marquette history, and played eleven years in the NBA. Kojis, one of five players to have his number retired at Marquette, was the first Warrior to be selected in a professional draft.

Marquette advanced to the NCAA Mideast Regional in Hickey's first season, and was ranked 20th and 15th, respectively, in the AP and UPI wire service polls. It was Marquette's highest finish in the polls since the 1954–55 season, when it was rated 8th in AP and 9th in UPI. Hickey's successful debut in Milwaukee earned him Coach of the Year honors from the Basketball Writers Association of America. "I thought he was one of the best coaches I have seen for preparing a game. Hickey used long practices," said Kojis, who added that Hickey's Warriors were rarely surprised by other teams.

"Eddie came in when I was a senior," recalled Harlan. "Eddie had good material left over from Jack Nagle. It helped him recruit. He had 'Tricky' Dick Nixon, Dave Erickson, Bob Hornak, and Ron Glaser."

"He knew basketball, but he was different," remembered John Stone, a 6'5" senior forward on Hickey's last team. "He treated Hank [Raymonds] just as badly as everyone else. They were afraid of him and they despised him," he said of the players.

A good example is the case of Joel Plinska, who was reportedly touted as a better player than Don Kojis in high school. He and Hickey were like "oil and water," Stone said. Hickey ran Plinska off the team because he did not run his "test pattern offense" properly.

"'You take no shot until you see the defense,'" Stone remembered Hickey telling the team. "The offense went two options and Plinska just put up a shot, and that was it."

Entering the 1963–64 campaign, Hickey had an impressive career record of 431-210. In his 25 years of coaching, he had suffered through just two losing seasons. He described his 1963–64 team as "green" because he had only three returning starters joining a talented but untested group of sophomores, led by 6'5" forward Tom Flynn.

"The previous three years, five guys did all the playing for Hickey," commented Ron Glaser. "He had no real experienced players that last season. I think a lot of the complaints came from those players who were sitting on the bench. I had a good experience playing for Hickey. I look at the positives that he brought to Marquette. Hickey was one of the few Marquette coaches with a winning record."

After losing four of their first six, the Warriors hosted Georgia Tech, Wisconsin, and Dartmouth in the second annual Milwaukee Classic, Marquette's holiday tournament. But the Warriors' bad luck continued as they lost the Classic. They did take the consolation game, however, defeating Dartmouth, 98-69.

But the beginning of the end for the 61-year-old Hickey came when his 3-5 Warriors visited Bernard "Peck" Hickman's Louisville Cardinals for a New Year's Day matchup. It would be the last time the teams would meet as independents, since Louisville was joining the Missouri Valley Conference the next season.

On New Year's Eve, during an early evening party that Hickey had thrown for the team, the old-fashioned coach decided to let the players set their own curfew. They agreed on a 1 a.m. bed check.

But a snowstorm hit Louisville that night and four of the Warriors missed their self-imposed curfew: Paul Carbins, Con Yagodzinski, Joe Price, and Jim Warras. "They set the time," Raymonds said of the players' decision.

"I received a call from coach Hickey New Year's Day," said John Stone. "I thought it was the trainer with our wake-up call. But it was the coach, and he was screamin' at me to come down to his room. I went down there. I didn't know what happened."

"'Those guys missed the curfew,'" Stone quoted Hickey as telling him. "'What do you think I ought to do?'" A stunned Stone did not know what to say. Hickey then told Stone to have the players come to him with an explanation before that day's game with the Cardinals, or "they're through."

"They never went to offer an explanation and he went nuts," Stone recalled. "The coup de grace was that the Louisville paper had a story that the 'Warriors were on the warpath' the night before singing at a piano bar, singing Everly Brothers songs.

"They [players] thought it was a joke. That he was kidding. They thought nothing would happen," Stone said.

Warras, Price, Yagodzinski, and Carbins all dressed for the game, but Hickey did not play them. He kicked them off the team for what he termed violation of training rules. All four had their scholarships revoked at the end of the academic year.

When the basketball team returned to Milwaukee, Hickey called a press conference and explained that he threw the players off the team for disciplinary reasons.

"I thought it was a minor violation," Stone said. "It turned out to be a real nightmare when he threw the players off the team. They were thrown out of school and it really screwed up their lives."

The nightmare was just beginning for the Warriors. After an easy 98-67 win over the University of Wisconsin–Milwaukee, Marquette proceeded to lose 15 straight and establish the most records for futility of any Warrior squad before or since.

Any solace Marquette would take from the win over UWM was short lived as the Warriors prepared to play the third-ranked Loyola Ramblers. The defending NCAA champions spanked Marquette 96-80 at the Arena for loss number 11.

Bradley then dropped Marquette to 4-12 with an 81-73 beating, which was followed by a 72-68 loss to the Wisconsin Badgers before 10,488 at the Arena. After Wichita State pasted the Warriors 100-63—the team's first 100-point loss since 1958—the team lost another player when reserve Pete Grant left the university. Hickey was well on his way to his first losing season since 1939 when he coached at Creighton. None of his basketball teams had ever lost more than 12 games in a season. And the most losses by a Warrior squad up to that time was 17, when Bill Chandler's Hilltoppers finished 6-17. But this Warrior squad was threatening to break that dubious mark.

The Warriors suffered their next two losses at the Arena to DePaul and the Air Force Academy before dwindling crowds. As the losing streak mounted, the *Marquette Tribune* took consolation in the fact that the freshman team was the best since the days of Nixon and Hornak. "Their improvement lends a ray of hope to next year's fortunes on the Arena floor," said the student newspaper.

The Warriors then headed to Detroit, where they were beaten by the Titans, 97-73. It was Marquette's tenth straight loss and seventh straight road defeat. And the road did not get any easier as the team headed to the Chicago Stadium to face Loyola. Not surprisingly, Marquette extended its losing streak at the Stadium to four, with a 99-81 loss to the Ramblers.

After the loss Hank Raymonds tendered his resignation as assistant coach, citing "personal reasons," according to the February 26, 1964, edition of the *Marquette Tribune*. While he was not certain what the future held for him, Raymonds wanted to stay in coaching.

Raymonds had been a very loyal assistant coach, according to those close to the program. "In the three years I worked for him I had just one Sunday off," said Raymonds. "He didn't even let me go home to help my wife move into our house."

Marquette's road woes continued in New York where the team lost 68-60 to St. John's, which dropped the team to 4-20. The *Marquette Tribune* noted the team's lack of confidence and opined that the only person who could inspire confidence in the players was no longer there: Hank Raymonds. A cartoon showing a wounded warrior with a broken tomahawk and split feather appeared in the paper and summed up the sorry season with the caption: "MU's deflated basketball hopes."

On the day of the team's final home game, a blizzard hit Milwaukee and only 3,675 people showed up at the Arena to say goodbye to the seniors as they lost to Detroit 100-76. It was the 15th straight loss, bringing the season record to 4-21. The bleeding finally ended with the last game of the season against Xavier in Cincinnati. Hickey wound up watching most of the game seated, according to *Milwaukee Journal* reporter Terry Bledsoe.

"Hickey was called for a couple of technicals in the first half," recalled Bledsoe, who was not allowed to travel with the team at that time for road games. Bledsoe did his assignment by listening to radio broadcasts of the games at the *Journal*, and he filed his story right there at the office.

"He refused to bring his team up from the locker room for the second half. The Xavier athletic director and basketball coach persuaded Eddie to come up for the second half. By the time that game was over, his fate was sealed." The Warriors won 98-95 and finished the season 5-21. It was the worst win-loss record in Marquette basketball history. It was of little consolation to those in power at Marquette that seven of the team's opponents that season went on to postseason play in the NCAA or NIT.

Average attendance at the Arena dropped along with team morale, from a high of 7,176 during Hickey's second season to 5,871 for his 5-21 finish.

Even though Marquette experienced a post–World War II surge in enrollment and football was popular, it was a lack of fan support that forced Marquette to drop the football program in December of 1960, much to the chagrin of the student body, which held campus protests in the succeeding seasons to bring back football. But the protests fell on deaf ears.

At one time Marquette's football program was competitive, if not financially lucrative. Marquette played in the first Cotton Bowl in 1937, losing to Slingin' Sammy Baugh and Texas Christian University, 16-6.

"Our fortunes were sagging in the 1950s," recalled the Reverend John P. Raynor, who served as Marquette president from 1965 to 1990. "We brought in Moon Mullins from Notre Dame in the '50s. Lyle 'Liz' Blackburn then came on to coach. And in the hopes of attracting larger crowds the football team left the 19,000-seat Marquette Stadium for the much larger County Stadium, which opened in 1953. They played before several hundred people there. They got a bigger place and a smaller crowd." Even Paddy Driscoll, who went on to a Hall of Fame playing career with the Chicago Bears, had been a football coach at Marquette.

Unfortunately, all that Marquette had to show for its involvement on the gridiron was a debt of at least $500,000, which weighed down the rest of the athletic program. After the disastrous 1963–64 basketball season the Jesuits were concerned that without some turnaround basketball would suffer the same fate as football. With the exception of NCAA tournament appearances in 1955, '59, and '61, Marquette had won just one basketball championship in its history: the National Catholic Invitational Tournament during Tex Winter's first year as coach in 1952. Winter, at 28, was then the youngest college coach in the country. However, even he left Marquette for Kansas State after the '52–53 season.

Marquette basketball had been televised since 1948, before professional basketball came to town in 1951–52 with the Milwaukee Hawks. Red Holzman took over the Hawks from Fuzzy Levane during the '53–54 season.

One of the big highlights for the basketball program took place in 1955, when Nagle's Warriors took on Adolph Rupp's Kentucky Wildcats in the NCAA East Regional. That Marquette team had won 22 straight during the season.

"I was in high school, I was 16," recalled David Foran, director of Marquette's News Bureau during the mid-1960s. "I was at a movie at the Riverside Theater on Wisconsin Avenue when all of a sudden they stopped the movie and just announced the score. Marquette had beaten Kentucky 79-71, and people in the theater cheered."

But by 1964, the athletic board decided that a new direction was desperately needed in order for the basketball program to survive. Hickey would have to go.

Hickey's fate had actually been sealed before the New Year's Eve disaster, according to Raymonds. After a December loss at Wake Forest, the Reverend James Orford of the athletic board met with Frank McGuire, who was then coaching at the University of South Carolina, to discuss a possible replacement for Hickey.

"At this time, Hickey was considered gone," said Raymonds, adding that Frank McGuire suggested Al as a replacement. "I said I'd hate to do it to the priests at Belmont Abbey, but Al McGuire is the only one I know who can do the job," noted Frank McGuire.

A few weeks after the season had mercifully ended for Marquette, rumors were circulating that Hickey would not be back for a seventh season. The university had given Hickey the option of resigning, according to Raymonds, but he refused.

University President Reverend William F. Kelley ended the speculation on April 3, 1964, when he announced that Edgar S. Hickey would not be retained as head basketball coach and athletic director. According to the announcement in the *Marquette Tribune*, his decision was based on an athletic board recommendation from several months earlier. The Reverend Kelley finished his statement by saying that "sometimes a change in personnel is required."

So ended the Hickey era at Marquette. It was the first time in his coaching career that he had ever been fired. The 62-year-old had compiled a respectable 92-70 record in six seasons at Marquette, taking the Warriors to two NCAA tournaments and one NIT. After a graceful exit at the basketball team's annual banquet, an embittered Hickey quietly disappeared from the coaching ranks and moved to Terre Haute, Indiana, where he managed a AAA agency. He retired to Arizona, and was inducted into the Basketball Hall of Fame in 1978.

After Hickey was fired, Stan Lowe, 60, was named athletic director. Lowe had been involved in Marquette athletics for 42 years. Speculation then started on who would become the next head basketball coach.

According to the *Marquette Tribune*, the university was searching for what it called a mystery man as its next coach. "'Mystery Man' because the board didn't want to tell the *Marquette Tribune* who they were looking for in a new head coach," said Sauceda, a language professor who later succeeded Lowe as AD. "They [athletic board] were looking for the best man out there at the time."

The Warrior players petitioned the administration to hire Raymonds because he was a known entity to the team. "Hickey had recommended me for the open Marquette job after he was let go," Raymonds recalled.

Raymonds was one of 50 applicants for the job. Another coach who was in the running was John Castellani, who coached Elgin Baylor and Seattle University to the 1958 Final Four, where they were defeated by Kentucky and Rupp's "Fiddlin' Five." Others considered for the job included state high school finalists Vic Anderson (Milwaukee North) and John Wilson (Dodgeville), DePaul assistant coach Bob Lukstra, and Jim Harding (Gannon, Pennsylvania).

CHAPTER SIX

Park Avenue

While it was true that Frank McGuire helped Al McGuire reach the third point on his coaching compass—Marquette University—there is more to the story. Frank did write a letter of recommendation for Al, but he was not responsible for getting him an interview with the Jesuit fathers in Milwaukee.

Al McGuire's friend and confidant Tom Brennan recalled that when it was clear Hickey was going to be fired, he called a friend who was president of a Wisconsin manufacturing firm and an influential Marquette alumnus. Brennan asked if he could somehow get McGuire an interview for the head coaching job. "I told this guy that if Al got the interview, he would get the job. That's how confident I was in Al's ability to sell himself."

The 35-year-old McGuire hardly seemed to be the "mystery man" Marquette was looking for to end its hoops nightmare. After all, Belmont Abbey was coming off an embarrassing six-win season and had won a total of 13 games in McGuire's last two years. He was certainly not the hottest coaching commodity around, and he was in no position to bargain for a Division One head coaching job.

"After the season, I drove to Al's house," said Brennan. "I'm sittin' across from him and he's laying on the couch with the flu. I think it was a Tuesday. I told him, 'I think I can get you an interview at Marquette.' 'Who the hell is gonna hire me after the season I just had? Nobody's gonna wanna look at me in the condition I'm in,' McGuire shot back.

"I said to him, 'If I get you the interview, will you go to Milwaukee?'" McGuire said that he did not feel ready for the challenge of a Division

One program. He was convinced that getting the job was a long shot. But Brennan and McGuire's family convinced him that he had nothing to lose by interviewing for the Marquette job.

"Al didn't want to go after the Marquette job because he didn't think he would get it," explained Pat McGuire. "He was a New Yorker who went south to Belmont Abbey and didn't think people [in the Midwest] would know him.

"He was reluctant, but he went [to Milwaukee]," continued Pat. "He took the camp bus to the airport and said he would be back the next day. That was Friday."

While Pat stayed in Charlotte with the kids, Al flew to Milwaukee and was met by the Reverend Leonard Piotrowski, who warned McGuire not to get his hopes up, that he might not get the job.

"Al became incensed," recalled Brennan. "Al then said, 'What do I want to waste my time coming up here for?' Father Piotrowski tried to calm him down and suggested that as long as McGuire was in Milwaukee, he might was well hear the good fathers out."

Needless to say, when McGuire arrived at Marquette for his interview with the athletic board, he was not impressed. "I said to myself, 'What the hell am I doing here, you know, in Milwaukee? I got so PO'd that I went in and said I'm gonna get this job. I went in and spoke for 45 minutes."

"Al reamed them out about Loyola basketball and Wisconsin basketball," Brennan recalled of the one-way interview. "He said, 'I told those guys how to play basketball in the Midwest and that I can recruit and do things within the rules.'"

After the interview, McGuire headed back to his room at the Pfister Hotel thinking that he probably was not going to be selected. As he was preparing for his return trip to Charlotte, the phone rang.

"Father Piotrowski called his room," Brennan said. "He told Al that the athletic board wanted to talk to him again. Al said, 'I don't have time to talk.' Father Piotrowski said, 'No, Coach, they want to offer you the job.'"

"I did not know one soul in Milwaukee," McGuire said at the time. "They must have been desperate, or they would have hired a first communion coach."

McGuire went back to the bargaining table with the athletic board and laid out his terms of employment, according to Brennan. He was offered a two-year contract. Before he left the meeting he told the board: "There is no leak of this news until noon tomorrow. I have to talk to the priests at Belmont Abbey first."

Back at the hotel, McGuire called home to break the good news to his family. Pat was not there, but daughter Noreen answered the phone. "Noreen, tell Mom I got the job, and have Tom meet me at the airport tonight."

When McGuire arrived at the Charlotte airport he told Brennan, "Abbott Walter Coggin has to approve what I've done." When they arrived at Belmont Abbey, sometime after 11 p.m., McGuire banged on the monastery door until the old abbott opened the door. Rubbing the sleep from his eyes, he asked: "Al, is that you? What do you want at this hour?" McGuire explained that he had been offered the head coaching job at Marquette. "God bless ya, Al. You're on your way," said the weary abbott as he released McGuire from his seven-year sentence in college coaching purgatory.

With the blessings of the Abbey monks, McGuire, the mystery man, returned to Milwaukee for his introductory press conference at Marquette University. It was during the return trip that the first apocryphal story involving McGuire and Marquette was told.

"When Al returned to Milwaukee, the university put him up at the LaSalle Hotel, which was scheduled to be renovated as an all-girls dormitory [Cobeen Hall]," Raymonds explained. "They put Al on the seventh floor and then there was a fire in the deli downstairs. Someone allegedly set the fire to collect on the insurance. But we got Al out of there OK."

When McGuire accepted the job, the locals thought that it was the legendary Frank McGuire who had been hired as the new basketball coach. After all, he was the only McGuire that basketball fans in Milwaukee recognized at the time.

"I do remember that Al was totally unknown at that time," said Bob Harlan, Marquette Sports Information Director (SID). "There were a lot of names and rumors mentioned to replace Hickey.

"WTMJ radio told me that it had a very good source who said the new coach would be Frank McGuire, who was then coaching at the University of South Carolina. I received a phone call from [Marquette President] Father Bill Kelley, who told me to come down to a press conference where the new head coach would be introduced.

"I went to the press conference looking for Frank McGuire," said Harlan. "Then I see a tall, gangly sort of guy come up and introduce himself. 'Hi, I'm Al McGuire,'" recalled Harlan, who later called *Milwaukee Journal* reporter Terry Bledsoe with the news.

"We got McGuire!" Harlan blurted out. "Wow!" said Bledsoe. "Frank McGuire." "No, it's not Frank," corrected Harlan. Bledsoe shot back, "It's Dick. He was a good player." "No, but you're gettin' warm," Harlan teased. "It's his brother Al."

"I recalled hearing from Father [James] Orford, who was the head of Marquette's athletic board, that he kept getting letters of recommendation for Al from people he would never dream of hearing from, like Ned Irish, Walter Brown, and Doggie Julian," said Bledsoe.

"I went down to O'Hare Airport with Harlan to pick him [McGuire] up in the springtime at 1 p.m.," remembered Bledsoe. "He was coming into town to house hunt.

"We offered to bring him to Milwaukee, but he wanted to talk to George Ireland. I was on deadline, and I had a portable typewriter and wrote my story in the car. Loyola University was his first stop [after being hired by Marquette]. He wanted to talk to Ireland because Ireland knew major college basketball. [At that time] he looked up to Ireland. There was no question. It was almost like Al was making a courtesy call to the pope."

"Al McGuire, 35, basketball coach at Belmont Abbey in Belmont, North Carolina, was appointed head basketball coach at Marquette University." That was how the announcement of McGuire's hiring as the ninth basketball coach in Marquette history appeared in the *Milwaukee Journal,* April 12, 1964. In the *Marquette Tribune* McGuire's young Irish face smiled out from the top of the sports section.

He had signed a two-year contract with the university reportedly worth between $12,000 and $15,000 a year, with annual raises of $1,000. McGuire felt that two years was enough time for the school to get a feel for his coaching style and personality. Recalled athletic board member Sam Sauceda, "Al called me 'Stan' for the first year. He told me that the people worrying about his salary figure will eventually see 'that I'm the cheapest for what they are getting in return for their money.'"

The new coach's first recruiting job was getting Raymonds to return to Marquette. McGuire hired him on the telephone, without ever having met him. The two had been briefly acquainted when Raymonds was head coach at Christian Brothers College in Memphis, Tennessee. In fact, he booked a game between CBC and Belmont Abbey when McGuire was still coach. "We paid him [McGuire] $750 to play us," recalled Raymonds, who left CBC to join Hickey's staff at Marquette before the game was even played. The Abbey lost by 16, and Raymonds never let McGuire forget it.

"A few days later, I got a call from Al," Raymonds said. "'Why don't you stay with me?' asked McGuire. I asked him, 'What are the arrangements?' He said, 'Don't worry about that, we'll knock 'em dead.' Hell, I didn't have anywhere to go. I resigned before Hickey was fired. Then I applied for the head coaching job."

McGuire had conferred with Hickey about the players and the program after being hired. And not long after that, he did his first interview with radio station WTMJ-AM. Host Larry Butler conducted the long-distance phone interview with McGuire from his home in Charlotte. When Warrior fans learned who the new head coach would be, they asked, "Al Who?"

McGuire said all the right things during his first interview. The new coach said that he appreciated the opportunity. He also mentioned that he had conferred with Hickey after getting the position. McGuire tipped his hat to the former coach, saying that he wanted to build on what Hickey had accomplished. But he was also very tentative in his responses to questions, carefully measuring his words. Warrior fans who listened to the broadcast that day heard a cautious new coach who did not exactly exude an air of self-confidence.

The questions quickly turned to scheduling and recruiting. "I don't believe in any cupcakes [easy opponents]. When you play, you play the best. I want to recruit the best boys, not the number two boys. I don't want Marquette to be an Avis. I want it to be a Hertz, because America is about winning.

"I'm going to give the maximum effort. This is a 365-day-a-year job. I want to have Marquette to the level where they had reached in the past."

McGuire's timing was fortuitous. When he arrived in Milwaukee the Green Bay Packers were in the middle of their dynasty and Vince Lombardi was achieving godlike status in the state of Wisconsin. Milwaukee was a National League baseball town, and though the Milwaukee Braves were going through some tough times in the early 1960s, they had made consecutive World Series appearances in 1957 and 1958, winning it all in '57. There was no such thing as professional basketball, hockey, or soccer in Wisconsin back in 1964. Milwaukee was well known for its beer and brats. While Schlitz's advertising proclaimed it to be the beer that made Milwaukee famous, the conservative, blue-collar town had a number of other well-known breweries, including Pabst, Miller, and Blatz.

Change was certainly in the air in Milwaukee, as it was in the rest of the country. There was a changing of the guard and the end of an era on April 5, 1964, when General Douglas MacArthur died. On April 11, McGuire was named head coach at Marquette. Hickey, like MacArthur, had been a military man; McGuire was not.

Henry Maier, a Democrat, was the mayor of Milwaukee, and 1964 was a presidential election year. President Johnson's War on Poverty was in full swing, and as the spring breezes blew off Lake Michigan, a number of politicians blew into town, including Alabama Governor George Wallace, Vice President Hubert Humphrey, and United States Attorney General Robert F. Kennedy, who gave the address at Marquette's eightieth commencement exercises that year.

In addition to the ROTC, the Peace Corps was big on the Jesuit campus, Hootenannies were still a big part of student entertainment at the Brooks Memorial Student Union, as groups like the Kingston Trio and the Lettermen performed. The previous year, the Congress of Racial Equality, (CORE), opened a branch on the Milwaukee campus. Later that school year, John Howard Griffin's book *Black Like Me* was creating waves on campus. Other student concerns in 1964 included the draft, birth control, papal infallibility, and peeping toms. Freshman enrollment set a new record of 1,668.

Up to that time, the most famous Marquette alumnus was Ralph Metcalfe, who as a Marquette student won silver and bronze medals in the 1932 Olympics in Los Angeles and a silver in the 1936 Summer Games in Berlin when he ran with Jesse Owens, much to the chagrin of Adolph Hitler. Known as Marquette's fastest man, Metcalfe was the only Marquette athlete to make two Olympic teams. He later became a U.S. congressman from Chicago. Another nationally famous alum was Don McNeill, popular host of the long-running radio show *The Breakfast Club*.

During the fall campaign, Barry Goldwater appeared at the student union and Vice President Humphrey made a return visit to the Arena, as did LBJ just before his landslide win in November.

Not unlike his situation at Belmont Abbey, McGuire had little talent to work with at Marquette. As a result, Warrior fans were willing to give him the benefit of the doubt. Needless to say, expectations for the team were not very high after the forgettable 1963–64 campaign. As at Belmont Abbey, McGuire said that his first two years at Marquette would be spent "building character."

The young, handsome, well-mannered New Yorker began working the phones to try to convince players to come to Jesuit-run Marquette.

"The Jewish boy is leery about going to a Catholic school," McGuire told Larry Butler in a WTMJ interview in 1964, joking about one of his recruiting phone calls. "I told him we wouldn't try to convert him."

When McGuire finally met his assistant Raymonds, the new coach said, "Introduce me to the people with money." Noted Raymonds, "When I came up from Memphis, I made $7,800 a year. I didn't know anyone with money in Milwaukee."

But apparently McGuire had some money. Once he found his dream home in Brookfield, McGuire asked Raymonds to buy it for him. "Then he gives me a blank check and signs it. He told me to fill in the amount ($28,000) to buy the house. I had never met the man in my life, and here he gives me a blank check. I didn't know if the check was any good, and he went back to Charlotte."

"A lot of times I do my business that way, very quickly," said McGuire on a WRIT radio special in 1977. "I am a calculating person. But I can read people. I think I got it from either being a bartender or bouncin' around the different parts of the country or from the pros. I read people very quickly. And 99.9 percent of the time my gut feeling is right. With coach [Raymonds], he was what you might call a straight arrow."

Between recruiting fans and players, McGuire put on a full-court press to sell himself to Milwaukee, Marquette, and the returning players. He was able to bridge a lot of gaps, including the generation gap.

"They [McGuire and Hickey] were about as opposed as two people could be," said Tom Flynn, captain of McGuire's first team. "Al held a pizza party at his first meeting with the players, which was something Hickey would never do. [But] I learned a lot from Hickey. I learned a lot from McGuire. Hickey was from another era.

"He [Hickey] was the Adolph Rupp kind of guy—old school," added Flynn, an all-stater from Milwaukee Messmer Catholic High School who was also recruited by Notre Dame, UCLA, and Michigan, but grew up with Marquette basketball.

"I was a Milwaukee kid. I had never been out of Milwaukee in my life. I used to sit and listen to Marquette basketball games on the radio. Playing at the Milwaukee Arena was a big deal. I probably deep down didn't want to do anything else."

McGuire next reached out to the students and the business community in Milwaukee. He was concerned about the morale on campus and came up with fresh approaches to build support for the team among the students, especially women. He held clinics during the basketball season on campus with his two best returning players, Flynn and Bobby Wolf. The weekly clinics focused on basketball basics, and after each session the women were invited to stay to watch the men scrimmage. And in order to recruit local lawyers and businessmen to his Warrior cause, McGuire would invariably say to the receptionist, "Tell him this is Mayor [Henry] Maier," and he was usually put through immediately.

"We tried anything we could do to get a story," recalled Raymonds. "We just tried to generate interest. Al started a season-ticket drive with the Marquette Minutemen, a booster organization. He set goals they never dreamed of setting."

"In order to create excitement and fill the Arena, he did a lot of Annie Oakleys [freebies]," explained Jerry Savio, who was transferred to Wonder Bread's offices in Milwaukee about the same time McGuire arrived. "He did quite a bit with nothing."

In his first address to the M Club, the university's sports letter winners, McGuire told the group, "My first love is football," and went on to talk about his playing days at St. John's Prep. "But I eventually realized that my best route to the pros was through basketball, and I switched."

Harlan was not aware of McGuire's football background and quickly learned how the new coach could win over an audience. "When we were walking back to campus, he told me, 'Bob, this was a football audience. Always tell people what they want to hear.' There was a real method to what he was trying to accomplish. He came in very silently, but he didn't leave silently."

McGuire's first address to the Tip-Off Club, the main basketball booster organization, was low key, according to club member Einar Olsen. "He was so soft-spoken that he was practically whispering. The other Tip-Off members were disappointed. But he wound up being the furthest thing from soft-spoken we've ever seen."

After working his recruiting pitch in Milwaukee, he needed some guys who could play. For that, he headed east to reopen the "underground railroad" of basketball talent from New York City.

Most of McGuire's returning players had a strong ethnic flavor. German, Irish, and Italian Catholics who hailed from Wisconsin burgs like Antigo, Menomonee Falls, Superior, and West Allis, as well as Milwaukee, with a few from the bigger midwestern cities like Chicago and Toledo. "Al had tough little Irish kids," recalled Bledsoe. "Flynn and Bobby Wolf were great Wisconsin kids."

"We used to wear haircuts called the 'Princeton Cut'—short, close to the scalp," recalled Wolf. "We wore cotton pants, shirts, and sweaters. I don't know if the university allowed jeans at all.

"We really lacked talent," admitted Wolf. "We didn't have the talent or height to compete. He had a lot of guys on that team who couldn't play Division One basketball. We had a lot of guys who knew that that was the last year they would play basketball. Al told them that they could keep their scholarships, but they weren't going to play on the team."

Since McGuire had been away from the New York basketball scene for a while, he needed another talent scout, like Fred Stegman, to give him the skinny on the hot high school players in the Big Apple. The street scout he relied on was a basketball junkie named Mike Timeberg.

Timeberg regularly attended five high school basketball games a weekend. "He was Al's recruiter in New York City," recalled Jim Chones, a 6'11" center who arrived at Marquette in 1969. "He'd go to the playgrounds to watch them. He was talkin' real slick, smokin' a cigarette, and he always looked like he was waiting for the subway."

"I got Al all of his New York kids," said Timeberg, who also assisted Frank McGuire, Don Haskins at Texas Western, and much later, Jerry Tarkanian at UNLV. "McGuire's players had to be NCAA eligible. Cazzie Russell couldn't qualify at Marquette, so he went to Michigan. Walter November and I didn't have a rivalry. He got ballplayers for George Ireland's Loyola teams in Chicago. The ballplayers he got wouldn't have been accepted at Marquette," noted Timeberg.

One of the first players Timeberg helped McGuire recruit was a nearsighted center from Harlem named Pat Smith, the seventh of ten children in a Baptist home. "I met Al through Mike," said Smith. "He [Timeberg] loved the game. He had a serious rivalry with Walter November, who was George Ireland's New York talent scout.

"At any given time," Smith continued, "they [Timeberg and November] would have 30 of the best ballplayers in the city in basketball tournaments. They were short tournaments, double elimination. Some were in the summer. I knew Timeberg through my brother Billy. Mike would have to come and get him so he could play in the tournaments."

"During my day," added Dean Meminger, "the Reliables and the New York Gems were the best teams in the playgrounds. Those teams were controlled by white guys, like Mike Timeberg. They [Timeberg and November] got the best players. Jerry Harkness of Loyola came out of the Reliables," noted Meminger, who attended Rice High School at 124th and Lenox Avenue in Harlem and was only the second player in New York City high school basketball history to be named First Team All-City three years in a row. The first was Lew Alcindor.

"I was playing with another organization with three of my high school teammates," Meminger recalled. "We entered the Ray Felix Tournament. I was a freshman or a sophomore. Mike happened to see us play. And for some reason the following season the team I played with had fallen apart. Mike recruited me. I played two years with the Gems.

"Mike Timeberg was the coach-in-title of the New York Gems," Meminger continued. "He sat on the end of the bench and we coached ourselves on the court. Mike Timeberg was a basketball junkie. It was fulfilling for him to be around great athletes and win and be successful. He lived on 56th Street and the Avenue of the Americas. When people like Mike came into our circles it was a big deal. Mike Timeberg happened to like Al and he steered players his way. Al was a New Yorker. Al took over the 'underground railroad' from Frank McGuire. It was Mike who helped Frank start the underground railroad to North Carolina."

"I never made any money out of it like the Howie Garfinkels and Tom Konchalskis of the basketball world," said Timeberg. "I did this because I wanted to build a champion out of the college teams that I was involved with. Al knew about me because of all the all-state teams we had, and he wanted some of those players at Marquette. I could have gotten Moses Malone, but Al said that he didn't want a guy who would last just one or two years and then go pro."

"He [McGuire] came to my home twice," said Smith, picking up the story. "In the summer of 1964, I was scheduled to go to Long Island University before I heard from Al," said Smith, who was an Honorable Mention All-City that year at Benjamin Franklin High School in Harlem.

Smith, a rock solid 6'3" 200-pounder, was a scrappy center who never played high school hoops before his senior year. "I was also recruited by Utah, New York University, and some New York–area schools like C.W. Post and St. Francis.

"When it came to college recruiters, usually you would meet them in hotels. But here was a coach who knew how to catch the subway to Harlem. I see this white dude bopping along out of the subway toward our apartment like he was walking the streets of Rockaway Beach, without any fear. I said to myself, this guy's different," recalled Smith.

"[When Al arrived] it took Pat's mother ten minutes to get all the bolts off the door," Flynn recalled of McGuire's recruiting visit. Al said, "'Who in the hell would want to break in there?'" The precautions were for good reason. His mother was head of the household since Pat's father had died two years earlier, and two of Smith's brothers had been killed on the streets.

"I was just runnin' around, playin' in tournaments," said Smith. "He talked more to my mother than me. He outtalked her. But he was talkin' education. I hadn't really heard of Marquette. But he was talkin' education. My mother had signed off on my letter of intent to Long Island. But she never mailed it after talkin' to McGuire. He impressed my mother. There were eight males in my household and we all played ball. She would size 'em [recruiters] up. She took a liking to McGuire.

"There was no bullshit about him. Al was very up front. Very honest. He talked more education than basketball. At the time, Al hadn't even seen me play. We had coaches and recruiters coming to the home all the time. You get used to it. McGuire was the exception."

When he traveled to Brooklyn to visit 6'3" guard Danny Nee, another Honorable Mention All-City from Fort Hamilton High School, McGuire brought his mother with him for some serious kitchen-table recruiting. "Al heard that I was available," recalled Nee. "I didn't know he was coming. I walk into the small kitchen at home, here's Al and his mom drinking tea and eating Irish soda bread. My father didn't know what Marquette was. He wanted me to go with my own kind, get a good job after high school and get in with the Teamsters.

"He [McGuire] talked the English I understood. A lot of the Midwest people didn't understand the things he said. I really believe that he had a plan of making that program great," said Nee, who took his father's advice and "went with my own kind" to Marquette.

After returning from New York, McGuire pulled a recruiting coup when 6'5" guard Blanton Simmons from Milwaukee North High School, considered the best player in Wisconsin in 1964, committed to Marquette. Simmons had scholarship offers from 75 schools, including Indiana, Michigan, Minnesota, and Wisconsin.

"He had never seen me play in person," said Simmons, who was the second leading scorer in the Wisconsin state basketball tournament. "He had heard from others about a 6'5" guard, 190 pounds. He wanted me to stay at home. [But] I had already made a verbal commitment to [University of Wisconsin coach] John Erickson.

"I wrote a letter to John Erickson before my senior season and told him I wanted to go to Madison. I wanted to play in the Big 10. They played my style," continued Simmons, whose pure, quicksilver shot off the dribble left defenders in his wake. He scored a record 36 points in the semifinals of the state basketball tournament before losing in the finals. During his four years under Milwaukee North High School coach Vic Anderson, Simmons's teams went 67-2.

"Al McGuire was one of the greatest recruiters I've ever known," continued Anderson. "He approached Blanton and Blanton's mother, but he did not approach me. Blanton was good on defense and offense. He was a complete player. I wanted a couple of my players to go to Marquette. Al was also one of the best salesmen I ever knew."

"He [McGuire] took me to lunch at my high school," recalled Simmons. "He was very charismatic. He said, 'I don't know you. But I'm just going to ask you to do one thing. Give me a call before you sign with anyone.'

"He guaranteed me that I would get a pro contract, that I would get a good look at the next level. Here's a guy whose brother [Dick] was a scout for the New York Knicks," said Simmons, whose father had died when he was a kid.

"I was 17. I was naive. McGuire also told me that Marquette had a great dental school, and that 'we'll get you porcelain jackets for your teeth for free.' That was something that my mother couldn't afford. It was taken care of my senior year. I committed to Marquette in mid-April 1964. Al McGuire was able to get the player that everyone thought would get away."

"Most of my players who were in the 'minus pool' would go to the dental school, which was next to my office," explained McGuire. "It was a dental class and the students would work on Blanton or another player during the class. That was not uncommon. We could do this without having any problems."

McGuire's promises were quite a bit different from those that other coaches around the country were giving Simmons during the recruiting process. "The coach at the University of Arizona told me that the school would be a 'nice opportunity for a colored boy.' Tulane wanted me to be the first black on campus," said Simmons, still surprised that such attitudes existed as recently as 1964.

"There were maybe a dozen black students at Marquette my freshman year," recalled Simmons, whose Milwaukee North High School was 100 percent black. "I attribute a good deal of the success that I had to making the transition to a 99.8 percent white school and surviving," said Simmons, who double-majored in speech communications and philosophy. "I grew up around high expectations and very literate people. I was exposed to a lot," Simmons pointed out.

"Being from New York City I had a lot of adjustment problems," added Pat Smith. "At night in New York City, you don't start to get dressed to go out until 10 or 11 p.m. In Milwaukee we had a curfew. McGuire and I had an understanding. Small things like that [curfew], you understand. But if you mess up, you do something wrong, then you had to pay. I was suspended a few times for different things.

"It was hard for me. Al wanted everyone at Schroeder [residence hall]. But at Schroeder, I had some problems with the people in the dorm. At Stewart Hall they had a small room. There was a deli in the basement where you could buy a beer. I said, 'Coach, here's where I want to be.' He said, 'Go ahead.'

"He had a hi-fidelity record player in his office. Sometimes when he was out, he would let me go in and play my records. After I graduated he gave me the set. Milwaukee was a cultural change. I was in Harlem one day, the next day I was in the Midwest. It took me two years to adjust socially. That was the toughest," said Smith, who was a history major.

Smith figured in one of the apocryphal tales told about McGuire. Reportedly McGuire received a phone call from the university bookstore that one of his players was caught shoplifting. The description of the player matched Pat Smith. McGuire called Smith into his office and asked him what happened. Smith's reported response was: "You worry about small stuff like that, coach?" "In his senior year, Pat was still shoplifting, but it started to bother him," recalled McGuire. "That let me know that I was getting through to him. That's why he's my favorite ballplayer."

Besides Simmons and Smith, McGuire's first class of freshmen included 6'9" center Jim Goodin from Indianapolis; 6'2" guard Brad Luchini, an Honorable Mention All-Stater from West Allis, Wisconsin; 6'4" forward Mike Curran, a two-time All-Conference star from Antigo, Wisconsin; and Gus Moye of Aliquippa, Pennsylvania, who had just finished a hitch with the Marines.

The new coach had his work cut out for him as the team met for its first practice, on October 15, 1964.

"In my first day of practice I knew then why I got the job. It was a complete abortion. There were no players. There was no nothin'. It was really the minus pool. Which was an asset in reverse because you were building from scratch and whatever you did was an accomplishment," he recalled.

The fans, students, alumni, and longtime Milwaukee fans knew the cupboard was bare. The talent left over from Hickey's last season at Marquette was not quite up to Division One standards. McGuire was desperately looking for any kind of talent to shore up the roster.

"My plan," McGuire told Harlan at the time, "is we're gonna recruit one blue chipper a year. By his senior year, he will be a star. That way we will have a successful program."

While there were no blue chippers that first season, McGuire did make some moves to help shore up the varsity, which featured three seniors, five juniors, and eight sophomores. Freshmen could not play varsity ball at that time. One of the moves was to bring back Paul Carbins, a 6'6" forward who was a good rebounder. Even though Carbins had been kicked off the team by Hickey, McGuire needed him.

"Piss on 'em. I want the kid," McGuire replied when told that Carbins was no longer in school. Carbins was somehow reinstated, and McGuire also offered another Hickey refugee, Joel Plinska, a scholarship.

McGuire's problems were compounded by the fact that Hickey had booked a killer schedule for the upcoming season. In addition to the usual home-and-home games with such traditional Catholic rivals as DePaul, Loyola, Xavier, and Detroit, the Warriors had to play NCAA champion UCLA, NIT champ Bradley, Minnesota (ranked 5th), St. John's (ranked 7th), Boston College (ranked 8th), and Villanova (ranked 9th), as well as two games against bitter rival Wisconsin. McGuire called it the toughest schedule in the nation, and though he predicted a "non-terrific" season, he told the students that the team would need additional support when the going gets tough.

After a month of practices, the fans had their first opportunity to see the new coach and his team in the annual preseason freshman-varsity scrimmage.

"[All of that week] before that game, I was walking around the varsity in the student union telling the players that 'you guys don't have a chance,'" recalled Simmons. "They knew it. I was a fun guy, but I was teasin' and laughin'." Added Smith: "We beat 'em [varsity] almost every day in practice."

Some 5,700 fans came to the Arena on Friday, November 14, and saw the freshmen, with Simmons and Nee, beat the returning varsity squad 70-66. It was the first time in school history that the frosh had beaten the varsity.

A nervous Raymonds coached the freshmen, who played the varsity tough throughout the contest. Late in the game, with the freshmen ahead by a few points, McGuire walked over to their shocked huddle.

"Al came over to our huddle and told us, 'Look, if you guys can beat us, you beat us,'" recalled Nee, who added that the words gave the freshmen the confidence they needed to win the game. Curran led the freshmen with 18, Simmons had 15, Nee had 11, Luchini 9, and Smith had 12 rebounds. But the varsity, who were led by Wolf's 14 points and Carbins's 13 boards, made them pay for it.

"The next day, we had a tough practice. The varsity practiced until they beat the shit out of us," said Nee.

After Marquette defeated St. Thomas 69-49 in McGuire's first regular season game as head coach, the team lost to Louisville and then Minnesota at Williams Arena. The Golden Gophers were led by Archie Clark and Lou Hudson. "Marquette lacked height, but you never lacked hustle," complimented Minnesota coach John Kundla, who defeated McGuire two out of the three times they played. Kundla was frustrated by the higher-ups at Minnesota because they did not want to play a Catholic school. However, he fought to keep the Warriors on the schedule.

Nonetheless, McGuire became increasingly frustrated with his inexperienced team, which was turning the ball over too often and getting consistently outrebounded. "If I had known the material was this bad, I would have never taken the job. You get kids like this with a three-cent postcard."

He also noted that his young team suffered from a lack of height and had a tough time counteracting Hickey's style of play. However, McGuire retained half of Hickey's plays to avoid complete confusion. He also borrowed from his old Knicks coach Joe Lapchick that season by instituting a freelance style offense, in which all of the players were in constant motion with no set pattern. Just look for an opening in the defense and score. "Al wanted an offense where all of the players touched the ball," Raymonds said.

Lacking offensive talent, McGuire leaned on what he knew best: defense. In order for his players to be prepared for his aggressive style of play, they needed to be in superior condition and fundamentally sound.

As part of the conditioning program, McGuire had his players run with the cross-country team at Washington Park. McGuire felt that this would cut down on knee and ankle injuries during the season. The players ran under the guidance of cross-country coach Melvin "Bus" Shimek.

"Hickey was more cerebral [in his approach to the game]. Al was much more physical," said Rocke Calvelli, who played for both coaches and is now an attorney in Milwaukee.

"He figured we were missing too many layups because we were putting our heads down. We had to jump over a card table and a chair in order to make the shot. Those symbolized the differences between Al and Hickey. Al was going to get us back to fundamentals, where we would score the basket and play the game instinctively."

One of the most physical practice drills was something McGuire used at Belmont Abbey called the "wheel" or the "knockout," where the players were forced to crawl under tables, jump over benches, and perform other kinds of boot-camp drills until they dropped.

"He had generally shorter practices than Hickey," said Flynn. "But he would work us to death. We'd run the lines on the court for a half hour. Guys were throwin' up, sprinting and sliding. I can remember cursing the guy out loud after a certain amount of fatigue. He wasn't a cream puff. He insisted on us being in shape."

"During our practices there would be wrestlers running on the track above the court, shotputters at the other end, gymnasts working out. It never did bother us," said Raymonds. "Al would let opposing coaches in. He loved it. Al was oblivious to the people or the crowd around him. Jerry

Tarkanian came to a practice a few years later and left in a cold sweat," Raymonds laughed.

The Warriors came home to play New Mexico State at the Arena, and pulled off the first of a number of comebacks that season. Trailing by 10, the team went on a 16-0 run to win 62-54. Flynn scored 23 points, Wolf had 14, and Carbins pulled down nine rebounds. McGuire felt that Carbins's rebounding was what made the team go early in the season, but he wound up fouling out of most of the games.

Former Marquette star and then Detroit Piston Don Kojis came to a practice and asked McGuire if he could work out with the team. "I asked Al, 'How do you want me to play it?' He said just play your regular game. I said, 'Al, I don't want to get hurt.' So I went in and his guys double- and triple-teamed me. It was getting rough, so I elbowed a guy. And Al calls a time-out and says, 'Hey, don't go rough on my player!' 'But Al, they're elbowing me,'" said Kojis.

"We played off a set offense where we would pass from guard to forward," explained Flynn. "Sometimes we played where we went into a double post and Carbins and I would pick off each other. With Paul, he was 6'6". He was a workhorse. He was big and strong, but he wasn't like Pat Smith, who was a leaper. Paul would screen you off the boards and you would stay screened. Voracious rebounder but not a good shot."

"One of the things that Al wanted to do was fill the Arena," said Raymonds. In fact, a week after the frosh-varsity game, photos were released to the local newspapers picturing McGuire at the Arena ticket window showing how quickly tickets for the Milwaukee Classic were selling. And having high-profile, nationally ranked teams come to Milwaukee certainly helped boost the gate. Athletic Director Stan Lowe said, however, that attendance figures were just educated estimates at the time since there were no turnstiles in the Arena, where the Warriors had played since 1950.

Along those lines, one of McGuire's changes for the team included having the freshman play an intercollegiate schedule instead of just scrimmages against the varsity reserves. Not only would this provide better competition for the frosh, but it would create more interest in their games, to which admission was a quarter. And to boost team spirit, McGuire put a hi-fi in the locker room.

Heading into the third annual Milwaukee Classic, the Warriors were 2-3. Having UCLA was a big draw, as was having two-time defending Classic champ Wisconsin and the Boston College Golden Eagles, coached by McGuire's old pro nemesis Bob Cousy. Hickey had booked the game with UCLA athletic director J. D. Morgan, according to Wooden, who said that while he was coach he did not control the scheduling of UCLA basketball games. "I let the AD handle it."

"He [Morgan] did know that I wanted to play one tough game on a trip to the Midwest. It usually was a Big 10 team, Notre Dame, and a double-header in Chicago. Morgan did all the scheduling."

The Warriors played UCLA in the Classic's opening game. Marquette was leading the Bruins, 24-22, with less than 20 seconds left in the first half.

"Right before halftime, Al wanted us to take a shot with six seconds left," recalled Flynn. "I took the shot with eight or nine seconds left. They get the rebound and Gail Goodrich hit a shot from beyond halfcourt that went in at the buzzer to tie the game."

While Marquette did hold Goodrich to 21 points and UCLA to 30 under its season average, the Bruins took charge in the second half, defeating the gritty Warriors 61-52. The teams would never play again, said Raymonds, because Marquette could never get a commitment from Morgan on return games.

In the consolation game, Marquette defeated Wisconsin 62-61 in a game McGuire described as a "whammy-breaker" because it ended the Badgers' three-game winning streak over the Warriors. Captain Flynn was the only Marquette player selected for the All-Classic Tournament Team.

Even though the Classic win over Wisconsin was a confidence builder for the team, the Warriors proceeded to lose three straight road games to Iowa State, Loyola, and DePaul at Alumni Hall in Chicago.

"Before the Iowa State game in Ames, Iowa," remembered Flynn, "Al told us: 'Oh, you guys are hung over.' He decided we could use a walk before the game. He tells us to get out [of the bus] and walk the rest of the way to the game. And then the bus leaves with Al. By the time we got to the game, the other team was already on the floor. We barely got dressed in time for the game." The Warriors lost by 11.

The game at DePaul was the first between Al McGuire and Ray Meyer. At that time the team benches were under one of the baskets in the small 5,300-seat gym. "I can remember the priests at Alumni Hall with their rosary beads hanging over the balcony railing every time a Marquette player was at the free-throw line, praying he would miss," laughed

Tom Collins, who was teamed with veteran Wisconsin broadcaster Merle Harmon in the WEMP radio booth for the games.

"We always got homered during games against Ray Meyer's Blue Demons," remembered Flynn. "Every time I tried to catch the ball, someone would hold my arm, and the refs wouldn't call fouls. Paul and I fouled out in the first half." McGuire became so frustrated, he begged Meyer for mercy.

"Al gets down on his hands and knees and crawls over to my bench," Meyer laughed. "Al said, 'You can take my car, my house, my wife, but please don't steal this game from me.' Al kneeled in front of me and begged for mercy."

After the first losing road trip of the McGuire era, the Warriors came home for a rematch with Ireland's Loyola Ramblers, on January 6, 1965. In order to shake things up, McGuire reached into his bag of tricks to make up for the dearth of talent on his team.

With three minutes remaining in the second half of a nip-and-tuck game and a slim lead, McGuire pulled out all of his starters and inserted five reserves: Joe Mimlitz, Billy Joe Smith, Dane Mathews, Craig Leonard, and Joel Plinska. They proceeded to run all over the floor, playing a scattershot offense and defense, and basically causing chaos for the Ramblers.

"He had five hatchet men, none over 6-foot-4," recalled radio play-by-play man Collins. "He inserted these reserves simply to disrupt the other team while the starters rested." And, he hoped, to keep the lead.

The result was fewer turnovers by the Warriors. The reserves kept Marquette in the game. McGuire brought back his starters and forced Loyola into overtime. Rocke Calvelli then hit the game-winning shot for the 71-69 final score. The 5,170 fans at the Arena were thrilled. Calvelli was lifted on his teammates' shoulders, and a smiling McGuire clenched his fists in glee on the floor. He later praised his team for never giving up.

Since the reserves came out onto the floor later than the starters, their game meal usually was scrambled eggs and not steak. That was the ostensible explanation for the genesis of the "scrambled eggs." After these reserves created havoc on the floor, McGuire would bring back his starters to try to get back in the game. It was similar to what he originally started at Belmont Abbey.

"It [scrambled eggs] wasn't a resounding, 100 percent success, but it was different," remembered Flynn. "He had more of a gambling mentality in that he tried to do things differently. That tells something about where his strengths were: mental aspect, emotions of the game, physical."

"That [scrambled eggs] was a football technique," added Savio. "Five guys in, five guys out. Al was a defensive coach. And Al was a great clock coach. If you got over 55 points on one of Al's teams, you usually beat him."

"In coaching, no one's as good as you think or as bad as you think. So there's only a half-step difference, which can be made up with enthusiasm or closeness, all for one," said McGuire.

The "scrambled eggs," who were also known by the nickname "Marquette Minutemen," helped preserve an 80-73 win over Xavier before 7,500-plus at the Arena.

McGuire now had momentum going into the rematch with the Wisconsin Badgers. McGuire actually thought that the Warriors could win, but that four of his starters would have to have a good game.

More than 300 Marquette students took buses to the Wisconsin Fieldhouse in Madison to support the Warriors. However, the team started out badly, missing its first 17 shots as the Badgers spurted to a 17-1 lead. By halftime the score was 38-25. In the locker room, McGuire told his players they could win the game. "He told the team they had to make up two points every five minutes," said Bledsoe.

When the Warriors came out of the tunnel for the second half, 75 Marquette students were lined up on either side of the players as they ran onto the court, loudly cheering them on.

Marquette held the Badgers scoreless for the first five minutes and narrowed the Wisconsin lead to five. The struggling Badgers hit a four-minute dry spell, and Marquette won 59-58 on a buzzer-beater by Rocke Calvelli. The Marquette students mobbed the floor and surrounded the team. Raymonds and the team managers did all they could to keep the students out of the locker room. McGuire called it the greatest comeback of his coaching career and biggest win ever.

McGuire described both games against Wisconsin as "sand fights" (hard-fought games). It was the first time since the 1937–38 season that Marquette defeated Wisconsin twice in one season. Even though both teams were having poor years, the game enlivened the rivalry and marked the first of many buzzer-beaters that would characterize the series during the McGuire era.

"The Marquette job is really very easy and very hard," McGuire summarized. "All you must do at Marquette is beat Wisconsin for the real diehards. That game every year is a killer."

"Al didn't go back on the bus with the team to Milwaukee after the game," recalled Mike Christopulos, who was covering the game for the *Milwaukee Sentinel*. "He rode back in a car with me and Rel Bochet, who was covering the Badgers for the *Sentinel*. He wrote the game story and I wrote the sidebar. Al wanted to go to the Lime House on Blue Mound Road in Brookfield. We took Blue Mound Road all the way from Madison to Brookfield."

"I used to go to the games before Al arrived [in Milwaukee]. I met him after the first Wisconsin game at Madison," recalled Walter Wong, a lawyer and owner of the Lime House. "I ran buses to Madison from the Lime House. In those days when we were down 22 points at the half, we'd probably close early. [But] when Marquette came back to win, I knew we would have a long night.

"The waitress said that Al was at the bar," Wong continued. "I told her to give Al's party a bottle of champagne on the house. Al wanted to take the bottle of champagne home. He came over and introduced himself. Then Al used to come occasionally to the Lime House. It wasn't a fancy place. It had atmosphere. He liked it. When the Holy Name Society had sports nights, he cashed his speaking fee checks at the Lime House."

"I liked going to the Lime House because if you got there by midnight, you could still eat," said McGuire. "The Chinaman would fix you a meal."

"I had no preconceived notion of coaches," Wong continued. "The only notion I had was, you win you're good, you lose you're bad. Al said to me, 'We'll probably get along if you don't talk to me about basketball and I don't talk to you about law,'" Wong continued. "We hardly ever discussed politics. Going out to eat, he liked the crummy places. The dirtier the joint, the better the food. He liked Mexican food. Those were the types of places he liked."

"At the Lime House, we played gin together in the back room and Walter would cook up some concoction," recalled Savio. "After games we would go to different people's houses. Al would invite the opposing coaches and he would naturally hold court. Every coach would come, usually. But Al took losses very hard. We never went to the houses after losses."

The excitement of the win over Wisconsin made even long-lost alumni sit up and take notice, according to Norman Ochs.

"Al gets a call in his office from a man who begins by telling him, 'I played football at Marquette in the 1920s. I lost touch with the school over the years. I kind of feel a loyalty and I'd like to do something for the university,' he told Al. It was an attorney named Victor McCormick.

"Al brought McCormick over to the dean's office, and McCormick says, 'I live in Green Bay. I'd like to build a dormitory.' No one was allowed to talk to McCormick after that, except Al.

"One day, Al and a friend went up to Green Bay to visit McCormick, who asked why Al was there. 'Well,' Al begins, 'we're having our annual dinner and we want you on the dais.' On their way back to Milwaukee, Al told his friend in the car that the situation wasn't right to ask McCormick about the dorm. His sense of people comes from his old bartending days."

While McCormick had pledged over $2 million toward the dorm, it is still not known how much the university received. Construction began after the season, and the final price tag of the cylindrical eponymous men's dorm exceeded $4 million.

Unfortunately, the Warriors suffered a letdown in a 79-67 loss at Detroit against Dorie Murrey and the Titans. But when they returned to Milwaukee, McGuire welcomed his old pro coach Joe Lapchick, who was on the victory lap of his coaching career that season at St. John's, which would later win the NIT.

"Al and Dick epitomized the New York City player that my dad liked to coach," remembered Richard Lapchick, founder of the Center for the Study of Sport in Society at Northeastern University. Lapchick added that his father was a "shy" person. "Run-through-the-wall guys. They were completely loyal. They would go beyond their talent. I remember that my dad was even more happy that Al became a coach."

While it was the Wisconsin game that gave Marquette regional notice in the Midwest, the game that earned McGuire and his inconsistent team national acclaim was a 28-point blowout of Lapchick's St. John's Redmen at the Arena on January 30, 1965. McGuire was not the gracious host to St. John's, which was ranked number seven in the country by UPI and featured Lloyd "Sonny" Dove.

The Warriors mixed their man-to-man and zone defenses, and then the scrambled eggs came in with nine minutes left in the half to stake Marquette to a 43-20 lead at intermission. A national wire service reporter who saw the halftime score reportedly did not believe it. But Marquette opened a lot of eyes with its 78-50 blowout, which improved its record to 7-8.

"I was hiding [during the game]," joked Lou Carnesecca, who was Lapchick's assistant and succeeded him the next season. "I think they [Marquette] were so charged up, we came in and got whacked. Joe was always nervous. You could see the tension. He was disappointed that we played so poorly."

"For the first time, fans saw what a good bench coach Al was," said Bledsoe. He described the upset as the "turning point" game that first season. "It took him a little while to learn the officials. By the middle of the second season, Al knew which ones he could work and those he couldn't.

"At the beginning, Al didn't know them [officials] and they didn't know him," explained Raymonds of the handicap that afflicts every rookie coach. "And he's a young coach and he's playing against established coaches. He had to get some kind of identity. And this is one of the reasons he did what he did when he started out. To get some identity, so that when he went up against a heavyweight, he would have a chance.

"Let's say a young coach goes up against a John Wooden. He doesn't have a chance. Especially if the teams are even. Your team has to be superior when you're first starting out. But as you go on, it starts to level off and the officials respect you. You see, officials are human beings, too. They know who's good. They know who's supposed to win. Not that they're gonna help you win. But they know who's supposed to win. See, when we first started out we weren't supposed to win. Who were we? So, we had to establish a reputation. During a game, Al would remind a ref, 'You missed one. Ah, you missed one there. OK, you gave us one there.'" During an especially tough night with the refs, McGuire turned to long-time team chaplain, Rev. Leonard Piotrowski, for help. "Father, they're (referees) killing me tonight!"

Officials worked in pairs back then, and since Marquette was an independent it was assigned Big 10 officials, according to Ed Maracich, who officiated more than 600 games between 1964 and 1988.

"Al started the assignment of referees when he went on the road. He requested his officials—Big 10. The next year when you come to my arena, you bring your referees," Maracich recalled McGuire telling opposing coaches.

"I heard that Al was very vocal, an exhibitionist," said Maracich, who as a guard for Loyola University played against McGuire when he was a senior at St. John's in 1951. "He tended to arouse situations on the court. The impression that I got was that he would try to bait the officials. Al was not a rules-conscious coach. Al was an active guy with the officials. He was trying to get his point across. I found him to be a fair type of guy. If he happened to lose, he would never hold a grudge. He set out to do a job that night and once it was over, it was over. In 14 or 15 years of officiating, I called one technical on him," said Maracich.

The euphoria of the momentous upset of St. John's quickly faded as the team lost road games to Brigham Young and the Air Force Academy. As it turned out, those two defeats were the beginning of McGuire's longest losing streak at Marquette: seven games. During the next 12 seasons no McGuire team would ever lose more than three in a row. After a loss at Colorado Springs, McGuire tried to boost the team's spirits. "Let's keep our heads up. We've been in worse boats than this. Get your heads up, c'mon."

The team headed back to Milwaukee for a game with another struggling independent, the Memphis State Tigers. The Warriors 11th loss of the season was marred by a bench-clearing fight with two minutes left. It started when scrambled egg Craig Leonard fouled Jamie McMahon.

Then the Tigers' John Hillman grabbed Leonard by the elbow and Hillman was hit in the face by another Marquette player. That cleared the benches and players began throwing lefts and rights. Leonard and Hillman were both ejected and Marquette was hit with three technicals. Said McGuire after the melee: "I'm numb. I don't know what to do, they were just a better club than we were tonight." McGuire praised the performance of the scrambled eggs, who scored over half of the team's points in the 82-70 loss.

Ray Meyer was not particularly impressed with the scrambled eggs when he brought his Blue Demons to the Arena for a return matchup. Marquette missed its first 15 shots in the 67-61 loss. "We had Marquette's offense well figured out in the first half," said Meyer, who was quoted in the *Marquette Tribune* as saying, "Marquette's scrambled-eggs unit played like chickens without heads."

But the veteran coach praised McGuire, saying, "Al has brought Marquette a long way since we played them in Chicago."

The losing streak finally took its toll on McGuire in St. Louis. The Warriors were scheduled to play Washington University, a game that Hickey had scheduled so he could spend some time at home with friends.

"Marquette lost 72-66 and Al got mad," recalled Bledsoe. "He walked all the way through Forest Park in St. Louis back to the hotel. I found Al in the hotel bar, and he never forgave Hickey for booking that game. That first year, you wondered whether Al was gonna get it done."

Next up for the Warriors were the Bradley Braves in Peoria. The NIT champs handed Marquette its sixth straight loss. It was also Marquette's eighth straight loss to Bradley. In fact, no Marquette team had beaten Bradley since Jack Nagle's 1954–55 squad.

Even though Marquette was playing poorly, the student newspaper continued to back the team in its editorials because the Warriors somehow seemed to bounce back after losses under McGuire. "But when a team has a losing record at this point in the season and still arouses fans to a fever pitch, it's unusual . . . This is a team that features instant excitement and built-in heroics," noted the *Marquette Tribune* on February 19, 1965.

In the team's next game against the Creighton Blue Jays, even the scrambled eggs could not prevent the Warriors from losing, 78-68. Uncharacteristically, McGuire refused to comment after the team's seventh straight loss.

Finally, it was the University of Wisconsin–Milwaukee that cured what ailed the Warriors. Marquette defeated the Cardinals (the team nickname then) 79-65, and had led at one point by 32 points. It was the 22nd straight time the Warriors had won the intracity game.

Marquette suffered its 16th loss at Xavier and its 17th at home to Detroit. McGuire was so frustrated that he left the scrambled eggs in to finish the Detroit game because the starters' press was ineffective. The Warriors finished the season against All-America Bill Melchionni and ninth-ranked Villanova on Senior Day.

The Warriors almost pulled off another upset of a highly ranked team. Down just 71-68 with five seconds left, the Warriors fell 73-69. McGuire apologized for not being able to get all of the seniors into the game. "I was trying to win the game in my own way," said the frustrated coach.

While McGuire's Warriors lost 10 of its last 11 en route to an 8-18 finish, Raymonds's "Little Warriors" freshman squad finished a respectable 11-3. The play of Pat Smith, Danny Nee, Brad Luchini, and Blanton Simmons was certainly a bright spot and held a great deal of promise for Warrior teams of the future.

"Beating Wisconsin twice in one season was a big coup for Al," said Flynn. "We lost to teams we shouldn't have lost to and beat teams we shouldn't have beat."

While the basketball team started to create excitement on campus, the ripple effects of racial disturbances in Selma, Alabama, were being felt all the way up in Milwaukee. In mid-March, some 700 faculty joined students in front of the Milwaukee Courthouse to protest the racial situation in Selma. CORE helped to lead racial consciousness-raising on campus. In that season's NCAA Finals, UCLA won its second straight title, by defeating Michigan 91-80.

After the protest, a group of students calling themselves Students United for Racial Equality (SURE) left for Selma to join other protest marchers around the country in support. At the time, it seemed there was an acronym for every cause. That spring of 1965, students' consciousness was also being raised by the steadily escalating war in Vietnam. And Motown's famous Revue even passed through Milwaukee at the same time its self-proclaimed "Sound of Young America" was vying with the British invasion for the hearts and minds of America's youth. "I remember meeting Stevie Wonder outside the Pfister Hotel," said Blanton Simmons.

Back on the basketball court, McGuire proudly told his first team at the first banquet that it was not any of the wins that gave him the feeling that he was getting through to them; it was one of the 18 losses the team experienced that first season of the McGuire era.

"When I saw the expressions of the players faces after we lost at Loyola, 83-71, I knew then that they felt as bad about losing as I did. That's when I knew that I had arrived."

Even the *Chicago Tribune* predicted better days ahead for the young coach. "In a year or two, he may begin proving what others in the profession already feel: that he's a genius for coaching."

Chapter Seven

Yellow Ribbons and Medals

In the wake of his 8-18 debut as head coach, McGuire was not about to push the panic button, even though the team won just a single road game. He was determined to stay the course by getting improved play from his returning class of players, continuing to play a top-flight schedule, and recruiting better ballplayers.

While it was the emergence of his scrambled eggs that kept the Warriors in a number of the games and garnered attention for the program, McGuire and everyone else knew that Marquette could not build a foundation on a gimmick.

"The scrambled-eggs unit is a sharp group of hustlers, but in the long run you can't depend on second stringers to win ball games," noted the *Marquette Tribune.* "Even though the team gave 100 percent, the fact remains that they are only mediocre players."

During that summer of 1965, Marquette opted not to join the proposed National Collegiate Conference, which was backed by DePaul coach Ray Meyer. The NCC would have included independents such as Memphis State, Oklahoma City, and such traditional Catholic opponents as Xavier, Dayton, Canisius, and Loyola of New Orleans. It was the fourth time Marquette had rejected such an idea, mainly due to travel costs.

In the wake of the assassination of Malcolm X earlier in the year, racial problems continued to emerge in Milwaukee and around the country. Another acronym appeared: MUSIC—Milwaukee United School Integration Committee. Problems continued to simmer just below the surface of inner-city America.

In order for the second-year coach to earn his "yellow ribbons and medals"—a term he borrowed from his track days at St. John's, which translates to success in recruiting—he had to get better talent. That was especially true since his contract was up at the end of the 1965–66 season. While nobody expected a miracle at Marquette, the administration did not want a repeat of the previous two seasons, which resulted in a combined 13-39 record. And going back to his final two years at Belmont Abbey, McGuire had had three straight losing seasons.

"Al always coached out of fear," recalled Raymonds. "Down deep, he's a worrywart. When his back's to the wall, look out! That's when he's at his best, not when things are going smoothly."

In order to compete with the deans of college coaching in Chicago—George Ireland and Ray Meyer—McGuire began to reach out to high school coaches in the area not only for networking purposes but for recruiting. McGuire also asked respected coaches from around the country to be guest speakers at his team banquet after each season.

To get his foot in the door with Chicago Catholic high schools, McGuire decided to go after the league's Most Valuable Player, Dan Quinn of Loyola Academy.

"Notre Dame wanted him, too," recalled Gene Sullivan, Quinn's basketball coach at Loyola, located in Wilmette, a suburb north of Chicago. "So Al comes in the door. He comes in with a nice, full-collar coat. Al's a handsome guy. He says to me, 'Gene, can you get the boy, Danny Quinn?' So I get him in my office.

"He's a quiet, shy kid. Al stands over him. 'Dan, I'm Al McGuire. I'm the new coach at Marquette University.' He's all over the kid," Sullivan laughs. "All of a sudden, McGuire tells him: 'Dan, we're gonna win if you come to Marquette and we're gonna win if you don't come to Marquette. You see, Danny, I'd like you to consider Marquette.' Later, I told Al that the kid really wanted to go to Notre Dame.

"Then Al says, 'Do you mind if I make a phone call?' Then he calls Johnny Dee, the head coach at Notre Dame. 'Dee, this is Al McGuire. I'm here at Loyola Academy. Are you serious about recruiting Danny Quinn?' After Al hung up the phone, he says: 'I just got your kid a scholarship to Notre Dame.'

"Al wanted to get out of the office for a drink in the middle of the day. So I brought him to Meier's Tavern for Silver Bullets [martinis]. Then

Al proceeds to tell me what was needed for success in Division One coaching and what he's going to do at Marquette.

"'You don't need any Xs and Os,' Al said to me. 'Recruiting, officiating, and scheduling are the three most important elements in coaching.' And then he tells me about this kid in New York he's recruiting, George Thompson. 'If I get him, we're bound to win a game or two more. Then, next year is my contract year.'

"Back in the mid-1960s, nobody had anything going as far as college basketball was concerned in Chicago," according to Sullivan, who sent Craig Leonard to Marquette from Loyola Academy. Marquette had a good rivalry with the other Catholic independents, Loyola and DePaul. It also had a pretty good one with Notre Dame, but the Fighting Irish stopped playing Marquette after the 1958–59 season.

"But Loyola University was *the* basketball team back then. Expectations were high for another [NCAA] championship in Chicago."

Johnny Dee had succeeded Johnny Jordan, and Ray Meyer had been a fixture at DePaul for a generation. Meyer, Jordan, and Ireland all played together at Notre Dame in the mid-1930s. "The established coaches in the Midwest didn't take him seriously at first," recalled Chicago sportwriting legend Bill Gleason. "They said, 'What does he know about coaching anyway?' But Al was very respectful of the other coaches. He revered Johnny Jordan when Jordan was at Notre Dame," stated Gleason.

"Jordan, Meyer, and Ireland were coaching all at the same time." said Sullivan. Harry Combes was at Illinois, Branch McCracken was at Indiana, Fred Taylor was at Ohio State, John Kundla was at Minnesota, Arad McCutchan at Evansville. Ray had had good teams at DePaul. Ray recruited Chicago. But not much outside of Chicago. Al just wanted to get one or two players a year.

"But midwestern basketball was still a plodding big man's game," explained Sullivan, who went on to become Dee's assistant at Notre Dame in 1967. "When you don't have [the] talent, you reach out for the gimmick defenses, which McGuire fell back on during his first year at Marquette."

"Al had a sarcastic feeling toward midwestern guys," said Flynn. "He would put them down. If you were stronger, but not as quick, he'd let you know about it.

"In the Midwest, we had Big 10 officials. There was more physical play in the Midwest. There was more body contact. Out east, nobody touched each other. They were much quicker to call fouls on incidental contact. 'I want thinner and quicker,' McGuire used to tell us. He liked thinner, faster, quicker guards, guys who could win on pizza and Pepsi, he liked to say.

Tom Brennan sent him one such player, but Al was not sure what he was getting when he met him.

"When Al and I went to the airport to pick up Jim Burke," recalled SID Jim Foley, "we saw a freckle-faced kid come off the plane. Al said to me, 'Oh, oh—Tommy Brennan sent me a relative.'"

"Some of those type of players included Burke, a whippet of a player, who had transferred from Wharton [Texas] Junior College but was from New York. He'd try to steal the ball and his momentum would carry him to the sidelines. He shot a two-handed set shot. McGuire liked the Smith brothers [Pat and Gene], New York kind of players," said Flynn.

Many of the players who were already at Marquette when McGuire arrived were physically tough, but they lacked the mental toughness that characterized players from the Big Apple.

The city game that McGuire grew up with in New York in the early '40s had evolved into more of a one-on-one game a generation later. As the late Pete Axthelm wrote in *The City Game*, "Each ethnic group and each generation of street ballplayers produced its special styles and legends, and each left its colorful brand on the sport. But more than that, each built a distinctive kind of pride—partly ethnic or racial, partly athletic, but much more than the sum of these parts. Veterans of playground ball describe it in terms of individuality, status, manhood. . . ."

"Up at Harlem, there was a lot of one-on-one, flash," explained Pat Smith, whose signing with Marquette opened up New York for McGuire. "But the basics were still there. The exclamation point was the dunk and no-look pass," said Smith, in describing the evolution of New York City hoops from a game of fundamentals to a game played above the rim.

This was the game that Smith knew. As a youngster, he grew up watching the famous Rucker Tournament at the Seventh Avenue park at 130th Street. As a second-team All-City player at Benjamin Franklin High School in Harlem, Smith and his brothers spent quite a bit of time on the playgrounds and in tournaments, not only in Harlem but in the Bronx, Queens, Manhattan, wherever there was a game in New York. "Everybody just gravitated to one park in the summer. You might be a senior in college or a freshman, and you played all day until you got tired.

"I would play ball seven days a week in the Bronx, Manhattan, Brooklyn. We played in Rockaway Beach all the time. As a freshman in high school, McGuire's Playground was one of the places we played at, usually on weekends, pickup games. It would take me one and a half to two hours on the subway. People came from all over the city. You knew that this was where the ballplayers were gonna be on certain weekends. It was a word-of-mouth type thing," remembered Smith, who played against Lew Alcindor and Charlie Scott, among others.

"There were some good point guards like Pablo Robertson, who was a mini-Magic. Wilt [Chamberlain] and Connie [Hawkins] would go against each other at Rucker in the Summer Leagues. I went to school with 'the Goat' [the late Earl Manigault]. We were on the same team together at Benjamin Franklin. He was a senior, I was a junior. It was interesting playing with the Goat. At Franklin, only the seniors played. The other seniors on that team were Willie Mangham and Larry Newbo," said Smith.

"I had heard of the legend [of the Goat], but he was another basketball player," said Meminger, a 6-foot lightning-quick guard. "Willie Mangham said that Earl would show you something different every time he played. He was an entertainer. The free-lance game of basketball was played by the guys who needed to have the ball in the playgrounds. But at the college and pro levels, the game is more structured. A lot of one-on-one players can't play in a system. They have to play with the ball. It's their ball. It's their show. That's the difference between playing in a park and playing on a team."

"I always watched Connie Hawkins, but I never played against him." said Smith. "Alcindor was younger than me. I was a year or two older then he was. It was fun playing against him, but I never checked him. Aubrey Matthews was a phenomenal leaper, but physical. He was built like a natural 6'6" power forward.

"I played against a lot of them [future Marquette stars from New York]. Ric [Ulric] Cobb lived 10 blocks from me. He played on a rec center team, Millbank in Harlem. I played against him in high school. He went to Hughes [now Brandeis] High School with Pee Wee Kirkland. Dean [Meminger] was younger than I was. I was a senior [at Marquette] when Dean came in, but we played against him in the summer when I came back to New York.

"I knew nothing about Midwest basketball at all [when I came to Marquette]," Smith continued. "But I was a New York player. It didn't matter to me where I played. In New York, everybody is so damn good, that if you think for one second that guy is better than you, you can forget it.

"When I was playing in New York you played against the pros. You learned how to play inside. If I can rebound in New York, I can play in about every game. I could jump," said Smith as he explained how he survived as a 6'3" center.

"When I got to Milwaukee, it was no big deal. It was kinda tame after you leave New York City. The intensity level was a lot lower in Milwaukee. They didn't seem to take the game as seriously. They [Midwest players] were slow. I was used to playing against people bigger than I was. My philosophy was to box 'em out and get the rebound."

"Pat Smith was the best athlete I'd ever seen," declared Simmons. "He was six-foot-three-and-a-half, and he was a center. He was the greatest physical specimen I'd ever seen. He was also the first player I ever saw with a natural."

"When McGuire came to Marquette, his personality was right out of New York," remembered Flynn. "To kids from the Midwest, he was foreign to them. He had a way of seeing through 30 miles of b.s. right to the kernel. I had never met anybody like him. He was cocksure about everything. I never experienced anybody quite like that before. In New York, that's the way people think. Impatient. That kind of thinking."

After the door into New York opened a crack, McGuire went after his first blue chipper, George Thompson. A star at Erasmus Hall High School in Brooklyn, Thompson was named to the All–New York City team with Lew Alcindor in 1965. Thompson averaged 23.5 points and 15 rebounds a game for a 22-0 team that won the city championship. He was considered the second-best player in the city after Alcindor. His high school coach, Bernie Kirsner, compared him favorably with one of his former stars, Billy Cunningham.

"During the summer I played against George Thompson," recalled Smith. "We would meet in tournaments. I played against him in some tournament in Brooklyn. I knew of him as a player. He was an inside man. That was his reputation." Not bad for a 6'2" guard/forward. McGuire firmly believed that basketball games are won three feet from the basket, and that Thompson was the perfect type of player to complement his back-to-the-basket 6'3" center, Smith.

"I played against George Thompson when I was a sophomore in high school and George was a senior at Erasmus High, back in 1964–65," recalled Meminger. "And I also played against Ric Cobb, who was also from Harlem, as was George 'Sugar' Frazier."

"What Al would do if he had somebody in mind is, he would ask me, 'What do you know about him?'" Smith continued. "Basketball-wise, Al knew. His questions were about the individual. He was interested in them as people and also whether they would fit into the Marquette program. He looked for heart more than for anything else. What are you gonna be like when the game is on the line?" asked Smith, whose brothers Gene and Billy committed to Marquette and Loyola, respectively, in 1965.

McGuire's recruiting strategy included not only blue-chip prospects, but junior college transfers and complementary players. "Tailenders are usually walk-ons or complementary players," he said. "I take one JC every second year. One blue-chip championship freshman. I take one or two transfers every year and a complementary player. We get the whole gosh-darned thing done for $1,500 without going out and spending $15,000 to $30,000. No one's gettin' ulcers or waitin' by the phone or gettin' gray hairs or burpin'."

McGuire's visit to the Thompson household in Brooklyn was memorable. "I remember a mouse running across the floor, back and forth in Thompson's apartment," he recalled. "And George's father, who had served in the Merchant Marines, was watching the television. I got up and turned the knobs. I said to him, 'Hey, I just traveled 1,100 miles to see you, I don't want to catch you just during commercial breaks.'"

Thompson remembers the visit differently. "First of all, there was no mouse. That's just Al embellishing a New York story. He was talking to my father and the TV was on. Al said, 'Well, can we cut the TV off? I want to talk to you about your son's future.' My father turned off the set and said, 'Wherever he goes, I'm behind him 100 percent. Don't try to sell me on it.' My father got up, offered Al a cup of tea. He then said to Al, 'You don't have to go through all that. He will get a college education wherever he wants to go.'

"I didn't want to take a lot of recruiting trips," Thompson continued. "I was fairly certain that I didn't want to stay on the East Coast. I didn't think I wanted to go out to the West Coast. But I didn't want to go to a place I considered a factory," commented Thompson, who is now vice president of corporate communication at Milwaukee's Briggs and Stratton.

Thompson signed a letter of intent to play at Marquette in May of 1965. "We regard him as the number two player behind Alcindor in the New York area," commented McGuire in the *Marquette Tribune* after the signing. "And we are sure he has the ability to be a top-notch collegiate performer."

"George Thompson was a freshman when I started as SID," recalled Jim Foley, who was Bob Harlan's handpicked successor for the job. "Al gave him the nickname 'Brute Force.' George was only 6'2" and I can remember one game when he went up for a rebound where his armpit was equal with the rim," marveled Foley, now a radio analyst for the Houston Rockets. "I gave Thompson the nickname 'Brute Force,'" insisted Timeberg. "You looked at his legs, he looked like a football player."

McGuire was never really big on names or details at Marquette. Foley remembered his first experience with the coach.

"The first day I met Al, I drove up in my nice white convertible. A friend had loaned me a $100 bill. That was all the money I had. Al said, 'I have to give a talk somewhere, but I need to go the dry cleaners to pick up a shirt.'

"So, we drive to the dry cleaners and Al says, 'I don't have any money to pay for the shirt. Do you have any money?' I said, 'All I have is a $100 bill.' He said, 'That'll do,' and I gave him the $100 bill. When he came back to the car, he said, 'We'll get along fine,'" Foley said, chuckling at the memory.

"When we worked together, Al was terrible with names," Foley continued. "If we came across someone he knew at one time but whose name he didn't remember, he would say, 'Hey, pallie, you know Jim Foley here.' And that would be my cue to ask the guy his name and then Al would take over the conversation, pretending like he knew the guy's name all along."

McGuire was also a creative accountant during his first two years in Milwaukee.

"The school accountant said to Al after the team returned from its first road trip, 'I don't have your first expense account.' So Al writes down on a piece of paper: 'Left Milwaukee with $300, came back with $140. Marquette owes me $160.' But the accountant said that Al had to refine his expense reports," explained Foley. After that, McGuire did a much better job of itemizing his expenses.

If the devil was in the details, McGuire preferred to have someone else deal with the devil. And that person usually was his assistant Hank Raymonds.

In addition to coaching the freshmen, Raymonds served as academic advisor and traveling secretary. He also was charged with selecting the team managers and mascot, Willie Wompum, a politically incorrect caricature of an Indian.

The nickname Warrior was selected by the university in 1954 because the previous choices—Hilltoppers and Golden Avalanche—were deemed inappropriate. Warriors was chosen because the first inhabitants in the U.S. were Indians. It also honored the memory of Father Jacques Marquette who came in direct contact with American Indian tribes during his explorations with Louis Joliet. The Warrior symbolized respect, spirit, and dignity.

The university had a new president that fall as the Reverend John P. Raynor succeeded the Reverend William Kelley. Marquette's enrollment was swelled by a flood of freshmen applications. There were now 11,914 students at the school compared with 10,828 the year before. But even with the continued increasing enrollment at the time, Marquette was not in great shape financially, what with the $500,000 debt inherited from the football program and the expense of running a medical school, according to Dave Foran, director of the university news bureau.

"In the mid-1960s, Marquette had serious financial problems. The Marquette Medical School was sucking the life out of the place. The toughest decision in the late 1960s was [whether] to close the medical school down," said Foran.

At that time, many on campus still opposed the Vietnam War. Yet 250 students sent a telegram of support to General William Westmoreland to show support for the U.S. troops.

During the course of his coaching career at Belmont and at Marquette, McGuire treated the good fathers with respect and deference. And, according to Foran, he especially held Father Raynor in high regard.

"Al said that he had never met anyone like Father Raynor, who could run a large institution and still be a priest," recalled Foran. "To McGuire's mind, the two were incompatible. 'I never forgot when I spoke with him that he was a priest,' Al said. He [Raynor] was a tough man as an administrator. But once he made up his mind, he stuck to it, and I think Al respected that," remarked Foran.

"In my era, that respect was automatic," said McGuire. "Respect for the clergy, respect for doctors. I always thought that a clergy's life was a lonely life. So every time that you could bring a smile to a priest's face it would increase your odds of breaking through upstairs. With Father Raynor, there was never any doubt that he was a priest."

Even though McGuire was boss, he delegated authority to people in whom he had confidence. Raymonds was a solid administrator and had a great basketball mind, according to former players and coaches. As a result, McGuire let Raymonds handle the Xs and Os and organize the practices. "I understood my position," said Raymonds. "He allowed me a lot of freedom. He trusted me. At least I thought he did."

"Al gave Hank a lot of credit," recalled Wolf. "Hank studied the game, he knew the game. [But] Hank was too serious. 'Take it easy, Hank,' Al would say."

Hank brought the players up for a retreat before the season. The guys brought up a couple of cases of beer and wound up skipping the retreat.

"'You guys, go home,' Hank yelled. 'You guys are gonna pay for this.' Al gets us in a big group the next day and then says, 'I should have known better,' and then we had a normal practice," recalled Wolf.

"Hank Raymonds was a nice man," said Simmons. "He would introduce me to former players [like Don Kojis], saying that *this* is the guy who is going to break all of your records. He wanted to help me improve. Whatever he would do, I would do. I felt that he had my best interests at heart. I was positive, happy. Hank's ego never exceeded that of the players. He knew the Xs and Os."

McGuire told the Tip-Off Club before the '65–66 season that he expected the team to finish with a .500 record because he considered the schedule soft. And, with a little luck, he said the Warriors might go to a postseason tournament.

After the varsity crushed the freshmen in the annual intrasquad game, 91-66, the Warriors played inconsistently throughout the year. They would win one, then lose one; win one, lose two; win four, lose three. It was that kind of year. Once again, they would play well against great teams and lose to poor teams.

It started out positively enough at the Arena, where the Warriors defeated Gene Bartow's Valparaiso Crusaders 80-79.

The team's second game of the season was against visiting DePaul on Tip-Off Weekend. To help promote the game, a basketball was dribbled from Chicago to Milwaukee and into the Milwaukee Arena, where Tom Flynn sank what was called the "Marathon Ball" before the game.

Entertainers Stan Getz and Jackie Vernon performed that weekend on campus, and Marquette lost to DePaul, 82-69.

The Warriors bounced back to beat North Dakota State and then lost at Davidson, where Lefty Driesell was still prowling the sidelines.

At Louisville, Flynn held the best sophomore center in the country—6'8" Wes Unseld—to 10 points, but Marquette still lost to the Cardinals 70-61.

Marquette started its longest winning streak of the season when it won the Milwaukee Classic for the first time, dispatching Bucky Waters's West Virginia Mountaineers 100-87 and edging the University of Washington 75-74 on a Tom Flynn buzzer-beater.

After beating the number seven team in the country, Wichita State, 95-76, McGuire returned to the site of one of his most famous games as a college coach: Evansville University. The Warriors won their first road game of the Evansville Tournament, defeating Yale in the opener, 74-68.

"They [Evansville] had a good team," recalled Wolf. "They didn't lose a lot at home. They were one of the top teams in the country. We lost by a half-court shot, 88-86." This time, however, McGuire did not promise to set up the house with ice cream.

Marquette continued its inconsistent pattern, with home losses to Wisconsin (73-72) and Loyola (87-65). Then the Warriors somehow came up with their second road win of the season, an 81-74 decision over Detroit, which had played in the NIT the previous season.

In the Wisconsin game, Badger coach John Erickson insisted on inspecting the game ball. Not to be outdone, McGuire then wanted to look at the ball. Erickson wanted to see the ball again. Ending this back-and-forth, the referee took the ball from the big kids and started the game.

The next game at Loyola was part of a doubleheader at Chicago Stadium, a Stadium tradition for 27 years. In order to drum up some interest for the upcoming game with the Ramblers, McGuire denied a published report that he had predicted a Marquette win because, as the story went, his team was better than Loyola. He did tell reporters that Marquette would key on Billy Smith, the Ramblers' leading scorer and brother of Pat Smith.

"That year, the 'seatbelt' rule was instituted," explained Gene Sullivan. "A coach could leave the bench only to make a substitution, call a time-out, or get a glass of water. You'd think it [Loyola game] was the NCAA tournament. Al's coat came off, the tie comes off, he's really emotional, and every time the ref would go by Marquette's bench, McGuire would be off the bench, and then he reached for the water bottle.

"Marquette was ahead by one with 12 seconds left. Loyola throws in the ball, and the clock hasn't started moving. They throw up a shot and it was tipped in by Corky Bell, and they won 85-84.

"When I see him after the game, I'm thinking that he will be uptight. But there he is. His tie is on, his hair is slicked back. I said, 'Gee, I'm sorry that you lost. It was a tough way to lose.' Al replied, 'Gene, a little controversy in the papers tomorrow. It's good for the program. You gotta look at the big picture.'" The game became known as the Long Count game.

Before games Al would record his radio show with Tom Collins in the visiting team's locker room. When the Warriors visited Alumni Hall to play DePaul toward the end of the season, Collins also interviewed Ray Meyer to get his comments on the upcoming contest.

"After I was through with Ray, a manager or trainer for DePaul thought that I was going to play back for Al what Ray had just said. When Meyer heard about it, he came into the men's room adjoining the Marquette locker room where Al and I were taping our segment and began flushing all of the urinals so that the tape would be bad. Ray flushed all of the urinals, walked out of the john, and we continued on with the show," laughed Collins. McGuire lost for the fourth straight time to Meyer, but the rivalry between the two schools was becoming more competitive and entertaining.

One of the biggest wins of the year came against Northern Michigan, which was one of the highest scoring teams in the country. Coach Stan Albeck came to the Arena with former Warrior Con Yagodzinski. Blanton Simmons scored a career high 30 points to lead the Warriors in the 105-94 win.

Simmons was reportedly the best pure shooter on the team, but before the season McGuire described him as "hot and cold and a great crowd pleaser. But he has a great shot and when he gets going, no one on the team is better."

The next day in the newspapers, McGuire described the sophomore's prolific performance as "lucky," according to a frustrated Simmons. "And he told me that I wasn't that good. He used to tell me that my game was like Sweetwater Clifton's. 'Don't do that, I just want straight vanilla.' He looked at me and said, 'I like Jimmy Burke better, and that's why he's startin' and you're not.'"

"Blanton was not a physical player," McGuire recalled. "He was soft. In those days I was trying to build Marquette University to a media level. I was very flippant in my early days at Marquette with all of my statements."

In all of the pictures of McGuire in the press guides, game programs, and team shots from his first three years, he looks young enough to be one of the players. "I remember when I first met him," said Collins. "He was a very young-looking man. He looked like a college student himself."

And while he was always pictured wearing a whistle, he never blew it. According to players and assistant coaches, McGuire would usually yell to get his point across. The whistle was for showin', not for blowin'. And one of the ways that he motivated his players was by getting inside their heads, as Flynn and Wolf both recalled.

"There was never a loss that I didn't feel bad about," declared Flynn. "But he tried to hit nerves. He told me that he thought I'd been fixing games. Compliments were not frequent. Then after he'd read you the riot act, he would say, 'I wouldn't yell at ya, if I didn't like ya.'

"Al was a motivator. He knew how to get the most out of our abilities. We used to get into it quite often. We were playing Air Force at the Arena. Al was yelling at me. I said, 'Go to hell, Al!' 'Well, it's about time that you get excited and play a little harder,' Al answered. He liked the confrontations."

"He would scream and yell at them and get on them, but five minutes later he would be patting them on the back," explained Raymonds. "He let the players know who was boss. He had to get certain things out of them. But Al was smart enough to not let the players leave the floor mad."

During one practice, while McGuire was holding court with the local media, Raymonds was working on a play with the team during a scrimmage. In the middle, McGuire interrupted Raymonds. "No, Hank, I want it run on the other side of the court." After Raymonds ran it McGuire's way, McGuire said in an aside to the assembled reporters, "I know Hank is right. I just have to remind him every once in a while who's coach."

McGuire's explanation for his aggressively verbal coaching style, which was chock full of what he called tugboat language, was that he was basically just trying to help the players reach their full potential.

"They prefer being a boy," said the coach. "I'm trying to make a person take one step deeper. These things are done in my world with verbal violence. It is my way of trying to get out what God has put in them. They think they did it. It has to come out. It's a mortal sin if it doesn't."

"When we went to practice, at certain times, if you could get him talkin', one hour would be gone out of a two-hour practice," said Pat Smith. "That's when he would go into his little lecture. I liked to listen to him. He was talkin' New York stories. I learned a lot. But you didn't want to hear him at halftime.

"It would depend on how you were playin'. If you didn't put in the effort, he'd go ballistic. That's when you tried to get a seat in the furthest part of the locker room."

"Al used to tell stories about growing up," recalled Wolf. "How they should relate to our life. One time, one of the players was having a problem with his girlfriend. Al gets us in a circle during practice, and he tells us that if we put all of the world's problems in a huge blanket that ours would not even compare to what other people are going through. And he was right."

As the regular season wound down, the Warriors found themselves at St. John's Alumni Hall in New York. The Redmen were waiting to avenge the previous year's 78-50 blowout in Milwaukee. While St. John's won the game 70-68 in Lou Carnesecca's first year as head coach, it was the only time that Little Louie would defeat McGuire in their four career meetings.

"I remember Al letting Jimmy Breslin sit on the Marquette bench," said Terry Bledsoe. "After the game, we went to Pep McGuire's, which was co-owned by Al's brother Johnny and Norton Peppis.

"There were two ladies sitting in front of the cash registers behind the bar, but facing each other. I asked, 'Who are they?' Johnny said, 'That's my aunt and that's Pepe's aunt. If one steals off the other, we're even.' "

"If you went into Pep McGuire's with a $5, $10, or $20 bill you never came out with any change," recalled Jerry Savio. "They [Johnny and Norton] couldn't get the money out of the register fast enough to go to the track. It was a race to see who could get to the cash register first at the end of the day. Norton Peppis used to date Connie Francis at one time.

When they broke up Pepe explained that she was startin' to use his name, so of course he had to break it off," Savio laughed at the recollection.

Pep McGuire's was a large, loud nightclub that was considered the biggest gold mine in Queens. These were still the days of mohair suits and houndstooth coats. Peppis, who was the administrator of the establishment, referred to himself as the genius and called Johnny, who was the people person, the enemy because he was always hoping for that one big score at Aqueduct. After ten years as a New York City patrolman and setting the record for sick days taken, he joined with Peppis to open Pep McGuire's. Al made it a point during the basketball seasons to keep his distance from John, according to family friends.

After winning their third road game, the Warriors finished the season with an 87-78 home win over the Detroit Titans.

"They [Detroit] had Jim Hiatt, Jim Boyce, and Dorie Murrey," recalled Simmons. "We had beaten them in Detroit, but McGuire credited me with orchestrating the defense that night. Jim Boyce was begging me to let them go to New York for the NIT. But I was never going to lay down for anyone."

Marquette finished 14-12 overall, and just ten points separated the team from four more wins. Marquette drew an all-time record of 106,955 fans to the Arena, averaging 7,130 at home and more than 5,600 on the road.

"When Al came in," recalled Terry Bledsoe, "no one knew what he had. Even in the second year, it wasn't a breakthrough season at 14-12, but it wasn't a disaster. Al and Hickey were at opposite ends of a spectrum. Al could offer good copy even if he lost. Hickey couldn't. Al is an original. I covered Lombardi on Sundays and had Al during the week. No one was the same kind of person Al was, and is."

"He became more of a magnet for the fans," said Flynn. "He enjoyed the combat. He loved a snake pit that was full. He got life from the fans. That was his milieu, also. When he heard the roar of the crowd. When the seats were filled, that's when he wanted to be there. He seemed to be preoccupied with filling the seats. He was constantly talking about looking in the top rows and seeing the seats filled."

"But to just go out and give a Pepsodent smile, it's just not my world. I cannot turn on without feeling something, " McGuire insisted. "Ya gotta feel it and if you feel it, it has been in my life that other people feel it.

I must feel something to turn on. You can't walk in and say now I'm gonna give a Rockne talk and punch lockers and kick chairs."

While the Warriors ended the season on a high note, the freshmen squad, a.k.a. Young Warriors, finished 13-4 behind George Thompson, who was quickly living up to his potential by averaging 23.7 points a game.

During the 1966 NCAA tournament, the game that literally changed the face of college basketball took place between Don Haskins's all-black Texas Western University Miners and Adolph Rupp's all-white University of Kentucky Wildcats. The Miners beat "Rupp's Runts," 72-65, which included Pat Riley. That game helped break down the white picket fence of bigotry in college basketball throughout the country, and was also the last NCAA finals appearance by Rupp.

After McGuire's second season, the *Marquette Tribune* weighed in with its view of the coach's future. "We can visualize only increased success for coach Al McGuire and the Warriors. McGuire's ingenuity, savvy, emotion, and his natural ability to attract quality ballplayers coupled with Hank Raymonds's vast basketball knowledge can only mean greater things in the years ahead."

Chapter Eight

Showtime

McGuire did not waste any time capitalizing on his moderately successful second season at Marquette. There were players to recruit and his contract was up for renewal. Among fans, expectations were high as the Warriors were about to begin their 50th anniversary season.

McGuire set up his first basketball camp in Waukesha, Wisconsin, in 1965, when Wisconsin high schools first allowed athletes to attend these kinds of summer camps. "Al had befriended a coach at Eau Claire, and Al worked for him," recalled Hank Raymonds. "But Al did not want a set fee; he wanted so much money per camper. And at [coaches] clinics, Al wanted to be paid per head. Then he later went to Delafield, Wisconsin, at St. John's Military Academy." Medalist Industries bought the camps from McGuire in 1967.

What started out as seven-day overnight camps for kids at $100 a head turned into a longtime business relationship between Medalist and McGuire spawning coaches clinics, sports books, and uniform making. Medalist later produced colorfully designed uniforms for Marquette each season.

Even though McGuire had never conducted a coaches clinic before, he stepped in boldly. A lack of experience seldom kept him from trying anything new.

"I received a call from McGuire two months after we first met," recalled Sullivan. "Al says, 'I'm terrified. What do I do? I gotta speak at a basketball clinic.' So I go with him down to Joliet Central High School, and all the way down in the car he keeps saying, 'I don't know what you do at a clinic!'"

"At the clinic, it was a big crowd," Sullivan continued. "The coaches are all Xs and Os. Al starts off the top of his head. He just tells stories related to basketball. 'I have to do things unorthodox. We play four on five, with one eye on offense,' said Al. He was forever trying to get a union for coaches. He's got a way of making you feel he's one of your closest friends," Sullivan continued. "He just can get through to people one-on-one.

"Craig Leonard, one of my high school players at Loyola, who played three years under Hickey and one under McGuire, said to me, 'With Hickey, everything was planned. With Al, after practice he would say to us, 'See you guys at the game.' And Al was gone," recalled Sullivan.

The new coach received commitments from Jeff Sewell, a 6'3" guard from Grafton High School, the top scorer in the state of Wisconsin, and Ron Rahn, a 6'5" forward from South Division High School in Milwaukee, considered the top forward prospect to come out of the City League in the previous five years. "Al always recruited a little white guard in Wisconsin to please the alumni out there," observed Chicago sportswriter Bill Gleason.

After the recruiting season, McGuire and Raymonds were rewarded for their efforts with three-year contract extensions, which were the longest ever for basketball coaches at Marquette, according to athletic director Stan Lowe.

Armed with a new contract which reportedly paid him in the neighborhood of $25,000 a year, McGuire felt relieved and confident and was ready to hit the road again, this time to try to recruit his first High School All-America player. He worked hard to get a 6'11" center named Bob Lienhard, out of Rice High School in New York.

When the youngster came to Milwaukee, McGuire was pictured in the papers escorting him around campus. Signs around school welcoming the big kid read, Welcome Bob Lienhard, High School All-American. It was unusual because McGuire hated to chase after players. But this was different, this was the first time he went after a high school All-American. Unfortunately, Lienhard eventually went to Georgia.

"The first time that I saw him speak was at St. Monica's parish in Milwaukee. There was a sports night there in April of 1966," recalled Dave Foran. "He was the main speaker and said that Lew Alcindor was the best player he had ever seen, and that he was trying to recruit him.

'If we had him here, we wouldn't lose a game.'" Alas, Alcindor went to UCLA to play for John Wooden.

While McGuire lost both Lienhard and Alcindor, he was able to get Braves' baseball star Eddie Mathews to help recruit a 6'5" forward out of Canton, Georgia, named Joe Thomas, whose parents worked in a textile mill. Thomas could both score and leap, according to Hank Raymonds, who was sent down to Canton to sign the player. As with a number of other recruits, however, McGuire never told Thomas's parents that Raymonds was coming down for a visit.

Thomas had transferred to Marist High School, a military academy where the son of Milwaukee Braves President John McHale was a student. "John (Jr.) asked me if I wanted to go to a Braves game at Fulton County Stadium, where the team had moved from Milwaukee.

"After the game we go into the locker room and I meet Hank Aaron, Del Crandall and Eddie Mathews. At the time I didn't know where I was going to go to college, and then Mr. Aaron and Eddie Mathews started talking about Marquette, this Jesuit school in Milwaukee. I was the second oldest of nine. I would be the first in my family to get a college degree. I was interested in academics from the start even though I wanted to play baseball and basketball. Both Eddie and Hank told me that at Marquette they really take care of their kids.

"Al told me, 'We're going to the NCAA tournament. We're gonna play on national TV. Either you can be a part of it or you can watch us win on television.' It was the confidence with which he presented that vision that convinced me to come to Marquette."

McGuire was confident as he prepared to address the Tip-Off Club before the season. He pointed out that the Warriors' days of sneaking up on people were over. This season Marquette would play its toughest schedule, with ten games against eight teams that played in either the NIT or NCAA tournaments the season before, including NIT champion BYU, runner-up NYU, and third-place finisher Villanova. The Warriors road schedule included stops at Madison Square Garden, the Palestra in Philadelphia, and Chicago Stadium.

"The goal that McGuire had set for his 1966-67 squad was getting to the tournament that season," said Flynn. "That was the start of the real McGuire era at Marquette. His players—George Thompson and others. It was pretty exciting back then."

"Marquette had a winning tradition before Al got there," noted Thompson. "They had good basketball before Al got there, but Al took it to the next level."

Even though McGuire was bringing in the most impressive talent the university had seen in years, he did not forget those players who had been loyal to him when he first came to Marquette.

One of those was Paul Carbins, whose eligibility would expire during the season. "Before Al rose to speak at the Tip-Off luncheon," recalled freshman team manager Goran Raspudic, "he told me, 'Don't let anyone out that door until we get enough money from the club members to pay Paul Carbins's tuition for his last semester at Roosevelt University so that he can earn his degree. He has too much going for him to be driving a CTA bus in Chicago.'"

McGuire's star captain Flynn was also on the receiving end of his coach's assistance. After winning the Chandler Memorial Trophy as the team's most valuable player for a record third straight year, and the McCahill Award as most outstanding student/athlete, Flynn was drafted by the Los Angeles Rams. Flynn did not make the cut as a pro football player, but he had planned to go back to school for an advanced degree.

"Al kept me on as an assistant from 1966 to 1969, and they [Marquette] paid for my law school," said Flynn, who was graduated from Marquette Law School in 1969. "He helped people and he didn't take bows."

Added Wolf: "My father died before that season. I didn't practice a lot after I came back. Al was real sensitive. He told me to take as much time off as I needed. 'Do what you think you have to do,'" he said. "He was my counselor. I think he always knew what was going on. It always sounded like he was in control, even though it seemed he was flaky. Either you liked him or you didn't like him. There was no in between."

McGuire's popularity as a speaker had grown quite a bit in his two years at Marquette. He was at the top of the list of speakers for many of the organizations on campus, in the city, and throughout the state of Wisconsin. During the 1965–66 season, McGuire delivered some 150 speeches. "I talked to the Elks, the Eagles, the Lions, the Tigers, the Leopards, everybody," he said. "You must do it [free speeches] once you get the job, "McGuire continued. "You do the whole menagerie on the arm, but never free again."

"Not long after I got to know Al, he became involved in speaking engagements," recalled Raymonds. "The first I remember was at a high school reunion in Wausau, Wisconsin, for $50. He scratched a few things on a napkin. I drove him. He wouldn't even give me gas money. It was way the hell up there. We drove forever. He had his shoes off in the car, with his feet up. He was very informal.

"After Al made a name for himself at Marquette, the Knights of Columbus wanted him to speak in Green Bay. It was a black tie affair. Al told me to fill in the amount I wanted—$700, $800. When they said OK to the amount, Al's response was, 'I might make some money in this speaking!'"

Warrior television analyst John Owens recalls a time early in the McGuire era, when the coach asked a Marquette faculty member to listen to one of his talks. "Al said to a speech professor at Marquette, 'I'm gettin' a lot of requests to speak. Sometime I want you to come to listen to me speak and critique it.' Some months later, the professor calls Al and said, 'Al, I heard you speak.' 'Well, what do you think?' Al asked. 'Al, you're so bad, you're good!'"

"Al had this book of 10,000 quotes," Owens recalled. "He would mark the quotes he liked. He would put a red dot on the ones he really liked. Those would always be stored in the back of his mind."

For the talks McGuire did not want to make, mainly because they were freebies, he sent one of his players in his place, often Tom Flynn or Bob Wolf.

"I dragged my butt to the churches," said Flynn, "I was like any other 19- or 20-year-old. It [speaking] helped me in developing my confidence. I may have had a dozen or more speeches in the Milwaukee area. Usually they were sports nights, Holy Name breakfasts, Catholic events. Sometimes I would meet Green Bay Packers stars like Henry Jordan, which made it fun, while not necessarily lucrative."

Before the 1966–67 campaign, McGuire promised the Tip-Off Club that he planned to speed up the Warriors offense with a more liberal fast break. This was possible because of the arrival of George Thompson, who was the breakthrough blue chipper in the Marquette basketball program. "Thompson must show more effort and play better without the ball. But George is the best. He should make everyone forget Tom Flynn real fast," crowed a proud McGuire.

"George was one of the finest players I had ever seen," said Flynn. "He was a 6'2" forward. He could jump. He had a wide body. He made moves in the air. George was something I had never seen before. Pat Smith was a 6'3" center. He was a scrapper. He was wiry tough. He was nonpretentious." McGuire had redshirted Smith the previous season so that he could play with Thompson and the other talented players in his recruiting class.

"George set the tone," noted Raspudic. "He opened the gate and made Marquette a legitimate power. I remember a game against DePaul where George guarded the Blue Demons' Earl Palmer. He was taller than George, but when George went up to dunk, Palmer went down and George stayed up."

"Every game that George gave his all, he threw up at halftime," remembered *Milwaukee Sentinel* reporter Mike Christopulos. "Al would say that if George didn't throw up, then he'd get worried." Concurred Thompson, "Before a majority of Marquette games I vomited. Once I did that, I was at ease. I guess you'd have to say it was tension. Any time I felt tension, I felt it there [in my stomach]."

But Thompson was not the best at following curfew, according to Chicago sportswriter Bill Jauss. "Al delegated the responsibility of bed checks to Hank [Raymonds]," explained Jauss. "Hank came back from the checks and said to McGuire, 'He hasn't been in his bed since midnight.' Al said, 'Hey, he's gettin' passin' grades, so leave him alone.'"

"Hank used to send trainer Bob Weingart around to our dorms for bed check," recalled Thompson, who has worked as radio analyst for Marquette basketball games on WISN since 1978. "Most of the time we were there. One of the great things that Al knew is that he knew people and knew how to deal with people. Al knew that I was deadly serious about winning basketball games."

With the excitement of the golden anniversary season, the Marquette Minutemen booster club set a season ticket sales record of 2,000, breaking the previous year's mark of 1,275. "Everything is ready for this year after two years of alibis," McGuire told the group. He also predicted that average attendance would exceed 9,000 per game and that the team would earn a bid to a postseason tournament.

Competition for tickets on campus became such that students began pitching tents on the grassy area of campus near Brooks Memorial Union, where tickets were sold. As the team's success grew in succeeding years, so did the number of tents.

The burgeoning success of the basketball team gave the university and city an opportunity to feel good, but it did not take their minds completely off the problems of the day.

In fact, some 70 percent of Marquette students had expressed disapproval of the draft. Students began protesting the draft and questioning U.S. involvement in Vietnam. Back at that time, a number of student organizations, such as SURE, were picketing particular venues in Milwaukee for discrimination. Sit-ins were becoming more common as students joined in the demonstrations for racial equality and women's rights.

But McGuire tried to stay above the fray. "He didn't address the politics of the day," remembered Raspudic. "Al would say, 'That's the world you're gonna be in. So wear your love beads now, but when you interview at IBM make sure you wear a white shirt. Take care of the business of making yourself successful.'"

"It was an era of great turmoil," remembered Bob Wolf. "You didn't like it [Vietnam War]. As far as things happening in the world, Al didn't talk to us about it.

"I was drafted," continued Wolf. "I had gone through basic training and went to Fort Hood. I called Al and asked him if he knew anyone so that I could play ball while I was in the Army.

"He knew Hal Fisher, the old Army coach. I worked my way into the gym. I told him where I was stationed. He told me, 'You can try out for the All-Army Team.' So I was player-coach for the Fort Hood team for two years. We traveled all over the world. It was a great experience," said Wolf.

The changes around the country had not yet affected the basketball program, but the players and the coaches would eventually be forced to deal with those touchy issues, especially as the team took on a higher profile on campus.

Meanwhile, back at the Arena, McGuire was continuing to create a positive excitement with his team and helping people forget about the problems of the day for a couple of hours on game nights.

"I don't remember an empty seat in the Arena," said SID Jim Foley. "We darn near sold out every seat during that season." Added Thompson, "Between the players doing their thing on the court, Al doing his thing, and the media, it was a big circus. People literally planned their weekends around Marquette basketball. Wherever he was, there was going to be excitement, conflict, entertainment. The day after a game people would say to each other at the water cooler, 'Did you hear what Al did last night?'"

McGuire was not a superstitious coach, but he had his eccentricities, according to Warrior broadcaster Tom Collins.

"He always wanted to take a walk before a game. I had to do a pre-game show. Sometimes it was in a men's room or even in the ocean. Before a game we'd walk across the Marquette campus in a half-hour."

"Most coaches were generally out there 20 minutes before the game," noted John Owens, who was public address announcer in the Arena during the 1970s. "Al didn't want to go through the boredom of layup drills and the stretching."

"We'd [the team] go out and warm up. We'd go back in. He'd stay in the locker room after everyone had left," explained team manager Goran Raspudic, whom McGuire affectionately referred to as Gorman Rudewitz. "There was a time not long after I started as manager, Al couldn't remember my name and he started calling after me, 'John! John! Come here!'"

"When Al was ready to go out onto the floor, he'd say, 'OK, let's go.' There were heavy burgundy curtains leading to the court. I'd push the curtains aside and he'd walk through. He looked at the four corner seats to see that they were filled. It was a dramatic entrance. The fans went crazy. With basketball success and renown came increased self-respect," Raspudic said. He noted the impact that the winning basketball program was having on the inferiority complex of the "little Jesuit school."

Two others who were at just about every home game during the McGuire era were Jerry Savio and Herb Kohl of Kohl Food Stores fame, later to become U.S. Senator from Wisconsin. McGuire was aware of their mutual business interests and introduced them.

"Herb was like Caesar at that time," recalled Savio, who worked at the Wonder Bread sales office on Vliet Street in Milwaukee. "I said, 'Al, maybe you can introduce me.'" Savio eventually wound up getting business from the Kohl's chain, and he obtained courtside tickets at Marquette basketball games for Kohl.

"I gave Al three peanuts from a packet that I always bought from a vendor before each game," Savio continued. "That was one of the routines we followed before home games."

"When he was at Marquette, Al never started a game until I arrived at the Arena," recalled Kohl, the soft-spoken senior U.S. Senator from Wisconsin who was a regular Monopoly partner on Thursday nights in the McGuire home. "Al thought that perhaps I was a good luck charm for the team."

"Before any game, Al would be laughing and joking, telling stories, relaxed. Then five minutes before the game would start, he'd walk out of the locker room and do a 180-degree [attitude] turn as he walked out onto the floor. He would walk over and shake hands with the opposing coach to see if his hands were sweating," said Owens. "When it was time to go to work, it was time to go to work."

After the starting lineups were announced, the Arena's public address announcer would lead the crowd in a short prayer before the playing of the National Anthem. And as the final words of the anthem were sung, the crowd would yell in unison: "Give 'em hell, Al!" The chant started out with a solitary voice echoing through the Arena early in McGuire's tenure and grew to a regular pre-game chant by the crowd at every home game.

"Before the game, the team would say a prayer, usually the Catholic 'Hail Mary,'" recalled Hughie McMahon, a freshman that season. "And six of the 12 guys on the team were Protestant. At the end of the prayer we'd say, 'Queen of Victory, pray for us. Let's kill 'em!'"

Marquette opened quickly with three big wins, including a 79-63 victory over NYU at Madison Square Garden. Their next game was at the Palestra against Villanova.

"We were leaving the floor of the Palestra after losing to Villanova 80-78," recalled Collins. "It was part of a double-header. It was a brutal game. A hard-fought game. Some guy came out on the floor and he tried to go after Al. Al punched him and the guy claimed that Al had chipped his tooth. The university offered to pay for his tooth," said Collins, but nothing more came of the incident.

McGuire's old college coach Frank McGuire brought his South Carolina Gamecocks in for the annual Milwaukee Classic. It was the first time the two coaches had faced each other since McGuire's days at Belmont Abbey. "Al asked me to get a case of Schlitz and a bottle of Cutty Sark and personally deliver it to Frank when he arrived in Milwaukee," said Foley. "Frank was thrilled."

Unfortunately, the Warriors lost the hard-fought contest, 63-61, but the elder McGuire came away impressed with what his protege had accomplished in a short time in Milwaukee.

"His players react the same way he reacted when I was coaching him at St. John's," said Frank McGuire. "Such quickness. I remarked to my assistant coach, 'You know, these guys reflect Al McGuire from the time they come on the court until the time they come off.'"

"Al always gave a little bit of his life when he played basketball," noted McGuire, "whether he was playing a three-man game on a concrete court in Rockaway or at Madison Square Garden. It made no difference to Al where the game was played because there was always a man to beat and a man trying to beat him. Al got tremendous enjoyment from both."

The Warriors took the consolation game of the Classic by pasting Fordham, 82-58. After beating Minnesota at home, the Warriors then lost to Don Donoher's Dayton Flyers and Ireland's Ramblers, before going on a five-game winning streak.

While Marquette lost 85-72 to Loyola, the team introduced its new uniforms at Chicago Stadium. The dark blue singlets featured horizontal white stripes and were dubbed Nash "Sand Knit," for the Wisconsin company that created them, J. M. Nash. It was the first time the team introduced new threads, and from then on Marquette would wear a new look for each season or for tournament play.

After the loss to Loyola the team was 5-5 and playing inconsistently. The players asked McGuire if they could hold a closed-door meeting without the coaches. McGuire agreed.

After the meeting, NIT champ BYU came to the Arena and were beaten 81-70 by the rejuvenated Warriors. Marquette won convincingly at Wisconsin and at St. John's, and then defeated Ray Meyer's Blue Demons for the first time under McGuire. The team won 16 of its last 20 after the players-only meeting. As it turned out, that was the turning point of the season.

"It [the season] was fun itself, but it was a lot of pressure," recalled Pat Smith of the games leading up to the season's conclusion. "Every game, Al would keep reminding us, 'This is the one that will get us the bid.' He would continue to repeat it until the end of the season."

Those constant reminders from McGuire, in addition to the tough competition on the road, brought the team closer together. One of the toughest games was a 94-92 overtime loss at Detroit that turned into a donnybrook. "Al ended up the night at a Detroit jail," recalled player Jim Langenkamp.

The players and the fans were leaving the court in the same direction and "a Detroit fan came out of the stands and got crazy and started yelling at me," recalled Pat Smith, who proceeded to knock the man down. "The police came and grabbed me. McGuire jumped into the fracas to get the cop off me, and he was later charged with assaulting an officer. He was charged, but it was dropped. That's the type of guy he was. He's always gonna take care of his players."

McGuire was freed by Detroit police after he paid a $27.50 bond. He was accused of slugging the policeman and loosening one of his teeth. After the incident, McGuire continued to insist that he did not hit anyone. He recalled seeing two guys with blue hats on top of Smith. McGuire thought that they were ushers. Later, the policeman who made the charge backed off from his original statement and said that he was mistaken. It was someone else who had hit him.When asked to comment about the incident afterward, McGuire's brief response was tinged with embarrassment: "If I were a university, I wouldn't hire me."

A confident warrior team went to Alumni Hall to face DePaul in that season's return matchup, but Ray Meyer's team was ready this time, and beat the Warriors 79-74. Ten more years would pass before Meyer would beat McGuire again.

"Al gave Ray the ultimate compliment," recalled Bill Jauss. "Ray kicked a guy off his team for fighting before a game against Marquette and lost. Al's response afterward was 'I wouldn't have the balls to do what Ray did. Ray threw his best player off the team. His principles were higher than winning a game. But my principles aren't that high.'"

"Al had so much respect for Ray Meyer," added Tom Collins. "Al would bend over backward for Ray."

Marquette went on to win six of its last eight games, including a narrow 81-80 decision over Loyola at the Arena. In this rivalry, Ireland would beat McGuire just once more.

"When I was a senior, Ireland played a box-and-one on me. Al hated it," said Bob Wolf. "Al said that he wanted to beat George Ireland more than anyone. Their personalities clashed when we were playing. Ireland didn't like Al's antics or the way he was working the refs."

"The rivalry didn't last very long," recalled Bledsoe. "We used to watch those double-headers. Loyola started to slip. Then Marquette made the NIT and things started to happen for Marquette. I always felt that Ireland resented the fact that McGuire was in the limelight."

"From a distance you could dislike Al," noted Sullivan. "He was flamboyant, well dressed. I think that Al was an outsider, an easterner. The media attention he got right away. He realized how important the media was in building a program. And he managed to get that attention before he became a winner. Al was a publicity hound in their minds."

"When Al came on the college basketball scene," noted Raspudic, "the old-time coaches were autocrats. [But] Al accepted people as individuals as long as they were committed to working together. Al broke a lot of taboos."

Marquette finished the season a strong 18-8, having lost no more than three consecutive games all year. While McGuire thought that this team might be on the NIT bubble (they were ranked 13th out of 50 independents), Fordham coach John Bach, who was a member of the committee, liked Marquette's chances of making the NIT. The team was honored with a congratulatory resolution from the Milwaukee Common Council and telegrams were pouring into the university from all over.

The third time turned out to be the charm for McGuire as his team finally earned a postseason bid when the National Invitation Tournament Committee came calling. McGuire and Marquette were in the national spotlight under the big top of college basketball's mecca, Madison Square Garden, then located at 49th Street and Eighth Avenue in New York. The invitation was special to McGuire not only because players enjoy it, but people who really know basketball can be found at the Garden.

It was showtime for the Warriors. But before the team headed to New York, more than 2,000 students jammed the Brooks Memorial Union for a send-off rally. After the rally, a woman wrote to the *Milwaukee Journal* to say how refreshing it was to see the students' spirits soaring because of school spirit instead of LSD or marijuana.

"I made them pack for ten days," recalled McGuire. "There was no point in going out there without figuring we were going to win it." In order to keep distractions to a minimum, McGuire had the players stay in a fleabag hotel off Lexington Avenue, where the lobby was closed at 10 p.m. and ropes were used to work the elevators.

More than a thousand Marquette fans traveled to the Big Apple for the 30th annual NIT, which was considered a major tournament at that time. All 14 teams were invited to New York to play in the Garden; there were no regional games.

"In the NIT it was Jimmy Burke and Bobby Wolf starting in the backcourt and Brad Luchini coming off the bench, Pat Smith, Brian Brunkhorst and George Thompson," remembered SID Foley.

The Warriors unveiled new uniforms from the J. M. Nash Co. They were dark blue with bold, horizontal stripes, according to Michael Micheli, who designed the uniforms for Nash.

"During the NIT tournament games at Madison Square Garden, Coach kinda relaxed," Smith said. "Myself, Thompson, Burke. It was comin' home. I had played in the Garden, so I loved playin' on that floor. Thompson was the same way. For the New York kids on the team. But for some of the others, they were still in awe."

"The best crowd was in the old Madison Square Garden in New York in 1967," said Wolf, still in awe. "There was a haze over the court. It had a lot of atmosphere."

"Marquette was an underdog in every game," remembered Jim Foley. "I knew we had to win two games in order to celebrate St. Patrick's Day in New York. It was a homecoming of sorts for Al."

"We started with Tulsa, who had Bobby 'Bingo' Smith, a first-round draft pick of Cleveland in the NBA. We beat them 64-60. Then we beat Providence and Jimmy 'Mayor of the Garden' Walker 81-80 in overtime. The bookies had us losing to Providence," said an indignant Pat Smith. "Jimmy Walker had a big rep," noted Thompson. "But we saw fear in his eyes early. Harlem and the Bed-Stuyvesant guys can smell fear. Jimmy was doomed."

"Al marched in the St. Patrick's Day Parade in New York with a lot of Marquette fans who came from Milwaukee for the NIT," remembered Tom Collins. "[During the parade] he decided that he wanted to go into a bar. We broke off the parade route and went in." Joining McGuire in the parade was Herb Kohl, who traveled to New York with Jerry Savio, Bob Roedl, Joe DuChateau, and Walter Wong, all part of Al's Rat Pack. Or as they referred to themselves, the Apple Dumpling Gang.

"We then beat the Thundering Herd of Marshall and George Stone, who was one of the top scorers in the country, 83-78," said Foley, who added that Marshall's most famous alum at the time was comedian Soupy Sales. "In the semi-final against Marshall, McGuire let us run with 'em," said Smith, who sprained his ankle in the game. "When the smoke cleared, it was us and SIU [Southern Illinois University]. I had had a good tournament. Defensive-wise, stat-wise. I was in a zone. No pressure," Smith declared.

All of Marquette's games were beamed back to Milwaukee and broadcast on local TV station Channel 18. "Many of the students were watching the games in the bars on Wells Street and farther down on Wisconsin Avenue," remembered David Foran. "After the win over Marshall, students began spilling out of the bars and dorms and running down Wisconsin Avenue."

The win set more than a thousand Marquette students dancing in the streets of Milwaukee, celebrating the Warriors' heading into the NIT final against Southern Illinois University. The celebration blocked traffic in the downtown area.

Jack Hartman's SIU Salukis were considered the number one small college team in America that season, and before the NIT McGuire had picked Southern Illinois as the favorite to win the tournament.

McGuire was feeling pretty full of himself and decided to take a walk through the old neighborhood and let the old gang see how well Alfie had done since he left Rockaway. But the old gang wasn't all that impressed, according to Norman Ochs. "Al came back to Rockaway the afternoon of one of his NIT games in 1967. Al is all over the sports pages, so he decided to ride down to the old neighborhood. People usually hung out at 116th Street.

"The guys who were hanging out when Al lived there years ago were still there. On the corner was Walter Moran and Johnny Cholakis and they're standing there. Al walks up to the guys with a sly smile on his face and he says, 'Hi guys, what's doin'?' 'Nothin' doin', Al. What's doin' with you?'" Al always had the ability to poke fun at himself, Ochs noted. Regardless of McGuire's success, he was still just another guy from the neighborhood, which put the whole NIT experience in perspective for him.

"[Muhammad] Ali came to the Garden and scrimmaged with us," recalled Langenkamp. "Ali was running up and down the floor with Jimmy Burke throwing up half-assed shots."

The Salukis had a guard named Walt Frazier, who was not that well-known before the tournament. Jimmy Burke had the assignment of guarding Frazier.

"In the NIT, we had three real tough games," said Bobby Wolf. "Every game was close, right down to the wire. We only had seven guys who could play. When we got to the final, after four games in five days, we were tired."

But win or lose in the finals, McGuire was back in the Garden, home to some of his biggest successes as a schoolboy, collegian, and professional. It was showtime again for McGuire, and he was on center stage.

"Southern Illinois had an outstanding team," recalled Wolf. "They were bigger, stronger, and more talented. But we were fired up." The Salukis were also five-point favorites in the afternoon contest, which was aired live on CBS, with Tom Kelly doing play-by-play and Frank Gifford doing the color commentary.

"I remember that I sat next to Al in the Garden in the '67 NIT finals," said Timeberg. "George had four fouls in the first half, and I told Al to take him out of the game. Al said, 'No, he won't get any more fouls.' And George didn't get another foul in the game. Al, as a bench coach, was one of the best, and Al could also dominate refs."

"I can remember coming in at halftime thinking, 'I'm tired.' Here we were up by 11 and we're dead," continued Wolf. "This isn't good. I had 14 points in the first half. They put Frazier on me and he shut me down. He could take over a game all by himself," noted Wolf, who was picked in the fifth round of the ABA draft by the New York Nets and in the seventh round of the NBA draft by the Chicago Bulls. Wolf was the first McGuire player at Marquette to be drafted.

"In the second half, he [Frazier] put on a show. Assists, rebounds, scoring. We never got more than one shot each possession. We had a 6'3" center in Pat Smith."

McGuire broke one of his cardinal rules of basketball, that the players who start the first half also start the second half.

"In the second half, Al put Dave Anderson in for me at center," said Smith, who had been injected with painkillers for his ankle. And that hurt. I couldn't do anything. At halftime we were up. Coach told us to maintain. Then Frazier went up on us. We were aware of him. I still think we should have won the game," said a disheartened Smith. Marquette team physician Doc Eichenberger was also trying to numb the pain in Thompson's foot. "I was worried about my foot, and by all rights I shouldn't have played in the final. Doc couldn't find the joint with this long needle.

I had the cortisone shot in my big toe and couldn't feel my foot. It was excruciatingly painful not being able to feel," said Thompson.

Marquette scored only 12 more points in the game's last eight minutes and lost, 71-56. McGuire made no excuses for losing the final. "We lost our poise, they didn't," was his simple explanation. He also praised his team and told them that they had nothing to be ashamed of in the loss.

The biggest complaint about the broadcast came from viewers in Milwaukee and other parts of the country, who felt that Kelly and Gifford were biased in their reporting, favoring Southern Illinois. CBS then apologized for the broadcasters, saying that higher standards were expected in a network telecast.

After the game, NIT MVP Frazier took the championship trophy with both hands and held it just above his head for all to see. It was against the Warriors that Frazier earned his reputation and a draft selection by the New York Knicks. In the NCAA Tournament, UCLA rebounded after its loss in the Finals the year before, when it defeated Dayton 79-64.

McGuire and Marquette had earned a newfound respect as a result of their first post-season appearance since the 1962–63 season, and the university earned $15,000 for the school's participation. Marquette was in the midst of building a very good basketball program, and Al McGuire was earning a reputation as not only a good court coach but something of a personality.

Marquette's strong run in the tournament gave the basketball program a high national profile and a boost in recruiting, which helped the small independent school in Milwaukee, Wisconsin, take the next step up the ladder of big-time college basketball.

Chapter Nine

Goin' Uptown

After the successful 21-9 campaign in 1966–67, expectations for the next season were ratcheted up another level by fans and media alike. McGuire attempted to dispel those high hopes for the upcoming season.

Not everyone believed him. The eighth annual *Basketball* magazine picked the Warriors 13th in the country, as did *Basketball News*. Associated Press weighed in with Marquette at 18th. This was the highest preseason praise any McGuire team had received.

In the 1967-68 preseason press guide, on which he appeared with Captain Brian Brunkhorst in front of the new Victor R. McCormick Hall, McGuire proclaimed that he was making no more predictions. He noted that it would be a challenging season without Bob Wolf and Paul Carbins, but returning starters—All-America candidate George Thompson, Pat Smith, Jim Burke, and Brian Brunkhorst ("the secret of our success")—would be able to pick up the slack. He warned fans not to expect another 20-win season.

Marquette's performance in the NIT made such an impression on New York high school phenom Dean Meminger that he included the Milwaukee school on the list of colleges he was considering.

"He [scout Mike Timeberg] got me into Madison Square Garden to see Marquette play in the '67 NIT," said Meminger, who had narrowed his college choices to UCLA, Michigan State, Cincinnati, Providence, and St. Joseph's among more than 100 colleges that recruited him.

"I met Al after the NIT," recalled Meminger. "At that point, I was impressed that they had some New York players and they had George Thompson, and I knew George. We shook hands and he may have said a few things to me. He was the original hippie coach. A maverick. One of a kind. He was raw. Most people are fake. That raw honesty touches people. I asked Al if he was going to stay at Marquette my four years, and he told me, 'Dean, you're born alone and you die alone.' He said if I came to Marquette, I would get a good education, and if I kept healthy and kept my attitude, I could play ball and be an asset to Marquette and Marquette could be an asset to me," recalled Meminger in a 1977 WRIT special.

"I had seen Walt Frazier and Southern Illinois play Marquette in the NIT. So I knew Marquette was on the come and I knew George Thompson was an accomplished player at Marquette.

"UCLA was already established. I knew that I could start there. And I was being subconsciously pushed to Marquette by Mike Timeberg. I met with John Wooden and [assistant coach] Denny Crum at UCLA. The lifestyle was different for me, California laid back. Everything was on a silver plate. What was the challenge? Every athlete wants to win a championship.

"Wooden told me I would be the heir to Mike Warren. With Kareem we could win more titles. He was the coach of the national champions. He wasn't gonna get down on his knees," said Meminger.

"I needed to get away from New York, however, to sever the umbilical cord. But out of respect for Digger [Phelps] and Lou [Carnesecca], I visited Fordham and St. John's."

While McGuire had never seen Meminger play a high school game, he had heard enough about him from Timeberg and his other New York players to know that the guard was the real deal. It was that summer of 1967, also known as the "Summer of Love," that Dean Meminger signed to play at Marquette.

"At Marquette, it was my show, but it was Al's system," said Meminger. "Al didn't change his system. He knew that I could handle the ball and he put me in situations that would allow me to play my game and still be within his system.

"He believed in a slow, half-court game. I've always been structured," Meminger continued. "My senior year in high school I was not even the top scorer on my team. I believe in winning and I believe in the team concept."

Contrary to popular belief it was not McGuire who dubbed Meminger "Dean the Dream." "I gave Dean the nickname," claimed Timeberg. "I gave Dean his nickname when he played for me on the New York Gems. George Thompson was a very good player, but the highest rated player that I got for Al was Dean Meminger coming out of New York."

"After signing to go to Marquette," explained Meminger "a journalist wrote an article about 'Dean the Dream' and it stuck. Just from that article I became 'Dean the Dream' Meminger. From the time I chose Marquette, the article said that I was a dream come true for Marquette."

"Dean was a smart guy," noted Thompson, "and a good ballplayer. I told him that we'd have one year together—when he was a sophomore and I was a senior. By the time he was a sophomore, Dean was an acknowledged star."

"Dean was a freshman when I was a senior," recalled Blanton Simmons. "He was a great talent. Incredible ball-handling skills. He could play offense and defense. In college, he was a great scorer because he could get to the basket a lot."

That turned out to be a fortuitous spring for McGuire. First his team reached the NIT Finals. Then he signed probably the best guard in America, and three days later he and Raymonds were given five-year contract extensions through 1972.

The freshman phenom Meminger was also the only player to leave McGuire speechless, according to "Voice of the Warriors" Tom Collins. "Prior to the season, McGuire set up clinics where he would bring his players to high schools in Wisconsin. Al told Dean Meminger to 'get up and show the boys how to dunk a basketball.' Meminger shattered the backboard. Al was just left speechless." The dunk had been outlawed before the 1966–67 season.

Marquette had another freshman join the team that season—Rick Majerus from Milwaukee. Majerus was not in Meminger's class, even though they were the same height, 6-feet. The big difference was that Majerus was 210 pounds and set the meanest picks in Marquette practices. He was the quintessential gym rat.

"Rick was one of the walk-ons," recalled Tom Flynn, who was working as a graduate assistant for McGuire. "Hank and I were going to keep five or six freshmen. We each took a piece of paper and wrote down who should be on the team. We both put Rick down. Rick Majerus went to Marquette High School, but he could not make the basketball team. We liked him. He did exactly as you told him. You couldn't deny him. He had such heart that neither of us could keep him off the team. He won his way into their [Al's and Hank's] hearts. I was his first coach."

"I was happy to contribute to Rick's development," Raymonds recalled. "For the freshman team at Marquette, I always put three guys on the team who never played high school ball. Rick loved the game. Rick was a basketball junkie. He'd come into my office daily and just talk basketball.

"When the Milwaukee Bucks worked out at Concordia College, Rick would go over there to watch the practices, and Oscar [Robertson] would always put him on his team because he set such good picks for Oscar," Raymonds continued.

Unfortunately, heart and determination were not enough for Majerus to make the Marquette varsity. After his freshman season, McGuire broke the bad news to Majerus that he would not get a chance to play hoops at Marquette, bluntly saying that he was the worst player he had ever seen. However, McGuire and Raymonds liked Majerus so much that they decided to give him another chance.

"[Later] we got him a grammar school coaching job. Then he became the freshman basketball coach at Marquette High School, where Gary Rosenberger and my son Steve were players," said Raymonds. "Later on Al had mentioned to me that we needed to find a young assistant coach since we weren't getting any younger. 'Why don't we just take Rick?' I said to Al. We first brought him on as a coach at Al's basketball camps. He also worked at our other camps. Rick was all basketball."

McGuire's fourth team started the '67–68 campaign with wins over three cupcakes. But as in previous seasons, McGuire invited top level teams to participate in the annual Milwaukee Classic. This particular season it was Florida State University and Louisiana State University, which featured sophomore scoring sensation "Pistol" Pete Maravich. The guard dazzled the nation during his sophomore year with Harlem Globetrotter-like moves while leading the country in scoring at 44.2 points a game. Even though the NCAA had outlawed the dunk that season, Maravich found ways to entertain with a basketball that had not been seen before. In a way, he was the precursor to another Magic who would come along ten years later, Earvin Johnson.

The Seminoles and Tigers squared off in the first game of the Classic, with Florida State winning behind Dave Cowens's 31 rebounds, while Maravich scored 42 points in a losing cause. Both stand as Milwaukee

Classic records to this day. Cowens and Maravich hold six Classic records between them and their teams hold four Classic records.

"[Purdue's] Rick Mount was a wonderful shooter," commented *Milwaukee Journal* reporter Terry Bledsoe, "but I don't know that I saw a better shooting performance than Maravich's in that Classic game in 1967."

The record crowds that turned out for the games were treated to a "classic Classic" by the four teams that year. Unfortunately, their beloved Warriors lost the Classic for the second straight year, 77-65, to Wisconsin. Wisconsin coach John Erickson enjoyed the Classics and the clinics the mornings of the game, featuring each of the four coaches who received $100 each.

Marquette did get back on track with an 80-67 win over Villanova at the Arena. With that victory, the Warriors began to protect their home court jealously—so much so, that Marquette would not lose another game at the Arena for six years, one of the longest home winning streaks in the country and one of the top 10 streaks in NCAA history.

"We took every game seriously," recalled Joe Thomas. "We knew we got homered on the road, but when teams came to the Arena, they knew they were going to be beat. They knew it and we knew it. We took no names, we took no prisoners in protecting our home court."

Said Ray Meyer: "They were a very poised team on the road. Nothing seemed to distract them. They expected to win. That team reflected Al."

But it was not just the varsity that was making noise. The freshman squad was giving the fans at the Arena quite a show themselves, behind the artistry of "Dean the Dream." The night Notre Dame's freshmen came to the Arena, some 10,000-plus fans made for one of the biggest crowds ever to witness an underclassmen game.

"When we played the Notre Dame freshmen at the Arena, their freshmen, which included Austin Carr, were ranked number one in the country," according to Raymonds. "We were 16 points down with 10 minutes left and we beat them. Dean picked off a pass and he waited for the defender to foul him. He made the shot and was fouled. It was Dean's play that forced the NCAA to institute the five-second count. It was because of the delay game that we ran with Dean at the point."

As the teams played well, not only were the fans drawn to the Arena, but the media was drawn to the team and their coach. Marquette was beginning to make regular appearances in preseason basketball polls. "It wasn't long after that they were in the polls every week," recalled Dave Foran.

So while Raymonds handled the Xs and Os and other details, McGuire handled the entertainment aspect.

"I saw the way that Al would deal with the Chicago media," recalled John Owens. "With guys like Bill Gleason [*Chicago American, Sun-Times*] and Bill Jauss [*Chicago Tribune*]. I was impressed even more so with [how he handled] the New York media, like Jimmy Breslin and Leonard Lewin."

"Back then the media guys were your friends," explained Gene Sullivan. "They never tried to hurt you. They went on the buses with us. The coaches didn't view the press with mistrust. You knew which ones to trust: Roy Damer, Mike Conklin, Bill Gleason, Bill Jauss, and Ron Rapoport."

As McGuire's reputation began spreading far and wide during the season, no less a personage than sports journalist and CBS essayist Heywood Hale Broun wanted to do an interview with McGuire at Joe Deutsch's, at 4th and Kilbourn, near the Arena. "Al wanted me with him at the bar," explained Tom Collins, who added that McGuire handled himself like a pro with the experienced reporter. "I remember Broun leaving Al's office and saying, 'That is a rare character,'" noted Dave Foran.

After making an appearance at one of McGuire's camps during the summer, Dick McGuire was surprised at how quickly Al's star had risen in Milwaukee. "I never knew sports figures were that dominant and that Al was so well known. Everywhere we went people knew him. I never went through that in New York. I couldn't believe he would be that popular."

"We all went uptown together," recalled Goran Raspudic, the second-year team manager. "I was part of a winning team. It was like manna from heaven. Al was always there for us. He had integrity. You would graduate from Marquette," added Raspudic, whose responsibilities included not only taking care of the socks and jocks, but making sure that the players made it to class on time.

According to Raspudic, McGuire had no hard and fast rules for his players, as long as they did not break the law and were on time for class. "Al used to say to the players, 'You can stay out until three in the morning as long as you can make it to post-time. Just don't tell me you're too tired to get up for class.' I would have to show up at McCormick Hall to wake the players up for their first class. If there were any academic problems with the players, then the curfews would go on."

To coincide with the team's first major in-season road trip to Hawaii, McGuire started the "Hawaii A Go-Go" contest where the winner would win a trip to the island to follow the team. The Warriors defeated Ohio State (64-60), lost to Houston (77-65), but won the consolation game 80-67 over Northwestern. But before Marquette played a game, McGuire reportedly sent player Jim Langenkamp back to Milwaukee for missing curfew.

"We lost so badly to Houston that Al said, 'the next kid who misses curfew goes right back to Milwaukee,'" said Langenkamp. "I was back in time, but Brian Brunkhorst was with his girl, so I went out for another hour and while I was gone they did the bed check."

At the time it seemed that a minor transgression would not warrant such a serious punishment, but it was not unusual during his coaching career for McGuire to pick his spots in order to make a point with his team. In this case, Langenkamp happened to be his whipping boy. He ended up becoming a surgeon, and the paths of the coach and player would come full circle many years later.

The Warriors won four straight at home before losing at Loyola and winning at Detroit. Marquette headed to the friendly confines of DePaul's Alumni Hall for a Saturday night date with the Blue Demons.

After McGuire finished his pregame show with Tom Collins, he greeted Ray Meyer on court as he adjusted his cufflinks saying, "Ray, where are the TV cameras?" It would not be too long before the cameras of Milwaukee's Channel 18 and Chicago's Channel 32 caught the brawl and blood.

As Pat Smith prepared to jump center with DePaul's 6'7" Bob Zoretich, the Blue Demons' leading scorer, both players started scuffling and then fighting just after the tipoff. Zoretich and Smith were both ejected. "In the first two minutes there's a fight," recalled Gene Sullivan, who was scouting the game for Notre Dame. "Both players get kicked out, but the players could stay on the bench after being ejected from the game.

"The game gets emotional. Al is orchestrating with any kind of a foul. Al would stand up, put his arms out. He's pointing to his bench. At Alumni Hall, all eyes were on him. The ref comes over. Al gets up and walks down the bench. He puts his hands on Pat Smith's shoulders. Smith walks the long distance and says something to Ray Meyer. Then Smith walks over and shakes Zoretich's hand," recalled Sullivan.

"When we played them at home [a 71-50 Marquette win], I outplayed Bob Zoretich," recalled Smith. "I outscored Zoretich. I outhustled him at the Arena. He was their leading scorer. He took offense to it. When we played at DePaul, he's the one that started the rough stuff, shortly into the game. You know, elbows and that type of thing. One thing led to another and we wound up fighting each other.

"I was just pissed because I was out of the game. It would have been no contest. He wasn't as quick as I was. He couldn't outjump me. We would have won the game anyway. Zoretich was still upset from the game before in Milwaukee. Especially against someone who's four inches shorter and lighter than he was. There was no need to fight him, but I wasn't going to back down."

"I remembered going over to the bench and telling Zoretich what I could do to him after the game. He didn't come outside," Smith said. "Ray Meyer charged that he lost his best ballplayer and all Marquette lost was a guy who couldn't see, and who couldn't throw the ball in the ocean if he were standing on the beach," Smith said of Marquette's controversial 58-53 win, which has since become known as the "Pat Smith game."

"Ray said, 'I'll never play that guy again,'" recalled Sullivan. "Ray had an idea that Al planned the fight."

"I always accused him [McGuire] of instigating it," said Meyer. "They pushed and shoved and maybe a punch was thrown. It happened so quickly and then my player was out."

It was the first time a McGuire-coached team had won in Chicago and the first time Marquette swept DePaul. McGuire would win the next 17 games against his old friend Ray Meyer.

"On the Monday morning after the game at our weekly breakfast gathering, we all read Ray Meyer's quotes in the Sunday papers that Pat was some stumblebum who couldn't throw the ball into the ocean if he were standing on the beach. That's where the idea to have Pat throw the beach ball into Lake Michigan came to fruition," recalled SID Jim Foley. "Al called a *Milwaukee Journal* photographer and went out with Pat that afternoon."

"Al had me go out to Lake Michigan in my basketball uniform in the middle of winter and throw a ball into the lake. Al just made light of the situation," said Smith matter-of-factly.

It was strange how the fates of both players turned on that particular game

"Zoretich never played up to where he had played before that Marquette game," noted Meyer. "He never had a good game after that." On the other hand, Smith's performance helped propel the Warriors to seven wins in their last nine games. "People didn't like losing to Marquette because I was a small center. I would get a lot of elbows," said Smith, who was dubbed the Evil Dr. Blackheart by George Thompson for his pugilistic basketball play. McGuire said if he were Smith's manager he could be heavyweight champion of the world.

For the team's final road games of the season, McGuire included a trip to Vermillion, South Dakota. McGuire liked to take his teams to parts of the country that many of the city boys would never see otherwise. He also liked to show his players how the other half lived.

"The night before the game against the University of South Dakota, Al, Tom Collins, and I went to the local bowling alley, had some sandwiches and a few beers," recalled Jim Foley. "We head back to the hotel at about 11 o'clock. As we're getting into the elevator, we run into George Thompson. Al says, 'George, what are ya doin' out so late? There's no Harlem in Vermillion.' To which George replies, 'Coach, there's a Harlem everywhere,' and he walked out into the night."

"It got to the point we just wouldn't frequent the same places," explained Thompson. "Everyone would go their separate ways. As long as it wasn't in the same place as he was headed!'"

"The next night," said Foley, "toward the end of the game, George and one of the South Dakota players looked like they were going to get into a fight. Behind the Marquette bench were seated a number of South Dakota football players, dressed in their lettermen sweaters. They were ready to go out onto the floor and get involved in the fracas.

"They didn't realize that Al was aware of their intentions. He then turns around and raises his arms and says: 'You football players get back in your seats!' He spoke and that football team immediately sat down in unison. It was as if Moses had parted the Red Sea," Foley laughed. Marquette won 75-65 and Thompson scored 25 points.

Marquette finished 21-5 on the year, and in the process McGuire's Warriors compiled the best back-to-back seasons in school history. Their reward was a ticket to the NCAA Mideast Regionals, the first time a Marquette team had made it to the NCAA tournament since the 1960–61 season. The team had been in and out of the top ten of the wire service polls most of the year.

To show their appreciation, the Sportsman's Club of the Milwaukee Athletic Club honored McGuire with a special dinner. His former Knicks coach Joe Lapchick attended, as did McGuire's brother John.

McGuire and Lapchick praised each other. McGuire noted the accomplishments of Lapchick and his having stood the test of time (he also used the occasion to lambaste those who would fire coaches for no reason, saying that coaching is a profession just like any other).

For his part, Lapchick noted that McGuire's greatest attribute was never being afraid to tell the truth. He added that McGuire made the Knicks because he was a competitor and came to play.

McGuire's four-year turnaround of the Marquette program had turned heads not only in the college ranks but in the pros. In answering reporters' questions, he had fueled speculation that he might leave Marquette for the pros one day. The previous year McGuire was quoted in the *Sentinel* as saying, "Nobody can coach the pros. The pro clubs don't need a coach, they need a master-of-ceremonies, like me."

In fact, one member of the ownership group that brought the Bucks to Milwaukee had approached *Journal* reporter Terry Bledsoe in February of 1968 to see whether McGuire was seriously interested in leaving the university to become coach and general manager for a paycheck in the neighborhood of $105,000.

"A friend of mine with the Bucks asked me if I would ask Al if he was interested in the coaching job," recalled Bledsoe. "So, I asked Al, and he said that he was interested. When [University Executive Vice President] Father Raymond McAuley found out, he confronted me and told me that I was interfering. I told him that a friend asked me if I would relay a message and I said that I would, that's all."

McGuire was under the impression that he had permission from the university to talk to the Bucks about the offer. He attempted to reach Marquette President Reverend John Raynor and McAuley, but both were out of town. McGuire next talked to Dean of Students Ed Kurdziel, who reportedly told the coach that he could not stop him from talking to the Bucks, but could not give him permission either. As far as McGuire was concerned, he owed it to himself and his family to discuss the matter.

"We were in New York and I said, 'Al, you're not gonna leave. You never got permission from the right person,'" recalled Raymonds.

"Father McAuley was the treasurer. He wouldn't let him out of his contract. He had a contract and Marquette was gonna hold him."

And as far as the university was concerned, a contract was a contract. The team had rewarded McGuire with a five-year contract that extended through 1972. Marquette was not going to budge.

"When we made a contract it bound both sides," recalled President Raynor. "The [athletic] board would make its contracts with the principal coaches. The vice president would endorse it. If it was a special crisis, well it would come to me.

"I never negotiated with Al. Father McAuley negotiated with him," Raynor explained. "I was kept aware of what was going on."

"Al's firm line when the university was going to hold him to his contract was, 'If they want to fight in the gutter, I lived in New York, I can show them how to fight in the gutter.'"

At noon on March 5, 1968, McGuire met with a number of his friends from the Tip-Off Club at the Holiday Inn Central in Milwaukee to explain his reasons for wanting out of his contract. Later that afternoon, he went to the Old Gym to talk to his players, reportedly to tell them that he hoped to be let out of his contract so that he could take the Bucks job.

An hour later, upon arriving back from Chicago, Father McAuley presided over a hastily prepared press conference.

"We cannot conceive of any less appropriate time than the present to discuss Al McGuire's availability for a coaching job in professional basketball," Father McAuley began. "The distracting and unsettling effect upon our entire basketball effort—on coaches, players, and fans—is particularly unfortunate on the eve of our NCAA tournament game with Bowling Green. At no time have we said or implied anything that would justify speculation to the effect that he is available for another position.

"As recently as last year Coach McGuire insisted that a five-year contract was desirable to assure the full realizations of his hopes and plans for Marquette basketball. We met all the terms of his contract, including the salary he requested. We stressed that a long-term contract imposed restrictions on both parties. He insisted on the security of a five-year arrangement knowing that we intended to hold him to the terms of the contract.

"On Thursday, February 22, I personally told Mr. McGuire that we would not consider releasing him from this contract. Under these circumstances I do not understand why he continues to negotiate with the local NBA franchise owners or why he decided to publicize the matter.

"In fairness to the thousands who have given Marquette basketball such enthusiastic support, we cannot entertain any thought of releasing our coach. As far as we are concerned, Al McGuire is our coach now and he will be our coach next year."

This was the first time that he had any real confrontation with the university authorities and McGuire was forced to back down. In order to add some levity to the whole situation, McGuire somewhat flippantly noted, "You know, the priests at Marquette take a vow of poverty, and they expect you to abide by it."

"I wanted to be the top paid coach in *any* sport," said McGuire. "I wanted it for a basketball guy to be the top paid coach."

"Al was so enraged that he got upset at Hank for not speaking out," noted Dave Foran. "Al was outfoxed by another Irishman."

Before his career ended at Marquette, McGuire had received professional offers to coach the Philadelphia 76ers and Cincinnati Royals, among others, but turned them down because he insisted on being paid one dollar more than the highest paid player.

"When the owner of the Royals called Al and asked him if he wanted to coach the team," recalled Hank Raymonds, "Al asked, 'If I tell Oscar [Robertson] to go over here, but he stays over there, who stays—me or Oscar?' The owner said, 'Well, Oscar is our number one guy.' Then Al said, 'That's all I needed to know,' and he didn't take the job."

After the hubbub subsided and the Warriors had their coach's full attention, they could get on with the important business at hand, the NCAA tournament.

After edging Bill Fitch's Bowling Green Falcons 72-71 in their first round game at Kent, Ohio, the Warriors prepared to meet mighty Kentucky and Adolph Rupp, in Lexington of all places. It was the first meeting between McGuire and the legendary Baron of the Bluegrass, and McGuire boldly predicted victory, saying that his team paid the price and deserved to be in the NCAA tournament.

"We were to play Kentucky at Lexington," recalled Raspudic. "Blanton Simmons warned us that something would happen in Lexington. Kentucky was all white. The next morning at breakfast, a waitress spilled coffee on Joe Thomas. We were not hospitably treated in Lexington."

"The black ballplayers had a hard time getting food service at that hotel," recalled Gary Brell. "It was a segregated state, Kentucky." Recalled George Thompson, "Kentucky had a stranglehold on the NCAA at that time. All the black players were referred to as 'boys.'"

"George Thompson was a prankster and a jokester," recalled Thomas. "At the restaurant George told us, 'You can't trust those southern rednecks. They might spill coffee on you.' Then, lo and behold, the waitress spilled a cup of coffee on me. I saw her stumble as she approached our table, so I knew it was an accident."

During the pre-game press conference featuring the four coaches in the regional, McGuire reiterated his boast that Marquette would beat Kentucky. He also complained about the fact that there was no coin toss to determine who would be the home team and wear white uniforms. Needless to say, Rupp was upset, but he did accede and allowed Marquette to wear its white uniforms. Kentucky was favored by six points.

"After the press conference," Hank Raymonds recalled, "Rupp says to the other coaches, 'Now why don't y'all join me in my limousine and come on my TV show tonight?' Al asked him, 'How much ya payin' me?' 'Nothin',' answered Rupp. 'Well, you're not gettin' this boy on,' shot back Al."

"At that time, Rupp thought that Al was a young upstart. But he had a lot of respect for him and a lot of respect for his team," commented Cawood Ledford, longtime Kentucky basketball announcer. "In fact, he had a lot of respect for the way Al had played at St. John's."

"That [regional in Lexington] was probably the most bad blood there ever was between Al and Rupp. Al was trying to psyche out Rupp. Al was always trying to get under Rupp's skin. Al was looking for any kind of edge that he could get because he knew that it was going to be a long night [when Marquette played Kentucky]."

"George Ireland and Adolph Rupp were among a minority of coaches who did not care for Al," recalled SID Jim Foley.

"Al was really awed by Rupp," according to Tom Collins. "Kentucky had great teams and had everything going their way, officiating-wise. Al never made any excuses after the game."

"It was a fun tournament," Pat Smith recalled. "It was everybody's first NCAA tournament. I don't know about expectations at that time. We weren't ready for the publicity, the pressure. The students partied all night. That was the last time that Al kept a team at an NCAA-sanctioned hotel.

"We knew Kentucky was really good. Dan Issel was there at the time. It was a good game. [But] we came out flat, they came ready to play. It was one of the first games that I felt we were overwhelmed. It was an all-white Kentucky team. I guarded Issel for a little while."

Issel did his job and Kentucky soundly defeated Marquette 109-87. It was the first time that a Kentucky team had scored 100 or more points in an NCAA tournament game. After the whipping, Marquette defeated East Tennessee State in the consolation game of the regional, 69-57, and Ohio State surprised Kentucky. "After our experience in the NCAA's," recalled Meminger, "I said to the team that we were going to beat them [Kentucky] next year." UCLA won its second straight title, beating North Carolina and Dean Smith 78-55.

Marquette had played in its first NCAA tournament since 1961. It was only the fourth NCAA tournament for Marquette, but it was Kentucky's 16th. As a result of the exposure, the Warriors finished the season ranked number ten in both the AP and UPI polls. The team also earned a number 12 defensive ranking, giving up just 64.7 points a game.

As the designated star in McGuire's "senior star system," Thompson's record-setting performances were also getting national attention. He received Honorable Mention All-America honors from AP and UPI. Other Marquette players getting attention—from the pros—were Brian Brunkhorst and Brad Luchini. Brunkhorst was taken by the Los Angeles entry in the 12th round of the ABA draft. He was also selected in the sixth round of the NBA draft by the Knicks, while Luchini was an 11th round selection of the nascent Milwaukee Bucks.

The ABA began play in the '67–68 season as the other pro basketball league, and distinguished itself with the red, white and blue ball.

Thompson's heroics were also felt at the Arena box office as the team shattered attendance marks for the third straight year with an average of 10,521 fans a game. "I put the people in the seats and you take them out of their seats," McGuire was fond of telling Thompson, who along with the other players were becoming big men on campus. But whatever celebrity status they achieved, the players were still students at Marquette and a part of the campus life.

"We were celebrities, but still we weren't," noted Smith. "We weren't separate from the student body. We weren't in separate dorms. We still intermingled. Students would say to us, 'Hey, good game.' You were a student first, athletics came later. When we came to school, there was no room to do a whole lot of failing. There were a lot of expectations."

It was those high expectations that would be most keenly felt by the black players on the Marquette team. In the late 1960s, America was fragmenting racially and the divisions were felt keenly on the nation's campuses. Young people were heeding the advice of LSD guru Dr. Timothy Leary by "tuning out and turning on"; the Beatles' experimentation with hallucinogens resulted in Sergeant Pepper and the White album, and free love was espoused by the Broadway musical *Hair*.

"From 1967 to 1969, one percent of Marquette's student body was black," noted Dave Foran. "Some of those black students were from foreign countries. But the Marquette team was significantly African American."

"Before Easter break in 1968, just after Martin Luther King was killed, I saw Blanton Simmons," recalled Raspudic. "He said, 'Don't go in the ghetto tonight,' which was in Milwaukee's inner core, east of 35th Street. As it turned out, there were riots that night."

"Marquette had New York blacks and white kids from Wisconsin," said Tom Collins. "They had some chemistry. There was a togetherness. They played as one. There were no real enmities or jealousies. Al had such tremendous respect from the players."

"The cohesiveness on our team, I don't know where it came from," mused Smith. "It was unique. We enjoyed each other's music. Otis Redding, Led Zeppelin, Eric Clapton. When Otis Redding died, we had a memorial for him on campus. We dated together, went to bars together. We hung out at the Avalanche, a bunch of bars on Michigan and Wells streets."

"We hung out at the Gym, the Black Spider, and Terranto, a black place on the North Side," said Meminger. "I used to hang out in the black community. We had to go to the North Side to do our own thing.

"My sophomore year I stayed at McCormick. After that I moved to 19th and Wells. No one else [on the team] had an apartment. My wife worked for Herb Kohl, and my apartment was known as the 'boogaloo palace.' Every two or three weekends we had a party at my place, where we played the Temps, James Brown, Marvin Gaye, Aretha. I had to be able to relate. I had to have some kind of connection. New York players were tough, guys who wouldn't back down. Players who would go to the wall for you."

In the late 1960s, race relations, or the "checkerboard," as McGuire called it, was a dicey proposition, especially at a school like Marquette which had a very small minority enrollment. "There were fewer than 40 blacks at Marquette at that time," recalled Mike Christopulos.

As the high-profile leader of the Warriors, George Thompson was approached by some of the activists on campus about boycotting the basketball team to protest what they called the "institutional racism" at the university. "Many of the minority students on campus believed that Marquette University was giving lip service to us," noted Thompson. One of the spokesmen for the activists at that time was Gus Moye, who played just one year at Marquette, his freshman season (1964–65).

"Auguste 'Gus' Moye was a smart, well-rounded individual," recalled Blanton Simmons. "He was a 6'4" forward from Aliquippa, Pennsylvania. He was a most engaging guy. He was 28 at the time. Gus was a role model to all of us. He never did get to the varsity level.

"George was more socially adept. Pat had a brother who had been murdered. We'd never been around white people. Who we were, many people thought we were inferior," said Simmons.

"In the spring of 1968, the revolution, or the insurrection, as it was called, was led by Gus and George," recalled Meminger. "It was during that time that blacks were taking a stand. George was the captain. They [activists] said if we do things without your support, we're gone. You guys [basketball players] have the clout. Are you down?

"I was into my nation-building at the time. The Black Power Movement, a term coined by Stokely Carmichael. How the institution was using us. It's still an old-boys network. I stepped across the tracks to live with you guys [white establishment] to be a good black guy. When do you step over to this side? It eats at your core," said Meminger.

"The players were being pressured to boycott the team," recalled Pat Smith. "Minorities were looking for concessions from the university. Marquette was being hard-nosed. There were pressures on the players to do something."

"There was a group on campus called RESPOND [a coalition of black and nonblack students]. They were trying to court more black students and get more minority faculty members at Marquette," recalled Foran. "It happened after the shooting of Martin Luther King. Stuff had been going on, on campus.

"They [players] signed a statement saying that they would no longer play basketball at Marquette. Jim Foley had called Al to let him know what was going on," explained Foran.

McGuire had left earlier that afternoon for a speaking engagement in Montello, Wisconsin. But he had a feeling something was up when he left Milwaukee. Thompson, Meminger, Simmons, Smith, Thomas, and Keith Edwards all signed the statement. Late that afternoon, the local headlines blared: Six Cagers Quit MU.

"George Thompson, Blanton Simmons, Gus Moye and all the players came out to where I was working in West Allis, Wisconsin, as a guard," contined Pat Smith. "We decided that if Marquette didn't give us concessions, we would leave the team. Al said to us, 'Make sure you know what you're doin'. We let the black campus organization know."

"George came into my office," recalled Raymonds. "Al was not in town at the time. I asked him, 'What do you want me to do, George?' So, I sent him to Father McAuley. And then I got a hold of McAuley and I told him that George was coming over. I said, 'If you lie to him, father, Al and I are gone.' Al came back later and met with the players in the early morning hours."

Recalled Thompson, "We wanted the word of somebody who was respected. It couldn't get any better than Father Raynor. If, in fact, he said anything, I had no need to doubt his word. He was a wonderful person."

"The university wasn't going to let us go, so they would have to negotiate," Meminger recalled.

"We left school," recalled Thompson, "and there was a black boycott. We dropped out of school for a couple of days. Gus and a few others were heavily involved. They recognized that we had a profile on campus and came to us. 'We need you guys so that people on campus will sit up and take notice.' There had been some real civil and earnest discussion, but as it turned out that wasn't the case," Thompson said.

RESPOND presented an ultimatum to the administration. It wanted a black hired full-time immediately as staff coordinator and scholarship coordinator. The students wanted a Minority Equal Opportunity Program at the university. As part of that, they called for an increase in the number of minority students and faculty members at Marquette.

Some 800 students began demonstrating on campus. Seven were arrested, including a priest. The Theology Department's faculty, expressing disgust with the failure of the administration to take steps to end institutional racism, threatened to resign from the university.

President Raynor promptly issued a rebuke to the demands, stating unequivocally, "This university will not be governed by coercion, nor will it respond to rash and loosely conceived program demands of such groups." Raynor did promise to form a broadly representative committee to work toward meeting demands.

"I knew where to get hold of Al," remembered SID Jim Foley. "He told me that he was going to wait until everything cooled down. When he came in, he picked the right time."

"Sometime after midnight [1:30 a.m.] we were there with Al and his players at the Holiday Inn Central. He invited us," noted Christopulos. "Al first asked Thompson, 'What are these guys doin' for you? They're just usin' you.'" McGuire went on to tell the players that they had God-given talents and should use those to better themselves. He added that quitting school was like cutting off their hands.

McGuire then met with Moye and the other activists at a nearby apartment. According to published reports, the shouting match between Moye and McGuire could be heard blocks away. "What Al didn't realize," explained Thompson, "was that there was and are some legitimate concerns that minority people had in their day. We had less hassles because we were ballplayers. But that didn't change the fact that we were minorities in a majority society. What Al was saying was his opinion. He was looking at it as a coach."

McGuire lashed out at the activists, priests, and others who tried to co-opt his players to their cause, according to Frank Deford's account in his story on McGuire, "Depression Baby," which later appeared in *Sports Illustrated.*

"The smooth-talking theorists he screamed at. The tough guys he ridiculed. He suggested to an idealistic white coed that she should take one of the black players home to her suburb for Thanksgiving. To a priest, he snarled, 'Don't come after these kids from the Jesuit house. You never bought a pound of butter in your life, and you're asking them to be kamikaze pilots.'"

McGuire diffused the situation early that morning. At 5:45 a.m. George Thompson released a statement saying that the players were going back to school. "We have met with Father McAuley and he has our best interests at heart."

"I think it was a couple or three days," said Thompson. "There was enough time to have passed that it got the attention of the city and Marquette administration. The administration then decided to make changes. Now they knew we were serious and they seemed to know the seriousness of the situation."

"Teams in the South had no black players in the 1960s," explained Foran. "With Al, who he perceived to be the guys who could do the job would be the ones on the floor."

"Al came along in an era when the black athlete was trying to find himself, and be accepted as far as society is concerned," said Raymonds. "There weren't any black athletes playing basketball down South. He came along at the right time. We would get calls from coaches in the South asking us, 'How do you handle the black player?' We said you treat them just like everyone else. These people played for Al because they knew he was doing something for them."

"Then Marquette made concessions to the organization," said Pat Smith. "When it hit the papers, what came out of it was a minority advancement program. We were serious about it. There was a lot of pressure on us."

"As a result of that stand, the university started the Minority Equal Opportunity Program, from which my wife was the first graduate," noted a proud Meminger. "The politically correct thing at the time was 'Let's do a minority program. We gotta give 'em a bone.' But what about the 200 years when you built the country on our backs?"

"It became the Educational Opportunity Program [EOP]," recalled Dr. James Scott, who was later named university vice president of student affairs. "Arnold Mitchum was named the first director of the program. He was taking his Ph.D. at Marquette. He did a good job."

Marquette was one of the first schools in the country to have a full-fledged EOP, according to James Sankovitz, a university vice president. He noted that Mitchum remains the EOP's national director.

But that was not the end of it. According to Foran, "The night of the Pere Marquette dinner, students blocked the door to the entrance. It was May 5, 1968. It was civil disobedience. A month later, Bobby Kennedy was killed."

Later that summer Tommie Smith and John Carlos raised their fists in the Black Power salute at the Olympic Games in Mexico City, a gesture that would be repeated during the upcoming basketball season.

And in Chicago, while the whole world was watching, what began as civil disobedience outside the Democratic National Convention turned into an uncivil disturbance as police battled—and battered—young demonstrators in the streets of Chicago, while inside the International Amphitheatre the beleaguered Democratic Party, still reeling from the assassination of Senator Robert Kennedy, nominated Vice President Hubert Humphrey for president.

What took place at Marquette was a microcosm of what was happening around the country. It was the beginning of consciousness-raising for players like Thompson, Simmons, Smith, and Meminger in determining who they were and where they fit into American society. For Meminger it was all about the importance of self-image.

"It [progress] doesn't happen in 50, 60, 70 years. Anything that was black, you hated. Self-hatred. There was not a healthy self-image for blacks." But McGuire was determined that the era he described as "hand grenades in their hands" would not impact his team. "Al said, 'Hey, we're not gonna have a checkerboard problem on my team.' We never had a problem in terms of race," noted Raspudic.

Joining Thompson, Joe Thomas, and the others for the 1968–69 campaign were sophomore guard Meminger, 6'5" center Ric Cobb, a transfer from Ranger (Texas) Junior College, and forward Hugh McMahon, another Erasmus Hall High alum and transfer from Frederick Military Academy in Portsmouth, Virginia, who became known as McGuire's original "enforcer." "An 'enforcer' is someone who wouldn't back down. I did whatever I could to play," said McMahon, a forward. "Not to be a tough guy, but if something was awry on the court, I was not backing down. Back then it [fighting] was an acceptable thing. That's how I got known." However, the team would have to do without their hard-nosed center Pat Smith, at least for the first half of the season.

"Al's expectations were that we were expected to be in the Final Four that season," recalled Smith, who was in his final year of eligibility. "I was suspended for the first semester. I didn't come back until the second semester. I didn't practice with the team. I was suspended a few times. He had reasons for doing it. We sat down and talked about it. He always had an open door policy. I had no problem with it. It was the first time in my life I wasn't playing basketball. I got time to study."

That season ushered in the Age of Aquarius as the Fifth Dimension soared to the top of the charts, as well as a "Ball of Confusion," the

Temptations' hit that mirrored the fissures in American society. That Top 10 hit started the psychedelic era at Motown.

Marquette still had a small lineup, with no starter taller than 6'6"; and that was Joe Thomas.

The Warriors won five of their first seven games. Then Bob Knight brought his Army Cadets to play Marquette in the Classic. Knight had a young player from Chicago named Mike Krzyzewski. It was the first time that Knight and McGuire had faced each other and McGuire came out on top, 62-42.

The Classic final went to overtime as Marquette continued its buzzer-beater mastery over the Badgers, 59-56. Other highlights included season sweeps of both DePaul and Loyola and an 11-game winning streak, the longest that a McGuire team had put together up to that time.

In order to get the team tournament-tough, McGuire had scheduled five of the last seven games on the road. At the University of Denver, Marquette was already assured a tournament bid, but ran up against a stubborn opponent.

Marquette was 18-4 and had already accepted a bid to the NCAA tournament. Denver had won just two games all year when Marquette came to town, according to Tom Collins.

"It was early in the second half and the Warriors were getting beaten," recalled Collins. "Al called time, walked out to the officials, and in a voice that could be heard all over the Rockies said: 'Hey, what are you guys tryin' to do to me? We're goin' to the NCAA, and these clowns aren't goin' anywhere.' When play resumed Denver was charged with traveling, charging, basket interference, and the Warriors went on a scoring run to win 65-61."

The team finished with a 22-4 record and a second straight trip to the Mideast Regionals. It was the third postseason in a row for the Warriors. But this time, McGuire expected bigger and better things from his experienced team.

After handling Murray State by 20 (82-62) at Carbondale, Illinois, the Warriors headed for a rematch with big, bad Kentucky at the UW Fieldhouse in Madison, which was as close to a home court advantage as Marquette could expect for a regional final.

"Kentucky had Pat Riley and Dan Issel. That game in my mind wasn't as big as the Texas Western–Kentucky NCAA final in 1966. But that Marquette-Kentucky game typified the 1960s: North against South. Their band was playing 'Dixie,' our band was playing 'Battle Hymn of the Republic.' White versus black. The confidence came from Al's demeanor and the guys who were on that team. When you rely on people and trust them, there's very little pressure playing in a basketball game," said Thompson, who called that regional one of the most significant games in his career at Marquette.

"In the locker room before the game, the Kentucky assistant coach knocked on our door while Al was giving us his pregame instructions," recalled Raspudic. "Al asked me, 'Who's at that door?' When I answered it, the Kentucky assistant asked, 'Coach Rupp wants to know which basket you want to take.' I relayed the message to Al," who told the young man to get lost, or words to that effect, according to Raspudic. During that regional, Rupp referred to McGuire as "son," which caused McGuire to shout back, "Don't call me son unless you're going to include me in your will."

Marquette outplayed the Wildcats in that contest, as McGuire used the home court advantage and revenge factor to his benefit, beating Rupp 81-74. "When we won that game, we showed that we had arrived," commented Thomas. "The next game against Purdue had almost become an anticlimax.

"Al had lost to Adolph in Lexington, but Al beat him in Madison," noted Jim Foley. "Al threw his coat in the air after that game and his wife, Pat, who was sitting next to me and said: 'Al, that's an expensive coat. But then we don't beat Kentucky every day,' she said." George Thompson leaped into the air with both arms outstretched as a coatless McGuire threw a victorious fist into the air as he walked off the floor.

"I thought that Al had a better team in 1969," recalled Cawood Ledford. "We had a pretty good outside shooter in Larry Steele, whom Marquette decided not to cover so that they could double Dan Issel. Steele could not hit anything he put up that night and George Thompson was such an all-around player. He had a super game against Kentucky."

That night, a Marquette booster somehow obtained the telephone number to Rupp's hotel room and made a crank call to the Baron in the wee hours of the morning. "I heard those Catholic boys put a whippin' on your boys today, what happened?" said the voice in a mock southern accent on the other end of the line. "Well, those Catholic boys have a pretty good team," Rupp reportedly responded before hanging up.

The Warriors still had not come down from that big win when George King's Purdue Boilermakers awaited Marquette in the regional final. The winner would advance to the Final Four.

"We had a helluva team. It was kinda quiet in the locker room before the game. It was the quietest locker room I had been in. I was reflective because it was the last game that I would play at Marquette," recalled Pat Smith. It would also be George Thompson's last game as a Warrior. He finished his three-year career as the all-time leading scorer in school history and still owns a number of records. He was a second round draft pick by the Minnesota Muskies [which later became the Pittsburgh Condors] of the ABA, and was taken in the fifth round of the NBA draft by the Boston Celtics.

"I'd heard of Al when I was at Purdue," recalled James Scott. "That game was televised back to Lafayette. I can remember Al taking off his coat and slamming it on the sideline because he wasn't happy with a call. I thought he was nuts. I can remember watching the whole game and still hearing the drums beating during the game. This was when they still let the school bands play during the games."

Both teams played well in that game, but Marquette was uncharacteristically skittish at the free-throw line. The game went into overtime. Marquette's tough 6'1" guard Jackie Burke was guarding sweet-shooting Rick Mount, who was having an outstanding game, according to Pat Smith.

The seconds ticked down in the overtime period with the score tied 73-73. "Bill Keller won the game for Purdue," recalled Gary Brell. Keller fed Mount the ball in the right corner and he put up his final shot of the game, a high arc that swished through the net at the buzzer. Marquette lost 75-73 and Purdue advanced to the Final Four, where they defeated Drake. And UCLA defeated North Carolina. In his last NCAA Final Four, Lew Alcindor helped UCLA soundly defeat Mount and the Boilermakers, 92-72.

"I'm still waiting for the rebound of Mount's last shot," said a dejected Pat Smith.

"That game would have put us in the Final Four," said Thompson. "I probably would have gone higher in the draft. I was drafted by the Baltimore Colts as a wide receiver and a D-back. The ABA came along and I got a no-cut contract."

After the game, all that McGuire could say was, "Rick Mount is the best pure shooter I have ever seen."

"It [Kentucky win] was the sky above and the mud below [Purdue loss] in 24 hours," said Thompson. "Beating their best [Kentucky]. And then we couldn't get any lower than after the Purdue loss. I took pleasure in spanking him [Mount] every time we played the Indiana Pacers in the ABA," concluded Thompson, who was named to the NABC's 25th Anniversary team.

After finishing with a 24-5 record, number 14 in both polls, and a number 12 defensive ranking, Marquette prepared for another season. Their experienced incoming squad would be filled with juniors and seniors, including Dean Meminger, Ric Cobb, Joe Thomas, Jeff Sewell, and Gary "Goose" Brell.

Marquette's three strong postseason appearances and as many 20-win seasons put the team squarely in the public eye, but the visibility of the basketball program was also helped by television. The die was cast in 1968, when the viewing numbers exploded for college basketball's first mega-event, Lew Alcindor and UCLA versus Elvin "The Big E" Hayes and Houston, playing in the Houston Astrodome.

Local stations such as Channel 18, which beamed games from around the country back to Milwaukee, as well as regional syndicates like Eddie Einhorn's TVS, made the deal not only for the UCLA-Houston game but also for independent schools, such as Marquette, to televise their rivalries. The take for the UCLA-Houston game was $27,500, according to Einhorn, who was involved with 25 Final Fours between 1956 and 1980. The exposure helped Marquette publicize itself and became a valuable tool in the recruiting process, a fact that was not lost on the publicity-conscious McGuire.

"After we started doing games with Notre Dame and Marquette, those schools were getting a recruiting edge with the television exposure," noted Einhorn.

"In the Midwest, it was Marquette," noted Dean Meminger. "During those ten years (1967–77) it was Marquette. When Marquette was on television and the star was Dean Meminger, that's recruitment. The big time was my sophomore year (1968–69). That's when people found out we were not Marquette, Michigan."

TVS's Einhorn worked with independents such as Marquette, Notre Dame, St. John's and South Carolina. "Back then conference teams didn't have the flexibility to do televised games on the weekends, due to the schedules," said Einhorn, who added that Big 10 teams did not want to play independents in the middle of their schedule. Einhorn also remembered McGuire from his playing days as the "quintessential New Yorker from the accent to the mannerisms.

"Frank McGuire was a friend of mine. But I didn't get to know Al well until I expanded TVS when I wanted to use Midwestern independents in my package. Al was good copy. His teams played good games. When you needed personality, I tried to make the coaches the personalities. My biggest were Wooden, [Digger] Phelps, and McGuire. They were the personalities in the business. I tried to build them up.

"Each coach was different. A different style. They were the personalities, but of course they backed it up with good coaching and good teams."

When asked what made McGuire stand out from his coaching brethren, Einhorn recalled, "He was always yapping about the timeouts. He was the first to utilize the TV timeout. 'You're gonna call one, aren't you?' he would ask me during games. He was always thinking. I used to be right near him on the court. 'Yep, Al, I'm gonna call one,' I would tell him during a game."

In Chicago, UHF channels 32 and 44 carried the games of Loyola and DePaul, whose games with Marquette were usually televised. One of the sponsors was Gonnella bread and the announcer was Red Rush (a.k.a. "the Swella Gonnella Fella"). "Loyola was playing Marquette in the Milwaukee Arena. It was packed to the brim," said Rush. "I had to have Al on the air before the game, and Al was trying to beg off by saying the game was about to begin. I said to him, 'Al, you promised.' Then Al pointed to the fans in the farthest corners of the arena and told me, 'They're here because of Marquette and they want to see the game.' I said, 'Al, don't you think they would rather see you on TV doing public relations for Marquette and have the game start a little late?' Then a big smile came across his face and he said, 'You're right, baby, let's go!'"

McGuire also became involved in television locally with his own television show, which aired during the basketball season. *The Al McGuire Show,* which was originally sponsored by Schlitz, usually opened with McGuire driving his Kawasaki motorcycle or Thunderbird with the top down through Milwaukee. The opening looked like a television commercial. And Snyder's of Oconomowoc was making the dapper Irishman look even better with their fancy threads.

Just a year after his set-to with the administration over his contract, McGuire inked a new five-year deal, which would take him through the 1973–74 season. He also received his first car—the Thunderbird—as part of the package. McGuire still had three years remaining on his 1967 contract, which gave President Raynor pause at that time.

"He had three years left on his contract and he renegotiated," Raynor recalled. "He was crazy to do so. [I told Al] he shouldn't bind himself for a number of years. 'Well, if we extend it,' I told McGuire at the time, 'we're all gonna live by it.' Al said, 'Don't worry, father.'" "If you're the president of a big institution, if you give 'em a job, expect them to do the job, was my philosophy," said McGuire.

In order to invest some of his newfound largesse, McGuire and some friends invested in Joe Deutsch's Restaurant and renamed it Time Out. It was quite possibly the first sports bar in Milwaukee. McGuire decked out the waitstaff in referee uniforms and oversaw the menu. While he promised to appear at the establishment a number of times each week, he rarely showed, according to those who frequented Time Out.

It was rumored the Marquette administration asked McGuire to divest himself of his one-sixth partnership at Time Out, where one of Al's bartenders was Hughie McMahon. "Father Raynor did not ask me to relinquish my interest there," explained McGuire. "It was an investment. But I didn't want to put the time in. Time Out was not a working investment for me. The other partners wanted me to be around the bar and make appearances. I just didn't want to do it."

Time Out was mere window-dressing for the coach. McGuire pretty much had the town to himself after Vince Lombardi left Green Bay after the 1968 NFL season. The Packers had won Super Bowls I and II and Lombardi decided to make a change. He was named head coach of the Washington Redskins in 1969. That season the expansion Seattle Pilots were a year away from becoming the Milwaukee Brewers, and the Milwaukee Bucks were getting their feet wet in the NBA with their franchise player, rookie Lew Alcindor.

For the 1969–70 season, McGuire's main worry was finding a big-time center of his own to complement his returning starters. While Ric Cobb could jump through the ceiling at 6'5", which prompted McGuire to dub him the Elevator Man, Cobb was not a natural center.

McGuire did not have to look far for 6'11" Jim Chones, who was right under his nose at St. Catherine's High School in Racine, Wisconsin. He became McGuire's third blue-chip player. Chones told his story to writer Terry Pluto:

"I was very interested in Grambling [State University in Louisiana] because they had a great tradition," said Chones, a high school All-America, "but I never heard from Grambling. Bill Fitch, who would later coach me with the Cavs, was at the University of Minnesota and he was recruiting me hard, but I wasn't interested in Minnesota. I made a visit to Michigan State and I liked that. Fitch told me, 'If you don't go to Minnesota, you should play for Al McGuire at Marquette.' But I hadn't heard much of anything from Marquette, and I was only 25 miles away.

"Late in the recruiting process, Al McGuire called me and said, 'On Friday, I'm going to come down to Racine and see you.' They came to see me in my beat-up old house with the vinyl floors torn up and looking like a map of the United States. There were roaches crawling on the walls, wood splinters coming off the walls. As we were talking, the roaches were falling off the walls and dropping onto people.

"I was totally embarrassed for Al McGuire to see how we were living. Al McGuire sat next to me in a beat-up chair. He said, 'Look, we want you to come to Marquette and I can talk about education and all the other good things we have to offer, but the real thing for you to know is that if you do what we tell you, you can be a pro and get the hell out of all this shit.'

"When Al left our home, my dad loved him and he told me, 'I want you to play for Al McGuire.' I had over 200 offers. I went to a Catholic high school and the people there wanted me to go to Marquette, although they tried not to put any pressure on me. Despite the fact that we were poor, I wasn't a street kid. I had five brothers and sisters, I used to have to be home at night and would baby-sit the younger kids in the family. We weren't allowed to swear at home. We went to church on Sundays."

Chones's parents, who were once sharecroppers in Mississippi, were among the first blacks to settle in Racine, according to Chones, who noted that he was also recruited by such nationwide powers as UCLA, Michigan, Louisville, and North Carolina.

"They wanted me to send back their questionnaires," said Chones. "I wanted to spend time at home. My dad was dying of cancer . . . My mom was washing dishes in a restaurant.

"I had people [recruiters] offer me homes, money, cars, but I didn't want any of that. If you give me the education, I'll play hard for you, I said.

"[With Al] it was honesty with a purpose. There was a method to it. He'll make an honest statement, but it is made so you will be emotionally dependent on him. After I signed, I didn't see him again until the first day of practice at Marquette for the 1969–70 season. My dad died a month into my freshman year. One of the first innovative things that I saw was players having their ankles taped. I never saw players getting their ankles taped," said Chones.

Recalled outgoing sports information director Jim Foley, "I went to Marquette with George Thompson. My last official function as SID was to announce that Jim Chones was coming to Marquette. And I went to the Milwaukee Bucks just as Lew Alcindor was coming in." Foley had joined the Bucks as vice president of public relations, a position he held for 15 years. "I earned my bachelor's degree at Marquette, but I got my master's with Al in four years."

Other players joining the freshman squad were George "Sugar" Frazier, a 6'3" forward from the Bronx, 6'4" forward Kurt Spychalla, of Schofield, Wisconsin, and the coach's son and namesake, Al "Allie" McGuire, a 6'3" guard from Milwaukee, who was also coveted by Dean Smith at North Carolina.

One player McGuire certainly figured to get was Brian Winters, who grew up on Newport Avenue, just a three-minute walk from 120th and Rockaway Boulevard, where Allie lived as a youngster.

"When I was growing up we were friends," said Winters. "We were six or seven. I went to St. Francis de Sales Grade School. The only time I remember Al coming over to the house, we were in the kitchen. He had come up to the house and just walked in. He didn't knock or ring the bell. He just walked in and said to my grandmother, 'Hi, Mrs. McDermott.' It was the spring of 1969. Al knew me and he knew my family."

"I grew up with Brian," recalled Allie McGuire, "until second grade. But after we moved to Charlotte there was a long time that I never saw him," adding that it was not necessarily a done deal that Winters would go to Marquette. "He did visit."

"I knew Allie had turned into a pretty good player at Marquette. I just told Al that South Carolina would be a better place for me. He was always cordial. When he came down to Columbia to do a clinic with Frank

McGuire, he had a rental car that he didn't use. So he gave me the keys. Al was a lively guy. He had a lot of intensity. He knew how to motivate a team. He had his own flair to him. He did something offbeat to create interest."

While it seemed a lead-pipe cinch that Brian Winters would come to Marquette, losing the prospect backed up McGuire's contention that he could not recruit kids with grass in front of their homes. "Give me the cracked sidewalks, the cockroaches, and the urine smell, and I can recruit you every time. But suburbia or grass in front of your home, no way!" he said. The only other All-America McGuire missed on in his 13 years at Marquette was Jim McMillian, who went on to star at Columbia and in the NBA with the L.A. Lakers.

While the 300,000 flower children were preaching peace and love at Yasgur's Farm during the Woodstock Festival in the summer of 1969, McGuire decided to take a dip in the ocean off Rockaway. As he was running in preparing to make his lifeguard dive, something gave in his leg. As he came out, he told his wife, Pat, that he was going to be sick. As it turned out, he had ruptured the Achilles tendon in his left leg.

After surgery, he was recuperating in a New York hospital when Eddie Bacalles and some of his New York friends came in to cheer him up with a game of cards. While he did not like to lose at recruiting, he was even more competitive in cards.

"We were having a pretty good card game," recalled Bacalles, a long-time New York barkeep, "when Al says that he has to go to the john. But he insists that we go in there and bring the cards with us. He figured that while he was in the john someone would fool with his cards. That's how competitive he is."

That season McGuire accepted a transfer from Casper (Wyoming) Junior College, Bob Lackey. The 6'6" power forward helped lead his Evanston (Illinois) Township High School team to the Illinois State basketball championship in 1968. Lackey was referred to McGuire by coach Don Peterson of Delaware University, who had been invited as the guest speaker for the Marquette team's postseason awards banquet the previous season.

Peterson wrote McGuire, "We can't touch him with our limited program. But you ought to talk to him. You won't be sorry." His postscript noted that McGuire could reach Lackey through a barber in Evanston.

"When no one else could get Bob Lackey to come to Marquette, McGuire said, 'I'm going to Evanston and I will bring him here,'" recalled Sam Sauceda, chairman of Marquette's athletic board.

"It was about 11:30 p.m. when I got there [at the barbershop], but the place was open," recalled McGuire. "[James] Gordon told us he would be glad to help, and he was the man who we made the original contact through."

McGuire later met Lackey's family. After a month's correspondence and a visit to Milwaukee, Lackey signed a letter of intent. He had offers from Texas, Northern Illinois, Northwestern, Iowa, and the University of Wisconsin.

Also moving up a notch his junior year was transfer Gary Brell. "McGuire asked me at practice, 'And who are you again?'" Brell remembered. "That's why everyone had a nickname. That's why nicknames were such a big thing in our school. I was Goose.

"We were playing Northern Illinois University in a scrimmage my junior year. One of their guys said, 'You're ugly. You look just like a Goose.' I did have a twitch," Brell said. "Ric Cobb heard it. And the name stuck. It was easier for Al to remember," said Brell, who had expressed his disapproval for the Vietnam war while a student, and would walk off the floor when the National Anthem was played before games. McGuire accepted Brell, even though they did have their run-ins. "There's something called individual dignity here [at Marquette]. I may not agree with Goose on the Vietnam issue, and I may not agree with everything the blacks say on campus. But, hey, at least it's occurred to me that they could be right and I could be wrong," McGuire said at the time.

"I'd be in his office a lot," Brell noted. "He actually gave us a lot of freedom. He'd send in one of the guys. Al didn't go into local hangouts around school. He didn't care if you went out and had a beer. But if he saw you, there'd be a problem. He'd have to deal with it," said Brell of McGuire's preseason dictum: "Here's where I go, the rest of the city's yours."

Later that spring Crosby, Stills, Nash and Young's "Ohio" eulogized the four students gunned down by National Guardsmen at Kent State University, opening the divide of the generation gap even further and deepening students' distrust of people over 30. Students were burning draft cards and women were burning bras.

"We really didn't have that tough a set of rules. One, you had to go to school. Two, you had to maintain a good G.P.A. Three, your time was your own until practice. Four, he expected you to play 100 percent. Five, he gave you personal freedom. Six, he didn't cut scholarships.

"He was one of the first coaches to insist that if you go to Marquette, you signed a contract to graduate," Brell continued. "They [Paul Carbins and Pat Smith] were still being helped by the school in their program. Fierce loyalty was here with Al toward his players."

In fact, McGuire said it would be his happiest day at Marquette when he saw Pat Smith graduate. In 1970, Smith graduated with a history degree and went on to work in a community outreach program in Milwaukee.

"We [black athletes] brought a lot to Marquette," said Dean Meminger. "There was some reciprocity involved. The university was very supportive in terms of making sure we got an education."

"He [McGuire] was a big fish that landed in a small pool," Brell continued. "Milwaukee really embraced him. He was involved in a lot of things. When he would talk about how coaches dealt with race relations on their basketball teams, he would say, 'I don't have a black problem. I have a white problem.' That was me," said Brell. "The black guys paved my driveway. What he meant was that because of their talent, they made him look good and successful. They [black players] knew it wasn't a racist statement. It was a compliment to our guys.

"It was a mix that fit really well," Brell explained of their team. "He kept that together. He would tell us, 'Hey, look. There's 40 minutes in a ball game. There are ten players on the court. Four minutes is the maximum you're gonna see it [the ball].' One of the greatest coaching philosophies was that you gotta learn to play without the ball."

In August of 1969, Marquette lost its athletic director when Stan Lowe died. "Al became interim athletic director after Stan died until December or January of 1970," recalled James Scott, who had come to Marquette to succeed Ed Kurdziel as dean of students. "Stan took the Arena seating for season tickets with him to his grave. The season ticket [seating arrangements] had to be reconstructed because it wasn't written down.

"Al came in to see me in October to talk about being athletic director," continued Scott, "I told him that the big question to consider is being able to handle basketball and administer the rest of the athletic department. We only had men's sports at that time. We didn't have women's sports until after Title IX was passed in 1972. Al came to me and said, 'I'm not going to be a candidate for athletic director.' It was later that Sam Sauceda of the language department came in and asked if he could be a candidate. He had just been elected chairman of the athletic board. Not long after, he was named AD."

Another goal for McGuire was to resurrect the basketball series between Marquette and Notre Dame. Fighting Irish coach Johnny Dee, who was hired the same year as McGuire, was all for it.

"Hickey screwed it up [the series]," noted Dee. "Marquette contacted me that they would like to start it up again. Marquette used to play a halfway decent schedule until McGuire got there. He admits it. He's very sensitive about it.

"Then you look at our schedule. We get to talkin' about schedules. It became a big item. In our area—Milwaukee to South Bend, Detroit, and Dayton. There were always six or seven teams fighting for one [at-large NCAA] berth. Marquette, Loyola, DePaul, Notre Dame, Detroit, and Dayton. We were all fighting for one or two at-large bids in that area."

Marquette lost to Michigan early in the season, but then reeled off 12 straight wins, including a 72-60 defeat of DePaul in Chicago and a 64-43 whipping of Wisconsin to win the Milwaukee Classic.

Marquette's winning streak ended during a Chicago Stadium doubleheader, where 15,864 saw Marquette lose to Loyola and Notre Dame defeat Illinois. "These were teams that were physically afraid of us," recalled McMahon. "When we played other teams, like Loyola, occasionally we would get together with some of the opposing players. But I remember at Loyola, the players telling us, 'We're not allowed to go out with you guys. You guys are crazy.' These people were afraid to play us. You could look down at the other bench in the Arena and you could see the expressions on the players faces that seemed to say, 'What are we doing here?'"

The Warriors then headed to South Bend to play Notre Dame for the first time since the 1958–59 season. Notre Dame had recently opened its new Joyce Athletic and Convocation Center (ACC). Previously, the team played in a 2,700-seat fieldhouse on campus.

According to Mike Christopulos, who covered the game for the *Milwaukee Sentinel*, Marquette had two chances to win, with 40 seconds remaining in regulation and with five seconds left in the first overtime.

"With 40 seconds left in regulation, the score was tied at 70. Marquette had possession and called time-out," wrote Christopulos. "After going into the delay, an official called for a jump ball with 26 seconds left, between Meminger and Notre Dame's Jackie Meehan, ruling that Meminger was not advancing the ball within five seconds.

"The rule book states that a jump ball will be called 'if a closely guarded player is either within a few feet of a front court boundary intersection or in his midcourt area dribbles or combines holding the ball and dribbling for five seconds.' The rule applies only if a player is in an area within 19 feet of the midcourt line. Meminger was farther down court, making the five-second rule inapplicable."

"The official made a bad call," admitted Gene Sullivan, who was an assistant to Notre Dame coach Johnny Dee at the time.

"Meehan controlled the tip and McGuire later drew a technical foul when he told an official what he thought of the call. Austin Carr, who led all scorers with 38 points, missed the free throw that would have won the game in regulation for Notre Dame."

With five seconds remaining in the first overtime, Marquette led 81-79 and had possession. All the Warriors had to do was run out the clock.

"We had the lead and they're pressing us," recalled team manager Goran Raspudic. "Al calls time-out and said whatever you do, don't throw the ball inbounds at this end of the court."

"They took a time-out," recalled Dee. The only thing we could hope for was to intercept the ball to send it into [a second] overtime. I called a second time-out, but I substituted some kids. I ended up with one forward and four guards."

"Jackie Burke inbounded a pass to Joe Thomas, who tried to pass to Dean Meminger," according to Christopulos. "Notre Dame's Mike O'Connell deflected the pass into the hands of his teammate Tom Sinnott. Sinnott quickly passed to Austin Carr who tied the game with a layup.

"'The game was over and all we had to do was throw the ball downcourt,' McGuire was quoted. 'We still had a tie game and five minutes to win in the second overtime. But we couldn't pick it up again, we couldn't get a spurt in the second overtime.' Joe Thomas later admitted that he should have just held onto the ball."

"He was absolutely out of his mind," said Dee of McGuire after the loss. McGuire said, "I never talk about officials after a game." While

McGuire usually was pretty good about leaving games behind, this one was a little hard to swallow.

The Warriors won their final eight games of the season, which included a 10-point revenge win over Southern Illinois, a 20-point win over Detroit, and a 19-point win over DePaul at the Arena that included some extracurricular activity featuring Jeff Sewell. "Jeff was giving one of the Meyer boys a tough time," recalled Gary Brell. DePaul's Tom Tracy "just cold-cocked Jeff and put him out cold," said Brell. "Jeff took this mellow attitude. He had a wife and a kid. He averaged 57 points a game in high school. Probably the best shooter I'd seen.

"McGuire could never get to him," Brell continued. "It happened before halftime," continued McMahon. "McGuire was incensed. He says to Jeff, 'I'll give you $50 if you go over to that DePaul locker room and clock that guy.' Jeff didn't react, said McMahon, "so Brell and I say, 'we'll do it for nothin' coach!'"

"Amidst all the protests and burnings that took place in the late 1960s, McGuire's players were pressured by groups on campus," noted Ed Janka, a former assistant basketball coach at John Carroll College who was a student at Marquette in the 1960s and a graduate assistant to McGuire. "The players wanted a moment of silence before the game at the University of Detroit. Al McGuire sees a lot deeper into people or situations than most people. That was one of his biggest assets as a coach and in business.

"Spencer Haywood and Scrappy Jackson were playing for Detroit. The Detroit guys asked us if we wanted to do a Black Power salute in honor of Malcolm X's birthday. They asked us, 'Are you down?' I went to all of the players on our team and asked if they would participate. Malcolm was our king. From where we came from he did the whole nine yards. He gave his life for his people," said Dean Meminger.

"I went to Al and he said, 'OK, fine.' We did it after the National Anthem was played. We did it on our side and they [Detroit players] did it on their side. It was just like Tommie Smith and John Carlos in Mexico City in 1968."

Marquette finished 22-3 on the year, the best record in the school's history, and the team finished eighth and tenth in the country in the AP and UPI polls, respectively. Its defensive ranking was number ten. In fact, before the season began, McGuire had predicted, "This year I consider us a defensive team."

And on the subject of polls, McGuire was quoted in Alex Thien's *Milwaukee Journal* column as saying, "I'm against them, even if we are in the so-called Magic 10. It seems that in football and basketball, because of polls, coaches are trying to bury each other. We're all in the same union . . . all bricklayers trying to build better homes. We're all hookers under the skin. I just don't think it's a good idea to see one team trying to beat another by 60 points."

While McGuire was criticized by coaches like Johnny Dee on scheduling cupcakes, McGuire's response was, "This year we added Notre Dame, Southern Illinois, Michigan, and St. Louis. You can sometimes build your schedule according to the other coach and his problems. I mean, I like to play DePaul late in the season because they come up with injuries. But Drake, I wanted early."

And scheduling may have played a part in the NCAA's decision in 1970 to send Marquette out of its region—the Mideast—to the Midwest, to play its early regional games in Fort Worth, Texas.

"I'm disgusted," McGuire said at the time. "I'm sick about the whole thing. They're [NCAA Tournament committee] treating us like patsies. We're rated eighth in the nation, and they're pushing us around.

"I'm deeply disappointed," McGuire was quoted in Mike Christopulos's account. "I feel a power complex within the NCAA has buckled under and tried to treat us as little brothers. Our heart was set on going to the NCAA tournament at Dayton. We have four starters back from the team that went to the finals of the Mideast NCAA Regionals a year ago. We have the finest record in my history at Marquette.

"I can't figure it out. When they told me this morning that we had been picked for the Midwest and not the Mideast, I was shocked. I couldn't believe it. It was absolutely crazy. We belong in Dayton. That's all there is to it. I tried to reach certain men on the committee and get to the bottom of it but the only person I talked to was from West Virginia (basketball coach Garland Moran). He said he voted us high.

"I'm not good at ethical politics. I'm better in the street. If you slap me, I'm going to punch you."

McGuire then questioned the ethics of the five men on the Mideast Selection Committee—Georgia athletic director Joel Eaves, Kentucky coach Adolph Rupp, Ohio State coach Fred Taylor, Georgia Tech coach John Hyden, and Moran.

"We're not a political power inside the NCAA," McGuire noted in a 1977 WRIT radio special. "The only independent school that's a power inside the NCAA is Notre Dame, and that's because of tradition. We have created something [at Marquette]."

"They worry more about giving a T-shirt to a ballplayer than their own ethics. The only thing you'll get from the NCAA is a straw hat in a snowstorm. I just can't see the thinking in what they've done unless we're building a mini-dynasty at Marquette and jealousy got involved. It might have been something between the committee members and me," McGuire speculated. "But if the knowledge of this gets out, it could hurt the NCAA."

McGuire continued, "If we can't represent our territory in the NCAAs with a 19-3 record, what do we have to do, go 23-0? They couldn't give us a reason why we weren't picked for the Mideast. If you go back to the schedules, the records, the UPI polls, the AP poll, anyway you go back, we should have been picked to go to Dayton. If you go back to the records, how can you put Notre Dame ahead of us? I can't recall another time when a team voted in the top ten of both polls has ever been moved out of its own territory like we were."

"After Al blasted the NCAA Selection Committee in 1970 for taking Marquette out of its region," recalled Mike Christopulos, "I called Adolph Rupp to get his reaction. Rupp blasted Al scathingly. Then ten minutes later, Rupp called back and asked if he could retract it, so I did."

"Al's biggest rivalries were the NCAA," pointed out Bill Jauss. "He cut through all the politics to make his point."

"Al was so upset and so persuasive that he was convinced that Rupp and the NCAA were out to get him," recalled David Foran. "He contacted the Marquette athletic board and persuaded them of what he believed to be the case, and that Marquette should go to the NIT. It was a spontaneous, emotional response. Many teams at that time were getting moved around in the pairings. They wanted to balance the regionals," said Foran, attempting to rationalize the committee's decision.

McGuire then informed his players of the decision, and his passionate explanation of his reasoning convinced his players that the NIT was the way to go. McGuire held a press conference at the university to explain the decision to the students and the public, which was met at first with disbelief, but then followed by a groundswell of support and sympathy for McGuire's position.

"Adolph Rupp and the committee wanted to send us to the Midwest Regional," recalled Thomas. "They wanted Notre Dame and Jacksonville in the Mideast . . . Rupp didn't want to play us again after what happened in Madison the year before," added Thomas, who was Team Captain that season.

"Initially," said Foran, "we all wanted to go the NCAA Tournament. They [NCAA] wanted to send us out of the Mideast Region. Notre Dame had a tougher schedule in 1969–70 season, but we had a better record than Notre Dame and a better schedule than Jacksonville. We said, 'Hey, you're gonna put us in a regional away from our fans.' Al asked us what did we think. We agreed with him that we should go to the NIT. We decided we're gonna follow Al. He planted the seed.

"After the decision was made, the day after it was decided that we were not going to the tournament, it was decided [by the Marquette hierarchy] that if Marquette was invited to the NCAA tournament in the future, we were going."

This position was further solidified when the university vice president Scott was informed via memo by Father Raynor that the recommendations from all concerned regarding the team's participation in tournaments would go through Father Raynor. In other words, the final decision would no longer be McGuire's to make alone.

The Warriors were once again headed to the Big Apple to play at Madison Square Garden. The latest incarnation of the venerable palace was at 33rd and Eighth Avenue. McGuire had put the pressure square on his shoulders and taken it away from his players, allowing them to do their thing. This was not the first time a team had rejected an NCAA bid in favor of the NIT. George Ireland chose the same route in 1962, but for less controversial reasons. The Ramblers reached the NIT semifinals, finishing in third place.

After Marquette arrived in New York, McGuire sequestered the team in a hotel where no one knew where they were. ABC's Howard Cosell wanted to talk to McGuire and called Milwaukee to find out how he could reach him.

"Merle Harmon arranged the interview," said Tom Collins. "We were in a hotel room on a piano bench and when Howard was ready to go he turns his back to me and says, 'Hello again, everyone, this is Howard Cosell with the great Marquette coach, Al McGuire. Al, it's great to see you again. How are you?' When we were done he bought us lunch across the street. Afterward, Al says, 'He went on about how he was my good friend and I never met the SOB!'"

Marquette introduced new uniforms for the NIT, solid blue singlets with thin gold horizontal stripes designed by Medalist Industries, with some input from McGuire. Their appearance prompted the nickname "bumblebee." Their warmups also boasted a patch commemorating the moonwalk of the Apollo 11 astronauts, for whom Marquette retired the uniform number 11.

"He got the Apollo 11 astronauts to come to Marquette to give us patches to put on our uniforms," said Brell, who had transferred from the University of North Dakota and UWM to play ball at Marquette. "He made an event out of something. Those astronauts [Armstrong, Aldrin, and Collins] came to Marquette."

After the NIT, the NCAA banned Marquette's "bumblebee" uniforms because they were deemed to have a "psychedelic effect" on opposing players, according to Hank Raymonds. It was the first time that the NCAA had banned a team's uniform.

Marquette's first NIT opponent was the University of Massachusetts Minutemen, who were led by a sophomore named Julius Erving, a rising star on the East Coast at the time, but well before he became known as "Dr. J."

"I knew he [Erving] was the leading rebounder in the country," recalled Meminger, who did not touch the ball for much of the first half. "He didn't have a great offensive game. He wasn't really concerning us."

"We'd heard about Julius," recalled Norman Ochs. "I told Al before the NIT, 'You really have to be careful of Massachusetts. They have a kid who can really play.' Jack Lynam was the UMass coach."

As Wayne Embry, then of the Milwaukee Bucks, recalled in Terry Pluto's book *Loose Balls*, "The next time I noticed Julius was when Marquette played UMass in the first round of the NIT. Al McGuire and Marquette really didn't believe that UMass could be any good. But UMass jumped out to a 12-0 lead and Julius had eight of those points."

McGuire's worst fears were being realized. Here he had brashly turned down the NCAA to come to the NIT, where his team was the favorite, and a player whom he considered an unknown was making his team look bad and making him look like a fool.

"McGuire called time-out and said to Hank Raymonds, 'Who the hell is that kid out there?' Raymonds said, 'That's Julius, coach.' 'Julius who? What d'ya mean, Julius?'

"By now, McGuire was ranting and raving, screaming, 'Who's this Julius guy?' Remember, all this was going on during a time-out. Raymonds said, 'He's from New York.' Al screamed, 'New York! New York! We get all the good players from New York. How come I didn't know about this guy?'

"Then Al grabbed Dean Meminger, who was from New York, and screamed, 'Dean, how come I don't know about this Julius guy?' Al was really beside himself. He grabbed Gary Brell on the bench, shook him, and said, 'Go out there and don't let him score another point.'"

Marquette put a box and one defense on Erving and "cut his head off," McGuire recalled.

"Half the time I was on Julius," recalled Brell. "I boxed him out at the free-throw circle, and he just went over me and tipped the ball into the basket. He reminded me a lot of Connie Hawkins," said Brell, whose teammates at Pius High School were Freddie Brown and Johnnie Johnson. Brell had also known Rick Majerus since grade school.

"He [Erving] didn't get big until he left school. I think he [McGuire] was kinda surprised that this diamond in the rough went to UMass," said Brell.

"We just played hard," Meminger recalled. "We may have had to make adjustments at halftime. When we decided to play our game in the second half, we shut 'em down."

The Warriors won 62-55. Next up was Mike Newlin and the Utah Utes, whom Marquette easily dispatched, 83-63. "We didn't have any close games in the NIT," recalled Brell.

Each morning of the NIT, a press conference was held. Before Marquette and LSU squared off, Tiger coach Press Maravich, who was Pete's dad, was holding court with McGuire. According to Marquette Vice President James Sankovitz, sportswriter Pete Axthelm asked Maravich what he anticipated from a defensive team like Marquette since LSU did not see much defense in the SEC during the regular season.

"Press said that 'Watching a team like Marquette play defense is like watching grass grow.' Al then grabbed the microphone from Maravich and retorted, 'Well, if watching defense is like watching grass grow, your ass is grass and I'm the lawn mower,'" to howls of laughter.

That night, "Pistol" Pete Maravich and the LSU Tigers were ready to play the Warriors. It was Maravich's senior year and he was still leading the nation in scoring. McGuire rotated fresh players in to hound Maravich the entire game, and he took just nine shots.

"Dean, Jackie Burke and Jeff Sewell played on Pete all night," said Thomas, who credited McGuire's triangle-and-two defense with holding Maravich well under his season-leading average.

"When he [McGuire] beat Maravich and LSU in the NIT, what he did in that game was intimidate him," noted George Affuso, one of McGuire's players from Belmont Abbey who attended the NIT Final with Abbey teammate Bill Dockery.

"So he [McGuire] had two guys follow Maravich all over the court. Maravich didn't get a shot off because you didn't let him handle the ball until late in the first half. And he just shut him down in the second half. He had like 20 points, 16 from the free-throw line," noted Affuso, recalling the same defense McGuire used at Belmont Abbey. Maravich *averaged* 44.5 a game during the 1969–70 season.

"We ran Pete Maravich into the ground," said McGuire. "We pressured him on offense and kept running on defense."

"We played 'Pistol' Pete well in the NIT in 1970," recalled Meminger, one of the players McGuire designated to hound the Pistol. "It was heaven. The NIT was big time back then. Pete Maravich could get only 20 points. He would acknowledge me when we saw each other later on. 'You see this little guy, here. He will follow you everywhere. Even to the bathroom,'" Meminger said of Maravich's compliments of his defense.

The Warriors would face St. John's in the finals, but they had some personnel problems to square away before tip-off. It was not certain whether Gary "Goose" Brell would be playing for Marquette in the final. He had skipped out on a team meal to spend time with his girlfriend.

"The biggest highlight of that season was when I was booted off the club," recalled Brell. "I went to visit my girlfriend's parents in Yonkers. We were supposed to go up to Power Memorial for practice. We finally got to practice. Then we had to eat the team meal.

"I went to the restaurant. I told the team, 'I'll see you later.' But Bob Weingart, our trainer, didn't think that my mind was in the right place. He pushed me, I pushed him, and we had a scuffle at the dinner table. And then I left, and I spent two hours in Yonkers.

"I got back to the hotel lobby and my bags were packed and an airline ticket back to Milwaukee was on top.[My teammate] Terry McQuade said, 'You're in big trouble.' The team manager, Goran Raspudic, was going to take me to Kennedy [airport]. Al was gone. I wanted to talk to him."

"We were preparing for St. John's," recalled athletic director Dr. Sam Sauceda. "Al told Hank to pack him [Brell] up and send him home. I saw Hank. I said we should put him up at the hotel across from Madison Square Garden. I left a message for Al. I told Hank to put Brell up at the hotel. I talked to Pat [McGuire]. Pat said to me, 'You did the right thing, because on his own, Al wouldn't have changed his mind' about sending Brell back home."

"Al had us in a hotel off Park and 38th right in the middle of the block," recalled McMahon. "It was a Park Avenue Petticoat Junction with a lot of Uncle Joes sitting around," he said referring to the popular television show. "Once you were in, you were locked in."

"No one got any sleep," said Raymonds. "We were going back and forth, and this is before the championship game. Al going back and forth like that took everyone's mind off the game."

Brell was later shown to his new hotel, "I got locked into a room across from the Garden. I tried to get out and see him [McGuire]. But the door was locked from the outside, and I had the bell guy open the door. I went out to look for Al."

"Al finally showed up at 3:30 a.m. I apologized to Bob Weingart. I said I needed to blow off some steam. I was mad. But this was our first chance to win a national anything. If we lost this game I'm gonna be the goat for all time in this town," Brell said he pleaded with McGuire, who was livid. "And I got to play. Otherwise I would have been back in Milwaukee."

By game time on March 21, 1970, the NIT final was something of an anti-climax for Marquette after all that it had experienced in the previous 24 hours. Marquette and McGuire were facing Lou Carnesecca and St. John's for the fourth time, with McGuire having won two of the three previous matchups. St. John's had beaten Bob Knight's Army team in a nip-and-tuck game that went down to the wire in the other semifinal.

St. John's was the alma mater of both coaches and sentiments were mixed. It seemed that McGuire's move to reject the NCAA bid in favor of the NIT had put the spotlight—and the pressure—squarely on him. But this was also Little Louie's final game as St. John's coach. He was leaving the Redmen to become head coach of the ABA New York Nets. "Financially, it was a good thing. I was making $11,000, $12,000, $13,000 a year at St. John's. With the Nets, I was making $50,000 a year," said Carnesecca.

Marquette won the game, 65-53, behind a balanced attack of 22 points from Jeff Sewell, 16 from NIT MVP Dean Meminger, 11 from Joe Thomas, 9 from Gary Brell, and 7 points and 9 rebounds from Ric Cobb, who said that he came home to win it for the people of New York. A crowd of 18,449 watched the Warriors beat the Johnnies at Madison Square Garden.

"I thought we had won the game in the first half," commented a relieved McGuire. "But you have to give Lou credit. He keeps coming at you. The only time I thought of that game [1967 NIT Final loss] was at the start of the second half. I was afraid if St. John's scored first, that might be it."

"The best defensive club I ever played against," commented Carnesecca. "They're marvelous. I hate to lose, but my kids didn't quit. Their whole team deserved the MVP award." The Johnnies were led by Billy Paultz's 15 points and 17 rebounds.

The NIT All-Tournament First Team included Meminger, Danny Hester and Maravich (LSU), Jim Oxley, and Mike Gyovai (Army). The Second Team included Ric Cobb and Joe Thomas (Marquette), Joe DePre (St. John's), Rich Yunkas (Georgia Tech), and Garfield Heard (Oklahoma).

"There is one way I say you can tell a pro in this game. When they put combination defenses on him—a triangle and two or something like that—he passes off. Unless the All-American passes off, his team is going to get beat," McGuire said of Meminger. "Dean Meminger was quicker than 11:15 mass at a seaside resort."

One of the most lasting memories from the awards ceremonies occured when Meminger held the trophy with both hands just over his head, a la Walt Frazier in 1967.

"I was real pleased with my seniors. They were fortunate enough to go out champions and they won it themselves," said McGuire, who now had his first championship at Marquette. In the NCAA finals' UCLA defeated Jacksonville, 80-69.

McGuire would not back down from the NCAA establishment, simply because Marquette was an independent with no conference affiliation like the traditional powerhouses in the SEC, ACC, and Big 10.

Normally a coach who played the percentages, McGuire gambled by standing up for himself and his team, and won. If McGuire had taken his team to the Midwest Regionals and Marquette had lost early on, there would have been little notice about the Warriors.

But because he chose to stand up and be counted at the risk of losing the NIT and making a fool of himself, McGuire received the respect not only of his players, the university, and the fans, but of other coaches around the country who felt that he showed a lot of guts.

"I'm not afraid to make a fool out of myself. The only thing I'm afraid of is having excuses when the game's over," he said. "I don't like excuses."

"Al beat the system," said freshman Jim Chones. "They [NCAA] didn't want us to play the Big 10 schools in the Mideast Regionals. 'We'll go to the NIT,' Al told us. We received a tremendous amount of visibility for standing up to the NCAA. He received a lot of respect from the players."

McGuire milked the maximum national exposure from his stand and winning the NIT, which was not a consolation prize by any means. It was still a prestigious basketball tournament with outstanding competition and Marquette was at the top of the hill. Even major dailies like the *Chicago Tribune* began assigning sports reporters specifically to cover McGuire and Marquette, two names that had become synonymous in the sports consciousness.

The nation now knew that Marquette was a national power, capable of playing with the big boys. And from all indications, it looked as if Al McGuire had all the pieces in place for a basketball dynasty.

Chapter 10

Dunkirk

Going into the 1970–71 season, the Warriors had Dean Meminger leading a tough and experienced squad which included the heralded 6'11" sophomore center Jim Chones. "Enforcer" Hugh McMahon was back, as well as Guy Lam, Gary Grzesk, Mike Mills, Terry McQuade, Bob Lackey, and sophomore Allie McGuire, who would be patrolling the point for his dad.

That summer, McGuire had reportedly been contacted by Father Ed Joyce at Notre Dame about the head coaching job there. "Johnny Dee was leaving Notre Dame at the end of the 1970–71 season," said McGuire. "I had our team at the Morris Inn in South Bend. Downstairs they had a little bar. I went down, and there were a couple of priests there. You know priests, they always travel in pairs. One of them might have been Father Joyce. They said to me, would I be interested in coaching the basketball team. I said to them, 'No, I'll never coach at another college in my life other than Marquette University.' I did say that I knew a guy at Fordham named Digger Phelps and that he was a pretty good coach. And then I thanked them."

As he had done through most of his career at Marquette, McGuire downplayed his team's chances for the new season. He said the team could produce "maybe a .500 season." The schedule included Minnesota, Detroit, Notre Dame, New Mexico State, DePaul, Fordham, Tulane, and Bowling Green. "But because of Lackey, I might have to push that up a couple of wins," McGuire joked. "I don't think I've ever seen anybody who goes to the backboard after his shot like Lackey does. That's something that comes from the crib, you don't coach that," said McGuire of his power forward, whom he had nicknamed The Black Swan for his physical grace.

After easy wins over St. John's (Minnesota) and St. Louis, the Warriors went to Minneapolis to play the Gophers. Although McGuire did not like playing at Williams Arena, Marquette prevailed by nine (70-61). While Marquette's narrowest win of the season was a three-point decision over rival Wisconsin in the Milwaukee Classic, their toughest game was an overtime classic against Fordham.

"Al brought one of his better early teams to the old Madison Square Garden to play Digger Phelps's Fordham team in 1971 before over 18,000," recalled Norman Ochs. "Seated behind the Marquette bench was Al's mother, Winifred McGuire, surrounded by her grandchildren. Wearing her 'Hedda Hopper' hat, she leans over to her granddaughter Kathy and says, 'Go over to Uncle Al and tell him that the twins are here,' in the middle of the overtime." Marquette went on to win, 85-80.

During the 1970 NIT, McGuire pointed out a poorly dressed man to Norman and Betty Ochs. It was Joe Thomas's father. "'That's the way that Joe dressed when he came to Marquette,' said Al. Sure enough, the door opens up and Joe Thomas comes out and he has this chocolate-brown jump suit on. He was walking out, looking like Harry Belafonte," recalled Ochs.

"'When I got him from the boondocks outside of Atlanta,' McGuire continued, 'that's how he looked,' pointing to Joe's father. 'Now take a look at him. That's what coaching is all about. I'm teaching life to these kids. If they ever learn anything at Marquette, they learn how to save a buck.'

"When Al had an academic problem with one of his ballplayers," Ochs continued, "he went to see the professor. 'You know,' Al would say to the professor, 'Not every one of my ballplayers is an All-American and not every one of your students is a Rhodes Scholar.' Al did some wonderful things for guys who wouldn't have smelled the inside of a college classroom."

Joe Thomas might be the best example of a former player who became one of McGuire's projects. After graduating from Marquette, Thomas played one season with the Phoenix Suns. McGuire reportedly told him, "Please save it [money he earned in the NBA] and let me help you get into law school [at Marquette]."

"Joe Thomas wanted to quit law school 15 times," recalled Ochs. "He graduated near the bottom of his class, but he's an attorney today in

Madison, Wisconsin. Al didn't forget his players after their eligibility ran out."

"After I was cut by Phoenix (before 71–72 season), I decided I was either going to law school or get my MBA at Marquette. "They [Marquette] could provide financial aid. My position was that I was going to do whatever it took to get my law degree. I narrowly survived my first year. It got better the second year. It was just getting accustomed to the volume of work. I graduated on time from law school. I was in the bottom 25 percentile of my class."

Thomas practiced private law and went on to become the assistant attorney general for the State of Wisconsin. "He [McGuire] was a surrogate father to most of us. He did take a lot of diamonds out of the rough and polish them."

In the 1970–71 season, Marquette's defensive ranking jumped to third in the country. The team allowed opponents just a 41.1 percent field goal percentage. The Warriors also outrebounded their opponents by more than 12 boards a game. Marquette had it going inside with Chones and Lackey, and outside with Meminger, who averaged 21.1 points a game. He was the first consensus All-America in Marquette history.

"It was said back then that Dean was a dream for Marquette and a nightmare for everyone else," recalled Dave Foran, director of the university's news bureau.

Marquette avenged its previous year's loss to Notre Dame, winning at the Arena 71-66. As part of McGuire's respect for coaches, he made a big deal of sportsmanship. According to Gene Sullivan, "Marquette started this thing where the players would run down and shake hands with the opposing coach. Johnny Dee thought it was a hot dog trick, so he gave each of the Marquette players a packet of mustard."

The Warriors swept their other Catholic independent rivals (DePaul, Loyola, Detroit, Xavier), and beat Lou Henson's New Mexico State Aggies—a Final Four team the previous year—to finish the season undefeated, a first for a Warrior team coached by McGuire. He was named 1971Coach of the Year by AP, UPI, *Sporting News,* and the basketball writers.

It seemed as if it would be clear sailing for the Warriors right into the NCAA finals, where they would likely face defending champion UCLA. Riding high into the 1971 NCAA Tournament (yes, the Mideast Regional) on a 39-game winning streak (including the final 12 games of the 1969–70 season) the Warriors were ranked number two in the nation in both polls, right behind the Bruins.

Needless to say, the Warriors were confident going into South Bend for their first game in the regionals against Miami of Ohio. It seemed as if nothing stood in their way. The Warriors took care of the Redskins 62-47. Next up was the Big 10 champion Ohio State Buckeyes coached by Fred Taylor, featuring Luke Witte and Jim Cleamons. The game was in Athens, Georgia, and once again McGuire created some excitement away from the court.

"Against Ohio State we were up by seven points when the game got away," continued Meminger. "I was hit with some charging calls. The officiating was terrible. I would catch the ball and didn't have room to come down with the ball. The whole team [Ohio State] was on me. Their focus was to put me in a situation where the officials had to make a judgment call."

"We were up by 13 at one point," noted Gary Brell. "We were really hurt. I was taped from my neck to my knees. Hughie [McMahon] was taped."

Frustrations were running high during the hard-fought game. Chones and Witte had a scuffle. The Warriors still led 57-52 with 3:25 left in the game. "We were down by one with three seconds," recalled Brell. "But Al's kid forgot to step inbounds. We lost the game and the season to the Buckeyes 60-59."

Marquette advanced to the consolation game, or as the players called it, "the loser's bracket," and soundly defeated Kentucky for the second time in three years, 91-74. Their final season record was 28-1. The dream matchup with UCLA never came to be that season. The Bruins played Villanova in the finals, winning 68-62.

"It was devastating. It was the first game that I fouled out of in my career at Marquette," said Meminger, who had also played his final game for the Warriors.

Meminger speculated that the NCAA "had it in" for Marquette and McGuire for not taking the bid the year before. "Al bucked the system. They weren't trying to keep him around in the tournament. When you go up against the system, in most cases you end up in losing situations."

"I liked the fact that he was a tough guy, a disciplinarian," continued Meminger. "It was his way or the highway. [But] his decision to suspend Gary played heavy on his head. I shouldn't have been in the game with four fouls," said Meminger, who was selected in the first round of the NBA draft by his hometown New York Knicks, and by the Indiana Pacers in the seventh round of the ABA draft.

That was little consolation for a player whose career and seemingly perfect season ended so shockingly. He wound up playing for the New York Knicks and Atlanta Hawks, and finished his career in New York. He played behind Frazier and Earl Monroe and also coached New York's entry in the first Women's Professional Basketball League, the Starz, the precursor to today's WNBA. He and George Thompson had their numbers, 14 and 24 respectively, retired.

And while one of the officials in the game represented the Big 10, the official who called the fouls on Meminger was a member of the Pac 8, Mel Ross.

McGuire reacted angrily after the game, calling the game an "abortion," and said that it was the first time in his coaching career that he seriously considered quitting. He also reached back to his favored military lexicon to describe the outcome, Dunkirk, disaster or extremely poor team performance.

The coach could not stay upset for long with the incoming nucleus for the 1971–72 season. Juniors Chones, McGuire, and George "Sugar" Frazier were joined by senior Lackey and super-sophomores Marcus Washington at guard and 6'9" Larry McNeill at forward. And a freshman from Pittsburgh, 6'8" center Maurice Lucas, whom McGuire said he recruited over a piece of pizza, was waiting in the wings. The Warriors were still considered the team to beat, and no less an authority than *Sports Illustrated* predicted that Marquette would be college basketball's next dynasty.

Trying out for the freshman team was a 5'11", 170-pound guard from Waukesha named Dave Delsman. "I played against Allie in grade school. He played at St. Dominick's in Brookfield and I was at St. Charles in Hartland, Wisconsin," said Delsman.

"The next time I met Allie I was a senior in Waukesha High School and he was a sophomore at Marquette. I played against him in the Milwaukee Summer Leagues. My last three years of high school I went to Al and Hank's camps in Beaver Dam, Wisconsin, and at St. John's Military Academy in Delafield."

Delsman had been awarded an academic scholarship to Carroll College in Wisconsin, "but I didn't get along with the basketball coach and

I asked the scholarship committee if I could go to Marquette. The committee membership OK'd it.

"Hank asked me if I'd like to try out for the freshman team at Marquette. He helped me get books. Luke [Maurice Lucas] and I were voted freshman team captains."

Delsman showed from the first practice that he would not back down from anyone, "I was next in line to get taped when Chones comes into the locker room and says, 'Hey, little man, I'm next.' I told him, 'I was here first.' Chones stared at me for ten seconds and then said, 'OK, little man.'

"We went up against the varsity every day," Delsman continued. "Luke never backed down from Chones. Lackey was the only guy that intimidated me."

McGuire also added a young assistant coach to his staff. This twenty-something graduate student who looked like a football lineman had coached two years at Marquette University High School and was now ready for the big time, according to McGuire and Raymonds. His name was Rick Majerus.

While Raymonds was pleased with Majerus's work with the Marquette freshman team, he was not totally pleased with his protege.

"Rick tried to emulate Al's do-now, think-later style, which caused him some problems early on," explained Raymonds. "Al used to do things and not worry about the consequences. Rick would imitate Al and then come to me with his problems."

The last line in Majerus's bio in the press guide from that time comes as close to describing his future as any: "Majerus . . . hopes to make a career of college coaching . . ."

"Marquette had the perfect troika to coach basketball," commented Chris Peppas, who was then sports editor of the *Marquette Tribune*. "Al was the lightning rod. Part of his strategy was, 'I'll take the technical in order to let the players perform.' Al's genius was his personnel management.

"Hank was the quintessential Xs and Os man. Rick Majerus was the missing link. He set the table for Al to sign the star players," along with Ed Janka.

There were some rumblings from some coaches, including Notre Dame's Johnny Dee, about the academic quality of the players McGuire recruited to his program. "I don't know how McGuire got some of those guys in there," wondered Dee. Former St. John's coach Lou Carnesecca said, "The Holy Spirit came down and touched them on the head. That's how they got into Marquette." "That's because they had very little success recruiting against me," McGuire explained.

But McGuire saw a lot of himself in the black players he recruited, according to friends. "I kind of understand them a little better than I think they realize," McGuire once said.

Respected *New York Times* sports writer Robert Lipsyte took McGuire to task in his "Sports of the Times" column: "But Al, doesn't it ever bother you, all this money spent on your basketball program, and there are thousands of kids in need to get into college who never will, because they can't play ball?" McGuire's response was, "[If] you start thinking philosophically about thousands and millions, you're defeated. Just help one kid at a time while you're helping yourself. He'll maybe go back and help a few more, and in a generation you have something."

"Back in 1971," said Howie Fagan of Medalist, "there was a total breakdown with respect to authority on campuses in the U.S. Medalist wanted to expand on the concept of the Al McGuire Basketball Camps. Norman Fischer wanted a sports education division to spell Al. It wanted to form the division with the philosophy of promoting the name and image of Medalist, getting product exposure to the coaches and to help improve the overall coaching profession."

Medalist formed an advisory board of prominent coaches, which included McGuire, Bart Starr, Dan Gable, and Norm Van Brocklin. "I was responsible for coming up with more concepts," noted Fagan, who, as executive director and division president of the Sports Education Division of Medalist, worked as McGuire's right-hand man.

McGuire's Medalist camps expanded to some 6,000 campers attending in five states in the Midwest, including Illinois, Michigan, Ohio, Wisconsin, and Iowa. The camps were so successful that Fagan and McGuire considered a camp in Ireland. However, the logistics were too difficult.

"Al would speak at the camps, especially at the St. John's Military Academy," continued Fagan. "Everything at the camps was structured in a time schedule. But when Al came to the camp, he would get the director and say, 'Tom, I want everyone in the pool. It's a hot day.' It would break the monotony of the day. 'It's hotter than hell. Let's have some fun.'

Those are the little things that he would do at the camp. He would bring something fresh, different, and surprising into the day," Fagan recalled.

"Hank [Raymonds] was national director of the camps and he had these booklets and three-ring binders, and was organized," Fagan continued. "Al would say, 'Hank, pick out the two most important things. Keep it simple.' Al knew what he could absorb."

After Jim Chones had settled in at Marquette before the 1969–70 season, he started to hang with the New York guys, which did not sit well with McGuire.

"I fell in with these street kids from New York who Al had recruited, like Dean Meminger and George Thompson," said Chones, "I'd never met guys like these who stayed out all night and talked back to the coach.

"One day, Al grabbed me and said, 'Listen, you stay away from those New York guys. Get your ass back to your room and stay there. You can't run with those guys. You're not like them.' I listened to Al about that."

By averaging 17.9 points and 11.4 rebounds as a sophomore during the Warriors undefeated regular season, Chones turned a lot of heads, including the pros. After the hardship defection of Spencer Haywood, teams in the nascent American Basketball Association began wooing college basketball's big men so that the league could compete with the NBA.

In Terry Pluto's book, Chones recalled, "Al said, 'Virginia [the ABA Squires] wants you to turn pro. They made an offer.' I said, 'How much?' Al said, 'A million for four years. I turned it down,' I said, 'You turned it down? Coach, that's a lot of money. I know guys who work in the mills for $20,000 and they're dying in there with all the heat and smoke and hot iron.'

"I later learned that most of that offer was in deferred money. I don't even think it was worth $100,000 a year. The rest would be paid out in 20 or 30 years. That was how those hustlers and sharks operated in the ABA.

"I already had it in my mind that I would go pro early," Chones continued. "I had paid attention to the Spencer Haywood case. I knew that it worked out for Spencer. I knew my family needed me. Actually, I was a good student at Marquette, a philosophy major. Unlike most basketball players, I enjoyed the academics. But I had to make some money.

"I also didn't enjoy our style of ball at Marquette. We were a very conservative, slow-down team, and I didn't think that was helping to train me to become a pro. I felt it impeded my progress," said Chones.

"When I asked Al why he turned down the offer from Virginia, he said, 'Right now, the money isn't the issue. I promised your dad that I would get you ready to be a pro, and I'm going to keep that promise. Mentally, you're not ready for pro ball. We're going to win a lot of games with or without you, but I'm not going to let you go until you're ready to turn pro, and you need another year.'

"I had tremendous respect for Al, so I believed him and I stayed for my junior year [1971–72]."

After two easy wins, the Warriors headed to Tennessee to play the Memphis State Tigers and Larry Finch. Chones had fouled out and "Sugar" Frazier was still feeling the ill effects of a broken foot.

"Memphis State was at the free-throw line with the chance to seal the win," recalled Raymonds, "when the Tigers were called for a lane violation by referee Ray Sonnenberg. We had the ball with a few seconds left and Frazier hit a 30-foot shot at the buzzer to win the game.

"Al's arms were upraised in triumph as he walked out of the arena. Their fans went crazy. The language those women were using as Al walked off the floor was something," marveled Raymonds.

The team continued its mastery at home with five straight easy wins, including a 15-point win over Minnesota and a 74-72 win over unbeaten Marshall in the Milwaukee Classic.

As collegial as McGuire was with his peers during his career, there were a couple of times when he did not speak kindly of a fellow coach.

After a convincing 55-40 win over Bill Musselman's Golden Gophers, who were led by Jim Brewer and Corky Taylor, McGuire said, "How's that for 33.9 defense!" in reference to the book written by Musselman when he coached at Ashland College. What really upset McGuire was the fact that Musselman would not shake hands with Bob Lackey. His players had formed a circle around the coach to shut out Lackey.

And when Marshall lost to Marquette in the Milwaukee Classic, Thundering Herd coach Carl Tacy refused to shake McGuire's hand after the game. "I didn't like the guy," McGuire said in *Sports Illustrated*. "He is a phony, an Elmer Gantry."

Marquette then won its fifth straight over the Wisconsin Badgers (72-60) before heading to Columbia, South Carolina, to play McGuire's mentor and namesake, Frank, in a nationally televised Sunday afternoon contest.

"It was a three-hour bus ride at night to Columbia," remembered team manager (72–76) Kevin Gleason. "Someone asked Eddie Daniels how far we were from Columbia. He said '30 drumbeats.' Lloyd Walton just rolled over laughing. Eddie was very funny."

"The first national one we did with Marquette was South Carolina. Both [teams] were going pretty good then," said TV producer Eddie Einhorn. "The two McGuires were the coaches. I always tried to get coaching matchups in those early days of college basketball on television, McGuire versus McGuire. McGuire versus Digger Phelps.

"When I was first approached about doing the game," Einhorn said, "I was told that the state of South Carolina's blue laws did not allow such activities on Sundays for religious reasons. I said I'd do the game if you get permission on Sundays. I'll put you on a national game. We changed a lot of games.

"It took an act of the South Carolina legislature in Columbia to approve the game. And it was played. The night before the Sunday contest, Dick Enberg and I worked the UCLA-Oregon game in Eugene, Oregon. We flew all night from Eugene to Columbia, South Carolina, to do the game.

"Sunday ratings were good enough," Einhorn continued. "Three games a year, regional games. As it became bigger I started doing more. That was part of the growth of the sport on a national basis. You had to pick All-Americas, coaches, and teams when working matchups attractive for television."

Television fans did get their money's worth when the Warriors and Gamecocks did battle—literally. "The shanty Irish against the lace-curtain crowd," Frank McGuire said before the game. "Lace-curtain?" Al shot back. "We lived in the back of a bar where drunks interrupted our dinner looking for the men's room." The game was highlighted in the January 17, 1972, issue of *Sports Illustrated* .

Chones and Lackey, decked out in the newest fashion statement from Medalist, a shocking blue uniform trimmed with black and gold, led the way for the Warriors as Kevin Joyce, Tom Riker, and Brian Winters, one of the few All-Americas who spurned Al McGuire, led the way for the Gamecocks.

The hard-fought contest became physical in the second half, according to Chones. "Tom Riker, who was the roughest, toughest guy in the

ACC, hit Bob Lackey in the face with the ball, which turned the game into a donnybrook."

According to Curry Kirkpatrick, writing in *Sports Illustrated*: Lackey elbowed Riker in the neck. Riker threw a left cross to Lackey's side—whiskers. Within moments several brawls had broken out—one featuring Chones against heavyweight Danny Traylor. "Let's stay out of this," Traylor said to Chones. "Can't do it," said Chones. "My man's in trouble." Then Chones opened a nasty cut under Traylor's eye.

Frank McGuire was in the middle of the floor, bodies whizzing past him, but Al McGuire remained on the bench with his reserve players. "A waltz," McGuire was to say later. "A bar-hall bouncer wouldn't take his coat off for this one."

"I thought that those 14,000 people were going to converge on us. I thought we were going to die," recalled Jon "Bingo" Berta, who owned a Milwaukee establishment at 50th and Vliet called Bingo's, which became a player favorite among Milwaukee watering holes.

After a good three minutes of heavy punching on both sides, order was restored; immediately a hefty South Carolina state trooper charged the Marquette bench and went after Lackey. The Warriors' Larry McNeill grabbed a chair, but he and everybody else were finally restrained. Lackey and Riker were removed from the contest.

"The dude sucker-punched me," said Lackey. "Then they throw me out. If I'm leavin', I want some action."

"I'll take kicks, knees, elbows, every shot he's got," said Riker, "but not after the whistle blows. The guy's a cheap-shot artist. It was bush league."

The Warriors won the fight and the game, 72-71. "The student against teacher situation tears your gut out," said Al before the game, which was the first time the McGuires had faced each other in six years. "I'd give anything not to play this game. But, really, I consider it a favor for me to do a favor for Frank. Maybe it's the first time ever I get to pay him back for all he's done. Loyalty—that's what he always taught us," noted McGuire, who described the relationship with Frank as "distant close."

"I'm not just blowing smoke rings at Frank," McGuire continued. "But he's got too much class to be a coach. Look at the clothes, those handmade shirts. I prefer not to get surly with him on Sunday, but I'm obnoxious and rotten on the road. I do it to get the crowd off my players and on me. But this man—I have to show respect. I don't know if I can wash out what this man means to me for the time it takes to win a game."

"It's like losing to a brother," said Frank, as the two embraced at center court."

The Warriors played poorly in wins over Nevada-Reno, Detroit, and Loyola before starting to roll.

But the donnybrooks were not always on the court, which gave the impression that McGuire really did not have control over his team and program. When Jacksonville came to the Arena for another nationally televised game on Sunday afternoon, February 16, Marquette was 21-0, and at the top of the college basketball world.

"The officials kept blowing the whistle," recalled a frustrated Jim Chones. "Al said to us, 'Do you think he's just callin' fouls on the brothers?' Ten minutes into the game a fight breaks out in the stands."

Recalled Chris Peppas, "Larry McNeill's wife, Gloria, who was working as a secretary at the Marquette Law School, had brought six girl-friends to sit in four seats. She had long fingernails and was squeezing a guy out of his seat. When he wouldn't leave his assigned seat, she began clawing at his knit sweater until there were several holes in it. Then she scratched his neck and drew blood.

"A fight broke out in the stands and the ushers escorted him from the Arena. Then she starts yelling at Larry to do something during the course of the game," said Peppas.

"They stopped the game," noted Chones. "Larry McNeill's wife [Gloria] was fighting some white guy in the stands. McNeill's wife was calling this guy 'honky-this, honky-that.' Al said to McNeill, 'Go get your wife.' So Larry puts his coat on over his uniform. While that was going on, Al said to me, 'I take back what I said before.'"

As it turned out, the guy Gloria McNeill was fighting was a former teammate of Larry's, Andy Friedrich, a sophomore from Westchester, Illinois. "He was a recruit who had a heart condition and couldn't play," recalled *Milwaukee Sentinel* sports reporter Dale Hofmann. "But Al gave him his scholarship for four years. They wound up hauling Gloria to the police station."

Marquette won the battle (and the game 88-79), but wound up losing the war. Some nagging injuries to players, a lingering illness that sapped Allie McGuire's energy, and a lackluster effort in some games made it a less than memorable undefeated season. Little did anyone know at the time, but it was after that game that Chones would make a decision that would have ramifications on the basketball program not just for that season but for the following three seasons.

In Terry Pluto's book Chones said, "Around January, I had seen Nick Mileti, who owned the [Cleveland] Cavaliers, and he was seeing if I was going to turn pro after my junior year and he also was feeling me out about money."

"He said that Cleveland, Buffalo or Portland would probably get my rights. Nick talked about $1.2 million for six years. Mileti had the long hair and gold chains and all that. I figured he'd get back to me, so I was stunned when he wrote out his offer on a napkin," recalled Chones.

"This was in the middle of the season and I had a preliminary offer from an NBA team, so the NBA wasn't very innocent in all this stuff either. About a month later, I got a call from Al to go see his attorney, Gene Smith. We had just beaten Jacksonville on national television. I saw Gene and he said, 'We've gotten another offer for you, and it's substantial.'

"I was really ready for the pros and Al obviously thought so, too, or he wouldn't have told me to see Gene Smith. Gene told me that the offer came from the New York Nets. They offered $1.5 million for five years plus a $500,000 interest-free loan. But I wouldn't see that $500,000 until I was 32 years old, and then I was to get $39,500 a year for 15 years. I knew that doesn't exactly work out to $500,000, but it had to do with taxes and things like that.

"As for the $1.5 million, it was paid out for ten years—so we were talking about $150,000 a year for 10 years."

"I made a deal with Roy Boe of the Nets for $1.6 million," McGuire told Bob Costas. "It was illegal at the time, but I didn't care. Nobody had a contract for that kind of money then. He said, OK, you got a deal. I think he was playin' with Monopoly money or somethin', but we had a deal.

"In the middle of the season, Boe comes to me and says, 'I want Chones.' I said, 'Ya got him. A deal's a deal.' He says to me, 'I want him now!' Now I'm 22-0, we're number two in the country.' He said, 'I want him *now*.'

"So I go up to Jimmy's apartment. I pick him up and drive him to Racine, Wisconsin, a 30-minute drive from Milwaukee. I said, 'Jimmy, ya just broke your leg.' Jimmy said, 'Whaddya mean, Coach?' 'You're goin' pro.' Then he started cryin'. I said Jimmy, 'What would you say if

I told you, you would be makin' $10,500 a week for the next four years?' Then he stopped cryin'."

The deal to leave in the middle of the season did not sit well with the Marquette administration, particularly President Raynor, who said to Al, "Can't you get Jimmy to stay one more year?" McGuire replied, "Father, if someone offered me $1.6 million I'd leave too. I looked in my refrigerator and it was full. I looked in Jimmy's refrigerator and it was empty."

It seemed that the Warriors' tank was on empty as the psychological effect of Chones's departure resulted in bad losses to Detroit (70-49) and New Mexico State (73-69) among its final five games.

Marquette would finish the regular season 24-2 and ranked seventh in both the AP and UPI polls. It was Marquette's sixth straight campaign of 20 or more wins and as many postseason tournament appearances under McGuire. It should have felt better, but it did not. Chones's departure in the middle of the season was a bad omen. The 1971–72 season, which started out with so much promise, became known as "the Screwed-up Season."

The Warriors accepted a bid to the NCAA Mideast Regional in Knoxville, Tennessee, but before the games began the NCAA required that the players who were considering leaving under hardship rules sign affidavits disclaiming any ties to pro teams or prospective agents.

McGuire told Bob Lackey to hold onto his affidavit until Marquette had a chance to scrutinize the document. The NCAA said that was OK as long as Lackey signed it the following Monday. The Warriors took out their frustrations on Ohio 73-49, and once again the Baron of the Bluegrass, Adolph Rupp, awaited McGuire's Warriors, this time in Dayton, Ohio.

Before the date in Dayton, the NCAA threatened to disqualify Marquette from the tournament unless Lackey signed the affidavit. The tournament committee said Marquette would be reinstated if Lackey signed the piece of paper. Lackey signed and the games continued.

This was also the last time McGuire and Rupp would face off against each other, since Rupp would retire after the tournament. And while this edition of the Wildcats was not nearly as good as his previous teams, they were still Kentucky.

Allie McGuire and Marcus Washington shot a combined 3 for 23, and the game was pretty much over. Al inserted a walk-on, Mark Ostrand from Sturgeon Bay, Wisconsin, recalled Norman Ochs. "Al tells the guy,

'Now, don't do anything silly.' A guy comes off the bench for Kentucky and hits eight out of eight. He killed Marquette. Ostrand gets shoved from behind by a Kentucky player and starts a fight. Marquette loses the game 85-69." Rupp evened the score with McGuire.

"The Kentucky player kneed me in the back," said Ostrand. "I just went after the guy. At that point it was emotional. There were some exchanges in the locker room that were not pleasant."

In a quiet Marquette locker room, frustration was setting in. No one was even thinking about the consolation game Marquette would play against Minnesota.

"Al started laying into Allie," Ochs continued. "Then Marcus Washington began to interrupt McGuire, 'Ah, c'mon coach. That's enough.' To which McGuire responded, 'Now I'll start on you. You're hangin' around with the worst group in the City of Milwaukee.' A half-hour later we went out for a drink and it was like it didn't happen."

"He does yell and he stays on you if he doesn't think you're living up," recalled Allie McGuire at the time. "He has whipping boys. Last year he was on Butch Lee constantly. Gary Brell, me, at other times. It's always somebody. Was my dad volatile? Yea. I remember him in his first year at Marquette when they went 8-18. Tom Flynn, who was a doggone good player, got a rebound and went down the court and threw a pass behind his back. My dad just went after him. If Marquette was going to be successful, they were going to have to work. He didn't care who you were.

"Marcus Washington was a super-talented guy," Allie continued. "But the minute he went back to the dorm, the guys would pat him on the shoulder, tell him what a great job he was doing—you're not taking enough shots, you're not getting the ball enough. All of a sudden, Marcus started to deteriorate a little. He started to hear the numbers, hear the agents saying you're not going to get drafted unless you start shooting. And this, I think, hurt Marcus. I think what makes Al McGuire great is that he cuts all that off."

"They [players] don't realize I know what the scouts are looking for," added Al. "Every pro scout exchanges information. If a scout watches you go belly up a couple of times, that guy spreads the word around like cancer."

Allie McGuire felt that wherever his father coached, that he would play for him. "I was at a lot of practices at Marquette. But basketball was never pushed. That's why I always liked being around the practices and players." After he had proven that he had the ability to compete at the highest level with the other All-Americas, Allie did not second-guess his decision. The other part of the equation was how he would deal with the sensitive area of playing for his father, whose home and locker-room demeanors were very different from each other.

"He's extremely quiet [at home]," observed Allie McGuire. "I don't mean he doesn't say anything. I think I'd be foolish to tell people he doesn't say anything at all. He's just not the same outgoing personality I think everybody sees."

When George Frazier challenged McGuire, telling him that he was just as good as Allie and should start, McGuire responded, "Sugar, I love my son. For you to start, it has to be a clear knockout. In order to start, you can't be as good as my son, you have to be better." End of conversation.

"That was my dad's battle," explained Allie. "My dad told George that his time would come. We were teammates. We had a good year and he was a quality guy. George was a good guard. He played 100 percent. My dad also said that if I had played for Dean Smith instead of him I would have been an All-American. That quote will live until the day I die. You become a scapegoat when you are a coach's son," concluded Allie.

The father asked sports information director Mike Gonring not to publish the team's field goal statistics so that his players' pro prospects would not be diminished. "It was because some of the players were off to a poor start," explained Gonring, who answered to Dave Foran. "Al said, 'If we didn't publish Ric Cobb's free-throw statistics last year, he would have been a pro.' Al said later at the NCAA tournament that in '10 years there will be no more statistics in sports.'" Also on the varsity was Hank Raymonds's son Steve—two coaching sons were on the same Marquette team.

The Minnesota game was an anticlimax, as the Warriors lost 77-72 to end "the screwed-up season." UCLA defeated Florida State in the Finals that season 81-76. Chones went on to play for the New York Nets and "I played terribly," he said. "I was 20 years old, very immature, and I got caught up in the New York City lifestyle. I didn't have an Al McGuire there to keep on my case. I was playing with a bunch of guys who had never made $25,000 in their lives and here I was with the million-dollar contract. It didn't make me real popular. I needed stability and found none.

The league was new, the team was young, our coach was Lou Carnesecca, who was new to the ABA and pro ball himself.

"People said things like, 'You make as much as Lew Alcindor; you should be as good as him.' I couldn't be that good; no one could. But I put all this pressure on myself and that just made things worse. People in the press were writing that I couldn't play at all. At Marquette, Al handled the press and kept the heat off of us. No one did that on the Nets. I remember when I left school and Al made his comment about his refrigerator being full and mine empty. That took a lot of pressure off me.

"After that first year, I was traded to the Carolina Cougars in the summer of 1973. I was labeled a 'head case.'" Chones then went on to to play for the Cleveland Cavaliers.

With the new season, it seemed that Marquette could recover its luster after the disappointing 1971–72 campaign. The Warriors had a record 72-game home winning streak and four starters returning, including team captain McGuire, juniors McNeill and Washington, and senior Frazier. Al McGuire, though, was looking at "an outside shot at the NIT."

While the team had lost Chones, and Bob Lackey to graduation, McGuire looked forward to having sophomore Maurice Lucas, "potentially the best player we've ever had here at Marquette," join 6'10" senior Mike Mills and McNeill on the front line.

Marquette won its first 11, including another memorable Milwaukee game in Warrior-Badger lore, as Marquette won its sixth straight Classic in two overtimes, a 75-73 win over Wisconsin.

Though just a sophomore, Lucas was up there with the other blue-chippers in Marquette history, according to Raymonds, "He could play forward or center. The greatest asset he had was being able to take a rebound and with one hand flick it downcourt. But Al would never run off a defensive rebound.

"In terms of strategy, Al always emphasized defense," Raymonds continued. "Defense still wins games. That's always there. That's a physical act. Intensity. When it came to offense, Al wanted one where all of the players touched the ball.

"We put together our number one pattern. He [McGuire] didn't like options. We added pattern number two so we could react to the defense."

When Lucas complained about the Marquette offense, likening himself to a robot, Raymonds told him, "Maurice, someday you're gonna be a million-dollar robot."

"Al also said that we needed two lockers for Maurice when he came to Marquette—one for him and one for his head," said Raymonds.

After three more wins, next up was Notre Dame. Digger Phelps came to the Arena with his Fighting Irish, featuring the talented trio of Gary Novak, John Shumate, and Gary Brokaw. Marquette had an 81-game home winning streak at the Arena that stretched back to 1967. It is still among the top ten home win streaks in NCAA history. Notre Dame, however, was earning a reputation as a giant-killer. It was in 1974 that Notre Dame ended UCLA's 88-game winning streak.

With time running down in regulation, it was neither Brokaw, nor Shumate, nor Novak who would take the last shot. In the far right-hand corner of the Arena was Dwight Clay whose shot swished through as time expired, giving Notre Dame the win, 71-69.

Marquette lost just two of its final 14 that season, and finished at 23-3, ranked fourth in the country in the UPI poll and fifth in the AP. Their first-round opponent in the Mideast Regional in Dayton was Miami of Ohio, which the Warriors defeated 77-62. Next up was Bobby Knight's Indiana Hoosiers, the first time the coaches faced each other since Knight was at Army when Marquette won by 20.

This time Knight's young team prevailed by six in Nashville, Tennessee, 75-69, in a game in which McGuire became physically incensed at some of the official's calls.

"He was angry with the refs," recalled Joan Bohmann, one of the Marquette cheerleaders. "He often would get emotional. But he would pull his tie away. His mouth would be open and veins jumping out of his neck.

"In disbelief that we were getting blown out, he stomped around like a little kid in little circles. Then he stormed toward the end of the bench. He started grabbing pieces of his hair out of his head. He was pulling clumps of hair out of his head," Bohmann recalled.

For the third straight year, the Warriors wound up in the loser's bracket, facing Austin Peay in the consolation game and winning by 88-73.

McGuire received more bad news after the season. He was losing his second player to hardship—Larry McNeill. Following in Chones's footsteps, McNeill decided to forego his senior year, which McGuire said was a mistake. "Young people will make mistakes. They don't know the size or the degree of their mistakes. Larry McNeill wanted to go pro. I said, Larry, don't go pro. It's gonna cost you $400,000. Plus your degree.

"So Larry had the misconception that I was talking about taking care of myself, having him back. I didn't care if Bo [Ellis] left. I don't care who goes. I'm born and I die alone. Now, it's true. Now it's four, five years later and Larry did blow $400,000. There's no way you can recover it," McGuire recalled.

McNeill was drafted in the second round by the Kansas City-Omaha Kings, but it was not the only loss for the Warriors that 1973–74 season. The team lost George Frazier, Allie McGuire, and Mike Mills and they also lost Willie Wampum, who was banned by Father Raynor before the season. Willie was eventually replaced by the "original Warrior," who was an actual Native American student in authentic Indian regalia. In October 1973, the country had lost a vice-president to resignation as it continued to wallow in Watergate. But earlier that spring, as part of President Nixon's "Peace with Honor," American troops began returning home. It was the beginning of the end of America's costly and controversial involvement in a war that nearly caused a civil war at home.

For the upcoming season, McGuire said he saw an either-or situation with his team—either roses or weeds, depending on whether the players get along, and whether they have "love affairs with the semi-agents who will tout them and blow their heads out of proportion."

Joining the Warriors were quicksilver 6'0" guard Lloyd Walton from Mt. Carmel High School in Chicago, built in the mold of Dean Meminger, and 6'3" senior transfer Eddie Daniels, one of Bobby Knight's players from Indiana. They joined Bo Ellis, who was given a chance to start that year, the first year that freshmen were eligible to play varsity under NCAA rules. Ellis claimed that McGuire visited him three times during the recruiting process, while the coach insists it was just once. "When I recruited Bo, I parked my car down near Parker High School in Chicago. When I came back, all that was left was the four hubcaps. The car was gonzo," said McGuire. "But I got Bo." While McGuire admits his car was not stolen, the story has become a part of the McGuire lore.

The Warriors went quickly out of the gate with ten straight wins, including overtime classics—one at Tennessee to Ernie Grunfeld and the Volunteers, and another Milwaukee Classic win over the Badgers, 49-48.

By this time, students were camping out for the limited number of tickets each season. The Arena was packed and McGuire liked to remind fans of that. "It was important to Al to announce that every game was a sellout," said John Owens, who took over as public address announcer.

"Al always said, 'Don't ever make anyone look bad.' My job was to be a part of the show."

Before the game against the Badgers, Chris Peppas asked Badger coach John Powless what it would take to beat Marquette. His curt answer: "Well, if they don't change the rules, then we'll have to score more points," and Powless stalked off.

During the season, McGuire usually used his philosophy-of-life talks to make a point. But he also used the talks to dole out punishment.

"Eddie Daniels ran up a big phone bill," recalled Delsman. "Al treated everyone with a team aspect. If one guy screwed up everyone had to pay. Al cut off everyone's phones until the bill was paid.

"When Al told us during one of his philosophy-of-life talks, we were all upset," continued Delsman. "Then he said, 'Hey, Eddie. Tell the fellows why their phones are being shut off. You know, Eddie. You can con yourself, you can con your teammates, you can con me, but you can't con Ma Bell.' He never treated anyone unfairly. 'You're working as a team,' he would say. 'Ya gotta respect the other guys.'

"He'd bring in authority figures before the season, like the FBI to talk about drugs, pimps, and gambling. 'Because you guys carry a lot more responsibility, you guys have to show it.' His advice to us was 'Never be the first one at a party or the last one to leave.'"

When Al was not at practice, either he was off on his motorcycle or practicing his golf game, according to Tom Collins. "Al was the greatest con man since Judas. He would cheat on strokes, have three clubs in his bag and wear gym shoes on the course. But he'd always win." During a benefit golf tournament named for Vince Lombardi, McGuire decided to lay down under a tree. Because he felt like it, he said later.

But he didn't like to lose at golf, according to Walter Wong, who belonged to the same country club as McGuire and Jerry Savio. "One time, Al lost and he walked all the way home to Brookfield."

McGuire had taken on more responsibility earlier that season when he took over the job of athletic director from Sam Sauceda, who decided to return to academia. Sauceda had been a longtime language professor at Marquette and had founded the university's outstanding program in Madrid, Spain.

"Al did well with it," said vice president of student affairs James Scott of McGuire's new responsibilities. "Al came to some staff meetings but

not always. Hank or Paul Prpish would go to the meetings in his place."
McGuire did not enjoy the administrative end of university life.

Scott told McGuire that it was important to put things in writing.
McGuire, a doer all of his life, usually just told people to do things. "At
one point, Al told me, 'Jim, don't send me memos more than a page long,
because I can't understand 'em. Don't send me more than a paragraph.'

"Al is a very bright fellow," said Scott. "He had ideas, a way to motivate. Then he moved on to more."

"Al is the best game coach I've ever seen," commented Greg Stack,
a manager at Marquette from 1972 to 1977. "Al is in charge. We would
be sitting in a huddle deciding on a defense. The [timeout] buzzer
would ring and Al would always look at the opposing coach to see what
he was doing. Ninety percent of the time we would stand. He'd look to
see if the guy was changing something by looking at his mannerisms.
His eyes, whether he would sit down or stand up. He would look at the
other coach and then change the defenses [of what he was originally going
to call] and nine out of ten times it would work," recalled Stack.

And it was Delsman, "Dels" as he was called, who was involved in
one of the most controversial incidents during McGuire's era.

"This was my junior season [1973–74]," recalled Delsman. "I thought
that I had a chance to be the starting point guard. I had played behind
both Marcus Washington and Allie."

"Delsman was coming off a surprise sophomore season," recalled
manager Kevin Gleason. "He went into the season thinking he had a legitimate shot to start at guard. It was his objective to start. He was going
after Marcus's spot. During the scrimmage, Delsman made it a point to
match up with Marcus."

"From the first day of practice," continued Delsman, "Marcus and I
were getting competitive. My freshman and sophomore years I guarded
Marcus. His sharp elbows always landed in my mouth.

"I had to put ice cubes in my mouth every day after practice. We got
in a couple of skirmishes. They had to pull us apart. I was starting to
punch. Marcus had hit me one time too many. 'Don't do it again,' I warned
him. I walked right up to him and we started fighting.

"I was getting the best of it. Al would let us go for a couple of minutes. Marcus was bleeding. Somebody grabbed me from behind. Nobody
grabbed Marcus, and he kept swinging. Al had come to practice 45 minutes late. Al had on this three-piece suit. He tried to calm Marcus down.

"Rick Majerus had a hold of me and Marcus came up to me. Al came in between us and said to knock it off. He said if anyone wants to fight here, they'd have to fight him first.

"For no reason, I hit him," said Delsman. "Then Al said, 'You S.O.B.,' as he took a swing at me. As soon as Al swung, I ducked. He fell down and I went on top of him. The players pulled me and Al apart. He just got up and said, 'I want you two out of here.'

"Hank Raymonds pointed to everyone in the practice and said, 'Everyone that's in here, I know who you are. If word of this leaves this gym, I know who you are.' Marcus went into the training room and I went into the shower. We ran into each other in the dorm later. He had a fat lip and I had a bump on my eye. Then Hughie McMahon yelled at me, 'If Al woulda got up, he woulda beat the shit out of you.'"

"I don't think there were any reporters at the gym during the Delsman incident," recalled Gleason. "And I don't remember anyone on the team thinking that this was something to be hush-hush about.

"During the preseason," Gleason continued, "McGuire almost encouraged fighting amongst the players. Al would say, 'None of you guys got into a fight yet. You're too soft, not intense enough,' He didn't seem at all upset there were fights between players. He thought it was necessary to develop a tough team."

"The next day," said Delsman, "I called up Coach. I showed up. He was in his sweats. I started to apologize. He said to me, 'Dels, work on your free throws. It's over.' I was sure that I was gone," said Delsman, still relieved to this day.

"Al called the team together to say that he wasn't going to hold a grudge. It was just kind of a spectacle," said Gleason. "Al wading into this was humorous to me. Al would talk to the team as a whole. They had a pretty good relationship."

The story was not reported in the press until the Final Four, when Jimmy Breslin asked McGuire if it were true. Breslin ran the story and it became another one of the legendary McGuire stories.

After losing to Frank McGuire at South Carolina, 60-58, Marquette won six in a row before losing at Notre Dame, 69-63. The Warriors lost just twice more in their final eight games, a 75-69 loss to Eddie Sutton's Creighton Bluejays, and 92-77 to Gale Catlett's Cincinnati Bearcats, who were led by Lloyd Batts.

But in between, the Warriors defeated Wisconsin for the ninth straight time on a snowy Tuesday night in February, 59–58. The teams played the most memorable game in the history of the series that night at the Arena.

The Badgers' coach John Powless, who was an assistant to Cincinnati's Ed Jucker in the early '60s, had two outstanding players in twins Kim and Kerry Hughes, and both teams played a tight nip-and-tuck game. "During the game, their father had ridden Al mercilessly," recalled Chris Peppas of the *Marquette Tribune*.

"One of the Hughes twins was on the free-throw line late in the game. When he missed the first shot, Al turned to Mr. Hughes and put his hand to his throat, indicating that his son was choking under pressure," Peppas continued. "When he missed the second free-throw, Marquette goes down and Maurice Lucas puts up a prayer at the buzzer to defeat the Badgers."

Immediately after the shot, McGuire jumped up onto the scorer's table with arms upraised. And as he is smiling at the crowd, Glenn Hughes gave McGuire his own upraised salute—a single middle-digit thrust into the air. McGuire had his moment of satisfaction. When told later on about the incident, McGuire noted that Mr. Hughes was just showing everyone that he knew Marquette was number one.

A photo ran in the next day's *Milwaukee Sentinel*, according to long-time reporter Mike Christopulos, but the editors had decided to run an edited version.

"They were great basketball games," Powless said of the Marquette-Wisconsin rivalry. "Because of the great games we had, it brought out all the Marquette fans to the Classic, but we could only get two tickets per player."

"Somehow the *Journal* obtained the same photo we ran," Christopulos explained, "and ran the unedited shot in its next day's edition."

Marquette was 22-4 and headed to the Mideast Regionals once again. And for the second time in his coaching career McGuire was named Coach of the Year, this time by the National Association of Basketball Coaches, at the end of the 1973–74 season.

The Warriors faced an overmatched Ohio University team at Terre Haute, Indiana, and easily dispatched the Bobcats 85-59. After a 69-61 win over Vanderbilt in Tuscaloosa, Alabama, McGuire was invited to the home of Alabama football coach Bear Bryant.

"Bear Bryant loved Al," recalled Jerry Savio, who was traveling with McGuire and the team. "We were invited to a barbeque at Bryant's home. We played golf. Bryant had an assistant assigned to us. When we tried to get rid of him, the assistant told us that Bear would kill him if he weren't taking care of our every need.

"At the party there was Duffy Daugherty of Michigan State and John McKay of USC, the Bear, and their wives. Then the Bear just raised an eyebrow and everyone scattered. And the Bear asked McGuire into his den.

"'Al, we're very impressed with what you're trying to do for coaches,' Bryant began. 'If there's anything we can do to help, we'll back you.'

"Al told me afterward, 'There was the man, organized, tough. Everyone knew that he was the man.'"

"I tried to get Al on the board of the National Association of Basketball Coaches," recalled Dean Smith, "but he said that he could do more as a maverick." Added Bob Knight, "I really believe in the time that I've been in college coaching that no one has more conscientiously tried to better the lot of coaches than has Al McGuire. I think on numerous occasions he's come out talking about things for coaches, he's talked about how coaches should be taking care of coaches . . . I really believe he's been a tremendous benefit to college basketball."

"My calls for a coaches union were for the assistants more than the head man," McGuire explained. "Coaches need tenure after three years. That should be a trial period for coaches. After that a coach deserves tenure just like any other professor."

Next up was Johnny Orr's Michigan Wolverines in the regional finals. This was the furthest a McGuire team had advanced since the 1969 regional final against Purdue. The Warriors just got by, 72-70, to advance to the Final Four for the first time in Marquette history. Next to winning the NIT championship in 1970, this was by far McGuire's greatest accomplishment as a coach.

"The Michigan game was an increasingly exciting game," recalled Gleason. "It was pretty close throughout. Maurice Lucas fouled out halfway through the second half. We put Rick Campbell in the game. He was from Gordon Tech High School in Chicago. He did a good job rebounding."

It was also the first time that UCLA had not reached the Final Four in seven years, making it an even more momentous occasion. "Kansas was a good draw," said Delsman. "We had a high confidence level. We felt if we put pressure on their guards we would do well."

Marquette easily defeated Kansas in a 64-51 semifinal, and faced Norm Sloan's North Carolina State Wolfpack in the finals. They were led by David "Skywalker" Thompson, who had a 44-inch vertical leap. The Final Four was held in Greensboro, North Carolina, which was basically a home-court advantage for the school, located down the road in Raleigh-Durham.

McGuire earned two quick technicals from referee Irv Brown with just over two and a half minutes left in the first half, which turned into a ten-point turnaround for the Wolfpack. They would go into the locker room with a nine-point halftime lead.

Marquette was led by Maurice Lucas who scored 21, Bo Ellis 12, and Dave Delsman 11. But State had balanced scoring from Thompson (21), Monte Towe (16), 7'4" Tom Burleson (14), Morris Rivers (14), and Tim Stoddard (8). Marquette whittled away at the Wolfpack's lead in the second half, but their tenacious defense kept Marquette from getting good shots. The Warriors lost by 12, 76-64 in the university's first NCAA final.

"I have no complaint with the way we played. We played just about as well as we could, but I didn't have a good coaching game," said McGuire.

Said guard Marcus Washington, "We stopped playing defense. I don't think we pressed as well as we should have. We weren't playing well right off the bat. I think we were a little tight."

"On the two technical fouls," noted McGuire, "I would say that I lost the game there. I would say that I gave them two five-point plays and that was it. I had a bad day. Officials never win or lose a game for anyone. North Carolina State is a better ball club than Marquette University.

"I think North Carolina State is a super ball club," McGuire said graciously afterward. "We gave them an alley fight for a while. But they have no weak spots . . . They've got an aircraft carrier in Burleson and a battleship in Thompson, and destroyers all over the place."

Concurred Marcus Washington, "This night in this tournament, North Carolina State was the best. I think we could have played better, but they are the best."

After the game, a frustrated Maurice Lucas told McGuire, "Thanks a lot for losing the game for us, coach." McGuire's response, "Well, Maurice, that makes up for all the games that I won for you."

Sophomore forward Bo Ellis summed up the championship experience and what the future held for the Warriors: "We'll be back. Not here,
but somewhere else in a championship game. This was the wrong place
and the wrong time, but we'll be back."

During that season, there were rumors running rampant that junior
center Maurice Lucas had selected Richie Phillips as an agent, or a "back
room lawyer" in McGuire's words. NCAA rules forbade a player still on
scholarship from retaining an agent. "Richie Phillips was the only man
who Al feared," said Hank Raymonds.

McGuire always had expressed concern that the NCAA kept an eagle
eye on his program. He felt that as an independent, Marquette could not
step over any fine line the association set up or the university would be
in trouble. So he was always careful about playing within the rules.

"I didn't fear him [Richie Phillips] as much as I didn't want Marquette
University hurt," explained McGuire. "As it got down to the short strokes
and then Luke wanted to come back to school, he had three agents: in
Pittsburgh, Phillips in Philadelphia, and Gene Smith here in Milwaukee.

"I said that this multiple agent thing is getting out of hand. Richie
ended up with Luke. I wanted to have the three fellows on a conference
call and clean it up. There was only one body [Lucas] here. We can't chop
it up. He can go on to his personal life," McGuire concluded.

"There was a question of whether he [Lucas] would stay at Marquette
or go pro," recalled Hank Raymonds. "We were playing a game at
Chicago Stadium, and Ed Badger of the Chicago Bulls, who had coached
Lucas in the World University Games the previous summer, was talking
to Lucas in the Marquette locker room.

"I told Al that Lucas may leave. Al then got 'Luke' in his office and
said, 'Maurice, it really doesn't matter if you go. The question at Marquette is, if I go.'

"Lucas then told Al, 'If it wouldn't have been for me, you would have
been under the table and not on top of it,' referring to the win over the
Wisconsin Badgers in the Arena the previous season."

"At the end of Maurice Lucas's junior year," recalled James Scott,
"Al found out that he got an agent. Al said that the second he [Lucas]
walks back on that floor we'll be in violation of NCAA rules. 'It will be
a problem and I will need some help,' he said. 'I have got to take care of
it. I'll call you when it's settled,' Al told me.

"Al said he knew what he had to do, and he couldn't explain it. I needed to let Dr. Quentin Quade know and I won't tell him any more than he needs to know other than you have to be out of town. Quentin said, OK, fine.

"Al called me a week later. Richie Phillips was indeed his agent. Richie didn't want to talk to Al. Al wanted Maurice to go on his own to the pros, and Al said that Lucas decided to do this."

Lucas declared early for the pros, as Chones and McNeill did before him. And just like his string of eight straight 20-win and postseason appearances, for the third straight year McGuire lost a superstar ballplayer. It is said that McGuire's only regret as a Marquette coach is not having the chance to see Chones, McNeill, and Lucas play together as the starting front line.

"I was regretful of the fact that we lost Chones and Lucas," said university President John Raynor. "Most players came back and got their degrees. I never bought the hardship case. That's greed. How about an education? What are your priorities in life? Does he want an education or what? Don't let the tail wag the dog."

Earlier that summer Richard Nixon resigned the presidency and Vice President Gerald Ford took the oath of office. When he pardoned Nixon, it ended what was called the long, national nightmare of Watergate.

The recruitment of Earl Tatum, whom McGuire nicknamed the Black Jerry West, is also interesting. "As a senior at Mt. Vernon (New York) High School, Bob Knight came out to see me," said Tatum. "And not just for basketball, I played baseball too.

"I was going to go to Indiana. They brought out the baseball coach *and* Bobby Knight to see me. I didn't really want to travel. The phone never stopped ringing. The mail didn't stop coming.

"I get a call one morning. Tickets were coming from Jacksonville. I told Jacksonville I wasn't coming. John von Bargen called and said, 'What do you want to go to Jacksonville for? Why don't you see my boy, Al McGuire?' 'You mean that team with the crazy uniforms?'" Tatum asked.

"Maurice Lucas picked me up at the airport. I stopped at a Holiday Inn at 17th and Wisconsin. Maurice and I had breakfast. Al was late. I was full. He apologized. I still had some bacon, waffles, and eggs on my plate," said Tatum.

"He came in and started taking the food off my plate with his hands. I said, 'Man, this man's all right.' That's when I knew I was coming to Marquette," said Tatum, laughing at the memory.

But what he had coming back for the 1974–75 season were no slouches either. Super sophomore Bo Ellis took fashion design classes at nearby Mount Mary College and designed the team's uniforms, led a group that included fellow Chicagoan and point guard extraordinaire Lloyd Walton, smooth-shooting junior Earl Tatum at forward, tough guy senior forward Jerry Homan, and freshman shooting guard Butch Lee, who was born in Puerto Rico but grew up in the Bronx.

"Lloyd Walton was never out of energy," said an admiring Tatum. "He was a smaller 5'10" guy but his heart was big. If he made a pass that he thought you should have had, he got on you about it. You could send him out there against the lions and tigers and he wouldn't back down."

After losing two in a row early in the season to Pittsburgh and Denny Crum's Louisville Cardinals, who were led by Junior Bridgman, Marquette won the Milwaukee Classic for the seventh year in a row.

But the holiday season was marred when the brother of sophomore cheerleader Joanie Bohmann was shot and killed in a Milwaukee robbery. Bohmann had planned to not return to cheerleading or Marquette, she was so devastated. In the midst of her grief, she received an unexpected phone call.

"Al called me at home and said, 'Hey, what's this I hear you're not coming to the game tonight,'" said Bohmann. "'It won't be the same without your cheerleading, Joanie. You get that uniform washed and be at the game tonight. We need you there.' That was all I needed. At the funeral, Al sent the biggest floral display."

The Warriors won six straight before losing to the Cincinnati Bearcats, led by Ron Hightower, and won their last 12 games of the season, to finish 23-3. UPI had the Warriors 6th in the nation, while AP ranked them 11th. In one of the season's last games, McGuire took Marquette to New York to play Fordham. "We went right from the airport to the press conference," recalled public address announcer John Owens, with Fordham coach Hal Wissel. "Al is the whole focus. Later a Milwaukee writer calls and asks Al if he would answer what the Fordham coach told him. Wissel said in the Milwaukee papers that Marquette doesn't play anyone. Al was incensed. 'Why didn't he just say it here in New York? We'd put 5,000 more people in the seats at the Garden.'

"The next night Marquette was leading 78-40. Al takes the starters out and goes to center court and says to Wissel, 'What do you think of our starters now?'"

In the 1975 NCAA tournament, and who should show up but the Kentucky Wildcats, Marquette and McGuire's postseason nemesis since his early tournament appearances. Adolph Rupp had relinquished head coaching duties to one of his longtime assistants, Joe B. Hall.

The young Warriors, obviously missing their superstar playing against Kentucky's thoroughbred talent, were beaten badly, 76-54, their worst loss since the first time they faced the Wildcats in 1968 and lost by 18. Kentucky went on to lose to UCLA, 92-85, in John Wooden's swan song as coach in the NCAA finals.

With four starters returning, including junior Bo Ellis, Butch Lee, Lloyd Walton and Earl Tatum, speculation in Milwaukee was that the 1975–76 team could very well be every bit as good as McGuire's 1970–71 squad that went through the regular season undefeated. "There was not one empty seat in the Arena at game time," recalled Tatum a 6'5" forward. "When we came out to do our drills, it was electrifying! Your head was clogged from the noise. The first five minutes of the second half, Al told us, "Go get 'em."

Joining the Marquette thoroughbreds was a young freshman shooting whiz, Bernard Toone, and complementary 6'10" aircraft carrier Jerome Whitehead, who had played for Bill Mulligan, one of McGuire's junior college contacts at Riverside City College, in California. McGuire placed the team's future on Ellis's success, "As Bo goes, so goes Marquette." But it was to be seniors Earl Tatum and Lloyd Walton who would be the designated stars that season.

Expectations had not been this high in years. McGuire had experienced players with talent. Save for an early loss at dreaded Williams Arena to Jim Dutcher's Minnesota Golden Gophers in overtime, 77-73, Marquette did not lose another game the rest of the season. Marquette swept Wisconsin, DePaul, and Xavier and defeated Notre Dame for the second straight year to finish the regular season at 26-1, the second best record in the McGuire era.

DePaul's Joe Meyer scouted the Notre Dame-Marquette game for his dad, and came back with this report, "He [McGuire] could orchestrate a crowd. Every time he stood up, the students derisively cheered.

Then he sat down. Then he stood up quickly and sat down and stood up quickly again.

"How he could do this in the midst of the game," marveled Meyer. "Here's the game going on and he's playing with the crowd. At the end, Marquette won. Al smirked and waved at the crowd. He did it to take the pressure off his players. He feels it. Some of it was fun. He loved the attention.

"He had a feel for people and a feel for the game. He didn't do the same thing with each player. He would change. He'd have to adjust to it. He'd just do it a little differently," said Meyer, whom McGuire referred to as "the Barracuda."

"During a game, when the fans would be getting on Al, he would look down the bench at us and give us a little smile, knowing that he had them," recalled student manager Greg Stack.

"In another game a few years earlier," Meyer continued, "we were playing in a matchup zone. Al and Allie were yelling at each other. They didn't know what we were in. 'It's a zone.' 'No, it's a man.' We had 'em confused. Al then yells, 'Chones, you get in the blocks. Lackey, you get in the blocks. Allie, you shoot.' The DePaul players at that time respected Al. Our players would talk highly of Al. 'We're playing Al McGuire.' We always talked about Al first," said Meyer.

McGuire's feel for people included the fans during and after a game. A Marquette student trainer recalled that after a game against Loyola in Chicago, "a Marquette booster was waiting outside the team's locker room looking glum after a Warrior win. When Al asked him what was wrong, the booster, who had come down from Milwaukee, explained that his car had been stolen during the game.

"Al reached into his pocket and pulled out some money. 'This will get you back home. Pay me when you got it.' That was how he was."

When the team went to Cincinnati to play Xavier, both Majerus and Raymonds were off on recruiting visits and McGuire was left to work the pregame preparations himself with sports information director Kevin Byrne, according to Arena public address announcer John Owens.

"The Xavier Fieldhouse had classrooms where Al met with the team before the game," said Owens. "Al told me to keep track of the fouls. Al starts telling us about Xavier. He said, 'Bo, you take the guy with the curly hair.' He didn't know their names or numbers. But he got them matched up by identifying the physical characteristics of the opposing players. It was in the days of the TV sitcom *Welcome Back, Kotter*. The classroom scene. All the players are sitting at small desks and Al is trying to determine who's guarding whom, playing Mr. Kotter."

Al not only had a tough time with names, but his own phone number. He rarely wore a watch and did not have a house key.

"Al asked me to call his wife," said student trainer, Mark Paget. "But Al didn't know his telephone number. We had to call his secretary for the number. Al's sitting on the floor of his office with his shoes off, papers all over the floor, wearing a suit and tie . . . he was a real free spirit."

Marquette finished second to Bob Knight's undefeated Indiana team in both the AP and UPI polls. It was the second time that the Warriors finished the season as the number two team. The first was in 1971 when UCLA was number one.

When the tournament began, everyone was pointing to the regional final with the possibility of the number one and two teams in the country meeting to decide who went to the Final Four. "That [1974 Final Four] may have made the game against Indiana even larger for Al," speculated Kevin Gleason. "He looked at a matchup with Knight as a very significant event. A measuring stick for Al."

Marquette easily defeated Western Kentucky 79-60 in the first round of the Mideast Regional, which was held once again at Dayton. A five-point win (62-57) over Western Michigan led to the much anticipated regional final against the Hoosiers, in Baton Rouge, Louisiana.

Before the game he decided to take a motorcycle trip to a leper hospital outside of Baton Rouge.

Trying to find a way to stop Knight's once-in-a-lifetime team would prove to be a difficult challenge for Marquette. But McGuire opted for the unconventional in order to give his team its best shot to win.

"One of the guttiest things I saw Al do was in the NCAA tournament in 1976. Indiana had Kent Benson, Scott May, Tom Abernethy, Quinn Buckner, and Bobby Wilkerson," recalled Owens. "There was no way that Marquette could match up with that talent, or so the speculation went before the game.

"Al was afraid that if he put Jerome Whitehead on Benson, Jerome would foul out. He put Bo Ellis on Benson and he put Jerome on Abernethy. Instead of putting Earl Tatum on May, he put Tatum on Wilkerson.

"Then he put Butch Lee on Buckner, and he put Lloyd Walton on Scott May. He bet that May would stay outside and shoot. There was no way anyone would match up a 5'11" guard, Lloyd Walton, on a 6'7" May."

Well, McGuire's strategy almost worked. The Marquette-Indiana game turned into a sand fight. The Warriors were down by nine with just a few minutes left. They narrowed it to three points, but two late technical fouls were called on McGuire and, as the coach would say, that's all she wrote. The Hoosiers spent the rest of the game at the free-throw line and continued their undefeated season with a 65-56 win. It was the second time that Knight had defeated McGuire in the NCAA tournament.

"We had very little time to prepare," noted Gleason. "That may have hurt us. Lloyd Walton and Butch Lee were both injured. Lloyd had a thigh injury. He was going around on crutches. Those two guys shot 3 for 18. I would have loved to have been at full strength against Indiana. Al very much wanted to win that game. It was a disappointment," concluded Gleason.

A frustrated McGuire said that if his team made the NCAA tournament the following season, he would not be there to coach them. He once again seriously considered calling it a career. After all of the success and the great teams that McGuire coached during his career, it seemed that his team's performances in the NCAA were the "minus pool" and his personal "Dunkirk."

CHAPTER ELEVEN

Seashells and Balloons

Despite the dashed expectations and lingering disappointment from the previous season, the summer of 1976—the nation's bicentennial—provided a font of optimism for McGuire's returning players, including senior Bo Ellis, who was confident of Marquette's chances for the coming 1976–77 season.

"We all had a taste of the honey [NCAA tournaments]. It was just a matter of getting it all together," said Ellis of his last Warrior team. "Before the season we knew it was there. We knew what our goal was. Coach gave us a lot of confidence. Al kept everything under control. He had his players thinking what he wanted us to do.

"There was never a doubt about how good we were. It was just a matter of getting a few breaks. We had been there so many times, it was a matter of getting over the hump," said Ellis, who was the designated star in McGuire's senior star system, where the plays were designed for the senior. Bo would get the ball.

That summer the team played a series of exhibitions in Brazil. And it was a memorable trip to say the least, according to Hank Raymonds. "We had a lot of problems. We almost were put in jail. And we almost decided to come home. And in so doing we were reminded that soccer players some years ago tried that and there was a riot and they were shot. So we told them that we would continue the game. So the next night, Al says to me, 'We're gonna play Puerto Rico.' He says, 'Hank you take 'em tonight. He says I don't want any problems. I'm gonna sit in the stands.' So as he takes off, his parting shot to me was, 'By the way, if they shoot you, I'll say a prayer for you.'"

The confidence of the team was such that the team picture showed them all dressed in different tuxedos, posed in front of a Rolls-Royce. The photo stressed the individual-as-team concept, where they all wore their own outfits but still stuck together as a team. The players were wearing the long hair, puffy naturals, flared bell-bottoms, poof hats, and platform shoes that were the fashion statements of the time.

Ellis was also the only Marquette player asked to try out for the U.S. basketball team that would play in the summer Olympics in Montreal.

"I really wanted Bo on the [Olympic basketball] team," recalled University of North Carolina coach Dean Smith, who was selected to coach the squad that would bring the gold back to the U.S. "I sat with Al during trials. We had a one-mile run the second day of the Olympic trials. Ellis started the mile run, but after the second lap he trotted off the track and quit the trials."

When the U.S. team gathered in Montreal in late August, it was heavily favored to win the gold. Few of the basketball experts expected Puerto Rico to be in the finals against the powerful U.S. team. As it turned out, Puerto Rico was led by Butch Lee, who was born in Puerto Rico but raised in the Bronx.

Lee scored 35 points to lead his native team to a near upset of the U.S. Later that evening, he was interviewed in a local nightclub by ABC. He was dancing the night away to the disco sounds of Tavares's "Heaven Must Be Missin' an Angel."

Smith was later criticized for not asking Lee to try out for the U.S. squad, but he responded that Lee would be a junior that season, and only those players who would be seniors that fall were eligible. Also, Lee was not born in the U.S.; he was born in Puerto Rico.

The Warriors also picked up another key element of the team during the summer, point guard Jim Boylan of New Jersey, who transferred from Assumption College in Massachusetts. Ironically, it was Dean Smith who recommended Boylan to McGuire.

"I made a decision that I wouldn't take transfers," Smith explained. "I wanted Jimmy Boylan out of high school. I told Al about him. I recommended Ulice Payne, Eddie Daniels. He liked them because where are they [transfers] gonna go?"

"Dean didn't have room for him," Hank Raymonds added. "Smith knew about him because North Carolina forward Mike O'Koren and Boylan grew up together."

As with Whitehead, Boylan was allowed to play right away after transferring because he had at least a B average, which was the rule then.

McGuire happened to be on the East Coast with friend and former Belmont Abbey player John von Bargen, who helped recruit Earl Tatum and Bernard Toone to Marquette.

"Al was at a clinic sponsored by Medalist in Newton, Massachusetts," recalled von Bargen. "Jimmy came to the hotel room where Al was staying. I let him in the room, and Al is on the bed, half asleep, face buried in a pillow. I said, 'Al, Jimmy's here.'

"Al sticks his left hand out and says to Jimmy, 'Gimme five. Now, don't tell me about how many points ya scored or how many rebounds or assists. All I wanna know is, can ya throw a bounce pass?' Jimmy says, 'Yeah, I can, Coach.'

"'I'll see ya at Marquette in September. Gimme five.'

"He stuck his left hand out to Jimmy. Jimmy gives him five and is out the door. Al didn't even look up at the kid," recalled von Bargen of the recruitment of Jim Boylan.

He also recruited a 6'6" forward from Chicago named Robert Byrd, whom McGuire nicknamed Blackbyrd. Walk-on guard Mark Lavin, also of the Chicago area, helped round out McGuire's last Marquette team for the upcoming season.

Joining Boylan, Lee, Whitehead, and Ellis were sharpshooting 5'10" guard Gary Rosenberger from Milwaukee; indispensable enforcer Bill Neary, who could not only take one for the team but give one back as well; forwards Ulice Payne and Jim Dudley, a transfer from Michigan State; probably the most gifted basketball player on the team, Bernard Toone of Yonkers, New York; and his only 7-foot center, Craig Butrym.

McGuire sought not only basketball talent but a new look for his team that season. For fresh ideas for the team uniforms he called the longtime editor of *Sports Illustrated*'s swimsuit issue, Jule Campbell.

"I got a phone call, and it was Al," recalled Campbell. "I was home sick in bed and the first thing out of his mouth is, 'How can I compete with you?' I assumed he was talking about the swimsuit issue. I knew who he was. That was how we met. He came to New York.

"My husband is the art director of *Fortune* magazine," Campbell continued. "He did sketches of uniform ideas. I did the socks blue and gold. I tried to make it [the uniform] avant garde and showy, because that's what Al is. It [the phone call] was a funny way to approach me. Creative. And it caught my interest.

"I asked him, 'How do you interview players?' He said that 'I throw a basketball to them when they come in my office. If they handle it, I can tell they are comfortable with it. If they can bounce a basketball while they are talking to me, I know they can play.'"

Jackie Stone, who worked with Medalist and was married to former Warrior John Stone, brought the uniform ideas to Medalist, which again produced the new telegenic look as it had done for the team and the cheerleaders for several years. Jackie Stone was a former cheerleader who owned her own salon.

It was his last couple of years that the motorcycle had become a big thing with Al, according to team manager Greg Stack. Whether McGuire would go to practice that day depended on which way he turned out of his driveway in Brookfield.

"My first few years I drove Kawasakis, then I went to the Hogs [Harley-Davidsons]. I never did use a helmet because I can't hear all of the sounds around me and it cuts off my peripheral vision," explained McGuire.

With three starters returning from the previous season, the Warriors were picked preseason number one in the country by UPI, *Basketball Weekly* and *Street & Smith's* magazine. *Sports Illustrated* picked Michigan number one, North Carolina number two, and Marquette number eight.

The Marquette team sped out of the gate, winning its first three games by an average margin of 24 points a game. It looked too easy at the start, and with the experienced group McGuire had, everything was looking like his trademark phrase, Seashells and Balloons, or happiness and victory.

Early in December of 1976, the nation had a new president in Jimmy Carter. Frank Deford of *Sports Illustrated* wrote a feature on McGuire that hinted the coach was ready to bring down the curtain on his career at Marquette. While he had talked about it occasionally since the devastating loss to Ohio State in the 1971 NCAA Tournament, no one really took the talk that seriously.

James Scott, the university's vice-president for student affairs and McGuire's immediate supervisor, recalled a late-night phone conversation on December 16, 1976. "I got a call at 10 P.M. from university vice president Dr. Quentin Quade, who happened to be sitting in Father Raynor's office. 'I'm meeting with Father Raynor and Coach McGuire, and he has let us know that he is retiring at the end of the year,' Quade told me.

"When I arrived, Al was there with Father Raynor and told me that he was leaving Marquette, effective at the end of the season. Al said he just felt that it was time to go. Father Raynor did not want to lose Al. He was such a winner and a major part of the university," recalled Scott, who added that Raynor gave McGuire his blessing nonetheless.

"He [McGuire] paid me a visit in December of 1976," recalled President Raynor." I had maybe known what was coming. His mind was made up. His desire was to terminate coaching at the collegiate level.

"I liked Al. I thought he did a magnificent job. He had to fight for every bit of his success. He was a good athletic director. He ran the department. He ran it well. He was a good administrator. He observed all regulations from the federal government in spending on other sports.

"While Al consistently reported surpluses with the basketball receipts, I reminded Al of his larger responsibilities as athletic director. As athletic director, he's got wider responsibilities to pay off the football debt. He ran a good ship. He pinched a nickel until it screamed. He built up the basketball program. He sold the program, got the competition up. He took something sleepy and made it a giant.

"I don't like the member of a winning team to leave," Raynor continued. "He has his own reasons. Before he left he wanted to thank us for our course of action [in not letting him out of his contract in 1968]. A big admission on the part of a big man. He was an honorable person. The profession is much more highly regarded because of his involvement in it. His teams had class. He was an excellent coach."

Raynor noted that despite McGuire's flamboyant personality, he had no problem with the university being viewed through the image of the high-profile coach. "He was not just a winning coach, but a real character who got people's attention. That made my job easier," said Raynor. "He was always good. He was always a gentleman. He was a positive contributor. He did it his own way with his own personality. The general reputation of the university was enhanced by Al McGuire."

"At times, my dad was bigger than the teams," noted Allie McGuire. "He was the team. He could fill up an arena. His means of success was to put a product out that was successful. That was what he created. Everywhere we went it was sold out. That was him. We were just actors for a short time on his play."

"When the athletic board met," recalled Dick Nixon, "one of them remarked, 'we have to find another Al McGuire.' I said, 'there is no other Al McGuire.'"

The shock waves could be felt all the way to Bingo's, an establishment that players and fans frequented where they were served and entertained by Jon "Bingo" Berta, whom McGuire affectionately referred to as Bingo Bango Bongo.

The next afternoon, McGuire took his players to a place called the Voom-Voom Room, which was located in the Time Building in downtown Milwaukee, where a luncheon was planned.

"Al said to us, 'I have something to announce,'" Bo Ellis recalled. "It took a lot out of him physically. He said it was time to do something else. He didn't really tell us he was going to quit. He broke down and ran out of the restaurant. He got emotional. We were kind of shocked. It didn't sink in until later in the season."

Later that afternoon, Medalist Industries announced that Al McGuire would preside over a press conference at 4 P.M. at the Wisconsin Club.

Medalist chairman of the board Norman Fischer announced that McGuire had been appointed vice-chairman of the board of directors, effective May 1, 1977.

After being introduced by Fischer at 4:10 P.M., a solemn McGuire stood behind a small lectern with a bank of microphones. Above him was a portrait of General Douglas MacArthur. In his brief but unemotional remarks, McGuire announced that he was retiring as coach. He thanked Marquette for all that it did for him and his family. When he was asked if he was definitely not coaching again, McGuire was affirmative. It was, in his words, "Tap City."

After noting that there was still a season of basketball ahead, McGuire told the gathering that "this is not a farewell, no last hurrah. I always said that all carnivals and merry-go-rounds come to a stop. It was time for me to go my way. I don't know what it is not to be a celebrity," according to Paul Levy's account in the *Milwaukee Sentinel.*

At age 48 and with a year remaining on his Marquette contract, McGuire felt that it was time to move on to the next stage in his life. And it was not coaching a professional team, even though he was reportedly the highest paid coach in the country.

In Roger Jaynes's account, "McGuire said that the idea of quitting 'had been in my mind for a number of years. But I had been concentrating on it for the last eight or nine months.'"

"Al's very smart," noted Mike Timeberg, his New York contact and retired hoops guru. "He didn't want to coach until he was 90 years old. He had other opportunities and that was the time to take advantage of them. He had a chance to go out while he was on top." And he did not have to worry about the pressure of repeating, if he won the national championship.

He would be joining Medalist Industries, whose camps and clinics he had run for ten years, to become vice-chairman of the board, which would actually pay him less money than he made at Marquette, according to McGuire.

McGuire said that if his number two-ranked Warriors made the NCAA tournament, he would go back on his promise of the previous season to never coach again in the tourney. He did hedge on whether he thought his final team could, in fact, earn a bid to that season's NCAAs.

He joked during the press conference that the reason he was leaving was temperamental sophomore Bernard Toone. After a 20-minute question-and-answer session, he speculated that the vice chairman's job is to put gasoline in the chairman's car.

"I remember talking to Al in December 1976," said Smith. "He said, 'We won't even make the NCAAs.'"

Other coaches weighed in with their feelings about McGuire. Lou Carnesecca was most impressed with McGuire's ability to know when to leave.

"He did what he wanted to do. He did it well, but he got out before they got used to him. They all knew he was his own guy. Al McGuire was a breath of fresh air. He came in with some new ideas. Another angle. Another play. He took us out of the gym and put us in the sun. He helped make coaches celebrities," said a grateful Carnesecca.

After a quick 4-0 start in McGuire's final season, Denny Crum brought his tough Louisville Cardinals to the Arena to play the Warriors the day after McGuire's announcement. Most of the students had already gone home for Christmas break. The Milwaukee faithful were still in shock as they filed into the Arena, and at game time the Marquette players were still stunned as well. They had had high expectations for a great season, and then McGuire dropped the bombshell.

The Cardinals were ready for a battle as they took the Warriors into overtime. Butch Lee scored 30 points, the team's last eight in regulation including the basket that tied the score at 67. With 20 seconds left, Lee made a steal and was fouled by the Cardinals' Wesley Cox.

Crum called a time-out to try to ice Lee at the free-throw line. Lee missed both free throws, sending the game into overtime. Louisville hit some big free throws down the stretch to win 78-75.

The team was still in a funk when Mychal Thompson and Ray Williams led Jim Dutcher's Minnesota Gophers into the Arena. The Warriors shot 16 percent in the first half and were behind by 24 points with just over 16 minutes to go. Marquette whittled the deficit to 59-57 with just under three minutes to go, but after a questionable technical was called on Bo Ellis, Minnesota won the game 66-59.

"We could have died after the Minnesota game, but we didn't," recalled McGuire. Afterward, Butch Lee boldly predicted that Marquette would win the NCAA championship that season.

In the Milwaukee Classic, Marquette beat Bill Foster's Clemson Tigers 67-49, a game in which Tree Rollins scored two points and got three rebounds. McGuire was not impressed with his troops after the game, "I don't think this is a great team. Great teams don't have droughts. We have to beat you with defense, muscling, and intensity."

The Clemson game was the beginning of a ten-game winning streak. The Warriors next scored a 64-57 win over the Badgers to win their ninth straight Milwaukee Classic, and then headed to Northwestern to face the Wildcats. Newcomer Bob Bach joined Uncle Tom Collins in the booth for the game as play-by-play man. Bach would come to be known as the Voice of the Warriors. After a Marquette basket his trademark GOOOD! could be heard all over Milwaukee on WISN radio.

"Al usually went on the team bus to the games in a shoddy-looking sweatsuit, and he changed into a suit and tie right before the game," recalled Bach, who added that Channel 12 did the Warrior telecasts. "Tom Collins did TV and I arrived from a small station in northern Wisconsin where I worked as a news and sports person. I did color with Collins. I did the play-by-play when Collins did TV.

"Coming to Marquette was culture shock," Bach continued. "The high school basketball team I covered was 2-18, the weakest team in an extremely weak league. Butch Lee was the only player that I knew on the Marquette team.

"The first time I met him [McGuire] was on New Year's Eve 1976 in the locker room before the game against Tex Winters's Northwestern Wildcats. He seemed very busy. The more contemporary term was intense. He was the kind of person where you got the feeling he had a lot of things on his mind.

"He had a way of speaking in short spurts. He knew he was quotable but he didn't show off," Bach continued. "You got the impression he was completely honest. There was no hesitation. He would give you the answers and substantiation to the answer. Not long, but always full. The two to three minutes of tape was almost always usable."

Marquette beat the Wildcats, 66-53, and in that ten-game streak on McGuire's farewell tour were wins over South Carolina and mentor Frank McGuire, and over Notre Dame and Digger Phelps. And Al had a little something for Digger before the game, according to Joan Bohmann.

"I was in the locker room with Al before the game," recalled the cheerleader. "I saw Al soaking his hand in a sink of ice cold water. "Al says to me, 'You're probably wondering what I'm doing, huh?' I said, 'No, but you can go ahead and tell me,'" Bohmann's curiosity sufficiently piqued.

"He wiped off his hand, put talcom powder on it and dampened his hair. 'It's all image!' Al told me. 'And it's all a psych out game.'

"I followed Al out and he shook Digger Phelps hand with an ice cold hand," said Bohmann. Phelps understood since he came from a family of grave diggers. Al's hand was cold as a corpse." The Warriors improved to 11-2 with a 78-69 win over the Irish behind 27 points from Lee.

Before McGuire's last appearance at Alumni Hall in Chicago, DePaul coach Ray Meyer and his staff planned a "Seashells and Balloons" send-off for Pat and Al.

"I wanted to give him a plaque and give Pat a seashell watch," recalled Gene Sullivan, who was athletic director at DePaul. "But [instead] we put 400 to 500 balloons in the ceiling, above the floor.

"[Toward the end of the pregame ceremony] I said, 'Now we'll celebrate with seashells and balloons,' which was the cue for the balloons to be released. But the balloons didn't drop as planned," explained an embarrassed Sullivan. "For the whole game, a balloon would float down, then another. And that was it. A rope broke and just two or three balloons came down." Marquette's balloon did not pop that night as it defeated the Blue Demons 85-64. The Warriors were 14-2 and ranked fourth in the country.

After ten straight impressive wins, the Warriors took the McGuire farewell tour to Cincinnati, where the number 11 Bearcats, coached by Gale Catlett, were waiting. Marquette had a shot to win with four seconds left. Lee collided with a Bearcat and fell to the floor while passing to Ellis. There was no foul and Ellis's shot was not in time. The Warriors lost, 63-62.

"At Cincy, Marquette seemed to get beat up pretty good," recalled Bob Bach, "but got the short end of the stick on officials' calls. Toward the end of the game, the Cincy players were mouthing off to Butch," said Bach, who added that Lee would eventually make them pay for their taunting.

The Warriors schedule had its last ten games split, with five at home and five on the road. McGuire always wanted his team to be tournament-tough and usually scheduled at least three games on the road to finish each season.

After a fairly easy win over Manhattan, 86-60, Ray Meyer brought his Blue Demons to the Arena, where they had not won since early in the 1965–66 season. In fact, the Warriors had won 19 straight over DePaul, a streak that stretched back to the 1967–68 campaign.

But DePaul won the game in two overtimes, 77-72, behind senior Ron Norwood's 23 points. Marquette was up 60-56 with just over four and a half minutes left, and Lee uncharacteristically turned the ball over while attempting to dribble through double teams in the Warriors' delay game. McGuire expressed doubts that the team could get a bid to the NCAA tournament.

Next up was Dick Vitale's University of Detroit Titans. Vitale had coached the team for just a few seasons when he brought his team to the Arena. Once again, the Warriors were in control at 57-52, but problems started after they went into their delay game. As McGuire would say, they let their sweat dry.

"I tried to pattern myself after Al McGuire," said Vitale. "Al McGuire represented a lot of the things that I believed in. It was a thrill for me when I got to play Marquette. I was in awe of Al McGuire. I used to watch him play for the Knicks, always hustling and diving after loose balls. What a down-to-earth, regular guy.

"One of my greatest wins was in 1977 at Marquette. The game went down to the last second. He's walking up and down the sidelines. We steal the ball with ten seconds and one of our guards, Dennis Boyd, threw it up and it went in with one second on the clock.

"After the game at the press conference, Al told the media, 'Why are you guys talking to me? This night belongs to that other young coach.'" McGuire also declared emphatically that Marquette would not get a bid to the tournament.

The Wichita State Shockers came to town for McGuire's last home game and Senior Night at the Arena. "I thought that the referees would throw me a party and bring the carnival down for me," recalled McGuire, who was hit with his first technicals of the season. After arguing a foul called on Jim Boylan, he was hit with a "T," which was followed by a shower of toilet paper rolls from the crowd. The second technical extended the Shockers' lead to 37-31.

But it turned ugly. A Wichita State player punched Bo Ellis, who did not retaliate. Both players were ejected. The officiating was poor—so poor that the fans began to get surly.

"At the end of the game, with Wichita State leading by 11," recalled Dave Foran, "McGuire called a time-out and asked athletics business manager Paul Prpish to get the police prepared to make sure the officials were able to get out of the Arena safely.

"McGuire had instructed Butch Lee and Jim Boylan to play catch until the clock ran out, resulting in boos raining down from the crowd. They didn't play well that year. They always played good defense," said Foran.

Marquette had not lost three straight at home or even five games at the Arena since McGuire's first year, when the Warriors lost seven on their home court. The Arena was not a pretty sight that night.

"That's what I remember most, was the boos," recalled Rick Majerus. Any hope that the team had of giving McGuire one last try for the brass ring seemed to have ended with that game as far as the Milwaukee faithful were concerned. It really looked like Tap City. Close the hymnals, mass is over, according to the gospel from Reverend Al.

The best thing that McGuire could do was get his team out of Milwaukee as quickly as possible and finish the season's last five games on the road as a spoiler. Before the Warriors headed on the road, McGuire told his team to simply take one game at a time.

They first went to Madison where they easily defeated Wisconsin 73-58 behind Lee's 25 points—the Warriors 14th straight win over the Badgers and a sweep of Wisconsin in McGuire's final season. His record against Wisconsin was 19-3. The Warriors' record after beating the Badgers was 17-6.

From there, the Warriors went to Blacksburg, Virginia, to take on the Hokies of Virginia Tech. This may have been the turning point game for the team in its final run. Lee took charge again with 22 points, six straight in the last minute and a half, to lead Marquette to a 75-70 win.

In what would turn out to be the worst-played contest in Marquette's last five games, the Warriors turned the ball over 30 times and Tulane gave it up 28 times as Marquette somehow won 63-44. Even though Ellis scored 26 points and pulled down 13 rebounds, Tulane shot just 27.6 percent. A win is a win, McGuire would say, and Marquette's record improved to 19-6.

At Omaha, Marquette used 56.8 percent shooting and strong rebounding to beat the Creighton Bluejays for the Warriors' 20th win against 6 losses. Notre Dame had an identical record in the battle of the great independents for an at-large NCAA berth.

Marquette's last obstacle was at Ann Arbor, where the tough Michigan Wolverines awaited. The Warriors led 40-35 at the intermission, during which a tearful McGuire informed his players that they were the last team selected for the NCAA tournament. Before the team went out for the second half, McGuire shed his lucky black three-piece suit, which he had worn since the Virginia Tech game. He promised to change it once the team earned a bid. "That suit stunk!" recalled cheerleader Joan Bohmann.

"I was responsible for making sure that McGuire's lucky three-piece suit was cleaned," recalled team manager Greg Stack. "Someone always carried it on and off the bus [usually 12th man Mark Lavin], but I had it cleaned and made sure Al's shoes were shined."

After McGuire put on a green suit for the second half, Bo Ellis fouled out and the team blew a six-point lead to lose 69-68. Their 20-7 record represented the most losses by a team up to that point to earn a bid to the NCAA tournament.

"Voice of the Warriors" Bob Bach learned what many of the journalists had known for years about what a great interview Al McGuire was. During the season, he had picked up quite a few, but none like the one before the team left Milwaukee to begin the tournament.

"If you asked plain old good questions, you'd get great answers," noted Bach. "Al mixed emotion with statistics in a unique fashion. He was highly self-assured. Al was always happy to get a few things off his chest and put the game behind him. When Al reached the point where he felt he had given all that needed to be said, he would say, 'That's it.'

"The best interview I did with Al never aired," Bach continued. "It took place in the old gym after the team's last practice before they left for Omaha and their first game with Cincinnati. It lasted about ten minutes. Solid questions, excellent answers. But as I went out to my car, I realized that the plug to the microphone was not plugged into the recorder.

"I said, 'I got to do it again.' Three to four minutes later, Al was gone from the old gym and the place was empty. He wasn't in the locker room and there was only one way to get in and out of the building. It was the best interview I never recorded.

"Once in Omaha, the night before Marquette played Cincy, Al was very relaxed, drinking a beer," recalled Bach, who noted that McGuire's lucky three-piece black suit had been lost in transit.

The Warriors started their tournament run on Saturday afternoon, March 12, 1977, at the Omaha Civic Auditorium, where they would play a grudge match against Cincinnati. Fortunately, before the game, the lucky suit was found and the Warriors were ready to tangle with the Bearcats.

"That was not an easy game for Marquette," recalled Bach, "especially after losing to the Bearcats toward the end of the season." The Warriors were down by three points at the half, and as the team was heading back to the locker room, McGuire and Bernard Toone exchanged words about his playing time.

"The exchange was verbal," said Toone, who was the first man off the bench for Marquette. "We got chest to chest. There was a little shoving, and it really inspired me," said Toone, who was restrained by Bo Ellis, while Hank Raymonds held onto McGuire. The only real casualty was Bob Weingart, who hurt his hand in all of the pushing and shoving in the locker room.

"Bernard and I had a verbal and physical get-together at the half," admitted McGuire. "But what that did was clear the decks and the rest of the tournament was a cakewalk."

"It was the standard Bernard-I'm-on-another-planet game," explained Bach, who noted that Toone played a half-hearted first half. "Al had a guy who was not concentrating on the game. Bernard had fabulous skills. But the one thing that upset Al was players who had great talent and did not make full use of it."

The Warriors went on a 13-0 run in the second half, behind 18 points off the bench by a suddenly inspired Toone. "Butch Lee pointed at two Cincinnati players toward the end of the game," recalled Bob Bach. "The Cincy players had mouthed off to him when Cincy beat Marquette near the end of the year, and Butch got even. And so did Marquette." The Warriors handled the Bearcats 66-51.

St. Patrick's Day found the Warriors in Oklahoma City for its Midwest Regional semifinal against the Kansas State Wildcats. Up to this point, McGuire had not received a technical in the tournament, but this game was different.

As the Warriors were running up the court, McGuire put his hand to his neck to let his players know that the Kansas State players were choking. But referee Jim Buckiewicz saw McGuire's signal and thought he was referring to the officiating crew, and he was hit with a technical. After that, McGuire was worrying about not only the game but his future.

Recalled Hank Raymonds, "After drawing the 'T', Al says to me, 'If we lose this game, I'm finished forever, Hank!'"

The Warriors were down ten with just under 12 minutes left in the game when Raymonds made a suggestion to McGuire, "I told Al to put Jim Dudley in the game. He scored six points for us and got some key rebounds that turned the game around."

Dudley was joined by Toone as the sophomores started a 17-4 run for Marquette. Dudley then stole a pass and fed Butch Lee for a layup to give the team a three-point lead with just 18 seconds remaining. It was not over, however, as Bo Ellis fouled Kansas State's Darryl Winston as he was tipping in a rebound. The referees ruled the basket no good and awarded him two free throws. Winston made the free throws, but the Warriors still won by a point, 67-66.

In the press conference after the game, McGuire delivered what was possibly the most emotional address of his coaching career, when he talked about the controversial technical foul, the NCAA's prepping of officials for the tournament, and his career. "After the game, Al went into a postgame interview room fuming," recalled Bach. "He was clearly on edge. He gave short, tight answers to reporters' questions, and then went on a 15-minute tirade. It was an impassioned plea to stop messing with McGuire and let his players play."

"I have a tremendous hang-up on the technical," began McGuire. "Either I'm sicko or someone else is sicko. Now, I was yelling that the

Kansas State team was startin' to tighten up. I put my hand on my neck and says, 'They are tightening up.' And the ref blows a *technical* on me.

"I've been through this bullshit too many times in the NCAA . . . I coach exactly the same no matter where the hell I am and every time I come to the NCAA, they end up calling technicals on me. Now it's *absolutely* wrong and I'm not a crybaby!

"I've been quiet for the last ten years. Now, either they're taking these officials and brainwashing them before they have my game. This has nothing to do with Kansas State. Kansas State should have beaten us. We were fortunate to win; we were lucky. Kansas State outplayed us, they were better prepared than we were, and they should have won the game. It just so happens we had a lot of time left and we caught them and we ended up getting a point or two ahead.

"The thing that got me aggravated is, I've been quiet about it for years. I've been through this thing from Athens, Georgia, with Ohio State, with Indiana, with them *all!* What the hell's going on? Guy calls a technical foul on me when I'm talking to the team, and the only way the guy can do it is because subconsciously he's been told, and then he won't come over and tell me. All I wanted to tell the guy is, 'Hey, I'm talking to the guys, not to you.'

"Look, I'm 25 years in the business, guys. I've never said a word against officials. In 25 *years*, and I've gotta go through that crap again. That's 25 years, and I'm not lying. Take any player that follows me here. I've never said anything about officials. Under no conditions, anywhere, anytime.

"Now, there's too much smoke in back rooms, or too much whispering or too much something going on. We're not that good of a ball club, I admit that. But to call a technical foul at that time of a game is a mortal sin. It's WRONG!

"Now, I'm not a psycho. One technical foul all year on me. Don't you think Notre Dame, Michigan, Creighton, and Florida, and all these games are big games? We got three times as many people at the gosh-darn games. I don't do any different in this league than I do at home or on the road.

"We have big rivalries with the University of Wisconsin and Minnesota and Northwestern. What happens when I come the NCAA? What are they trying to prove? Now, it doesn't make any difference to me. I'm on my way, but I don't want to blow it for these guys. I would not say a word here if we lost. There was no way I could say a word. But I'm, I'm just to a point. Why do you think I made a statement last year? Why? I'm not an irrational person. I'm not an irresponsible person. But someone has to talk to somebody. I'm not looking for no breaks tomorrow night or any night. I never wanted a break from any official. I can't even tell you these guys' names.

"I have never rated an official in my life. I have never blackballed an official in my life. And I have never had a preference list in my life. In 13 years, I've never spoken to the commissioner's office. *In 13 years!* And I gotta come up here with the NCAA pulling this crap. And that's what it is. But that's a competent official. He wouldn't be here if he wasn't competent. And someone brainwashed him and they've been brainwashed before.

"And that's the reason I wouldn't coach anymore in the NCAA. It's . . . it's . . . it's been a zoo. Now I'll go by any rules and I should have gotten it off my chest seven years ago and left seven, nine years ago. It has nothing to do with the officials. I'm talking about when the subconscious of the official is reached. In some smoke-filled room. Somewhere they're prepping them. No official calls a technical foul on a guy. The official had his back to me running down court. I'm yelling to the guys on my team. I'm saying, 'Hey, they're choking.' He turns around and blows a technical. And then he won't talk to me.

"So, peace. I got it off my chest and maybe it was me. It was a cancer and a pus that was in there the last ten years. So I'm glad it's out. And that's it. I'll never again say anything.

"I'm not talking about an individual official. I'm talking about the *selection* and the *prepping* of the officials before the game. That's what I'm talking about and they can have equal time and everything else they want.

"What the hell! A man spends 25 years of his life in a profession and every time he comes to something like this he looks like an idiot? Who the hell wants to look like an idiot out there? So, peace. I'm sorry and so on, but I'm glad to get it all off my chest.

"So, maybe I hurt some people. I'm sorry. But it's about time that some people started to realize that I'm not a bum in a bowery, or a wino in a hallway or a pimp on a corner. I know my profession! And I know it *well*. And I've worked at it *hard*. All my *life* I worked at it hard. They won the game. They save me from not being able to say this. Butch shouldn't have taken the last shot. I gave him hell for taking the last shot.

"I do not accept anything in victory that I won't accept in defeat. He had no right taking the last shot. The clock was more important. And that was it. Now they know what it is to play for me."

Paul Galvan, one of the Final Four officials that year, acknowledged that NCAA representatives do meet with the officials before games.

"In just about all NCAA tournaments, NCAA representatives on the tournament committee would always meet with the officials the day before the games for an hour or an hour and a half. At that time you would get the game assignment. And there is a Rule 10.9 on bench decorum, and we were told that it was to be strictly enforced," said Galvan, who worked Final Fours in 1974, '75, '77, '86, and '87. But '77 was the only year he worked a championship game. "The briefing officials never discussed before games that I've officiated that this coach does this or this team does that."

From then on, McGuire's memorable tirade became known as the St. Patrick's Day speech, and could very well have been the spark the team needed in its next game against the Wake Forest Demon Deacons, on Saturday, March 19, at the Myriad Convention Center in Oklahoma City. "It was the most unforgettable thing I heard him say," said Bach.

While the Demon Deacons had a three-point cushion in the second half, Toone scored nine of his 18 points during a 14-2 run that helped push the Warriors over the top. After a topsy-turvy relationship with McGuire that season, Toone led the team to a convincing 82-68 win. It was the second Final Four in three years for the Warriors. The team was headed to Atlanta's Omni, "the Mecca of the South," to play in the Final Four.

As in previous tournament years, McGuire did not keep his players in an NCAA-sanctioned hotel. He housed the players in an as-yet unopened Hilton hotel away from the hubbub of Atlanta to keep distractions to a minimum. There was not even a phone on the premises.

"He bunched everyone else at the Radisson Hotel in Atlanta," remembered Norman Ochs. "Al made that the headquarters. But he found a hotel halfway around the circle. That way nobody could reach him or his team.

"On the day of the semifinals, I had eight people and Al said, 'I'll give you the tickets when I get to Atlanta.' At the Radisson, there was a young man from Milwaukee who holed himself up in a broom closet of the hotel, but did not have a ticket for the Final Four. Every time he saw McGuire, he reminded him about getting him a ticket."

The sunny Saturday semifinals featured UNLV and the University of North Carolina in the first game, followed by Marquette and the University of North Carolina–Charlotte, which had been a Division One school only since 1972. Even though it was UNC-Charlotte's first NCAA tournament, they defeated a heavily favored Michigan team to get to Atlanta.

"The atmosphere was exciting," recalled Bach. "I remember it wasn't what I had expected. I had the dual role of doing color and reporting on the games for WISN. I filed reports, et cetera. It was exhausting at the finals. I never did see UNLV play Carolina."

"The first game is starting at 12:30 P.M. and Al is still not dressed," Ochs recalled. "And Pat is looking for some privacy so she can get dressed.

"Al tells me, 'My secretary is bringing up 24 tickets.' The secretary walks in with the tickets. Al then says, 'I got one left over. Normy, give this to the guy in the broom closet. He hitchhiked all the way from Milwaukee.' The kid got a ticket. Al didn't even know the guy's name. Al thinks differently. He liked the kid's gumption, traveling all the way from Milwaukee and didn't have a ticket for the game.

"Before the game," Ochs continued, "McGuire tells Lee Rose, the coach of UNC-Charlotte, 'We've played a hundred schools with names like yours, but I'm not sure that we can beat your team.'"

Marquette was favored in the semifinal and started out accordingly. Unlike the earlier contests, the Warriors sprinted to a 23-9 lead against the 49ers. Marquette, however, lost a good deal of its lead when it went into the delay game.

"They were tight," McGuire said of UNCC after the game. "This was showtime. This was something they had never experienced before. All of a sudden they found themselves and played their game."

UNC-Charlotte went up 35-30 when Bo Ellis was whistled for his fourth foul with just over 14 minutes left. The nip-and-tuck game started to go the Warriors' way when Jerome Whitehead scored six points in a 14-4 run to put Marquette back on top. Charlotte's team leader, guard Melvin Watkins, then fouled out with a minute left. Butch Lee hit a couple of jumpers, but "Cornbread" Maxwell tied the score at 49 with three seconds left in regulation.

McGuire called time and took a walk to the far end of the court, looking at the height of the scoreboard.

"Al knew how high off the court the scoreboard was," recalled sports reporter Bill Jauss, who was covering the game for the *Chicago Tribune*. "He was just doing that to freeze UNC-Charlotte."

McGuire's excuse for the time-out was that he wanted to make sure that Butch Lee could launch a court-length pass without hitting the Omni scoreboard, which was suspended at center court.

"McGuire was calm. He was exceedingly calm," recalled Greg Stack. "He came back and strolled to the bench. He said, 'Butch, you should have no problem throwin' it.' The pass was intended for Bo, but it went off his hands."

"I was the referee for the inbounds of the ball," said Galvan. "Charlie [Fouty of the Big 10] was about at the free-throw line extended at the other end of the floor. I broke downcourt as Butch threw the ball. Then all of a sudden, the ball went up."

Lee flung a baseball pass down the court toward Bo Ellis's outstretched hands. The ball deflected off Ellis's hands to Jerome Whitehead who was being guarded by Maxwell. Whitehead turned and went up to dunk the ball, but the shot was partially blocked by Maxwell. The ball hit the backboard, bounced off the rim, and dropped through the net as time expired.

"Marquette University came to a complete silence with those three seconds," recalled Dan Kelly, a sophomore at the time, who was crammed into his dorm room with ten other people watching the game on a 12-inch color set.

Back in Atlanta, "It was very noisy," Galvan continued. "The minute the ball went in the basket there was total chaos. Players were jumping up and down. I was at the other end of the floor. When I turned, Al was coming toward me. I just stopped. Coach Rose was still in his bench area. I asked Chuck if he had heard the horn. Chuck said, 'No, I didn't hear the horn.' I counted the number of seconds, I thought I heard a horn, but I wasn't going to guess. If you're not sure, you're not gonna guess," explained Galvan, the trailing official on the play.

"McGuire was running out onto the court, he had his hands out to the sides saying, 'It's good! It's good! You've got to count the basket!' It wasn't in a threatening way," Galvan recalled of McGuire's pleadings.

"After the play, Al was there, two inches away from his [Galvan's] ear. 'Goaltending and a foul! Goaltending and a foul!' Al must have said it 50 times," Stack continued.

Galvan then told McGuire, "If you move out of the way, I'll let you know if they're gonna count the basket. In order to get down to where he could talk to me, he was bending down with his hands to the side.

"At that time you could feel the coliseum come to a hush. When there was not a signal, everyone started standing around and going toward the scorer's table. Everyone was wondering what I was going to do. I've always met with the timer and scorer. I told the timer, Larry Carter, at halftime and before the game, if I come to you, you have to tell me if the ball was in his hands or in the air."

When it was clear that Galvan was heading over to Carter at the scorer's table, McGuire made a beeline and cut off coach Rose's access to the timer. "Al made his presence very clear at the scorer's table," remembered Pat Lloyd, a longtime Marquette season-ticket holder who sat with his wife, Polly, in front of the McGuire family at the Omni. "Al pushed him [Lee Rose] out of the way. Al was very demonstrative. We were in an SEC [Southeastern Conference] area. There were a lot of UNCC and UNC people there," noted Lloyd.

"You know that basket was good! You know that basket was good!" McGuire repeated as he interspersed what he called tugboat language in his sentences to emphasize his point. McGuire recalled that while he burned the timer's ears with his colorful words and phrases, Rose spoke in the manner of administrators who spend their time in ivory towers with the memos and pipes.

Galvan worked to get both coaches away from Carter as McGuire persisted in his pleadings to count the basket. "Will you let me find out?" said a frustrated Galvan as he pushed both coaches about eight feet away from the scorer's table.

"It was a three-ring circus," remembered Bach. "I admired Galvan for the way in which he controlled the situation."

"I asked him twice," Galvan said of his queries to Carter, the timer. "'When the horn sounded, where was the ball? You're telling me when the horn sounded, the ball was in the basket.' I was at the head of the circle extension near the bench area. McGuire and Bernard Toone were standing behind me, with his hand above his head signaling, 'The basket's good! The basket's good!' [When Carter told me it was good] that was when I turned and made the signal that the basket was good and the game was over, Marquette had won."

Back in Milwaukee, "When the referee turned and dropped his arm," said Kelly, "Schroeder Hall began to shake. Kids went into ecstasy. Within minutes the dorm emptied."

"Lee Rose then asked me, 'Are you sure the basket counts?' 'Yes, it counts, Coach.' 'That was a good ballgame. You called a good game,' he told me." Added Bob Bach, "Lee Rose was a wonderful gentleman. He got the word and left the court without a complaint."

The Marquette section of the Omni exploded in cheers as the 49ers team and staff made their way to the locker room after congratulating McGuire and the Warriors. In a rare show of emotion, McGuire hugged Butch Lee after the basket was signaled good.

"David Cawood of the NCAA came in after the MU-UNCC game to get a statement from me to give to the press," remembered Galvan. "Al had not drawn any technical at that game. He and coach Rose were excellent. Coach Rose took it as a gentleman. He took defeat as an outstanding coach and professional."

"After Marquette had beaten UNC-Charlotte," said Bach, "I remember leaving the arena that day overhearing the University of North Carolina fans saying they were not going to have any problems with Marquette." "We took a lot of taunting from the ACC fans those two days," added Pat Lloyd. "They told us, 'Wait till you play the real North Carolina on Monday night. Wait till you see the real Tar Heels. It's gonna be a different story.' We said, 'Wait till you see this independent team from the Midwest.'"

Back in Milwaukee, students continued to spill out of the dorms and bars and onto Wisconsin Avenue down to Lake Michigan to celebrate as they had for previous NCAA and NIT victories. Ten thousand students poured down Wisconsin Avenue. While the championship game was not until Monday night, the opportunity to celebrate a big win was too good to pass up. "People were stopped in the middle of Wisconsin Avenue screaming for several hours," remembered Kelly, who added that even though the bars were filled, there was a "nervous, excited anticipation of the grand finale on Monday night."

That night the sports programs in Milwaukee and throughout the country were talking about those improbable three seconds. The UNC-UNLV game, which UNC won 84-83, was given second billing in most sportscasts. "That was probably the most replayed three seconds in the history of college basketball," McGuire said after the game.

Both Marquette and North Carolina had Sunday to practice for the Monday night final. McGuire and Hank Raymonds put in a game plan they thought might work for the final. They decided to turn the tables on Dean Smith's vaunted "Four Corners" strategy and put in their own delay game. After seeing how quickly the team picked up the new wrinkle, Raymonds and McGuire said of Carolina's Four Corners, "Bring it on."

"Around the game itself," recalled Bach, "I seemed to remember the Marquette players appearing as if they were great underdogs. There was an 'us versus them' mentality. Marquette's shootarounds were loosely structured. They were businesslike, but very relaxed. They didn't seem to be in awe of the place."

On Championship Monday, McGuire decided to get away from it all and take off on his motorcycle. He wound up heading to Social Circle, Georgia, outside of Atlanta, where former NFL quarterback great and Medalist "coach" Norm (the Dutchman) Van Brocklin had a pecan farm.

"When I arrived," recalled McGuire, "the Dutchman thought that I was the veterinarian there to deliver his calves. I said to him, 'Hey, who the hell do you think I am? This is Al.' The Dutchman was rough. He thought his players were spending too much time with the hookers downtown."

"He [Van Brocklin] showed Al around the farm, showed him how the farm operated," noted Norman Ochs. "After a while, McGuire looked at his watch and said, 'I'd better get started back downtown.'"

As the story goes, McGuire was late getting back to Atlanta and was stuck in traffic. "There was a traffic jam near the Omni," continued Ochs, who was on his way to the game at the time. "And I look over to the left of me in traffic, and there's Al, sitting in a friend's car heading to the game!"

Earlier that day, James Sankovitz, Marquette vice president of government relations, had been sent to the airport to pick up Wisconsin Governor Patrick Lucey for the game. When switching planes in Detroit, Governor Lucey had met University of Wisconsin hockey coach "Badger" Bob Johnson, who was preparing his team for the NCAA hockey finals. When asked why he was going to the NCAA basketball finals, Governor Lucey simply told Johnson, "Because they invited me."

"We take the trooper car into the Omni," continued Sankovitz, "and there's Al, walking by himself toward the arena. He says, 'Hello,

Governor.' The governor then says, 'Why aren't you with your team?' 'They know what they have to do. I'm not sure I know what I have to do,' replied Al, and he kept walking."

At first the Omni security people refused to let McGuire in because he had no identification to prove he was indeed Al McGuire. Besides, there were reports that a Dean Smith impersonator had crashed a number of NCAA parties throughout the weekend, and the security detail at the Omni was not taking any chances, especially with some guy claiming to be Al McGuire.

Finally Hank Raymonds arrived to vouch for him, and the coach was finally allowed in for his last game as coach. "He was always late anyway," shrugged Raymonds.

NBC was preparing for the 8 P.M. tipoff with Dick Enberg, Curt Gowdy, and Billy Packer ready to call the action. Enberg described the game as McGuire's "Auld Lang Syne," and Gowdy said of McGuire, "He's the most quoted, most colorful, and most controversial coach in the game, but he's been a winner all the way."

Each coach was then given an opportunity to say a few words before the game. Dressed in three-piece suits, they looked like salesmen instead of coaches. Smith had sideburns just like some of the players, although Bo Ellis wore the mutton-chop style favored by many ball players in the late 1970s.

Carolina's Dean Smith complimented Marquette, calling the team the "best rebounding team in the country," and noted that Ellis was the "smartest and quickest defensive player in the country."

McGuire said, "They [Marquette players] paid the maximum price to get here. I feel they are on top of their game. I think it will be a dynamite game. No way will I blow it with a technical. Milwaukee, we're heading back home tonight, and I hope with a big trophy."

Smith's Tar Heels, though a slight favorite in the championship game, had to play without center Tom LaGarde. "[Walter] Davis had played with a broken finger. [Phil] Ford couldn't shoot from outside with his bad elbow," said Smith, who was coaching his fifth career Final Four. "I had no idea how we'd come out over UNLV."

While there certainly was a great deal of sentiment for McGuire since he was coaching in his final game, quite a few people in the basketball fraternity were pulling for Smith to finally win the brass ring after so many trips to the Final Four.

In Milwaukee, half-barrels of beer flowed in every TV lounge on the Marquette campus. There was a sprinkling of rain in the early evening, and at game time there was a nervous excitement, according to Kelly.

Officiating the game were Reggie Copeland and Galvan, who had refereed the 1974 Final Four contest between UCLA and North Carolina State. "That was very memorable because North Carolina State upset UCLA," said Galvan. "Players like Walton, Thompson, who were NCAA greats. It was a great basketball game with great talent.

"But 1977 perhaps was the memorable one. That was the only one where I refereed the championship game. And since these were the last games of a great basketball coach, that made them memorable. That was a big news item with him, with the press. This was his [McGuire's] last tournament. After the semifinal game, I'm assuming that everyone was rooting for him to go out as a champion. Playing North Carolina, with another great coach, Dean Smith, it was memorable.

"To an official, working in the NCAA championship is like the Super Bowl. To be selected is an honor, regardless of whether it's a semifinal or a championship," noted Galvan, who said to McGuire before the game that he hoped that the championship would not end like Saturday afternoon's game. "He seemed more relaxed in the championship game than in the semifinal game. He was relieved he was in the championship game."

A soft rain began falling in Atlanta just before the game started. Marquette won the tip-off, and both teams started out tight with Bo Ellis missing a jump hook and the Tar Heels being whistled for a three-second violation.

The game's first points were scored on a free throw by Carolina's Mike O'Koren. Ellis scored the game's first field goal, but picked up two quick fouls forcing McGuire to switch to a 2-3 zone to protect Ellis, the only Marquette player ever to play in two Final Fours.

The confident Butch Lee was smooth on the floor with his stutter-step dribble drives and "always in control," according to Enberg. "Butch Lee had a level of self-confidence unmatched by any other guard," marveled Bach.

Marquette's trapping defense forced Davis into two quick fouls. Not long after, Phil Ford hit the Tar Heels' first field goal. During the first television time-out, the horn-heavy strains of Chase's "Get It On" could be heard as the network went to break. McGuire had his arms up, directing from the sidelines. Smith and a limping McGuire met with Galvan to question a foul call. McGuire had hurt his foot kicking the scorer's table after a call he found questionable.

"We had a foul, then a false common foul and a dead ball foul," explained Galvan. "They don't shoot those technicals. I had to explain why they were not going to shoot the free throws. They [coaches] mostly listened. I got both together to explain it."

It seemed that on this night, Butch Lee's jumpers were falling easily. Early in the game, Carolina seemed to have quite a few second-chance shots. But after Warrior sharpshooter Gary Rosenberger checked in, the Warriors switched to a 2-1-2 zone. Up to that point, it was a nip-and-tuck contest.

Rosenberger hit his first shot, a long-range jumper, to give the Warriors a 12-11 lead after ten minutes of the first half. Marquette stayed in the zone and began playing big under the boards.

With just over six minutes to go in the half, Marquette went into a stall, which best utilized Lee's one-on-one moves and helped put the Warriors up 21-20 with 6:30 left. Marquette stayed in a zone, this time switching back to the 2-1-2.

At the 5:28 mark, Davis picked up his third foul and Bo Ellis was starting to make his presence known with rebounding and shooting. Enberg described him as "lightning in a bottle."

Behind Ellis, Marquette increased its lead to 11 points as the chants of "*We are Marquette*" echoed throughout the Omni. At about that time, drops of rain began to fall from the ceiling and form slick spots on the court. With 1:38 left, Marquette continued to play keep-away, but a Warrior was called for a foul. "What foul?" McGuire asked as he got off the bench.

Carolina's John Kuester looked exhausted as he headed to the free-throw line. After the free throws, Butch Lee went coast to coast to give Marquette a 12-point cushion. McGuire almost fell out of his chair, and the Warriors went to the locker room leading, 39-27.

"'Okay, fellas, you're halfway home,' McGuire began his final half-time talk. 'Do not get overconfident. These guys are gonna come back,'" recalled team manager Greg Stack. "Al was afraid because of the lead there was gonna be a letdown. He predicted that if that happened, Dean would go to the Four Corners offense. We spent a helluva lot of time on the Four Corners."

McGuire said later that the Warriors probably played the best 20 minutes of basketball in his 25 years of coaching—especially defensively, where he thought his team was on top of it. He was also surprised by the 39 points his team scored in the first half.

Warrior fans on the Marquette campus were cautiously optimistic as the second half began, even though the half-barrels on hand were quickly running out, as well as at the local liquor stores. And the rain begin to fall a little harder.

North Carolina won the tip to start the second half and the Warriors opened in a man-to-man defense. O'Koren scored the first field goal and blocked a Butch Lee shot on the other end. When O'Koren appeared to double-dribble in front of the Marquette bench, McGuire complained strongly to Galvan.

The Tar Heels whittled Marquette's lead to 39-31 on another O'Koren jumper off a Warrior turnover. McGuire quickly called time to stem the Tar Heel tide.

After another basket gave North Carolina a 6-0 run to start the half, North Carolina went to a full-court press. The teams traded baskets, and then a foul was called on Marquette, which sprang McGuire from his seat and set him to pacing, strutting, hands on hips, looking up and down the scorer's table. Another O'Koren jumper trimmed the margin to 41-37.

McGuire pointed and yelled, asking for a time-out. He was yelling at the officials, "What's going on?" His square face was taut with anger. Frustration was setting in for McGuire as his Warriors went cold during a 10-1 Carolina run.

After the time-out, Marquette came out in a zone, but Tar Heel zone-breaker John Kuester hit again to narrow the margin to two, 41-39. The Warriors' troubles continued. Walter Davis tied the game at 41. McGuire orchestrated the offense from the bench as North Carolina then went into a zone. The Warriors turned the ball over and the Tar Heels increased the second-half run to 14-2.

Jim Boylan broke the Marquette dry spell with a jumper to put the Warriors ahead 43-41. McGuire kept his team in a 1-2-2 zone, but Davis tied the game again at 43. Smith countered with a 1-3-1 zone and Carolina scored off a Tom Zaliagiris steal to take the lead for the first time since early in the first half, 45-43.

NBC analyst Billy Packer predicted that Smith would soon go to his Four Corners. Marquette initially returned to a man-to-man with just under 13 minutes left and tied the game at 45. McGuire switched to a 1-2-2 zone and Smith, as expected, went into his Four Corners.

McGuire then began orchestrating from the sidelines, gesturing to his players to back up and then come back to defend Carolina. Since the game was tied, the defensive team, Marquette, still had to come after the offense at the five-second count. McGuire said that he was "Mickey-Mousing" Smith's Four Corners.

"I think, several times, I know North Carolina had the ball, and McGuire would always say to me, 'We don't have to go out, do we?' I'd nod my head. He kept his bunch back and stayed within the rules," remembered referee Galvan.

"I wanted to pull them [Marquette] out of the zone," recalled Smith. "We'd gone to the Four Corners every game we were ahead. Al was smart, and he didn't come out. We thought we'd get one [basket]."

McGuire remained in what he called a one-man zone defense with his "aircraft carrier," 6'10" center Jerome Whitehead, underneath the basket, to cut off any backdoor opportunities for Carolina. He coolly continued to direct his players from the sidelines.

"He's like Leonard Bernstein, a little more from the woodwinds," said Dick Enberg, commenting on McGuire's conducting during the two minutes that Smith had stayed with the delay. Over that period of time, North Carolina had still not taken a shot. "It dried their sweat and they lost their momentum," said McGuire.

Marquette was able to get the ball back, and Jim Boylan gave the Warriors a 47-45 lead with 8:22 left. Bernard Toone pulled down a rebound on a Walter Davis miss. The teams exchanged turnovers as Phil Ford gave it to Butch Lee and then Lee gave it right back.

Ford attempted to save a ball from going out of bounds. When he did not immediately get back to the court, McGuire asked the officials to wait until Ford was ready to rejoin his teammates. "Classy gesture," complimented Packer.

There were seven minutes left and Marquette turned the ball over on a bad Lee pass into the paint. Boylan then fouled Davis, who tied the game at 47. Marquette took the lead at 49-47 and then went up 51-47 when Davis goaltended on a Boylan layup.

Marquette went to a 1-2-2 zone as Carolina inbounded with 5:20 left in the game. Lee missed a layup and Kuester hit a jumper to narrow

Marquette's lead to 51-49. Carolina then went to a full-court press. Bo Ellis drove the lane beautifully and was fouled by Kuester.

At the 3:43 mark, Boylan slipped on the Omni court made slick by the water dripping from the arena ceiling. Carolina got the ball on the Marquette turnover, but Whitehead stole it back for the Warriors and McGuire called time-out with 2:28 left.

All of the Marquette players stood around McGuire, who addressed each of them. All eyes were on the coach as he gestured, put his hands on the shoulders and heads of the players as he made his point. Just as the huddle broke, he pulled Whitehead aside.

With Marquette leading, 51-49, Kuester fouled Lee and fouled out of the game. With exactly two minutes remaining, McGuire put in *his* Four Corners, and Whitehead was fouled in the bonus situation. Then came a television time-out.

Whitehead made both free throws to give Marquette a 53-49 lead with 1:56 left. Everything seemed to be going Marquette's way, until Bernard Toone was fouled, poked in the eye by O'Koren. When Toone swung his elbows in retaliation, Lee tried to restrain him from an altercation, but a technical foul was called against Toone. McGuire put his hands to his head in disbelief. "I do remember having to tell Toone to just play," said Galvan. "'Let's play ball and let's cut that stuff out,' I told him. He [Toone] didn't have a negative attitude the rest of the night."

Toone missed his free throws. Davis made the technicals for Carolina. Smith then argued his case with the referee as team captain Bo Ellis looked on. Marquette still led, 53-51.

McGuire asked Galvan to explain the double foul and jump ball. Al bent over, then started clapping after speaking with the referee. Marquette won the jump ball and O'Koren fouled Boylan, who hit both free throws for a 55-51 Marquette lead, with 1:25 left.

Ellis was then fouled by Davis while going for a rebound. Ellis hit both free throws for a 57-51 lead. Davis then went coast to coast for a layup, narrowing the lead to 57-53.

Marquette's band began to play the school fight song. O'Koren fouled out and Ellis hit both free throws for a 59-53 lead with 1:02 left. Davis was fouled by Ellis and hit one of two free throws. Marquette led 59-54 with 47 seconds left.

McGuire looked up at the clock. It seemed as if he were taking in every second of the game, remembering what was happening. Phil Ford fouled Rosenberger, who made both shots for a 61-55 margin. Butch Lee then drove for a layup, which clinched the game. Marquette had a 63-55 lead with 26 seconds left. As he walked along the sidelines, McGuire pumped his fist in a quick, downward motion, as if to say, "That's all she wrote." He knew then that he had the championship.

McGuire put up one finger, pointing out what needed to be done. Signaling to his players with his hands, he was still coaching with the game in the bag.

With 19 seconds left, McGuire was still looking at the clock. Marquette fans broke out their gold pom-pons. Jim Boylan hit two free throws for a ten-point Marquette lead. McGuire continued to look at the clock. He pointed at the clock as Rosenberger looked at it with him. The Warrior lead was 65-57.

With 11 seconds left, North Carolina fouled again. At eight seconds, McGuire's eyes began to tear up. "It's tough for him to show his emotions," noted Dick Enberg, as the crowd began to chant, "*We want Al. We want Al. We want Al. We want Al.*"

In Milwaukee, "I turned off the volume on our set," said Kelly. "At that moment, you could feel Schroeder Hall shaking."

"We may have had a time-out and I looked down and he had his hands in his face," recalled Galvan. "I remember saying to myself, that's a great accomplishment, to win a national championship. He was into every tick of the clock. I'm glad I was a part of this," said Galvan, who added that he did not let McGuire's last game distract him from the task at hand.

McGuire buried his head in a towel as Hank Raymonds put his arm around his shoulders and gave him a congratulatory hug. Then McGuire wiped his eyes and Raymonds and Majerus shook hands with each other on the bench. Raymonds tightened his rolled-up program and punched the air with it.

Marquette's lead was at 67-57, as Lee deflected a pass out of bounds. Davis then scored the last basket of the game, giving Marquette its 67-59 final margin and its first national championship. Marquette was the last independent to win a national basketball championship. Dean Smith rushed over to shake McGuire's hand, as Bo Ellis began taking down one of the nets. He thrust his arm through the hoop in celebration. "Basketball's Don Quixote," declared Enberg, as McGuire began to accept the congratulations of his family and friends.

In Milwaukee "Ten thousand kids overflowed with jubilation down Wisconsin Avenue," recalled Kelly, who joined the run down to the lake in the steady rain. "I sat on the trunk of a Buick Regal with five other guys and a girl. Eight kids on the hood and the driver had to lean his head out the window in order to drive."

Back in New York, McGuire's brother Dick was watching at home and kept repeating, "I can't believe it's happening to Alfred McGuire."

"As Al passed me on the way to the locker room," recalled former SID Jim Foley, "he said, 'Jim, you changed your hair.'" While McGuire was taking in his greatest moment, he somehow was able to deflect attention from himself.

From there he went into the locker room, where the only person with him was Marquette SID Kevin Byrne. When asked why he was going in there during the celebration, he replied, "I'm not ashamed to cry. I just want to cry alone."

When he returned to the court, coach of the national champions, he smiled broadly and exchanged hugs with family and players. It was his moment, but he wanted to share it with the players.

In the postgame press conference, McGuire's simple explanation for the win was that North Carolina "fell apart in the second half. We hung in there."

When asked how he felt, McGuire replied, "Emotionally drained. I'm pleased for the guys. It doesn't seem real. Ya know, you think about something like this, but I've always been an alley fighter. I don't usually get into the silk lace situations. It seems like it is preordained, but I don't like to use the words of the TV announcers, the cliches.

"I was not emotional until a five-second count triggered me. I trigger easily. As a coach, you have to be constantly alert. Right now, I feel washed out. Once the avalanche came and we were tied [at the start of the second half], I tried to stop the avalanche by delays and I called time-outs. Usually we try to do it by contact lens time-outs, or something like that. You have to stop the momentum, no matter what.

"At the end of the game, I sat there and thought of all the locker rooms, the dirty jocks, the PALs [Police Athletic League], and the other things that a New York street fighter knows when growing up."

With Al McGuire it was life imitating art, as later that evening Sylvester Stallone would pick up the Oscar for best motion picture for *Rocky*. Al McGuire was one of those fighters of the world whom Stallone thanked for his inspiration. Also, the rock group Queen had just released its new single "We Are the Champions," which was quickly edited into a video that made all the local Milwaukee television stations.

"I was happy for Al," said Dean Smith. "I thought they played extremely well. Al was smart and he didn't come out [for the Four Corners]. We thought we'd get one [basket]. Ellis blocked Bruce Buckley. He's certainly a great coach. He has a good feel for the game. He just goes with the flow. His way was best for him. He definitely kept you from doing what you wanted to do during a game."

"There were more North Carolina fans that night at the championship," recalled Pat Lloyd. "But even after the game, the Carolina fans complimented us as we left. It rained pretty hard, but no one mentioned it. A lot of the fans came back with us on the charter flight. People were handing out 'Al McGuire for President' buttons."

In Milwaukee, the rains continued to fall steadily all evening as it seemed that every one of Marquette's 12,000-plus students stormed Wisconsin Avenue. Climbing on top of light poles, jumping on top of cars and taxis, riding on top of city buses, hanging from traffic signals and business shingles. "Students climbed on top of Milwaukee buses and walked the length of the bus roof from back to front," recalled Dan Kelly.

The 1600 block of Wells Street was a solid mass of reveling students. "Within hours, the campus bars were drunk dry," recalled Kelly.

The students began running to Lake Michigan to celebrate the city's first national championship since the Milwaukee Bucks won the NBA title in 1971. The city had not seen a celebration this wild since the old Milwaukee Braves beat the Yankees to win the 1957 World Series. On the minus side, the celebration cost the city more than $11,000 in damage.

"The effect that the team had was to send Milwaukee into delirium," recalled Bob Bach. "It was evidenced best when the team returned to Milwaukee. At 2, 2:30 in the morning, fans had jammed the Mitchell Field [airport] concourse. It was wall-to-wall people. They had been drinking. It was scary. I was not pleased to be in the middle.

"Jay Whitehead had tears in his eyes. You had no control over where you were going. The team had their uniforms stolen. The positive was that it put Milwaukee on the map. The fact that he won it in his last game was the zenith." McGuire had wisely ducked out a back gate to avoid the crush of the fans.

Students driving back from the airport followed *Milwaukee Sentinel* newspaper trucks as they dropped papers at each vending box throughout the city and took every paper from the boxes as souvenirs. At McCormick Hall that night it appeared that torches were being tossed out of the dorm windows. But it was actually telephone books being set ablaze that were falling to the ground. The flagpole at McCormick Hall was toppled. After the game, another student took his black-and-white television, opened the window, and let it drop. Explaining why, he said, "It was the most beautiful thing I had ever seen and I'll never see anything on that television as beautiful again."

Many students did not attend class the next day. Many did not get up until rather late the next day. And when they did, they discovered that University President Reverend Raynor had not canceled classes. A pep rally was held on campus a few days later where a tired Al McGuire and players were honored by the school for their accomplishment. McGuire, a happy Warrior, thanked everyone from his co-coaches to the university to the players and the fans.

Toward the end of the press conference, someone reminded McGuire about an engagement he had made before the tournament. "Al, I guess our lunch is off again for next Friday." McGuire said, "I'll be there. You buyin'?" "Yeah." "I'll be there."

McGuire received a congratulatory phone call from his mother, Winifred, saying how proud she was and, "Alfie, I'm glad ya got out clean."

After the game, McGuire told a friend, "I'll be talking for the next ten years."

CHAPTER TWELVE

Merry-Go-Round

Throughout his career, McGuire had often talked of taking a trip to New Zealand. Most people thought it was a daydream of a middle-aged, crazy coach, or just Al talking. It was a trip that he was serious about taking—someday.

While someday never comes for many people, McGuire's someday came after the national championship, when Marquette rewarded him for his success.

"When Al won the title, Marquette gave him a free trip. Al knew that I had spent three months in New Zealand," recalled former UCLA coach John Wooden. "He asked me if there was anything that I thought that he should see. I gave him a number of names of people I met from my trip earlier, people that I thought he should see.

"I contacted these people to let them know Al would be there. I began to hear from these people later and they said, 'Your friend never showed up,'" recounted a puzzled Wooden.

"Al told me that he had received these letters of introduction from John Wooden," recalled Ernie Vandeweghe, "but Al said, 'If these people meet me they'll never want to have anything to do with Wooden again.' So he threw the letters away."

"I asked Al why he didn't look up my friends in New Zealand," continued Wooden. "He said, 'Well, John, the real people of a country are found in the pubs, and I knew that you didn't go into pubs or drink. So I didn't look them up,' said McGuire, who went by the pseudonym, Reggie Sinclair of Manitoba.

"He hitchhiked up and down those islands of New Zealand. The next time he went to New Zealand he shipped his motorcycle and drove around the country.

"Al tried to get Norman Fischer of Medalist and me to take a motorcycle trip to New Zealand. He wanted me to come to Milwaukee and learn how to take care of a motorcycle before we left. But I don't know anything about motorcycles," said Wooden.

"You always knew where you stood with Al. He was a most entertaining and delightful personality. In a sense we're different personalities, but down deep we're the same. We can respect the differences in others, without being critical. I think Al is a character. That's not a criticism. But that brings on more publicity and attention to coaches. Al is different and draws more attention," said Wooden, who added that the most outrageous thing his own players would hear out of his mouth was, "Goodness gracious, sakes alive!"

"[Another time] Al was heading to Ireland and England to see his aunt," continued Wooden. "Al's mother told him to make sure he gave them some money. When Al saw the size of the place they had, he said, 'They should be giving some money to me.'"

"They call me eccentric," McGuire said in 1976. "They used to call me nuts. I haven't changed."

Unlike Wooden, McGuire did not keep an office at his university after he retired. He packed everything up and brought it home, eventually opening a small confessional box of an office in Mequon, Wisconsin.

He also promised after the championship that he would not attend a Marquette basketball game for five years, in deference to his successor, Hank Raymonds. McGuire wanted to give Raymonds the space to establish himself as a coach and put his imprimatur on the Marquette basketball program, without having to worry about McGuire looking over his shoulder.

It would not have made any difference if McGuire had stayed away from Marquette for ten years. His long shadow dwarfed the university and the city, not unlike what the modern Bradley Center has done to the old Milwaukee Arena, making his legacy difficult to escape. Northwestern University coach Kevin O'Neill, one of the coaches who followed McGuire at Marquette since 1977, probably summed up McGuire's legacy best: "Al McGuire was the best thing and the worst thing to happen to Marquette University. He was the best for the university because he brought a national championship here, but he was the worst thing for the coaches who had to follow him."

"To Marquette, it was the renaissance of Marquette," Allie McGuire noted of his father's impact on the school. "Basketball went big time, but it [success] made academics at the university as well. Marquette is still considered a top academic institution. He gave the Marquette basketball program a foundation that will always be perceived as successful."

Not long after his New Zealand trip, McGuire put on his wingtips and began to go to work as vice chairman of Medalist Industries. While he downplayed his role as someone who put the gas in the chairman's car, his responsibilities included everything from public relations to overseas marketing. He also was a member of Medalist's management committee which dealt with labor issues.

Despite the fancy title of vice chairman of the board of directors, it was clear that McGuire was not on any fast track to take over Medalist anytime soon.

"He [Norman Fischer] saw incredible potential. He thought that the sun set on Al McGuire," recalled Howie Fagan, who was executive director and president of the sports education division of Medalist when McGuire coached at Marquette. "Norman had a vision of what Al could do for Medalist Industries. Al had a nice contract and Medalist had the reward of having an Al McGuire. It was a symbiotic relationship. There was a split in 1978 and there was a professional parting of the ways. And they both went their separate ways."

"I'm an Einstein of the streets and an Oxford scholar of common sense," McGuire said. In other words, his true genius was not given room to blossom at Medalist. So, in the spring of 1978 he announced his surprise resignation, saying that it was time to move on.

"At the time I didn't know about NBC comin' along. They [Medalist] wanted me to wait two years before taking over as CEO. Norman and I just separated. There was no falling out with him. I said, 'Norm, I only got one life.'"

Since his retirement from coaching, McGuire has said on numerous occasions that Milwaukee was his home by choice. He and his family have lived in the same home in Brookfield since 1964. Even with all of his success, McGuire has never wanted to "go Hollywood," because he said he could never tell the real people from the phonies, with all the gold chains, sunglasses, and fancy cars.

He is comfortable with the conservative blue-collar city and citizenry where he could be Al McGuire, but where he could also disappear into the meadows and ponds of Wisconsin on his Harley and commune with nature or play with his toy soldiers. "The Irish have a tendency not to be social climbers," McGuire once said. "Even Mayor Daley lived in the same house all his life in Chicago."

In order to touch people and make a real difference in their lives once again, McGuire looked for a way to "put something back in the kitty," or give something back to Milwaukee for all that it did for him. In cooperation with Children's Hospital and the *Milwaukee Journal*, he founded Al's Run with the *Journal*'s Bill Dwyre in 1978. The event, with a five-mile run and a three-mile walk, was designed to benefit the pediatric and neonatal intensive care units of the Milwaukee hospital.

While the course for the first run was being planned, longtime friend John Owens remembered a run he took with McGuire, "When they first started Al's Run in 1978, we were down at the lakefront running three miles. We ran into some guys who asked us if we wanted to come over to their boat after our run.

"As we kept running, I asked Al why he didn't get his own boat. 'I'd rather that my friends owned the boat,' Al told me," Owens laughingly recalled of McGuire's legendary frugality.

A drizzly Saturday morning, September 28, 1978, greeted McGuire and the 4,100 runners for the first Al's Run. It was held near the Marquette campus on Wisconsin Avenue. Proceeds from the 1978 and '79 events went to the Variety Club/Al McGuire Limb Bank at Children's Hospital.

Since 1980, proceeds have benefited the pediatric intensive care unit at the hospital, and the unit has since been named for McGuire and the *Milwaukee Journal*, which provided administrative staff to organize, manage, and promote the run. In 1992, the event was turned over to Children's Hospital, which handled all operational duties with the newspaper continuing as title sponsor through 1994. Briggs & Stratton became sole sponsor of the 20-year-old event in 1997, through which nearly 400,000 participants have raised $3 million for the hospital.

Prior to the first event, McGuire had reportedly never run a straight five miles in his life, and that included his track-and-field days at St. John's Prep. His run grew from 4,100 participants its first year to twice that in 1979, 14,000 in 1980, 23,500 in 1984, and up to 29,700-plus in 1988, the run's high point.

"It's the greatest feeling in the world," said McGuire, "to be in the middle of Wisconsin Avenue on a podium, look into a sea of gold and green T-shirts, and know that not one guy or gal is forced to be there— that there is no monetary gain for them. To me, this is true charity."

It was at about this time he began his toy soldier collecting. "I started toy soldiers when Larry Bird was a junior at Terre Haute (1978)," said McGuire. "It's a nice pastime. I don't go to shows. My enjoyment is the hunt."

Some 30 years after his "DickandAl" playing days with his brother on the New York Knicks, McGuire joined another Dick at NBC—Dick Enberg. In 1978, NBC offered McGuire an opportunity to become a college basketball analyst, joining play-by-play man Enberg and analyst Billy Packer as a threesome. McGuire agreed to take the challenge even though he had no previous network experience. Throughout his life, McGuire had always been a performer, never a spectator in anything he did. But as a fairly high-profile analyst he would get to keep his hand in basketball and remain a celebrity.

"Al had four lives," remarked Norman Ochs. "Rockaway Beach, the Knicks, Belmont Abbey, and Marquette. But his fifth life was as a broadcaster."

"I was just thrown in at NBC," McGuire recalled. "You learn when you're with somebody good [Enberg]. I am really a workaholic. Breakfast ends. Lunch takes a little longer, and dinner's forever."

In an early pregame broadcast from Duke University's Cameron Indoor Stadium, McGuire was decked out in safari gear with a hunting hat, chair, and whip and threw peanuts to the Duke crazies as they were getting revved up for the Blue Devils game that afternoon.

As McGuire approached the roaring students, he cracked the whip and barked at Enberg for peanuts. As McGuire was throwing the peanuts, Enberg was trying to get McGuire's attention to do a station break. "We'll be right back after these commercials. *Hi ya doin'!* McGuire yells. Then Enberg quickly corrects McGuire, who says, "Oh. From your local stations. *Beautiful*," as he thrusts the whip in the air, really having fun with the crowd.

"Dick always liked Al," recalled Eddie Einhorn, vice chairman of the Chicago White Sox and founder of TVS. "We were driving from the hotel to the arena. Al was in a cab with myself and Enberg. He was getting ready to do his first game with NBC. The advice I gave him was, 'I gotta lotta guys who work with me that are terrific in the cab ride to the arena. But they lose it at game time. Be yourself.'

"And that's just what he did. That's why he's so good. No one can do it like him. Personality is the whole thing," continued Einhorn, who did not realize at the time he was dealing with a "prime time" player—someone who is ready when the curtain goes up at showtime, in McGuire-speak.

"[Dick] Vitale has a different act," said Einhorn. "There are very few personalities in the basketball business. But he was the first. Billy Packer's straight and he's very good. [But] it's a different approach."

During his career as a broadcaster, McGuire has continued to insist that he does not know much about Xs and Os, and gives credit to other coaches by saying that they were much more knowledgeable about the game than he ever was. For example, when he gets together with Indiana coach Bob Knight, McGuire insists he never talks basketball, only people. However, if he does not know something about a game or a team or a player, he is not afraid to ask a question.

"When Al began working as a color basketball analyst for NBC with Dick Enberg," recalled University of Nebraska coach Danny Nee, "he called me when he found out I was working as a part-time coach for Digger Phelps at Notre Dame.

"He called me to get names and information and scouting reports. I'd give him as much as I could in *his* language. Al was spontaneous. Al was a street guy who had intuitiveness," said Nee. "When I watched him broadcast, I said to myself, 'I can't believe he's getting away with this shit!' He was so observant and knowledgeable about people. Al would always have to do it his way. He never did anything according to convention. Through it all, Al McGuire stayed Al McGuire. There's a pureness he always had. The man doesn't have an ego. The only other guy who doesn't have an ego is Dean Smith."

McGuire also tapped Hank Raymonds, his Xs and Os man from Marquette, for strategy. "For 14 years you never ask me a thing about strategy and now you want to know?" laughed Raymonds, who was surprised at how much of an expert McGuire became as a result of his work on NBC.

"Al would always call me from courtside," recalled Howie Garfinkel, founder of the 5-Star Basketball Camp. "He would say, 'whaddya got on Notre Dame?'"

In addition to Enberg and Packer, one of the other broadcasters to work with McGuire early in his career was the University of Kentucky's legendary radio play-by-play man Cawood Ledford.

"We did an all-star game in Louisville," recalled Ledford. "He did color and I did play-by-play. He's very glib and obviously knows the game. Al was the first one to point out that players were tired by the way they grabbed the ends of their shorts at the free-throw line.

"So many of the ex-athletes they [networks] brought in were too technical with their analysis," continued Ledford. "He had the great vocabulary to put it in laymen's terms."

After his retirement from coaching and as he began to distinguish himself as a broadcaster, McGuire was beginning to receive not only recognition but awards. In 1979, President Jimmy Carter named McGuire to the President's Council on Physical Fitness and Sports, where he served for three years, part of that time as chairman. McGuire was asked to return to the council after Ronald Reagan's election, but declined due to the amount of travel involved.

McGuire has insisted over the years that Billy Packer, his foil, was the better interviewer. But a look at McGuire's tapes from 1979 through 1981 shows a very fluid question-and-answer style, as he interviewed subjects as varied as Nancy Lieberman-Cline, Ralph Sampson, Marianne Stanley, and Jerry Tarkanian. He seemed very good at putting his subjects at ease and then asking just one question. There was no long-winded preface filled with minutiae that the audience already knew. McGuire asked the questions he thought viewers might like to ask.

He also claimed that he rarely prepared for his broadcasts. McGuire's questions certainly made it sound as if he knew what he was talking about and that he had done his background work. There were no notes, clipboard, or legal pad in front of him. There was also a genuine curiosity about the subject; he never insinuated himself into the interview. And McGuire listened to the answers. If there was any fault at all about his early work it is that he let his subjects go on too long with their replies and he was too respectful to interrupt them.

"His two greatest strengths are that he not only prepares well but somehow makes it sound as if he is not prepared," noted Michael Hirsley, formerly the media critic for the *Chicago Tribune*. "You have to have the style and delivery and that's what has set Al McGuire apart from other color analysts. He's a street-smart Caucasian coach who understands New York basketball."

Added Bill Raftery, "His life is his preparation. He has the great facility to get the most out of a moment. He knew how to get it done. Even early on in a game, he gets a feel for it. He understands how a game should go. He has a good, good feel for the utilization of his personality."

"I thought Al was innovative and clever in his broadcasting," commented Utah Jazz president Frank Layden. "He's a dese-dems-and-dose kind of guy, but he's really kind of a philosopher. He's a sharp guy and better prepared than he lets on."

"What would really get my late wife, Marge [her name was Margaret Mary]," recalled Ray Meyer, "is that he'd call her *Mary Margaret* on the air. But Al does his homework, he prepares himself to go on the air."

"One time Al, Dick, Billy, and I came to ESPN to meet Scotty Connal, formerly of NBC," recalled Dick Vitale. "Packer is watching the monitors and tapes while Al went to sleep on the floor of Scotty Connal's office. Al says, 'Wake me up when it's time to go,'" laughed Vitale, who added, "Don't let him fool you. He's ten miles sharper than most."

McGuire's propensity to label reserve players with colorful nicknames was demonstrated in the 1979 final between Indiana State and Michigan State. With less than a minute to play, the shoe of Spartan reserve Jamie Huffman started to slip off his foot as he was attempting to make a play. As Huffman struggled to pull the shoe on and catch up with the play, McGuire quipped, "That's 'Shoes' Huffman."

In interviews with personalities who have proven difficult for other analysts in the past, McGuire's conversational style and deference for the subjects have allowed them to relax and tell their stories. This was especially true of his early interviews with Bob Knight and Larry Bird in 1980 and '81. Without fawning, McGuire was able to get more out of them than had others.

McGuire fell back on cliches occasionally to make his point or to visualize a question. And if he couldn't remember a word he was looking for, he would say so, but still used the visual representation to get his point across.

And he was not afraid to go out on a limb and make bold predictions and statements. In the 1980 NCAA final between UCLA and Louisville, McGuire predicted in the second half of the game that if the Bruins' Kiki Vandeweghe missed a shot, "UCLA will not win another NCAA championship for the rest of this *century!*" As terminal as that prediction sounded 20 years from the millennium, the Bruins did win another title in 1995.

McGuire also claimed that the NBA would deal with expanding player size on a regulation court by someday measuring all of the players on each team and if they exceeded a certain height, the teams would have to sit out one of the players. He also predicted that the NBA would never send its players to the Olympics. But if one of his predictions comes true, everyone remembers who said it—Al McGuire.

In their four years together at NBC, McGuire, Enberg, and Packer made one of the most entertaining teams in sports broadcasting history. McGuire was the eccentric personality, Packer was the Xs and Os man, and Enberg—"Dixie" to McGuire—was the combination courtside official and traffic cop, the one who kept things moving.

An exchange between McGuire and Packer at halftime of the Virginia-BYU NCAA tournament game in 1981 best shows how this trio worked so well together. The controversy revolved around a goaltending call against Virginia center Ralph Sampson.

"I thought Billy was right," began McGuire. "He put his hand on the lefthand side of the basket, which is against the rules, and he did—"

"What rules?" asked Packer, a half-smile creasing his face.

"You can't bang the backboard, Billy," McGuire said with all seriousness.

"Well you certainly can touch your own backboard," shot back Packer, laughing.

"Not bangin' and shakin.' Any type of shakin' of the backboard is illegal," McGuire insisted, as Packer broke up in laughter. "Billy, how much money ya got? How much money ya got, pal?"

"I got two punches in the arm that says you're wrong," said Packer, doubled over in laughter. All the while, Enberg was going back and forth with the microphone between the two, in a 1980s version of "Who's on first?"

An innocent-looking McGuire said to Enberg, "Now, you can't hit the backboard with your other arm. I'd bet my life on that. And the other thing which happened."

Packer was doubled over with laughter at this point and said, *"Please!"*

Enberg interjected, "Well, wait a minute, you called it an illegal play at the time."

Packer was still laughing heartily, and said, "No, it's illegal because the ball was in the cylinder. He doesn't know the rule, he doesn't know the rule," as all three broke up in laughter.

"You know why it worked?" McGuire told Bob Costas during a 1989 taping of *Later.* "Because there's love between us. And it wasn't a con game. I can read a con game quick. And it's hard to con a con. I'm on my third body. I've been around a long time.

"And what happened is that Billy and Dick allowed me to become a part of them. There's no room on the microphone, especially in basketball, for three people. And it worked because of the wholesomeness of it."

It also worked because while McGuire and Packer would go at each other, there was nothing mean-spirited about the exchanges. When McGuire thought that perhaps Packer had gone too far in showing off his knowledge of the history of the game, McGuire had no qualms about bringing his partner down a notch, and then he referred to him as Ocean Mouth.

"I was bartending at Friar Tuck's on Third Avenue," recalled McGuire friend Eddie Bacalles. "During a game between Purdue and Syracuse, Billy Packer brought up the great players who wore number 44 at Syracuse. As Packer went through his recitation, Al said, 'And don't forget Eddie Bacalles!' Which drew looks from both Packer and Enberg, but Al didn't care. He was just looking for a way to butt in on Billy. I received phone calls from all over the country."

"Billy knows the game and I have a feel for it," said McGuire in Jeff Pryor's *Milwaukee Journal* article." Our strong point when we worked together was our contradiction of each other in a positive way, not in a phony way. Because we would yell at each other and the balance of Billy being technical and me being humorous was the key to our success together, I think."

"See, there are a lot of things that Al can't do. Al couldn't do play-by-play," added Packer. "That would be out of the question. Al can't read cue cards. He can't wear an earpiece because he can't talk and listen at the same time. Al would have no organization whatsoever as a play-by-play announcer.

"We decided at the University of Texas-Southern California game that we would get the guy who was holding Al's cue card to drop it," Packer continued. "Well, it comes time for Al to say his bit and the guy drops the card and, of course, Al has no idea what the player's name is. So Al says, 'Well, Old Treetop can really clean the glass . . . he's a high jumper, he's a flyer,' or some garbage like that. Al never did call the player by his real name. He just gave him a nickname. There are stories like that as long as my arm," laughed Packer.

"One time Al and I were doing a promo for the network and we couldn't get it right after a few times. Finally, the producer ditched the cue cards and told us to do it off the top of our heads, and we did it in one take," laughed Ray Meyer.

"Al can't read!" said Ray Meyer in half-shocked laughter. "But Al would do anything for me or my family. Al even told me to get on the advertising bandwagon and endorse a product. He said, 'Ray, you'd be perfect for Geritol!'"

"Al realized he had a perfect foil in Packer," explained *Chicago Tribune* sportswriter Bill Jauss. "Their sparring back and forth was the impetus for the billion-dollar NCAA tournament."

"Al is always himself," noted ESPN's Dick Vitale. "Billy is all vanilla. I'm all the nuts and whipped cream and everything else thrown in," said Vitale.

"I love to hear Al and Dick Enberg," noted John Wooden. "The colorful things that he said, but his method of presentation. The way he would state things was entertaining and informational as well. Billy Packer's informative about the game, but I'd rather hear Dick and Al. I enjoy Billy in a different way."

"Another early game Al did for NBC was between Kentucky and North Carolina," recalled Norman Ochs. "Kentucky was up by 12 points with two minutes to go and Joe B. Hall begins substituting. Al says, 'It's too soon to call a time-out.' And Packer and Enberg start to give it to Al. 'I'm not jokin' guys, two minutes with Dean Smith is an eternity.'

"With 20 seconds left, Kentucky's lead is down to three points. And while Kentucky does win, Al made his point by finishing with the following saying: 'You don't kiss the cheerleaders and shake the hands of the parents until the game is over.' That was his version of 'The game isn't over till the fat lady sings,'" noted Ochs.

As McGuire, Enberg, and Packer gained fame for their broadcasts over the years, their friendship grew, even though their verbal sparring made it appear as if they were enemies.

In fact, McGuire and Enberg began spending time on Herb Kohl's dude ranch in Jackson Hole, Wyoming, where the deer and the antelope played. It was hard to imagine a city slicker like McGuire at home on the range, but that was the case.

"For many years, Al came out every year," recalled Kohl, a U.S. Senator from Wisconsin. "We would go in September and spend a week or five days. We would go riding, fishing, hiking. He would come out in the summertime. It's Al's kind of setting because it's informal, outdoorsy, jeans, flannel shirts, cowboy hat. He's not a cowboy, but he doesn't find his greatest enjoyment in nightclubs."

"Al likes to go off on walks, up a mountain," noted Walter Wong, who was a part of the group. "He liked to be active. We always went to little saloons. We would make small bets on what a guy would do when he came up to the plate in a baseball game on television. We would drink beer, watch TV, and make bets.

"Dick always went riding with us in Wyoming. We would go a half-day in the mountains. He always had good jokes. Al and Dick would ride each other. Dick would say, 'I know every nickname for every school.' Al would say, what about 'Wyoming State University?' Dick said, 'There is no Wyoming State University.' So they decided to make up a nickname for the school and Al came up with the Porcupines."

"Wyoming State was a team that we made up as we were riding," added Jerry Savio. "We started out by saying, 'I'll name the mascot, you name the team.' Al says, 'Porcupines.' We said, 'There's no school with porcupines as a mascot. What's the school? 'Well there is one now— Wyoming State,' Al said. I told him, 'There is no such school.'

"Al got on TV with Dick and Billy and they said the number 26 school in the country was Wyoming State. Then they said that the team played in the Kohl Arena. Then a guy from the *Chicago Tribune* picked it up and wrote a story about it. We were selling hats and T-shirts, blue with a red porcupine, with the slogan 'Go, Porks, Go!'" laughed Savio.

As with many of the great television teams that have broken up over the years, so too did this NBC trio. As McGuire would say, they had a nice run for four years. After the 1981 NCAA tournament, Packer left NBC for CBS. Packer had been with NBC since 1976 and received an attractive offer to jump ship. Even though Packer was gone, McGuire continued to work with Enberg in a one-on-one relationship and began to come into his own as an analyst. In fact McGuire was nominated for two sports emmys in 1987 and 1988 as outstanding sports personality analyst.

"Overall, Al and Billy were two personalities with tremendous appeal," noted Enberg. "One relies on his basketball knowledge, the other relies on his personality. I know there is still a question in many viewers' minds whether Al and Billy really do dislike each other. It's so amusing. They have a really good personal relationship because they are so secure in their work, although they had some verbal fistfights on the air . . . Boy they could really belt each other verbally.

"I've got a feeling we'll all work together again. It might take a miracle. But somehow, some way, I hope it happens, and I think Bill and Al feel the same way," said Enberg, who affectionately referred to McGuire as the Leo Gorcey of College Basketball because he still retained his Noo Yawk accent.

In February of 1982, McGuire made his triumphant return to Marquette, after a five-year absence as promised, for what McGuire referred to as the Vatican Championship between Ray Meyer's highly rated Blue Demons and a pretty good Marquette team coached by Hank Raymonds. McGuire was returning as a big success in his new career as network color commentator.

The night before the game, McGuire addressed a standing-room-only crowd of students on campus at Brooks Memorial Union for a pregame pep rally. "If you win tomorrow, you could be dancin' on Bourbon Street," he predicted, much to the delight of the students.

On game day, McGuire was well prepared and very fair in his analysis of the teams' strengths and weaknesses, especially noting the talent differential between the teams, with DePaul having the All-Americas and Marquette, having just one, Glenn "Doc" Rivers. DePaul had too much ammunition and won, 67-66, but it was a good battle for the folks at home watching on NBC.

"In all of the assignments in my twenty years of broadcasting, I don't sandbag," McGuire insisted. "I'm not fluff, but I'm not a patsy. I don't dodge problems, but I don't create problems. There is always something in coaching that's in the shade. I'm not gonna sandbag you. After 20 years these coaches know I'm not a house man."

Two years later, when McGuire and Enberg broadcast Meyer's last basketball game as a coach at Chicago's Rosemont Horizon, McGuire quipped that "Ray Meyer has been around so long that he held the ladder for Dr. Naismith when he put up the first peach basket."

As McGuire's national profile continued to rise with his work at NBC, so did his requests for speaking engagements. "I've done over 2,000 corporate speeches," estimated McGuire, whose topics generally range from "The Will to Win" to "Commentary on Today's Sports World." He reportedly receives in the neighborhood of $5,000 to $10,000 per speech, depending on the function. And, he never uses agents, or, as he calls them, back-room lawyers.

"No one negotiates for me," explained McGuire. "I have used different speaking agencies in the past. They represent you. But I tell them what I want. I look for time, money, position, or prestige. I negotiate for one thing. I'm in there for a reason. I don't negotiate the *obvious*. If you see me dressed in a suit talking to more than four people someplace, I'm getting paid for it."

In order for people to reach him, McGuire formed Al McGuire Enterprises. While that is an impressive name, his office does not match the name. Located in a small industrial park not far from his home, it contains a desk, a chair, a telephone, a message pad, and boxes on the floor— opened and unopened—filled with sentimental bric-a-brac and items that even he cannot identify. He does have a secretary, and if you are lucky you might be able to catch him mornings during the week.

And when he speaks before a group (and it is always a packed crowd) his presentation appears to be completely extemporaneous. It could be the St. Patrick's Day parade in New York, the Azalea Festival in Wilmington, North Carolina, a benefit dinner for the Ronald McDonald House in Chicago, a college booster group at the NCAA Final Four, or an event for a fellow coach—McGuire hits home with his message while entertaining the audience.

"He knew what he was about," said former Warrior Pat Smith, who now works for the Maryland Police Training Commission. "He spoke for two hours and didn't have a note or anything," Smith recalled of a McGuire talk at the University of Maryland. "They were entertained for two hours."

During a speech at the University of Notre Dame, the students in the Joyce Athletic and Convocation Center were giving him a hard time when McGuire answered back, "Hey, if you don't let me do what I want, I'll go back to Marquette and bring back football."

Since 1980, McGuire has been the entertaining emcee for a variety show at the annual Azalea Festival. It gives McGuire an opportunity to head back to North Carolina to see friends and acquaintances from his Belmont Abbey days. He also dons his dude ranch outfit. Each year, McGuire organizes and helps stage the family-oriented show, which is held at Legion Stadium. With his uncanny penchant for remembering some physical quality about people (if not their names) McGuire recognizes the faces of people who come back year after year for the festival.

When McGuire made his second visit to Marquette in January of 1986, he was there not as a broadcaster but as a visiting famous ex-coach/dignitary/guest. CBS was broadcasting the Sunday afternoon game between Marquette and number one-ranked North Carolina—a double digit favorite, even in the Milwaukee Arena. It was the first time the two teams had met since the 1977 NCAA championship game. But this time Rick Majerus was coaching the Warriors, while Dean Smith was still leading the Tar Heels.

During the pregame warmup, McGuire joked with CBS broadcasters Billy Packer and Brent Musburger that Majerus was losing weight, but "with Rick it's hard to tell. It's like tossing a deck chair off the *Queen Mary*," quipped McGuire.

As he was introduced to the crowd, McGuire raised his arms above his head and looked up to each corner of the Mecca as the chants of "*We want Al. We want Al. We want Al!*" filled the packed arena. It was SRO, just like in the old days; even the four distant corner seats were filled.

The outclassed Warriors stayed close to the Tar Heels, which included Brad Daugherty, Jeff Lebo, and Kenny Smith. When Marquette went ahead late in the game the electricity level in the Mecca matched that of earlier days when Majerus's boss was on the sidelines. Unfortunately, some of the stadium denizens were too raucous. Coach Smith was hit on the back of the head with a penny and Kenny Smith was hit in the face with a penny at the free throw line. Marquette wound up losing the game, 66-64. While McGuire helped wake the echoes of the glory years of Marquette basketball, his presence could not push the young Warriors over the top.

During his coaching days, McGuire was known as a physical coach, someone who watched the opposing team to see which player was tired, or what a coach was doing. And that translated to his announcing as well. When North Carolina State was involved in a televised ACC battle on

NBC, Vinny Del Negro of the Wolfpack went to the basket and was fouled hard. McGuire stood up from his spot at courtside and stared at the player until their eyes met. McGuire then predicted that Del Negro would make both free throws, which he did.

But McGuire can become so focused that *he* may not be all there. "At the 1987 Final Four in New Orleans," recalled Ray Meyer, "Al and Dick Vitale were answering questions from kids in the audience. Afterward, as Al is being whisked away in his limo, his wife, Pat, is running after him down the street yelling, 'Al, you forgot me!'"

Toward the end of McGuire's run at NBC, he was broadcasting fewer than 20 games a year, including a number of Notre Dame basketball games, since the peacock network was broadcasting the university's football and basketball games exclusively. McGuire still had the opportunity to tape preseason and postseason specials such as the "Al McGuire Show" and his "All–Al McGuire Team," many of which were produced with the help of his son Robbie. McGuire also helped broadcast the 1988 Summer Olympic basketball games from Seoul, South Korea, which was a first for him.

Over the years, he has worked with a number of different play-by-play announcers, including Tom Hammond, Marv Albert, Don Criqui, and Tim Brando. But it seemed that Dick Enberg was able to bring out the best in McGuire. He knew which buttons to push. As they continued to work together at NBC, they became closer and spent more time together.

"If I ever write a book, chapter 13 will be on Al McGuire," remarked Enberg at a speech before the National Restaurant Association several years ago. "The one thing that I learned from Al is that you have to stop and smell the roses.

"One time we were in Milwaukee at his place and we had some time on our hands before we had to catch a plane for a game we were doing the next day. So, we're driving along a back road and Al says, 'Why don't we stop at this antique shop?' So we go in and Al is taking his time, talking to the owners. All of a sudden I realize that it's getting closer to the time that we have to be at the airport. Al said, 'Take it easy, Dick. We'll get there. If you don't stop to see what's at the side of the road, you might miss something.'"

"What I remember most was his unpredictability," commented Albert. "Every point he would make during a game he'd punch me in the shoulder. Al didn't like to be out there [on the floor interviews] by himself.

He wanted another person out there with him. The punching got to be kind of a joke."

"Al used to carry his suit in a garment bag and his shoes in a shoe box," Albert continued. "I saw him one time outside of our hotel talking to a guy about toy soldiers, but it looked like they were making a drug deal! I felt sorry for his wife Pat because he kept piling all these boxes of soldiers in their basement," said Albert.

Recalled Howie Fagan: "Early one morning Al drove to Oconomowoc Lake and was playing with his toy soldiers on a picnic table. Nobody was there but a former Marquette player who was jogging through the park. The player gets closer and does a double take. 'Coach, is that you?'"

In addition to his humility and sensitivity, one of McGuire's best qualities is that he is able to turn humor on himself. He has never really taken himself too seriously, which is most evident when something happens that keeps him in the spotlight.

"He was extremely honest on and off the air," Albert continued. "I was able to kid him. The games I did with Al went too fast."

"Al was also very perceptive. When Michael Jordan was a freshman he predicted that he would become a big superstar," said Albert.

McGuire was at UNLV doing an interview with Runnin' Rebel forward Larry Johnson. Both were seated on a small, raised platform for the television spot. "I asked Larry why he was turning down the pros to come back to UNLV. He said to me, 'I wanted to go back to school to get my degree.' When he told me that, I was so shocked that I fell off the platform and broke my Achilles tendon."

When he returned to Milwaukee to have the tendon repaired, the surgeon was none other than Jim Langenkamp, a former McGuire player and current Marquette team physician. Back in 1967 Langenkamp missed a McGuire curfew during the team's road trip to Hawaii for the Rainbow Classic. McGuire sent him back on a plane to Milwaukee.

"I said, 'Jim, I hope you forgive me for sending you home from Hawaii. And I hope you get the right leg.'"

Probably the greatest honor that McGuire has received, other than the national championship and his Coach of the Year awards, was his induction into the Naismith Memorial Basketball Hall of Fame in 1992. He has downplayed his accomplishments, saying that he did not belong with the greats already enshrined there. He also expressed his disappointment that his brother Dick had not been inducted first.

At the summer ceremonies, five tables of family and friends were on hand in Springfield, Massachusetts, to help McGuire celebrate his induction, which was the capstone to a memorable career as coach and broadcaster. His honor escort was none other than North Carolina coach Dean Smith. McGuire looked out at the gathering before him during his speech and singled out those who helped make it possible.

"Ladies and gentlemen. You see these five tables here. I would like all of these people to stand up for a moment. These people are my life. They are the ones responsible for me being up here today," said a humble and grateful McGuire, who has received a number of other Hall of Fame inductions since then, including the City of New York, New York City's Basketball Hall of Fame, Marquette University's Law School and other booster groups on campus, Belmont Abbey, St. John's, and numerous other groups around the country.

Since he left coaching in 1977, six different men have taken over the reins of the Marquette basketball program. Since his retirement, Marquette has not regained the high national profile it enjoyed under McGuire. In the subsequent years, the university has treated its former coach with deference and respect. In fact, in 1997, on the 20th anniversary of his championship, Marquette retired the number 77 in his honor.

The '77 championship banner hanging from the ceiling of the state-of-the-art Bradley Center is as faded as the memories of the Warrior's only national championship. McGuire's legacy and presence is the only connection that students, alumni and loyal Milwaukeeans have with that championship season. It is all they have to hang their hopes on. O'Neill's 1993–94 team was the last to appear in a Sweet 16.

These days, McGuire drops in on Marquette practices now and then. Mostly he watches the players in order to prepare for his work on the team's Conference USA broadcasts during the regular season. During one of Kevin O'Neill's practices a few years ago, McGuire needed some help from the young coach.

"Al came in one day and asked if he could borrow my car," recalled O'Neill. "I said sure, but what happened? He said, 'Oh, I locked my keys in the car.' So I gave him my keys. That's Al."

In 1992, it was announced that NBC was dropping college basketball in favor of a lucrative telecast deal with the NBA. NBC agreed to let McGuire out of his contract early so that CBS could negotiate his services for the forthcoming NCAA tournament, which it had telecast for the previous few years.

A CBS representative contacted McGuire and asked to meet him at Wrigley Field for a Chicago Cubs game. McGuire, who was never a baseball fan, even growing up in New York, told him that he did not go to ball games. So, McGuire style, they met at a local watering hole to seal the deal. McGuire was now back on the same network as Packer and talk started that they might do some games together.

The network assigned him to games at the Bradley Center in Milwaukee, where McGuire continued to set himself apart from the rest of the CBS analysts during a subregional game between Georgia Tech and USC.

Freshman James Forrest of the Yellow Jackets hit a shot at the buzzer and McGuire yelled, "*Hoooly mackerel, hoooly mackerel, ooooohh!*" as he expressed his unbridled enthusiasm at the terrific finish of the game that came to be known as the "Thriller in Milwaukee." That was how he began his career at CBS, and he did it in a rather unforgettable way. In fact, CBS continued to include his spontaneous reaction to that last second shot as a part of its network promos for the tournament and regular season games for the next couple of years.

"Al started out as one of my heroes and now I look to him as a friend," said Bobby Cremins of Georgia Tech. "I can go to him any time I have a problem."

McGuire's freely flowing and spontaneous commentary during the games so impressed the *New York Times* that it dubbed him the James Joyce of the airwaves.

"My dad's contribution to basketball is the excitement that he brought to it," said Allie McGuire, a senior vice president for Fidelity Investment.

"Al will miss something during a game every now and then, but then he will come back with a real gem," noted the *Chicago Tribune*'s Michael Hirsley. "[Because of his past reputation] Al gets the benefit of the doubt."

After Syracuse advanced to the 1996 Final Four, McGuire concluded his interview with coach Jim Boeheim by doing the Al McGuire version of the "Cuse in the House" hip-hop with the Orangemen. It cracked up CBS studio host Mike Krzyzewski so much that he used a telestrator and slow-motion camera to illustrate the nuances of the "Al's in the House" dance.

At the 1997 regional finals, Minnesota coach Clem Haskins asked to talk only to McGuire, who finished his interview with Haskins by kissing him on the cheek, and then he found time to reprise his McGuire hip-hop with the Gopher players.

"I was happy for him," McGuire noted. "I did a show on his daughter, Clemette, when she was at Western Kentucky. I was happy that he got to the Final Four. There's something very exciting about getting there."

He did his hip-hop once again during the 1998 regional finals with the Stanford players after they advanced to the Final Four, and while it might be getting a little old, it certainly is different and more entertaining and memorable than most postgame interviews. "I danced with the Stanford group. It's just a thing. Everyone was so sky high. With a team that's supposed to be a Final Four squad, like Duke or Kentucky or UCLA, I don't know if it [the dance] would work. When it becomes something that you force, I would not dance if it's not there."

Longtime friend Jerry Savio noted that what has made McGuire successful in his professional life is consistency, "Everyone else changed [in the broadcast business], but he didn't. He's getting more work now than ever."

McGuire's star rose to such a height at CBS in his later years that he is now considered a hoops guru, and the network had him broadcast more regular season games during 1997–98 than at any time during his CBS tenure.

"I haven't seen anybody like him," marveled Eddie Einhorn. "The fact that he's still got staying power in a totally different world, he's still active and still contemporary, are tributes to his style and personality. He has a way to say X,Y, Z like no one else says it and makes it funny and unique. It's still good today. He's the most interesting guy on TV."

That could also explain why McGuire has been chosen by one of the local television stations in New York to do color commentary on the St. Patrick's Day parade. His stories about growing up in New York and St. Camillus Church have entertained people in the Big Apple for the past few years.

McGuire still rides his motorcycle without a helmet around the burgs of Wisconsin, cruising for his antiques and toy soldiers, and stopping at roadside cafes and garage sales, letting the day come to him. He enjoys the discovery and staying in touch with people from all walks of life, learning something about life and himself in the process.

He also will unexpectedly pop into the basketball practices at Marquette, simply lying on the floor in a torn T-shirt and jeans. Or he will drop in at a UWM practice, where his former Marquette player Ric Cobb now coaches the Panthers.

"One day I let Al talk to the players, and after he was done my players said, 'I don't know what it was Coach McGuire was trying to tell us.' And then I tell the players that I still can't figure out what he's talking about," joked Cobb.

The McGuire touch probably can best be illustrated in a story that McGuire's brother-in-law, Gene Mann, tells about the 1997 Al's Run, which was the last year that McGuire was officially connected to the fundraiser.

"The morning of the race, Al and I get up early before Pat and Kathleen and head down to Wisconsin Avenue. Al sees where they are serving free coffee and rolls on the Marquette campus. He finds a large cement flower pot to sit down on, and has some coffee. Before long, little kids are coming over, sitting on his lap and having their pictures taken with him.

"People are coming over and thanking him for starting the run," Mann continued. "Kids who have been helped over the years by the hospital are coming over and having their picture taken with him, and Al is orchestrating the whole thing. The kids and their families are asking for his autograph. Al was in his element and loving it. There was nothing planned. It just happened. I have never seen anything like it before. It was the most beautiful thing I have ever seen."

"His observations about life have always been on the mark," commented Senator Herb Kohl. "Al's a person who has a sense of what ordinary people are thinking about. He connects with people's values. It's not something out of left field. He connects with what every person is thinking.

"Al McGuire is very much a man of his times. He will comment on the human nature element of it, the common sense of it. He's a common-sense kind of guy," observed Kohl.

"Al McGuire is a loner. He's unique, but in other ways he's an enigma, a puzzle. But if you become his friend, well you're a friend for life," said Tom Collins. Concurred Butch Lee succinctly: "Al spoke the words of wisdom."

Wherever Al McGuire has touched down in his life, he has left a positive legacy. His seven years at Belmont Abbey, his 13 years at Marquette, 14 years at NBC, and the many other places he has graced with his presence. But you will not find him on the internet. He has no web page. There is no "seashellsandballoons.com" on AOL. Al McGuire's software or makeup is different from anything you will find on any computer, anywhere.

As McGuire himself says, "You can't get personality or common sense from a computer." Even with all of his success and fame, he remains down to earth, never forgetting where he came from. "That comes from his Irish-Catholic roots in New York," commented Georgia Tech coach Bobby Cremins, whose mother knew McGuire's mother in New York. "Al's a rare bird."

But what is it that makes a coaching legend. Is it wins, titles, Final Fours? Is it his 10 All-Americas or his 15 professional players? He has also had countless players who became doctors, lawyers, coaches, CPAs and government workers. Men who made something after basketball.

"When determining the success of ballplayers outside the arena you have to know where the bounce started. In other words, what background they came from. Then how high is the bounce with their lives after basketball? How far the ball bounces from where they started or how high they go. That's how you measure their success."

McGuire continues to ride the merry-go-round of life, letting the days come to him. "Remember to congratulate the temporary," he said recently at a fundraiser for the Ronald McDonald House. "That means to stretch out the day, live for the moment, and make every day just a little bit more special."

And as he heads into the autumn of his life, Al McGuire continues to touch people with the singleness of his approach while enjoying his special run.

His remarks after the 1977 Final Four still apply today: "It's been an extended love affair. It's been a merry-go-round that's been beautiful. So the merry-go-round stops and I get off and it starts for other guys. And I just hope that they do good by it. It's done very good by me."

Sources

By far, most of the material in this book came from my interviews with players, coaches, administrators, alumni, media people, and McGuire family and friends, who are named in the Acknowledgments section in the front of this book.

I also drew from radio and television broadcasts.

In April 1977, just after the Warriors won the national championship, Milwaukee radio station WRIT-AM broadcast a special tribute, "Al McGuire: Seashells and Balloons." John Wooden, Hank Raymonds, Allie and Al McGuire, among others, were on the show, and I have quoted some of their remarks throughout the book.

I also have noted some of Al McGuire's remarks from his appearance on *Later with Bob Costas*, an NBC television series, in March 1989. Of the printed sources, I found especially valuable Roger Jaynes's three-page retrospective in the *Milwaukee Journal* on March 22, 1987, "Seashells and Balloons: 10 Years Later," as well as Frank Deford's "Welcome to My World" feature in *Sports Illustrated* in 1976 and 1977. Jeff Pryor's "Odd Couple Swaps Hookshots," *Milwaukee Journal*, January 29, 1984, reported on McGuire and Friends in broadcasting.

Other useful articles appeared in *Sports Illustrated:* Michael Crosby's 1973 piece "Nostalgia: In Three-on-Three in Rockaway, the Ball Went Thisaway and Thataway"; Pete Axthelm's "When the Real McGuire Stood Up" (March 20, 1967); and Curry Kirkpatrick's "Get Da Shootah, Said Da Faddah" (January 10, 1972) and "You Know Me, Al. Right, Frank, and I Hate to Do It," (January 17, 1972).

Most of McGuire's recollections of his days at Dartmouth appeared in an article by Jim Kenyon, "Back Where It All Began—Al McGuire Got His Start at Dartmouth," in the *Valley News* of West Lebanon, New Hampshire, March 3, 1986.

"Mother dies, but McGuire celebrates her life," Roger Jaynes, *Milwaukee Journal,* September 16, 1986.

"Insight Magazine–*Milwaukee Journal,* January 16, 1977.

"The Boys Hoop It Up," Pete Coutros, Sunday *New York Daily News,* March 8, 1992.

Northliner Magazine, Fall 1974.

"Depression Baby," Frank DeFord excerpted from "World's Tallest Midget."

"Funny Basketball at Belmont Abbey," by John Kilgo, *Sport Magazine,* March, 1960.

Of the books I consulted, Milton Meltzner's *Brother Can You Spare a Dime? The Great Depression, 1929–1933* (New York: Mentor Books, 1969), provided much of Chapter 2's historical background about postwar America in the 1920s. Pete Axthelm's *The City Game: Basketball in New York from the World Champion Knicks to the World of the Playgrounds* (New York: Harper's 1970), described the game McGuire grew up on. Neil D. Isaacs's *Vintage NBA: The Pioneer Era—1946–1956*, told about McGuire's experience in the NBA in the 50s. Terry Pluto's history of the ABA, *Loose Balls: The Short, Wild Life of the American Basketball Association* (New York: Simon & Schuster, 1990), provided details from the 60s. *The NBA at Fifty* (New York: Park Lane Press, 1996), edited by Mark Vancil, provided statistics. *Seashells and Balloons, The Words of Al McGuire,* (1977 Franklin Publishers, Inc.) and *The Encyclopedia of Television,* 1994, edited by Horace Newcomb.

Chuck Sullivan gave me the poem in Chapter 5.

JOSEPH DECLAN MORAN

Joseph Declan Moran has worked the past 20 years as a journalist and editor in his native Chicago. His work has appeared in the "Suburban" *Chicago Tribune, Pioneer Press, Daily Herald,* Lerner-Pulitzer Newspapers, and *The Sporting News.* He has served as an editor for a number of foodservice, ethnic, and association trade magazines. Moran's interest in sports, especially college basketball, was spurred during his undergraduate days at Marquette University, where he earned his bachelor's degree in journalism in 1980. He earned his master's degree in broadcast journalism at Northwestern University's Medill School of Journalism in 1985. *You Can Call Me Al* is his first book. Joe and his wife, Kristen, reside in Chicago's northwest suburbs.